Library Association Record, Volume 4, Issues 7-12

Library Association

TV-6016
BP 12.1.7

Lowell fund

The Library Association Record

THE ABERDEEN UNIVERSITY PRESS LIMITED

THE

Library Association Record

A MONTHLY MAGAZINE OF LIBRARIANSHIP
AND BIBLIOGRAPHY : EDITED
BY HENRY GUPPY

THE OFFICIAL ORGAN OF
THE LIBRARY ASSOCIATION

VOL. IV., PART II.
(JULY—DECEMBER, 1902)

London
PUBLISHED BY THE LIBRARY ASSOCIATION
AT WHITCOMB HOUSE, WHITCOMB STREET
PALL MALL EAST, LONDON, S.W.
1902

VOL. IV.   JULY, 1902   No. 7

THE

Library Association Record

A MONTHLY MAGAZINE OF LIBRARIANSHIP AND
BIBLIOGRAPHY

EDITED BY

HENRY GUPPY, M.A.

LIBRARIAN OF THE JOHN RYLANDS LIBRARY, MANCHESTER

London:
PUBLISHED BY THE LIBRARY ASSOCIATION
AT WHITCOMB HOUSE, WHITCOMB STREET
PALL MALL EAST, LONDON, S.W.
Price One Shilling Net

PUBLICATIONS
OF THE
LIBRARY ASSOCIATION.

CONTENTS.

LIBRARY ASSOCIATION RECORD.

All Advertisements for the RECORD and the LIBRARY ASSOCIATION YEAR BOOK should be addressed MANAGER, 176 Milkwood Road, London, S.E., and should reach the Office not later than the 20th of each month

(vi)

The Library Association Record,

JULY, 1902.

ON A CO-OPERATIVE BASIS FOR THE CLASSIFI-
CATION OF LITERATURE IN THE SUBJECT
CATALOGUE.

By E. Wyndham Hulme, Librarian of the Patent Office, London.

THE present paper being the last of a series on the construction of the subject catalogue, I may be permitted to resume the conclusions arrived at in former communications.

(*a*) All subject catalogues are class catalogues in the sense that their headings are general names or names of classes. Hence the only distinction which can properly be drawn between the types known as dictionary and class catalogues is that they differ in the arrangement of their classes. Other assertions, such as that the dictionary type is more specific than the class catalogue; or, that the class catalogue is more philosophical than the dictionary catalogue in its division of subject-matter, are generalisations drawn from the comparison of particular instances, and are not true if affirmed of all members of either class.

Dividing subject catalogues by their formal distinction we obtain three types, which may be tabulated as follows :—

Library subject catalogues based upon

(*a*) Class order of headings, *e.g.,* Dewey class catalogue.

(*b*) Mixed alphabetical and class order, *i.e.,* main headings in alphabetical order with further subdivisions arranged in their natural order, *e.g.,* Mr. Fortescue's subject indexes.

(*c*) Alphabetical order, *e.g.,* catalogue of the Surgeon - Generals' Library.

23

There are, of course, numerous intermediate types. It should be noted that an alphabetical arrangement of the formal sub-headings (Bibliography, History, etc.), is seldom, if ever, adopted.

(*b*) Distinctions based upon different methods of subject registration are of infinitely greater importance than distinctions of formal arrangement. The three rational methods of subject registration are :—

(1) *Class or Superior Entry*, *e.g.*, a work of "Physics" entered under the superior heading "Science".
(2) *Specific or Coextensive Entry*, *e.g.*, a work on "Physics" entered under that heading.
(3) *Analytical or Inferior Entry*, *e.g.*, a work on "Physics" entered under the inferior headings "Electricity," "Light," "Sound," etc.

Substituting imaginary circles as representing the relative extent of the above classes, then in (1) the whole of the circle (Physics) is included in the larger circle (Science) ; in (2) the two circles include the same area, in (3) they intersect at certain points in virtue of their common subject-matter, *viz.*, Electricity, Light, Sound and so forth.

We have now a clear mental picture of what is meant by class, specific and analytical entry. The distinctions are based upon the relative area of the work registered compared with that of its subject-heading. It is not suggested that it is possible to construct a catalogue by a strict observance of any one of these three rules, but they serve as a standard by which any catalogue can be readily tested, and its properties at once made known. For instance, in the class entry catalogue, the subdivision of literature falls short of the classification inherent in literature. In the catalogue based upon specific entry, the extent of the two classifications is identical, while in the analytical subject catalogue classification is carried beyond that of the literature registered.

The relative merits of the three systems have already been discussed in some detail. I propose, however, to examine more fully the principles upon which analytical entry may be said to be based.

Analytical entry is, as we have seen, a resolution of a

whole into its parts, and the registration of the parts under their proper subject-headings. A library catalogue so constructed would form a general index of the matters contained in that library. And the application of the same rule of registration to the literature of the world would result in a "universal index of matters," such as was outlined by Mr. F. Campbell on several occasions. But the logical objections to this rule of registration are somewhat formidable.

"It is," says Mill (*Logic*, 6th ed., i., 135), "a fundamental principle in logic that the power of framing classes is unlimited so long as there is any (even the smallest) difference to found a distinction upon. Take any attribute whatever, and if some things have it, and others have it not, we may ground on the attribute a division of all things into two classes; and we actually do so, the moment we create a name which connotes the attribute. The number of possible classes is, therefore, boundless. . . ."

If, therefore, analysis is to be the rule of subject registration, at what point is analysis to stop? A work, for instance, on Physics naturally resolves itself into its component sciences, Light, Sound, Heat, etc., but each of these is indefinitely divisible. Unless, therefore, we are prepared to accept the volume, the section, the chapter or the paragraph, or some other bibliographical division as the halting-point of our analysis, it is difficult to see upon what lines operations are to proceed. In a book index all facts of importance must be registered, but can it be pretended that a need exists for a general index of the world's literature upon the same scale? Admitted that we want a fact recorded, do we also require a record of the number of times and places in which its statement has appeared? Obviously no! Such a scheme should be limited to the registration of original matter, *i.e.*, the first enunciation of facts or theories and subsequent modification thereof due to further research. But this limitation implies special qualifications and discretionary powers with which the cataloguer is not invested. The latter is bound to enter works according to rule and not by a critical estimate of their place in literature. It follows that while the unrestricted use of analysis leads to no useful result, its selective exercise lies without the province of the cataloguer. Analytical entry cannot form the basis of construction of the subject catalogue. We hark back, therefore, to specific entry as formulating the best guide to the extent to which classification should be pushed.

Specific entry is the classification of works as units under headings directly suggested by the ambit of these units. The warrant for the resulting classes is purely literary. Such a scheme may be likened to the survey of a locality on a given scale. Its merits consist in the faithful reproduction of existing contours and boundaries. Rival workers in the same field of equal powers of observation must arrive at substantially identical results. The elimination of the personal equation alone constitutes a feature which should recommend the scheme to the librarian. But like all other rules the rule of specific entry requires certain modifications.

Subject-matter, although indefinitely divisible, does not consist of classes of equal value. A work, therefore, may be said to be composed of a definite number of subject-groups which form the primary divisions of its subject-matter. Now, if a specific literature be assumed to exist singly and in combination for the three groups a b c, we obtain the following class-list :—

$$a+b+c$$
$$a+b$$
$$a+c$$
$$b+c$$
$$a$$
$$b$$
$$c$$

The nexus between subject-groups in literature is determined either by real affinity, convention or fancy;[1] in either of the former cases, if it is found to be constant over a considerable body of literature, it will probably persist in the future. But a class-list of the above type will be of uncommon occurrence. If the elements $a+b+c$ are constantly combined one or more of these combinations will preponder-

[1] When the nexus between subjects is purely fanciful, works may either be analysed or entered under the nearest class-heading.

ate and it will generally be feasible to reduce the class-list to

$a+b+c$ (to include the occasional combinations
a of any two of the elements)
b
c

Or, if preferred, such occasional combinations can be entered analytically with the monographs.

Thus, if the "laws of industrial property" are found to comprise three subject-groups, (*a*) Patent Law, (*b*) Trade Mark Laws, (*c*) Designs Law, "*Graham on Designs and Trade Marks*" may be entered either under the class-heading $a+b+c$ or analytically under *b* and *c*. The rule holds good in combinations of higher numbers of associated subject-groups. The procedure is to ascertain first the extent of a work, secondly, whether the nexus between the subject-groups is persistent. If the latter question be decided in the affirmative, a definition clearly delimiting the area of the associated subject-matter must be made, and the work registered thereunder.

It will be found a good working rule in cases of doubt as to how to define a group to extend the survey until some literary warrant is found for the new class-heading. Thus works on "washing, bleaching, dyeing and finishing fabrics" may be grouped under "Textile Fibres, Chemical Technology"; while works on operations preparatory to and including "spinning and weaving" will fall under "Textile Fibres, Mechanical Technology".

Thus by accepting the work as the unit of our classification, we obtain complete registration at the cost of single entry or a fraction over for each work treated. But whether we analyse as suggested above or enter concretely, the class-list remains unaffected, and the result to the searcher is practically the same.

Next as to the principles of correlating the subject-headings. It is submitted that the proper function of the class-list is to bring into juxtaposition works possessing common subject-matter. Correlation, therefore, should be based upon a careful quantitative estimate of the subject-matter common to two or more groups—quite apart from a consideration of their real affinities. Thus in the class-list, the class "carving" should stand next to "cookery," and the "phylloxera" to "viticulture," because this arrangement provides the searcher with the easiest method of obtaining additional information in passing from the general to the specific heading, or *vice versâ.* Cross references must follow the same rule, *i.e.,* they must be based upon actual survey and not be regarded as philosophical statements of real affinities. We may now take stock of our position and compare our rules with the requisites of logical classification.

Logical classification requires " that every class or general name (for our purpose every subject-heading) must bear a certain and knowable meaning ". We agree—but add that this need not be construed as meaning that our subject-headings should consist of formal definitions. For the purpose of book classification it will be sufficient if, when a term or phrase possesses several distinct meanings the heading is reserved for works conforming to its general acceptation, while other and less-known meanings are referred out. In the construction of subject-headings we are concerned with the history of words only in so far as a knowledge of their history enables us to distinguish literary classes which philologically are confounded under a common phraseology. A reference to Dr. Murray's *Dictionary* will generally serve to warn us of impending danger in this direction. Take for instance the history of the word " chemistry," which formerly stood for (*a*) alchemy and (*b*) the science and practice of medicine according to the method of Paracelsus and his school.

This science is generally known under the name of Iatro-Chemistry, which is thus connected both with alchemy, from which it sprang, and pharmaceutical chemistry and the practice of pharmacy, to which it gave a great impetus. Thus our class-list will run as follows:—

> Alchemy.
> > Iatro-Chemistry. *See also* Medical and Pharmaceutical Chemistry.
> > Chemistry.

Phædro's *Art of Chemistry*, which is a work on vulgar pharmacy of the Paracelsian school, will be registered either under Iatro-Chemistry or Pharmacy.

Again it is an axiom of logical classification that a class shall be created wherever one is needed—"wherever there is anything to be designated by it which it is of importance to express" (Mill, ii., 213). To this we demur that we are concerned with the classification of books and not of knowledge. Our classification is confined to the unit which we have provisionally fixed at the "work".

So far then our scheme may be described as consistent with the principles of logical classification. But in formulating the rules for co-ordinating our classes we take our final leave of logic and its teachings. For the problem of logical classification, according to Mill, is "to provide that things shall be thought of in such groups and those groups in such an order as will best conduce to the remembrance and to the ascertainment of their laws" (Mill, ii., 264). This at once distinguishes logical and literary classification. There is, however, a close, but accidental connection observable between the two systems; due to the fact that the nexus between literary subject-matter is to a large extent determined, in scientific literature at least, by the observed natural affinities of things.

Thus the primary division of chemical science is into organic and inorganic chemistry. The latter is again subdivided into metalloids and metals. Metals are again subdivided into natural groups beginning with the alkali metals and terminating with less well-known groups, such as the metals of the rare earths and so forth. Finally each group is resolved into its constituent elements. The logical class-list, therefore, may be supposed to run as follows :—

> (a) Chemistry.
> (b) Inorganic Chemistry.
> (c) Metals.
> (d) Metals of the earths.
> (e) Aluminium.

For each of the above groups a specific literature exists, and to this extent, therefore, the two systems are identical. The philosophical classification of chemistry, however, serves

only to account for a small fraction of chemical literature.
Thus from a selection from the same stock of chemical facts
we have works on chemistry arranged by its operations, or
its applications to industry, or in its general bearings upon
the health and welfare of the community or its sections;
and for each of these groups due provision must be made in
our class-list. In short, philosophical classification, so far as
it is recognised in our class-list, is there by accident. The
co-ordination of the subject-headings is the result of a
quantitative survey of the association of literary subject-
matter. To what causes that association is due is not
material. It is sufficient for the cataloguer to ascertain the
fact of the nexus and to co-ordinate accordingly.

Hitherto we have been content to treat of subject registration from the standpoint of the "work" which was
provisionally accepted on the unit of our classification.
We must now modify this statement in certain particulars.

By general consent publishers' series are now disregarded,
the components of the series being treated as independent
units. A difficulty often arises in the case of collected works,
owing to the use of the double title-page; the one asserting
the place of the treatise in the collection, the other occupying
the place of the ordinary title-page. This use of the double
title-page is rapidly extending in foreign scientific literature.
Such works may be said to possess a twofold existence,
sectional and independent. As a matter of library economy
it is necessary to resort to analysis to avoid the double
purchase of the work. In such cases where the work is
entered analytically by its parts there should be no serial
entry; but where a work is entered as a unit a contents-list
should be given in the subject catalogue. All duplication
of entry in the subject catalogue detracts from the value of
the class-list as a systematic guide to research. Duplication
must be distinguished clearly from analysis. To enter a
work on the geology of Cornwall, or the insect enemies of
a plant under the double subject-heading suggested by the
titles is duplicate entry. The choice of heading is not
material, and will be settled with reference to local requirements; but the system of classification, whether based upon

place or subject, or upon subject or subject-limitation, should be uniform throughout the class-list.

Again, analysis is contingent upon the existing scope of co-operative cataloguing. The forthcoming International Catalogue of Scientific Serial Literature will render the analysis of many scientific serials as unnecessary as the work of Poole and his continuators has that of general literary serials. The rules for analysis are therefore in their nature conditional. The co-operative index of literature and the library subject catalogue will always overlap at some points, while the extension of co-operation will tend to force subject registration in the library catalogue back into its true channel of specific entry.

The purpose of our essays now stands revealed. It is to suggest a positive basis for subject registration based upon a survey of the association of subject-matter in literature. By the persistent association of subject-groups in literature the units of the class-list, *i.e.*, the subject-headings, are called into existence, and by a quantitative estimate of their common subject-matter these headings are co-ordinated to form the class-list. Without such class-list there can be no uniformity in subject registration, and without uniformity systematic research is rendered a matter of great difficulty.

According to this view the function of the subject catalogue is to present a series of class-headings co-ordinated in such a way as to provide the literary searcher with *alæ seu scalæ* by which he can pass from the specific to the general, or *vice versâ*, without perpetually stumbling against the re-entry of the same work. In the notated class systems this advantage is obtained at the sacrifice of specific entry; broad generalisations being substituted for the ultimate divisions of literature. But in these days of specialisation we cannot afford to limit the efficiency of the subject catalogue in this way.

The relation of class- and shelf-lists may be alluded to briefly. The limits to which shelf classification can be profitably pushed is determined by the number of combinations of the notation marks employed. Thus a higher degree of differentiation on the shelves is compatible with the use of

the same symbols in the specialist library than is attainable
by the larger collections.   The classification of literature in
the subject catalogue being devoid of notation is free from
such limits.   But while it is idle to attempt to impose upon
all libraries the same system of shelf classification, it will be
seen that the value of all shelf systems depends upon their
approximation to the scheme of classification based upon the
rule of specific entry.   For in shelf classification a work must
be treated as a unit, and the recognition of literary unity is,
as we have seen, the basis of the rule of specific entry.   Shelf
systems, therefore, are in their nature an abridgment of that
larger system of classification which is inherent in literature,
the laws of which we have, however inadequately, attempted
to formulate.

Again, in the author and title catalogue uniformity of
entry is secured by a general adhesion to a code of rules, the
authority of which has been established by long usage.   In
the subject catalogue we seek to substitute a standard list of
subject-headings based upon an accurate survey and definition of the anatomy of literature and correlated according
to a quantitative estimate of their common subject-matter.
The acceptance of such scheme of classification leaves to
the librarian a choice of alphabetical or class order for
his catalogue, for the mechanism of the system is inter-
changeable.   The advantages of such a scheme are obvious.
The librarian gains by the economy of his time, the library
by the reduction of the printer's bill, the searcher by the
increased efficiency of the catalogue and the ease with
which the search can be extended from one catalogue
to another.   Co-operative class-lists could circulate in all
libraries with marks showing in what collection the work
could be consulted, with the special mark of the individual
library, of course, superadded.   The compilation of comparative statistics would be simplified, and the co-ordination of
library work in a given district materially advanced.   The
theme is a tempting one, but we have already strayed too far
from our central proposition, *viz.*, that uniformity of subject
registration in the library catalogue is practicable and within
our reach if we will only seek to attain to it.

REFERENCE LIBRARIES IN SMALL TOWNS. [1]

By HERBERT WALKER, LIBRARIAN OF LONGTON PUBLIC
LIBRARY.

CONSIDERABLE attention has of late been deservedly
paid to the question of Reference Libraries at the
meetings of this Association, and while it has been discussed
from the point of view of the great provincial city, and the
aristocratic London suburb, it may not be out of place to
look at the same matter from the point of view of the smaller
manufacturing town.

It has been assumed that the reference department
represents the crown and apex of library work, that it
possesses some virtue not to be found elsewhere. Its readers
are designated by the name of Student (with a capital S).
It alone shows signs of grace, while other departments are
utterly depraved. The reading-room, we are told, is given
over to betting and halfpenny sensationalism, and the lending
library to the circulation of ephemeral twaddle, with the
consequence that these two must be looked upon as necessary evils, and the serious attention of the librarian devoted
to the more worthy reference department. It is a pity such
statements should be made, as they only give the enemy
occasion to blaspheme. The reference library may be the
apex, but an apex presupposes a base, and to pay particular
attention to one and neglect the other is perilously like
building a pyramid the wrong way up. It is a dangerous
process, in these democratic days, to maintain a public
institution in such a way that large numbers of contributing
ratepayers are, through no fault of their own, shut out from
participating in its advantages, for it is admitted that reference

---

[1] Read at the Nottingham Meeting of the Library Association, 5th June,
1902.

libraries appeal to the few rather than to the many, and after all, it may be reasonably argued, that if by means of your reading-rooms you can raise the general public taste from *Police News* and *Comic Cuts* to the level. of, say, the *Strand Magazine*, to say nothing of the scientific and technical papers to be found there, and by means of your lending libraries raise the female taste from Bow-Bells novelettes to such books as *John Halifax, Gentleman* and *The Heir of Redclyffe*, to go no further, you are doing far greater service than if by means of the reference library some learned antiquary should be able to compile a paper on Runic inscriptions for the local Pickwick Club. Education is not to be despised if it is elementary.

Almost every public library report bears evidence to the fact that this theory of special virtue is very widely spread. It is fast crystallising into a dogma, and such being the case, it would be interesting to get to know what these reference library students really are. I went into a large reference library the other day, and to look at a railway time-table I was obliged to write my name, address and occupation on a slip of paper, while the attendant marked in blue lead the precise minute I took the time-table and the precise minute I returned it. Through this procedure I lost my train, but I was compensated by the knowledge that I figured as a student in that branch of science in which time-tables are included. In another large library I went through the same process to see *The Athenæum*, and in yet another, I was informed that the illustrated weeklies could only be seen in the reference department. Others, again, openly include issues of current popular magazines, and others, juvenile reading in boys' reading-rooms in their reference library statistics. All this may be very necessary for purposes of management, but it hardly bears out the high claims made for reference libraries. And in other libraries where such details of management are not necessary, in the majority of cases where there are large reference issues reported—that is, large as compared with lending library issues (I am not referring now to such cities as Liverpool, Manchester and Birmingham), it will be found that the figures are dominated by the figures of one particular class, generally called miscellaneous and magazines. This is somewhat disquieting, for serious study and miscellaneous reading are not often found hand in hand, and it is hard to understand why the busy man who hurriedly turns over the pages of the current *Punch* in the reading-room should be classed as an idler, while the gentleman who spends a couple of hours over the bound volumes of the same periodical in the reference library should be received with open arms as a student.

Then again, the cultivation of reference libraries leads to a system by which readers desirous of perusing standard contributions to any branch of knowledge are denied the privilege of taking such books home, but are required to visit the reference library for the purpose. There is thus a forcing process going on. Readers are forced into the reference library against their will. A friend of mine in a large industrial centre recently asked me to recommend a few books on a subject then attracting public attention. I named a few of a popular character, but my friend wrote back saying that the library of his city was no good, the books could not be obtained for home reading but only for reference, that he had no time to visit the library day after day, and so he would be obliged to do without reading them. Other libraries publish lists of books added to the reference library. Amongst them are often such books as *Huxley's Life* by his son; Nansen's *Farthest North*, Morley's *Cromwell*, etc. Why such books as these should be kept in the reference library, I have never been able to understand. If nothing but ephemeral twaddle is put in the lending library, we cannot complain that nothing but ephemeral twaddle is taken out. The character of lending library reading depends to a great extent not on the public taste but on the character of the library itself. As is the library, so are the readers; and if such books as those I have mentioned are kept for reference only the reference library issues may be magnified, but the lending library reading is of a correspondingly feeble character. There is only a certain amount of literary energy in a town. If it is consumed in the reference department, there is nothing left for the lending; while if the lending department is made most of, true reference library work is practically non-existent. Statistics, I think, will show, that there is a connection between a good average of solid reading in a lending library and a poor reference library, and between a low average of solid reading and a good reference library.

All this seems to indicate that the librarian of a small town must choose between one and the other. He cannot maintain both in a proper condition of usefulness, and which to adopt must depend upon circumstances. If the town is largely residential, and its inhabitants people of leisure and culture, reference libraries may doubtless flourish, but in a manufacturing district, where the vast majority of people earn their daily bread by manual labour, and make up for their lack of classical attainment by native integrity of character, good lending libraries are far more suitable and are productive of far better results. In such a town as this, people cannot be induced to use the reference library except for the elucidation of minute points. Standard books, books on abstruse subjects, scientific and technical literature will readily be borrowed for home reading—indeed there is a brisk demand for these—but the same and better books in the reference library remain untouched. More than this the librarian is constantly receiving applications for permission to take home many such works as are kept for reference, even publications of the British Museum, the general excuse being that the reader has no time to stay in the library, and there is no part of the librarian's administration which is so much criticised, and which he finds so hard to justify, than the inclusion of books in the reference department and not in the lending. Under such circumstances as these it is not to be wondered at that the lending department receives the bulk of his attention, and under such circumstances it is hardly the thing that he should be charged with neglecting his true function, that it should be said that the desire for big figures possesses an unholy fascination for him, and that those departments of work to which he directs his energies should be the recipients of such unmerited abuse as is now the fashion to bestow upon them.

But still, reference libraries are necessary even in small towns, and the question remains as to the character they should assume. They cannot undertake to be libraries of research. That duty must be performed by the national libraries, and by the libraries of those great provincial cities which are as truly metropolitan in character as is London itself. The ideal of a good education is sometimes said to be, "Everything about something, and something about everything". The librarian of a small town should endeavour to apply this ideal to reference library work. It goes without saying that he must have the usual books of reference, encyclopædias and the like. It goes without saying that he must collect the literature of his own district, though even this with discretion, for expensive works of an antiquarian character need not be duplicated sometimes even in a county, and the public library is not called upon to compete with the private collector for fancy editions. In this connection the term "local literature" sadly needs defining, both as to what is literature and as to what is local. Again, it goes without saying that the small reference library must contain all of value dealing with the local industry. Here also discretion is necessary, and the historic and dilettante aspects of the question subordinated to the practical. For the remainder, at least one standard work on each and every subject under the sun should be kept for reference. These works can be supplemented by those in the lending library if need be, for in the small town the two departments should be worked together, but a visitor to the library should be able as far as possible to obtain for immediate use the most authoritative contribution to any branch of knowledge that he is interested in, independent of the chance of the books being in the hands of a borrower from the lending library. And such books as are kept for reference should be comprehensive rather than particular. Stanford's *Compendium of Geography and Travel* may be a suitable work for reference, but records of individual journeys are better for lending. Such books as Macmillan's new *History of the English Church* and the *Cambridge Natural History* should be placed in the reference department, but particular studies of, say, the Reformation or the Oxford Movement, or of particular branches of zoology should be allowed for home reading. A good foundation for a small reference library might be laid by taking the hundred great divisions of Dewey's classification and obtain a comprehensive treatise dealing with each, and afterwards filling up the subdivisions as occasion afforded. The Library Association might do a less useful thing than publish a selection of books suitable for such a purpose, and the problem of reference libraries in adjacent towns could be solved by each town selecting different books as representative of the subjects chosen.

One other note on this subject. The literary side of a library should not be overlooked. We live in a materialistic age, and while we pay attention to scientific and technical literature, let us not forget Shakespeare and Milton. The best critical editions of the classics should find a place in the small reference library. There is a danger of libraries becoming obedient handmaidens to technical instruction, and providing books out of their limited income which should properly be a charge upon the ampler funds set apart for educational purposes. This should be jealously watched, and this class of work should not monopolise the attention of librarians to the exclusion of those great masterpieces of literature which will live on long after the latest scientific treatises have become obsolete.

THE LIBRARY INDICATOR: PRO AND CON.[1]

By A. Cotgreave, Librarian, West Ham Public Libraries.

IN dealing with so well-worn a subject as that of the merits and demerits of library indicators, I fear that, in the first place, I shall have a difficulty in submitting anything sufficiently fresh or original to be worthy of your attention, and that, in the second, I am imitating somewhat the rashness of certain beings of whom it was said, they rushed in where much superior beings feared to tread, especially as my remarks are more pro than con. However, I must hope that my paper will be judged as one not dealing with any particular form of indicator, but with indicators collectively; and with that view I have collected models from every inventor, where obtainable, for your inspection, and have also provided a pamphlet containing notes and illustrations of various designs for your information.

The indicator is generally believed to have been first adopted at a Manchester Branch Library, for the sole purpose of saving the time of the staff, previously wasted in looking for books which were out on loan. It does not, however, appear to have effected much improvement as it was ultimately discarded, and the old method of checking lists of books by

---

[1] Read at the Monthly Meeting, held at 20 Hanover Square, 15th May, 1902.

Note.—In connection with this paper, it should be explained that arrangements had been made for one descriptive of the various indicators known, but that owing to the extensive amount of matter received by Mr. Cotgreave from various quarters, it was found impossible to do justice to the various indicators (some twenty or more) in a single paper, and consequently a short paper, " Library Indicators: Pro and Con," was hastily substituted at the last moment, supplemented by an exhibition of indicator models, illustrations, etc., kindly lent by various gentlemen. Mr. Cotgreave desires to take this opportunity of expressing sincere thanks to these gentlemen for their assistance, and regrets that he was unable to take advantage of it, and to state that he hopes at a later period to publish an article, probably illustrated, giving the accounts of the various indicators which they assisted him to gather together.

the shelves reinstated. During the last twenty or thirty years several improved designs have been brought out, some of which have been in use for many years at a large number of libraries, and even now, in spite of the agitation and craving for change—sometimes even a bad change rather than none —the authorities of these libraries are still convinced that the indicator is the best system. The principal opposition to indicators appears to have been instigated by a certain class of librarians or readers who are averse to mechanical aids of any kind in a library when they can possibly be dispensed with. They will view with equanimity scores of useful designs for every purpose elsewhere, even in their own homes, but are suspicious of, and opposed to any proposition to save the time of the library staff or improve the work by mechanical aids, and raise all kinds of bogies to aid in their opposition. The following may be summarised as the stock objections to the indicator :—

    1. That it is mechanical and out of harmony with its surroundings.
    2. That it prevents free intercourse between the library staff and the readers.
    3. That the borrowers complain of inability to get the books they require.
    4. That tickets get misplaced by careless assistants.
    5. That it takes up considerable space.
    6. That it does not expedite the service.

I will take the above in the order enumerated, and in reference to No. 1, the objection to the indicator on the score of its mechanical character, I contend that the time saved by its use for purposes of a non-mechanical nature should more than condone its mechanical transgressions and infirmities. Besides, to be consistent, these objectors should taboo everything of a mechanical nature, instead of which I have noticed that some libraries, where the indicator is excluded, are filled from one end to the other with various designs of American iron book-presses, with mechanical self-adjusting shelf supports, the prominence and engineering, machine-like appearance of which pale the books and everything else into insignificance. Then again they have dusting machines, and other mechanical aids to which they make no objection.

With No. 2 objection, *that an indicator prevents intercourse between the librarian and his readers*, I fear I shall, in the classic words which appear in a certain paper refuting an objection to open access, have to describe it as a "sheer hollow turnip of a bogie," and endeavour to show by quoting a former argument of mine on the same subject that this objection is largely sentimental. There might be something in it if the librarian were always at the counter, and had to work the indicator himself, but in very few libraries is this the case.

Indicator or no indicator, he will generally locate himself in his office, or some quiet spot where he can attend to his catalogue, book-lists, committee work, accounts, or other important matters, for which, where the indicator is used, he has double the time at his disposal, and when his services are specially and legitimately required by any borrower they are more available, as the sub-librarian will be at liberty to do part of the work that would otherwise fall entirely upon his chief. More intercourse than this, in the lending department, is not desirable, as it is apt to lead to intimacies and continual conversation on subjects not connected with the library, thus setting the staff a bad example, and encouraging readers thus favoured to ignore the catalogue and other arrangements for the service, and interrupt and impede the assistants in their work.

Yet another consideration: however able, well-read and impartial any librarian might be, he could only personally attend to a few out of the large number of readers at a public library, a number which is constantly increasing. Further than this, he would be frequently asked for books on all sorts of out-of-the-way subjects, to many of which there might be only a few references in altogether unlikely books, references of which he could not possibly in all cases be aware. To quote from an article in the *American Educational Review* on the "Libraries of Europe": "The librarian of the Bodleian once gave a gentleman, Mr. J. Howard Gore, a batch of titles of works on a subject of which he was a historian and bibliographer; several of these were new to him, which fact led him to the conclusion that nobody knew all the literature of any subject, and that a good subject catalogue or index was the best guide ". My own opinion, which I believe is shared by many other librarians, is that the best guide, at any rate in a busy lending library, is a catalogue, or series of catalogues or handlists containing an index or synopsis of the principal and most useful subject-contents of the best and most suitable books in the library, a guide which would not be subject to forgetfulness, or absence on account of meals, illness, etc., but would be an ever-present help, not only to the readers, but to librarian and staff as well, and which would be available to fifty readers as to one at the same time. Possessing such an aid the librarian need only give his services to those readers who require advice as to the special character of any work on science, history, politics, etc., appearing in the catalogue, or as to some plan of reading. Further than this a librarian ought not to be expected to go, and in fact is not able to go except to a limited extent. I venture to say that readers frequently ask for works containing information on subjects which could not be found for them without the aid of some such guide as I suggest, and if the librarian himself has to use such a guide, even if only as a reminder, why not place it within reach of the readers and the staff and thus save his own time for duties which *must* be performed by himself and cannot be relegated to others.

In the reference department, where at the outside not more than twenty or thirty readers per day would require advice or information from the librarian, his personal services might very properly and usefully be given ; but even here, if a card catalogue is used, valuable references and notes can be continually inserted that would be of great and immediate assistance, and always available to the readers.

3. *That borrowers complain of inability to get the books they require.* Those who make this objection to the indicator must pardon me if I characterise it as somewhat strained, as it appears so obvious that when a book is actually out, no system, not even " Open Access," will cause it to be in. But it should on the other hand be equally obvious that, as with an indicator the books are available for reissue directly

they are returned, there is more likelihood of obtaining popular books than by systems where they are kept idle until they are marked off. There is also the economical side, that owing to this feature, with an indicator fewer copies of a work might be required.

4. *That tickets are misplaced by careless assistants.* Well we know that mistakes are made by careless assistants with any system, and I know of none which will prevent it, but beg to point out that many overlook the fact that practically every fault or mistake in an indicator is or can be found out, whereas by some other systems they are hidden. Take the old ledger system; when the entry of a returned book could not be found it was passed over and the book put on the shelf, and when overdues were got out and lists checked, the book was either found on the shelf, at binder's, or in posting book as reissued. With the indicator no such escape is possible, as the borrower's ticket must be found upon return of book or the mistake admitted. Hence the indicator frequently receives undeserved blame on this account instead of praise for the way in which it brings the carelessness of assistants to light, and consequently tends to improvement in the work.

5. *That the indicator takes up considerable space.* It certainly appears to require more space than some systems, *e.g.*, the ledger, or card charging methods, but I think this objection is more fanciful than real; for instance, there must be somewhere for the borrowers to stand while waiting their turn to be served, and it certainly appears to me that the system by which they are served the quickest and which thus keeps the number down, should require the least space. It must be admitted that as a library grows in extent and popularity, so the indicator will grow, and consequently require additional space; but so will the books, the papers, the number of readers, and in fact everything connected with the library. Therefore, why should the indicator be the only thing to be condemned for growing? This, like other arguments against the indicator, seems, to say the least, unreasonable and somewhat like those urged by the wolf in the fable, when he wished to find an excuse for eating the lamb.

6. *That the issue is not expedited by the use of an indicator.*
This objection is, I need scarcely say, made only by those
who have not used indicators, or who have since using
them been engaged in libraries where open access has been
adopted. It is possible that, as with open access, each
borrower finds his own book and the staff have merely to
record the loan, the issue may be as rapid as with an indicator,
although I believe the borrowers have in some cases to wait
their turn to be admitted to the shelves, and in all cases
many of them will remain browsing among the shelves a
considerable time ; but for the much larger number of libraries
which use neither indicators nor open access, but depend
upon ledgers, card charging, or some other system neces-
sitating the searching for books from long lists handed in by
the borrower, it is obvious that the time required to serve
each borrower will on an average be doubled or even trebled.
As an illustration let us take an indicator library and suppose
that only one assistant is on duty at the issue desk while
several borrowers are waiting there. Each one in turn hands
in his ticket and asks for the book or books he requires, which
the assistant obtains and issues to him without delay. Now
what happens without an indicator? First, a long list of
the most popular books is handed in, all or nearly all of which
are generally out. Consequently, the assistant, instead of
being able to immediately obtain the books required, as with
the indicator, has to make a tedious and often heart-breaking
search at several parts of the shelves, dragging a ladder with
him, only to find continually that not a single book on the list
is in, while all the time some of them may be actually among
a heap of others waiting to be marked off, which in an
indicator library would have been on the shelves. Secondly,
the borrower is not only annoyed at having to wait so long,
but is quite exasperated when he is informed that out
of the twenty or thirty numbers he has taken considerable
trouble to select, none are in, and it is feared that in many
cases he doubts the truth of the statement. One special
advantage of the indicator in this connection is that the
borrower, instead of waiting a long time at the counter for
his turn which is very irksome to an active mind, is engaged

in checking his list by the indicator, and in addition feels much more satisfaction in ascertaining for himself whether any of the books he requires are in or not. Should the borrower fail to find any of the books he requires in, which will as a rule only happen when he requires novels, it is an easy matter for him to ask the assistant to give him an interesting book or even a few to select from, and in such case I feel confident that he will generally be better satisfied with the assistant's choice than if he had been allowed to roam among the shelves and select for himself. In saying this, I wish it to be understood that I refer only to works of fiction and their readers. Readers of higher class books will generally find the books required shown in by the indicator.

The following are the claims most generally advanced by those who advocate the use of indicators :—

1. That it saves the time and labour of the staff considerably.

2. That it prevents a good deal of undesirable or unnecessary conversation between the staff and the readers.

3. That it prevents friction between the staff and the readers.

4. That it not only enables the librarian and principal assistants to give more time to their special work, but also to assisting readers.

5. That it gives satisfaction to the readers by enabling them to ascertain for themselves whether the book required is in or out, and also in the greater rapidity with which they are served.

6. That it adds to the working value of a book.

7. That in some indicators the records of the books are brought together and centralised in such manner as to give information frequently required, in a much quicker and effective manner than by any other system.

It is scarcely necessary for me to go into the merits of these various claims, as I have already done so to some extent in dealing with the arguments against the indicator, but no doubt further light will be thrown upon the matter if the discussion I hope for is excited by my paper. If any of my remarks appear unduly assertive, I must plead that my paper concerns a somewhat contentious matter, and beg that such remarks will not be taken as personal or offensive, which is far from my intention.

THE PUBLIC LIBRARIES (IRELAND) BILL OF 1902.

WE have received from Mr. MacAlister, the Honorary Secretary of the Legislation Committeeof the Library Association, a copy of " A Bill to Amend the Public Libraries (Ireland) Acts," which is at present before Parliament.

The Bill is the work of the Legislation Committee of the Library Association.   It has been handed over *en bloc* to the Irish Party, who have undertaken to see it through the House of Commons.   The clauses, though few in number, have been carefully considered, and are the result of a very large correspondence with the friends of Irish libraries both in Ireland and this country, extending over more than twelve months.

One object in printing the text of the Bill is to make it clear that the credit of initiating the measure rests with the Library Association.   Notices of the Bill have appeared in the newspapers, where it has been assumed that it is entirely the work of the Irish Party, and in justice to the Library Association we venture to state the facts of the case.

[2 EDW. 7.]

A

BILL

TO

A.D. 1902.   Amend the Public Libraries (Ireland) Acts.

BE it enacted by the King's most Excellent Majesty, by and with the advice and consent of the Lords Spiritual and Temporal, and Commons, in this present Parliament assembled, and by the authority of the same, as follows :—

Short title and con- struction.   1. This Act may be cited as the Public Libraries (Ireland) Act, 1902, and shall be construed as one with the Public

Libraries Act (Ireland), 1855 (herein-after referred to as the principal Act), and the Public Libraries (Ireland) Act, 1894.

2. The principal Act may be adopted for any rural district Rural dis-by the rural district council, and the provisions of the Public trict coun-cils may Libraries (Ireland) Act, 1894, shall, mutatis mutandis, apply adopt the to such rural district and rural district council as if the same principal Act. were an urban district and urban authority respectively.

3. On the adoption of the principal Act for a rural district, Library the rural district council shall be the library authority for authority. such rural district.

4. The amount of the rate to be levied in any district for Limitation which the principal Act is adopted shall not exceed the sum on expen-diture. of *twopence* in the pound, and section eight of the principal Act shall be amended accordingly.

5. Any library authority may enter into agreements with Use of the managers of any school for the use of such school as a schools as libraries. library, and for the care of the books, and the management of the library, upon such terms as may be mutually agreed by and between such library authority and school managers.

6. Any county council may, out of the funds at its dis- County posal for technical education, make a grant-in-aid to any councils may make library authority for the purchase of books by such library grants. authority, or towards the maintenance of any public library belonging to or established by any such library authority.

7. The Libraries Offences Act, 1898, shall apply to any Offences. library established under the principal Act.

8. The provisions of the Public Libraries Act, 1901, Byelaws. enabling a library authority to make byelaws, and otherwise relating to such byelaws, shall extend to Ireland with the substitution of the Public Libraries (Ireland) Acts, 1855 to 1902, for the principal Act, and of sections two hundred and nineteen to two hundred and twenty-three of the Public Health (Ireland) Act, 1878, for sections one hundred and eighty-two to one hundred and eighty-six of the Public Health Act, 1875, and of the expression "sanitary authority" for "local authority".

LIBRARY NOTES AND NEWS.

UNITED KINGDOM.

ABERDEEN : *Extension of the Public Library.*—A meeting of the Aberdeen Public Library Committee was held on the 17th June, Lord Provost Fleming in the chair. Plans for the erection of a new reading-room at the central buildings and a branch reading-room at Torry were submitted. Considerable discussion took place over the question of the greatly increased expense that would be involved by the new plans. It was stated that, whereas when the original plans were drawn up it was estimated that the extension of the central buildings and the erection of two branch reading-rooms would cost £6,000, the estimated cost of the central extension would alone amount to nearly £7,000. Mr. William Johnston remarked that when Mr. Carnegie was communicated with on the subject, they had submitted plans to him estimating the cost of the new buildings at £6,000, and it was on that understanding that Mr. Carnegie had given a donation to cover the entire cost. As honourable men, he thought they should place the matter before Mr. Carnegie, and inform him how matters stood. It was eventually agreed to submit the whole position to Mr. Carnegie, and await his reply before proceeding further in the matter.

BATH : *Valuable Additions to the Reference Library.*—The library of the late Mr. J. W. Morris, which was purchased by the joint subscriptions of a committee of Bath citizens and some of his pupils and presented as a memorial of him to the Bath Public Reference Library, has now been arranged in two sections. The portion purchased by the citizens, numbering close on 2,000 volumes, consists chiefly of historical and biographical works, also many volumes of local interest, as well as illustrated works on botany and natural history. These add considerably to the value and to the utility of the library, which was previously sadly deficient in this class of literature. Each volume has a tasteful label placed inside with the inscription : "This Book formed part of the Library of the late J. W. Morris, Esq., F.L.S. It was presented to the Bath Public Reference Library by a committee of citizens as a memorial of his valuable services to Education, Literature and Art in the City."

The pupils' section numbers 1,000 volumes, and forms a representative collection of the works of the best English writers, including specimens of early English literature, a collection of historical tracts of the Cromwellian period. In the window of the building apportioned to this section a tablet of inlaid Italian walnut has been placed, bearing the following inscription : "The Pupils' Memorial to the late J. W. Morris, F.L.S. A record of his greatness as a teacher.—B. 1830, D. 1901." These volumes have also a label inside to distinguish the gift, worded as follows : "This Book formed part of the Library of the late J. W. Morris, Esq., F.L.S. It was presented to the Bath Public Reference Library by some of his pupils as a memorial of their gratitude for all he taught them."

A carved escutcheon has been placed on the centre book-case containing the library, which is a replica of Mr. Morris's own book-plate.

BIRKDALE: *Gift of a Site for a Public Library.*—Mr. C. J. Weld Blundell, Lord of the Manor, and chairman of the Birkdale District Council, has offered as a Coronation gift to Birkdale a site for a public library and reading-room, and £1,000 towards the erection of the building.

BIRMINGHAM: SELLY OAK: *Offer of £3,000 from Mr. Carnegie.* —Selly Oak is now almost the only populous suburb of Birmingham which has not a public library, but this long-felt want will shortly be supplied, thanks to the public-spirited enterprise of Mr. Olivieri, vice-chairman of the King's Norton District Council and the remarkable munificence of Mr. Andrew Carnegie, who has already distributed great sums in promoting educational and philanthropic institutions in England, as well as in Scotland and in his adopted country. When all the world was talking of these princely benefactions some months ago, it occurred to Mr. Olivieri that if the great want of Selly Oak was brought to the notice of the Steel King he might be induced to do for the working class community there what he has recently done for Stratford-on-Avon —to give the sum necessary to build a public reading-room and free library. Mr. Olivieri wrote several letters to Mr. Carnegie, pointing out that in a manufacturing district with a population of about 20,000 there was no public institution to provide for the intellectual recreation of the people, and supporting his application by offering to provide a suitable site at his own expense. In answer to his last appeal he has received a very gratifying letter from Mr. Carnegie's private secretary. The reply is as follows:—

"SKIBO CASTLE, ARDGAY, N.B.,
"*17th June*, 1902.

"DEAR SIR,
"Responding to your representations on behalf of Selly Oak. If the district adopts the Free Libraries Act and levies an adequate rate under it, Mr. Carnegie will be glad to furnish the sum you mention (three thousand pounds) to erect a free public library building for Selly Oak. The town will require to provide a site free for the building."

Mr. Olivieri read this letter at a meeting of the Selly Oak Coronation Committee on the 19th June, of which he is hon. treasurer, and also at a meeting of the Selly Park and District Coronation Committee, of which he is chairman. He expressed the hope that the District Council would lose no time in taking the necessary steps to establish a free library, which he thought would be a very fitting way of celebrating the Coronation. He also announced that he was prepared to give a site for the building at the corner of Dawlish and Teignmouth Roads, or, if another site was found to be more suitable, he would contribute £100 towards the purchase of it. Councillor Olivieri has given notice to the King's Norton District Council that at their meeting on 9th July, he will move the adoption of the Free Libraries Act for Selly Oak. Thanks to the exceptionally liberal gift from Mr. Carnegie, which is three times as much as Stratford-on-Avon received, it is estimated that only a ½d. rate will be required to maintain the library.

BRENTFORD: *Offer of £5,000 for a Library Building from Mr. Carnegie.*—At a meeting of the Brentford Free Library Committee it was announced that Mr. Carnegie had promised to give £5,000 towards a free library at Brentford if a site were provided. The present library is inadequate for its purposes. No doubt is felt in the town that they will be able to raise sufficient money to buy a site.

CARDIFF: UNIVERSITY COLLEGE: *The Salisbury Library.*— The Council of the South Wales and Monmouthshire University College, Cardiff, have definitely decided that the Salisbury Library now stored at the college in rooms adjoining the College Library, shall be merged in the College Library. The effect of this decision is that the suggestion, approved by the Court of Governors, that the Salisbury Library should be transferred on terms for a period to the Cardiff Free Library, is abandoned. The Senate of the college, and indeed, the academical section of the whole of the University of Wales, were absolutely opposed to the suggested removal. A meeting of the Salisbury Library was held at the college, Mr. Ivor James presiding, when it was resolved to recommend the Council to appoint Mr. W. Phillips, B.A., a member of the college teaching staff, to prepare during the vacation a card catalogue of the library, and to appoint Prof. Powel as hon. curator.

GLASGOW: PARTICK: *Mr. Carnegie Offers £10,000 for a Library.* —Mr. Andrew Carnegie has, it is understood, written to Mr. Charles Taylor, author of *Partick Past and Present,* who has been in communication with him for some time, stating that he is willing to give the burgh of Partick the sum of £10,000 for the purpose of providing a free library, on condition that the Town Council adopt the Free Libraries Act and find a site. The sum will, it is expected, be sufficient to provide a large central library at Partick and a branch library at Whiteinch. So far, the Town Council have received no official intimation of Mr. Carnegie's offer, which has been made only in a private letter to Mr. Taylor. The question of a free library has never been discussed, either by the Council or by any of the committees, although, as a matter of course, it has been spoken of privately. Mr. Carnegie's offer comes therefore as a complete surprise to the Council and to the inhabitants, as there has been no talk whatever of providing a library. The gift of a library to Partick at this time is peculiarly fitting, as the burgh attains its jubilee this year.

KETTERING: *£8,000 from Mr. Carnegie to Build a Public Library.* —On the 12th June, Mr. Andrew Carnegie signified his intention of presenting to the town of Kettering the sum of £8,000. for the purposes of building a free public library.

KINGSTON-ON-THAMES: *The New Public Library.*—The Corporation of Kingston-upon-Thames is about to erect a new public library, at a cost of £6,000. The library is at present housed at Clattern House, on the ground floor, the municipal offices occupying the first floor. The premises are quite inadequate ; the reading-rooms are generally overcrowded, and the shelving accommodation in both lending and reference departments has long been exhausted, and additional cases have been erected in basement and hall. Last year the Corporation authorised the Library Committee to obtain plans and estimates for a new building. The services of Mr. Basil Champneys were secured as assessor, and eight architects were selected to submit plans, Mr. Alfred Cox being successful. In the Tramways Bill promoted by the Corporation in 1900 authority was obtained for the allocation of a site on the Fairfield allotments, and for the borrowing of £6,000 for forty years. The income from the 1d. rate is not sufficient to meet the annual expenses after repaying the instalments of principal and interest on such a loan ; but in the local Improvement Act of 1888 authority was given to raise the limit to 2d. in the £, with the consent of the burgesses. In accordance with the provisions of that Act, a public meeting was held on the 14th May to consider the following resolution submitted by Councillor Lyne, chairman of the Library Committee: " That this meeting of burgesses, duly convened pursuant to the Kingston-upon-Thames Improvement Act, 1888, hereby consents to the increased annual contribution out of the rate for library purposes from 1d. to 1½d. in the £, such rate to take effect from October next ". The Kingston Municipal Society opposed the scheme, and the *Surrey Comet*, in a leaderette headed " Tit for Tat," argued that as the Corporation had not acceded to the resolution passed at a recent public meeting held in connection with the extension of the arc lighting, it would be " a fair enough rejoinder " to wreck the library scheme. At the meeting an amendment was moved " that the question be postponed for twelve months," on account of the present severe pressure of taxation, both local and imperial (the local rates have just been reduced by 4d. in the £). The promoters had the best of the argument, for it was pointed out that if the question was postponed the provisions of the Act of 1900 would lapse. The amendment was eventually withdrawn, and the resolution carried with only ten dissentients. There were about 300 present.

LEICESTER: *Mr. Carnegie's Gift of £12,000 to Build a Central Library.*—At length it is the turn of the borough of Leicester to share in the princely generosity of Mr. Andrew Carnegie. The munificent Scotch multi-millionaire has offered the Council a gift of £12,000 to build the long and much-needed Central Free Library. He accompanies his handsome benefaction by the two very reasonable conditions he almost invariably imposes under such circumstances. One is that the site shall be given. The other is that the proposed library shall be adequately maintained by the rates. To neither of these terms should there be the slightest objection. The second, of course, goes without saying, and merely means that the Corporation in the future, as in the past, shall continue to maintain its libraries from and by the rates. Nor can the Corporation have any hesitation in providing the requisite site. The solitary question at issue will be the most central and convenient one that can be placed at the disposal of the Free Libraries Committee for the purpose. Sooner or later a judicious choice will be made; the work of construction will be commenced, and Leicester will ere long be endowed with a Central Library in some degree proportionate to its legitimate and growing demands. For the moment the predominant sentiment must be that of thanks to Mr. Carnegie for his benefaction. Many must have hoped that one of the local manufacturers or merchant princes would have provided the requisite amount from their abundance, and thereby recognised the doctrine of ransom, and done honour at once to the community and themselves. As no such munificence has come to the rescue of the Free Library Committee in their emergency, it is satisfactory to realise that Mr. Carnegie has recognised the need of the borough and provided the desired gift.

LEWISHAM: *Mr. Carnegie Offers two New Branch Libraries.*—At a meeting of the Lewisham Council on Wednesday, the 18th June, the Mayor announced that Mr. Carnegie had offered to give two new libraries to the borough for Brockley and Lower Sydenham working-class centres, making four which the borough will then have. The offer was accepted with the heartiest thanks. The borough recently adopted a 1d. rate instead of a ½d. one.

LIMERICK: *Steps Taken to Comply with the Conditions of Mr. Carnegie's Offer.*—It has been unanimously decided by the Council that a sum of £2,500 be borrowed for the purpose of complying with Mr. Carnegie's offer to provide, on certain conditions, the sum of £7,000 for a new free library building in the city. The sum of £50, if added to the estimates every half-year, would be sufficient to meet the payment of principal and interest on the sum it was proposed to borrow from the Board of Works. It was pointed out that in order to comply with the conditions they required to raise a sum of £350 per year. At present they could only levy 1d. in the £ for the purposes of a free library, and this would only amount to £279. If they got this loan from the Board of Works, and invested it, the interest would make up the balance between the £279 already in existence, and the annual amount required to meet the conditions.

LIVERPOOL: LYCEUM LIBRARY: *The Year's Work.*—The annual meeting of the proprietors of the Liverpool Library, Lyceum, was held on the 23rd May. The committee's report showed that 53,477 works had been issued during the year. The income for the year was £1,176 7s. 8d., which included a balance from the previous year of £41 2s. 3d. The expenditure was £1,153 0s. 6d., thus leaving a balance of £23 7s. in hand. The amount spent in the purchase and hire of books was £438, an increase of £64 on the sum paid the previous year. Various improvements had been made, all of which the committee believed would be much appreciated by the body of the proprietors. The president, in moving the adoption of the report, said he was glad to be able to say that the interests of the library had advanced more during the past year than they had done for many years previously. He paid a tribute to the ability and devotion of the librarian (Mr. Hutt), under whose administration, he said, many valuable improvements had been made. Among a set of new rules approved was one which says that the library shall in future be kept open till half-past five o'clock on Saturdays, instead of closing at 2.30 as hitherto. A proposal by Mr. T. J. Smith to increase the annual subscription from 25s. to 30s. was referred to the committee for consideration.

LIVERPOOL PUBLIC LIBRARIES: *Progress with the Toxteth Branch.*—That the Libraries Committee of the Liverpool City Council, under the chairmanship of Sir William Forward, are not relaxing their efforts to open out new avenues for the diffusion of good literature, will shortly be more amply demonstrated than ever. Already the library system in Liverpool is widely extended, and its benefits to students and readers considerable; but in order that even greater literary advantages may be enjoyed several new and highly equipped branches of the parent institution in William Brown Street are at no distant date to be established in various parts of the city. Of these, the Toxteth Library is so near completion that arrangements are now in hand for its formal opening—an interesting ceremony which, it is pleasing to hear, will be performed by that active and sympathetic supporter of the free library movement in England and America, Mr. Andrew Carnegie. This library is regarded by those having practical knowledge of such matters as a model of its kind. The exterior of the building is of a graceful and pleasing design, and may certainly be considered a very fine architectural addition to the south end of the city. Its interior, which, after all, is the main consideration, leaves nothing to be desired. Light and commodious reading-rooms for men, women and boys are now provided in Toxteth for the first time, all of which will be furnished with a wide selection of suitable magazines, periodicals and newspapers. In addition, there will be a free lending department, through which 26,000 volumes are available for general circulation. The new general catalogue now in the press, though recording books in all departments of literature, shows to how great an extent the needs of the student, the craftsman and the artisan have been considered by the committee. A special catalogue for juveniles is also in hand.

LONDON : **BETHNAL GREEN** : *New Building Wanted.* — A meeting to celebrate the twenty-sixth anniversary of the founding of the Bethnal Green Free Library was held on the 12th inst., in the central hall of the library in London Street. The Mayor of the borough (Mr. Chas. Edward Fox, J.P.), accompanied by the Mayoress, presided in state, and there was a very large attendance. In the brief *resumé* of the report, the committee congratulated the subscribers and their friends on the announcement that the King had consented to continue his patronage of the library, and that the Prince and Princess of Wales were their vice-patrons. Owing to the exertions and generosity of their supporters the library was now free from debt, but at the present moment there were no available funds whatever. A regular income in the shape of annual subscriptions was earnestly to be desired, while for the erection of the new building—now rendered so urgently necessary by the rapidly increasing number of readers—a sum of £20,000 was required. The returns for 1901 showed that the number of borrowers had reached the total of over 2,300 daily, and was steadily increasing. The free lectures, concerts, etc., and the evening classes, it was stated, had been continued with much success ; special mention being made of the free educational classes conducted by Mrs. H. Wynne, which had been of great practical service. Since the opening of the institution more than a million people altogether had been benefited by its different agencies. The committee, in closing their report, regretted that, up to the present, no one had come forward to offer a site and provide a building to meet the ever-increasing demands upon the present limited space of the library, and to furnish proper housing for the valuable books contained within its present miserably inadequate accommodation.

The Mayor of Bethnal Green, in opening the proceedings, drew attention to the fact that the library was not supported by a compulsory rate, but was kept up entirely by voluntary subscriptions. This was a fact of which Bethnal Green, as one of the poorest districts in London, might well be proud. The meeting was brought to a close by the passing of the usual votes of thanks, to which the Mayor, in briefly responding, warmly congratulated the Library Committee on the invaluable assistance which they had received from the indefatigable services of Mr. G. F. Hilcken, their able and energetic librarian, through whose unwearied efforts had been achieved much of the success of this most flourishing institution.

LONDON : **POPLAR** : *To Receive £15,000 from Mr. Carnegie for Branch Libraries.* —At the meeting of the Poplar Borough Council on the 19th June, the Mayor, Mr. W. Crooks, L.C.C., said that he was present when the freedom of the Plumbers' Company was presented to Mr. Andrew Carnegie, and that gentleman made a statement that in New York there were seventeen branch libraries which he had given on condition that they were afterwards maintained by the people. Knowing the need of the borough for such institutions, he (Mr. Crooks) set to work to see if a similar compact could not be made with Mr. Carnegie. He entered into correspondence with that gentleman, and he was now able to announce that he had received from Mr. Carnegie an offer of £15,000 for the erection of two libraries, one at Bromley and the other in Cubitt Town, on condition that they were maintained by the borough and the costs of the sites borne by the ratepayers. The Council decided to accept the offer, and votes of thanks were passed to the donor and to the Mayor.

MAIDENHEAD: *Mr. Carnegie Offers £5,000 for a Public Library.*— At an informal meeting of the Maidenhead Town Council held on the 20th June, which was attended by a large number of burgesses, Mr. W. F. Good, the Mayor, made the pleasing announcement that Mr. Carnegie had written him that day offering to present the town with £5,000 for the erection of a free public library. The only stipulation is that the town shall maintain the library and provide a suitable site. The offer was received with great enthusiasm and thankfulness. There is a feeling that the necessary funds to purchase the site should be raised during Coronation year.

MAN (ISLE OF): *Appeal for Help to Mr. Carnegie.*—Mr. Hall Caine has been in communication with Mr. Carnegie with a view to enlisting that gentleman's sympathy and interest in the Isle of Man. A letter has been received by Mr. Hall Caine from Mr. Carnegie containing what is considered a most important and generous proposal relating to free libraries in the Isle of Man, but the precise terms are not yet made known. This much, however, is authoritative, that assistance from Mr. Carnegie is only to be forthcoming provided the Manx people make an effort on their own account. A rough scheme of free libraries is consequently being prepared, which it is thought, with Mr. Carnegie's generous aid, might be attained. Mr. Hall Caine is interesting himself in the movement with the view to formulating a plan for submission to Mr. Carnegie. It is suggested that the scheme might in some way be identified with the Coronation.

MERTHYR TYDVIL: *Mr. Carnegie Offers £6,000 for Library Buildings.*—During the past few years the Merthyr District Council, through their Free Libraries Committee, have been engaged in maturing the scheme for the establishment in the Merthyr parish of free libraries under the Free Libraries Act. A year ago Mr. F. Sydney Simons, Mr. Arthur Daniel (a former chairman of the Free Libraries Committee) and other gentlemen approached Mr. Carnegie with a view of enlisting his assistance. Mr. D. A. Thomas, M.P., interested himself in the matter, and nothing more of it was heard until Mr. Simons, the present chairman of the Merthyr Free Libraries Committee, received from the senior member for Merthyr a communication with enclosures setting forth that Mr. Carnegie would furnish the £6,000 required for library buildings at Merthyr Tydvil under his (Mr. D. A. Thomas's) scheme of 2nd June, *viz.*, five branches at £700, one at £1,000, and a central library at £1,500. This was in consideration of sites being provided, and not being a burden on the library revenue under the Act, and that the whole of that revenue resulting from the maximum assessment would be devoted to the purchase of books and general up-keep of these libraries. Mr. Carnegie was induced to do this because of his indebtedness to the Welsh element in America, many of whom had rendered him service. Mr. Carnegie said: "They are a great people, the Welsh". He bracketed them with the Scotch. The revenue for the up-keep of the reading-rooms is £900. One freehold site has been given by Lord Windsor at Troedyrhiw, and there are leaseholds at Penydarren, held at a nominal rent of 1s. per annum, from Alderman Thomas Williams; at Abercanaid, rented from the Windsor and Mackintosh estates; and at Aberfan, rented from Mr. Griffiths's estate. The chairman of the Free Libraries Committee thinks some scheme will now have to be propounded for the purpose of providing for the acquisition of the freehold of the various sites. Possibly some of the local landlords will exhibit a generous disposition in the matter.

MONTROSE: *£7,500 from Mr. Carnegie to Erect Public Library Building.*—At a meeting of the Montrose Town Council on the 9th June, Provost Melvin intimated the receipt of a letter from Mr. Andrew Carnegie regarding his offer to provide a building for a free library in Montrose. Provost Melvin had informed Mr. Carnegie that the rate of 1d. in the £ would only yield about £250, and the donor had replied in the following terms:—

"DEAR SIR,

"Hearty congratulations upon your success. The revenue stated will not be great for a free library for a town of the size of Montrose. Several towns have agreed to supplement the revenue under the Act by a regular contribution from the Common Good. Thus Bo'ness, to which I have given £5,000, contributes £50 per annum from that source. Montrose appeals specially to me, and I shall be glad to give £7,500 to erect its free library buildings. This, I think, you will consider ample, it being beyond the usual allowance in proportion to population and maintenance funds."

The Council agreed to tender their thanks to Mr. Carnegie for his handsome gift, and the Provost gave notice that at next meeting he would move that competitive plans be advertised for.

NORTHAMPTON: *£5,500 Given by Mr. Carnegie for a Public Library.*—It was announced at a meeting of the Northampton Town Council on the 23rd June, that Mr. Andrew Carnegie had given £5,500 to the borough for the purpose of erecting a free public library on a central site to be acquired by the Corporation. Mr. Carnegie has contributed £500 towards the endowment of the Queen Victoria High School for Girls, Stockton-on-Tees. The people of Stockton are raising an endowment of £6,000 as a memorial to her late Majesty. Mr. Frank Brown, J.P., initiated the scheme by the gift of the site worth £2,000, a contribution of £2,500 towards the cost of erection, and £500 for the endowment fund, which now amounts to £4,572.

NORWICH: *Proposed Alterations.*—The annual report of the Free Library Committee, which has just been adopted by the Norwich Town Council, states that the statistics show a slight falling off in the issue of books, due to a decrease in the demand for fiction; while it is gratifying to note that history and travel, natural history and biography, showed an increase of 740 issues. The reference department has been freely used, the total issues being 12,777. During the year 506 books and 326 pamphlets have been added. The stock, including the local collection, now numbers 19,253 volumes and 8,543 pamphlets. No use has been made of the rooms at the top of the building, vacated by the School of Art. Their possible use and suitability for relieving the pressure in the men's reading-room by transferring to them the newspapers and their readers, had been under the consideration of the committee. The cost of preparing the rooms for that purpose, of special superintendence, heating, etc., and the probability of objection of readers to mount so many stairs, led the committee at their last meeting to order a report to be prepared on an alternative scheme, of covering the land available at the back by a capacious and healthy reading-room on the ground-floor level, free from these disadvantages. The attendance on Sundays has been counted bi-quarterly, resulting in the following averages: In the men's room, 175; in the women's room, 39; total, 214.

PERTH: *Sandeman Public Library.*—At a special meeting of the Library Committee held on the 22nd May, Mr. Minto announced that he had been appointed chief librarian at Brighton, and intimated his resignation. He expressed the hope that the committee would relieve him of the duties a few days before the beginning of July, when he commenced work in the South. Lord Provost Macgregor, in moving that the committee accept Mr. Minto's resignation, paid a high tribute to the manner in which the library had been conducted by him since his appointment. While they congratulated Mr. Minto on his appointment, they were very sorry to lose the services of an efficient public servant. The way in which the whole institution had been engineered and conducted throughout reflected upon Mr. Minto's ability very brilliantly. They very warmly congratulated him on the excellent appointment he had been privileged to receive from the community of Brighton, and they offered him their good wishes for his future prosperity. They thought Mr. Minto ought to receive their public acknowledgments of the appreciation of the community of Perth for his services. Mr. Minto returned thanks to the Lord Provost and the committee. In view of an offer by the Perthshire Society of Natural Science to hand over their museum to the town free of cost, it was resolved to arrange for a joint meeting of the Town Council and the Library Committee to be held on 5th June.

WORKINGTON: *Gift of £7,000 from Mr. Carnegie for a New Public Library.*— The following letter from Mr. Carnegie to Alderman J. Fletcher, Deputy Mayor, was made public early in the month of June :—

"SKIBO CASTLE, ARDGAY, N.B.,
"*5th June,* 1902.

" DEAR SIR,
"Mr. Carnegie has considered your statement about Workington, and notes that the Free Libraries Act has been adopted, the revenue being £382. Mr. Carnegie will be glad to provide seven thousand five hundred pounds (£7,500) sterling for the erection of a free public library building, the town to furnish site. When this has been done and you are ready to proceed with building, cash payment will be arranged."

The magnificent gift is the outcome of Mr. Fletcher's persistent labours, together with that of the Public Library Committee, during his term of office as Mayor in 1900. Imbued with the hope that the great philanthropist of the United States and Great Britain might help the public library needs of Workington, he made representations to Mr. Carnegie, showing that the present building in Pow Street was altogether inadequate owing to the increase in the population, the growth of the library consequent on the gift of books by Workington people and the enterprising book club. Alderman Fletcher was greatly aided by Mr. Purves, the librarian, who had closely studied the position of affairs at the libraries in other towns to which Mr. Carnegie had materially contributed, and both at that period were sanguine that their appeals for help in the interests of the large population of iron and steelworkers would ultimately be successful. Mr. Fletcher, in all, wrote four letters to Mr. Carnegie, and it was in August, 1900, that a reply was received from Mr. Carnegie, stating that the matter would have his consideration. Nothing further transpired until the letter given above, which, on the inside margin, bore the addresses of Mr. Fletcher and Mr. J. S. Randles,

M.P., containing the assurance of this handsome gift was received, as was stated last night, by Mr. Fletcher. The Corporation possesses a splendid site in the centre of the town which is admirably adapted for the purpose, so that Mr. Carnegie's stipulation can at once be complied with. Workington people are fortunate at last, and they will attest in proper spirit and in the right way their lasting debt of gratitude to Mr. Carnegie, their educational benefactor.

OFFICIAL GAZETTE.

Cowan (Violet).—Miss Violet Cowan, who has been appointed assistant in the reference department of the Sandeman Public Library, Perth, is the youngest daughter of Samuel Cowan, author of the book on *Mary Queen of Scots and the Casket Letters.* Miss Cowan has had an exceptionally good education, both in this country and abroad, and so far as books are concerned has been brought up among them. She is, besides being well versed in modern literature, widely read in a most unusual degree in philosophy, of which she has made a special study, in both psychology and ethics, and on its historical side. She is also acquainted with several languages, including Greek and Italian, which last she studied in Florence, along with music and painting. She has also some knowledge of mathematics. Such a wide range of reading makes her especially fitted for the work of the reference department.

Soper (H. Tapley), Sub-Librarian of the Stoke Newington Public Library, and Hon. Editor of the *Library Assistant,* has been appointed Librarian of the Exeter Public Library.

NOTES AND QUERIES ON PUBLIC LIBRARY LAW.

UNDER this heading we continue from time to time to publish questions on the operation of the Public Libraries Acts which have been submitted to the Hon. Solicitor of the Association, together with the answers he has given.

All questions should be addressed to the Hon. Solicitor, H. W. FOVARGUE, Esq., Town Hall, Eastbourne, who will send his replies direct to correspondents, on the distinct understanding that both question and answer are to be published in THE LIBRARY ASSOCIATION RECORD.

The Establishment of Newsrooms.

Question.—I shall be very glad to know if my committee have power to establish a newsroom without a library at either or both of the two new districts recently included in the borough? My reason for asking is that there does not seem to be any desire for a library but only a newsroom.

Answer.—I know of nothing to prevent your library authority erecting newsrooms in different parts of the borough.

Payment of Property Tax.

Question.—I am instructed by our secretary to consult you on the subject of the liability of subscription libraries and literary societies to pay property tax.

To make my meaning clear I will state our case. We are the proprietors of a block of buildings in one of the principal streets of ————, consisting of shops on the ground floor and library premises on the second floor. Hitherto we have regularly paid property tax on the *Shop Property*, but up to the present year there has been no claim made against us with reference to the library rooms, and we, being a literary society, have considered ourselves exempt. This year the Commissioner claims payment on the *Library Premises* also. It has occurred to our secretary that you, as a Library Association, may possibly have had a similar case brought under your notice. Is it usual for literary societies to pay property tax? Can you refer me to any volume in your *Transactions* where this subject is ventilated?

Answer.—The liability of literary and scientific institutions to pay rates and taxes is discussed in *Chambers' Law Relating to Public Libraries and Museums* at pages, 139, 190 and 300.

I presume the shop property and the library premises are separately rated, and I am certainly of opinion that the library premises are exempt from property tax. I think you should refer the Commissioners to the case of Manchester Corporation *v.* Macadam (75 L.T.R. 229), where it was held by the House of Lords that a public library was a literary institution within the meaning of the Act, and therefore was not liable to pay property tax.

Product of Library Rate.

Question.—As it is impossible for us to carry out the provisions of the Library Acts with the net product of a 1d. rate, would you be kind enough to furnish me with particulars as to procedure in towns which recently have increased their rating powers for library purposes?

Answer.—The only method by which several towns have obtained increased powers of rating for public library purposes is by a Local Act.

As to Interest on Accumulation of Rates.

Question.—This borough was formed in November, 1900, by the amalgamation of Woolwich, Plumstead and Eltham. The Libraries Acts were extended to Eltham last year, but both in Woolwich and Plumstead they had been adopted, and the rates levied, for a year or two before the formation of the borough, though nothing had been done beyond commencing to build at Woolwich and preparing plans at Plumstead. Consequently, at November, 1900, there was an accumulation of the 1d. rate in both parishes (a loan having been taken for building at Woolwich). The Plumstead Commissioners handed over to the new borough £2,700 (accumulated rate *and interest*), and a larger amount was received from Woolwich parish. When the borough was formed these accumulations were included in a General Borough Fund, and the Library Committee have recently discovered to their consternation that they have not been credited with any interest since November, 1900, though they now have a balance to their credit of about £5,000, which they are about to capitalise for a new building.

The reason given for receiving no interest is that the General Borough Fund itself has been overdrawn, and has not received any interest (or rather it has not earned sufficient to pay the Electricity Committee, which have had similarly a much larger amount in the General Borough Fund, its interest, so that the Library Committee are getting none). We are pressing the Finance Committee to allow us this interest, which we think is certainly due to us, and are sending the following recommendation to their next meeting :—

"That the Library Account be credited with the whole of the interest which would have been allowed by the bank upon its balances if a separate banking account had been kept since the 9th November, 1900."

We have suggested a separate banking account, but this they refuse, nor do we wish it provided we get the same interest. Incidentally they tell us that we should soon be overdrawn if we had a separate account, but this would only be because it is their custom to credit our account with the proceeds of the 1d. rate once a year, and at the *end* of the year.

Answer.—I have no hesitation in saying that equitably the Library Fund is entitled to interest on the unexpended balance, but whether they could legally force the Council to pay it, is a matter upon which I should have to have further information.   Especially I should like to see a copy of the resolution appointing the Library Committee and any conditions imposed by the Council in the delegation of their powers, but I think you had better await the result of your application to the Finance Committee. I think the suggestion that the Library Account would have to pay interest, because the amount of the 1d. rate is not paid over until the end of the year, quite untenable.   The Council would have no power to charge interest against the yield of the library rate.

Erection of New Library Building out of Borough Fund.

Question.—This public library is under the control of a Municipal Town Council.

The general management of the library is delegated to a Committee entirely composed of members of the Town Council.   The Committee find the library has outgrown its accommodation and that a new library is necessary.

Is there any objection to the Council erecting a new building and paying for the same out of the Borough Fund, *if they are willing to do so ?*

Answer.—No, provided the Borough Fund is more than sufficient for the purposes to which it is applicable under the Municipal Corporations Act, 1882, and there is a surplus in the Fund (see section 143 of the Municipal Corporations Act, 1882).   If a rate has to be levied, it can only be done under the Public Libraries Act.

NOTEWORTHY BOOKS OF THE MONTH.

(Compiled by GUTHRIE VINE, M.A.)

The classification of each work according to Dewey's System of Decimal Classification is given in square brackets.

ALEXANDER (J.). The conquest of the air : the romance of aerial navigation. With a preface by Sir H. S. Maxim. [588.6] 8vo. 160 pp. *Partridge.* 2s. 6d.

BODMER (G. R.). Inspection of railway materials. [625] 8vo. 164 pp. *Whittaker.* 5s.

BURNE, *Lieut.* With the Naval Brigade in Natal, 1899-1900. A journal of active service kept during the relief of Ladysmith and subsequent operations in Northern Natal and the Transvaal under General Sir Redvers Buller. [968.2] 8vo. 168 pp. *E. Arnold.* 7s. 6d.

CHALMERS ( ), and HUNT ( ). On trade unions. [331.88] 8vo. *Butterworth.* 12s. 6d.

CHASE (F. H.). The credibility of the book of the Acts of the Apostles. Hulsean Lectures for 1900-1. [226.6] 8vo. 330 pp. *Macmillan.* 6s.

COLENSO (R. J.). Landmarks of artistic anatomy. [743] 4to. 64 pp. *Baillière.* 3s. 6d. *net.*

CONWAY (J.). Recollections of sport among fin, fur and feather. [799] 8vo. 334 pp. *Digby, Long & Co.* 6s.

CUMMINGS (W. H.). God save the King. The origin and history of the music and words of the National Anthem. [784.4] 8vo. 132 pp. *Novello.* 3s. 6d.

DAY (E. S.). An old Westminster endowment : the history of Grey Coat Hospital as recorded in the minute books. [372.9421 and refer from 377.7] 8vo. 302 pp. *Rees.* 3s. *net.*

DEBRETT's dictionary of the coronation. [394.4] 8vo. *Gale & Polden.* 3s. 6d. *net.*

DIAZ DE BIVAR (Rodrigo), called *El Cid.* Poem of the Cid. Translation by Archer M. Huntington. Vol. II. [861.12] 8vo. *New York, Putnam [De Vinne Press].* £6 6s.

DRUDE (P.). The theory of optics. Translated from the German by C. R. Mann and R. A. Millikan. [535.1] 8vo. *Longmans.* 15s. *net.*

DUFF (A.) Theology and ethics of the Hebrews. (*Semitic Series.*) [296] 8vo. *Nimmo.* 5s. *net.*

DUTT (R.). The economic history of British India : a record of agriculture and land settlements, trade and manufacturing industries, finance and administration. From 1757 to 1837. [886.54] 8vo. 484 pp. *Paul.* 7s. 6d.

ELISABETH, *Madame.* The life and letters of Madame Elisabeth de France. Followed by the journal of the Temple by Cléry, and the narrative of Marie Thérèse de France, Duchesse d'Angoulême. Translated by K. P. Wormeley. [944.04] 8vo. 340 pp. *Heinemann.* 21s. *net.*

ENGLAND, Church of. The coronation Prayer Book. With the service for use in Westminster Abbey. [264.03] 8vo. *Frowde.* 12s. 6d. *net.*

FIELD (J. E.). Saint Berin, the apostle of Wessex. The history, legends and traditions of the beginning of the West Saxon church. [274.2] 12mo. 248 pp. *S.P.C.K.* 3s. 6d.

FRASER (J. F.). The real Siberia. With an account of a dash through Manchuria. [915.7] 8vo. 296 pp. *Cassell.* 6s.

FROST (T. G.). A treatise on guaranty insurance. [368.8] 8vo. *Sweet & Murray.* 22s. 6d. *net.*

GREEN (R.). Anti-Methodist publications issued during the 18th century: a chronologically arranged and annotated bibliography of well-known books and pamphlets written in opposition to the Methodist revival during the life of Wesley : with an account of replies to them. [016.287] 8vo. 184 pp. *C. H. Kelly.* 3s. 6d. *net.*

GREGORY (A.), *Lady.* Cuchulain of Muirthemne : the story of the men of the Red Branch of Ulster. With a preface by W. B. Yeats. [898.2] 8vo. 380 pp. *Murray.* 6s. *net.*

HANNA (Charles A.). The Scotch-Irish, or the Scot in North Britain, North Ireland and North America. [941] 8vo. 2 vols. *Edinburgh, Schulze.* £2 2s. *net.*

HARPER (C. G.). The Holyhead road : the mail-coach road to Dublin. Illustrated by the author, and from old-time prints and pictures. [914.2] 8vo. 2 vols. *Chapman.* £1 12s.

HAVELOCK, *the Dane.* Havelock the Dane : an old English romance. Rendered into later English by Emily Hickey. [821.19] 8vo. *Catholic Truth Society.* 1s.

HEADLAM (C.). The story of Chartres. Illustrated by H. Railton. (*Mediæval Towns.*) [944.24] 12mo. 374 pp. *Dent.* 4s. 6d. *net.*

HUTTON (F. W.). The lesson of evolution. [575] 8vo. 110 pp. *Duckworth.* 2s. 6d. *net.*

INGLE (H.). Manual of agricultural chemistry. [631] 8vo. 422 pp. *Scott, Greenwood & Co.* 7s. 6d. *net.*

KEEN (F. N.). Tramway companies and local authorities : a collection of special provisions contained in private acts of Parliament of tramway companies, and relating particularly to the interests of local authorities. Compiled and arranged by F. N. Keen. [388] 8vo. 296 pp. *Merritt & Hatcher.* 10s. *net.*

KIRCHERSEN (F.). Bibliography of Napoleon : a systematic collection critically selected. [016.94405] 8vo. 198 pp. *Low.* 5s. 6d. *net.*

KURZ (L.). Guide to the chain of Mont Blanc. [914.449] 18mo. *Unwin.* 10s.

LENDON (E. H.). Method of cuignet or retinoscopy. [617.73] 4to. 2 vols. *Baillière.* 10s. 6d. *net.*

LILLY (W. S.). India and its problems. [354.54] 8vo. 344 pp. *Sands.* 7s. 6d. *net.*

LITTLE (A. G.). Mediæval Wales, chiefly in the 12th and 13th centuries. [942.9] 8vo. 160 pp. *Unwin.* 2s. 6d.

MABINOGION. Mabinogion : mediæval Welsh romances translated by Lady Charlotte Guest. With notes by Alfred Nutt. [891.66] 8vo. 378 pp. *Nutt.* 2s. 6d. *net.*

McGIFFERT (A. C.). The apostles' creed : its origin, its purpose, and its historical interpretation. A lecture, with critical notes. [238.1] 8vo. 214 pp. *T. & T. Clark.* 4s. *net.*

MAN (E. G.). Papal aims and Papal claims. With remarks on apostolic succession. [262.13] 8vo. 304 pp. *Sonnenschein.* 5s. *net.*

MAYSON (W. H.). Violin making ("Strad" Library). [787.1] 8vo. 108 pp. *Strad Office.* 5s.

MERRIMAN (R. L.). Life and letters of Thomas Cromwell. [942.052] 8vo. 2 vols. *Frowde.* 18s. *net.*

NIELD (Jonathan). A guide to the best historical novels and tales. [016.8] 8vo. *Elkin Mathews.* 5s. *net.*

OSTWALD (W.). Principles of inorganic chemistry. Translated by A. Findlay. [546] 8vo. 814 pp. *Macmillan.* 18s. *net.*

PASSOS (J. R. dos). Commercial trusts : the growth and rights of aggregated capital. [331.1] 8vo. *Putnam.* 5s.

PAUL (E. J.). The imperial army of India : its history, mechanism, government, equipment, etc. [354.546] 8vo. *Thacker.* 4s. *net.*

RICHARDSON (W. H.). A short bibliography of Abingdon in the county of Berks. [015.4229] 8vo. *Frowde.* 2s. *net.*

SAUNDERS (T. B.). Professor Harnack and his Oxford critics. [230] 8vo. 92 pp. *Williams & Norgate.* 1s. 6d. *net.*

SAUSSURE (César de). A foreign view of England in the reigns of George I. and George II. The letters of C. de Saussure to his family. Translated and edited by Madame Van Muyden. [942.07] 8vo. 396 pp. *Murray.* 10s. 6d. *net.*

SIDGWICK (H.). Philosophy : its scope and relations. An introductory course of lectures. [104] 8vo. 270 pp. *Macmillan.* 6s. 6d. *net.*

SMITH (E. M.). The law of master and servant, including therein masters and workmen in every description of trade and occupation. [347.6] 8vo. *Sweet & Murray.* 28s.

TAYLOR (A. J. W.). Refrigeration, cold storage and ice making : a practical treatise on the art and science of refrigeration. [621.5] 8vo. 612 pp. *Lockwood.* 15s. *net.*

THOMSON (B.). Savage Island : account of a sojourn in Niué and Tonga. [996.1] 8vo. 242 pp. *Murray.* 7s. 6d. *net.*

TOMPKINS (H. W.). Highways and byways in Hertfordshire. Illustrated by F. L. Griggs. [914.258] 8vo. 362 pp. *Macmillan.* 6s.

TOZER (H. J.). British India and its trade. (*International Commerce Series.*) [382] 8vo. 104 pp. *Harper.* 3s. 6d.

WATSON (T. E.). The story of France from the earliest times to the consulate of Napoleon Bonaparte. [944] 8vo. 2 vols. *Macmillan.* 21s.

WHITMAN (A.). Print-collector's handbook. [760] 8vo. 172 pp. *Bell.* 15s. *net.*

WILKINSON (J. R.). A Johannine document in the first chapter of St. Luke's gospel. [226.4] 8vo. *Luzac.* 1s. 6d. *net.*

A FEW NOTEWORTHY FOREIGN BOOKS.

ADAM (*Madame*), *i.e.*, *Juliette Lamber*.   Le roman de mon enfance et de ma jeunesse.   [848.89]   Paris : *Lemerre*.   18mo.   3 fr. 50.

BAUDRY DE SAUNIER (L.).   Les recettes du chauffeur : manuel pratique indiquant les procédés et les tours de main indispensables au conducteur d'une automobile, les remèdes aux pannes, etc.   Nouvelle édition.   [621]   Paris : *Dunod*.   8vo.   10 fr.

BERGER (C.), et GUILLERME (V.).   La construction en ciment armé : théories et systèmes divers, applications générales.   [623]   Paris : *Dunod*.   8vo (486 figures) and atlas in 4to.   40 fr.

CALLOU (L.).   Cours de construction du navire.   [623.8 and 623.9].   Paris : *Challamel*.   2 vols.   8vo (1100 figures dans le texte).   40 fr.

CHEVALIER (Ulysse).   Étude critique sur l'origine du St. Suaire de Lirey—Chambéry—Turin.   [246]   Paris : *Picard*.   8vo.   5 fr.

DUMOULIN (Maurice).   Précis d'histoire militaire : révolution et empire.   Fasc. ii. : Campagne de 1793.   [944]   Paris : *H. Barrère*.   8vo.   3 fr.

ENLART (Camille).   Manuel d'archéologie française depuis les temps mérovingiens jusqu'à la renaissance.   1ère partie, Architecture.   1.   Architecture religieuse.   [918.44 and refer from 723]   Paris : *Picard*.   8vo (405 figures).   15 fr.

FINZI (Giuseppe).   Dizionario di citazioni latine ed italiane.   [808.8 and refer from 870.8 and 850.8]   Palermo-Milano : *Sandron*.   8vo.   L. 8.

GASTAMBIDE (M.).   L'enfant devant la famille et l'état : étude de législation comparée.   [821.1, 331.8, 173.6, 179.2, etc.]   Paris : *Rousseau*, 8vo.   8 fr.

GRUYER (F. A.).   Chantilly.   Les portraits de Carmontelle.   [757]   Paris : *Plon-Nourrit*.   4to (40 héliogravures).   100 fr.

GUILBERT (C. F.).   Les générateurs d'électricité à l'exposition universelle de 1900.   [621.3 and refer from 537.8]   Paris : *C. Naud*.   8vo (615 figures).   30 fr.

HARIOT (Paul).   Atlas de poche des fleurs de jardins les plus faciles à cultiver.   128 planches coloriées.   [716]   Paris : *P. Klincksieck*.   16mo.   6 fr. 50.

LECLÈRE (A.).   Étude géologique et minière des provinces Chinoises voisines du Tonkin.   [555.12 and refer from 951.2]   Paris : *Dunod*.   8vo.   10 fr.

LESUEUR (Daniel).   Le meurtre d'une âme : roman.   [848.89]   Paris : *Lemerre*.   18mo.   3 fr. 50.

LOTH (Arthur).   Le portrait de N.-S. Jésus Christ d'après le Saint Suaire de Turin avec reproductions photographiques.   [246]   Paris : *Oudin*.   8vo.   1 fr. 50.

MOUSSU (G.).   Traité des maladies du bétail.   [619]   Paris : *Asselin et Houzeau*.   8vo (187 figures).   15 fr.

PORTALIS (Baron Roger).   Adélaïde Labille-Guiard (1749-1805) Peintre de mesdames de France et du comte de Provence.   [927 and 757].   Paris : *Rapilly*.   8vo (avec reproductions).   20 fr.

RABELAIS : Œuvres accompagnées d'une notice, . . . d'un commentaire, etc., par Ch. Marty Laveaux (Collection Lemerre).   Tome v.   [847.32]   Paris : *Lemerre*.   8vo.   10 fr.

RAZOUS (Paul).   Les scieries et les machines à bois : exploitation en forêt, scieries fixes, ateliers de menuiserie, machines diverses, tonnellerie, accidents.   [674]   Paris : *Dunod*.   8vo (332 figures).   15 fr.

RICHER (Dr. Paul). L'art et la médecine. Illustré de 345 reproductions d'œuvres d'art, tableaux, statues, etc. [**709** and refer from **610.7**] Paris : *Gaultier, Magnier.* 4to. 30 fr.

RIVOLI (M. le Duc de). Les missels imprimés à Venise de 1481 à 1600 : description, illustration, bibliographie. [**094** and **761**] Paris : *Rothschild.* Folio (orné de 5 planches sur cuivre et de 350 gravures, etc.). 250 fr.

SERAO (Matilde). Il paese di Cuccagna : romanzo napoletano. [**853.88**] Napoli : *Trani.* 16mo. L. 4.

SOULIER (Alf.). Traité pratique de l'électricité : sonneries électriques —téléphones—éclairage électrique—rayons—télégraphie sans fil. [**621.3** and refer from **537.8**] Paris : *Garnier.* 18mo (gravures). 3 fr. 50.

YRIARTE (Charles). Françoise de Rimini dans la légende et dans l'histoire. [**920.7** and refer from **945.04** and **851.1**] Paris : *Rothschild.* 16mo (Imprimé en trois couleurs sur papier de Japon). 10 fr.

LIBRARY ASSOCIATION : PROCEEDINGS AND NOTICES.

Monthly Meeting, 15th May, 1902.

THE Fifth Monthly Meeting of the Session was held on Thursday, 15th May, at 20 Hanover Square, at 8 o'clock.

Mr. L. Stanley Jast presided in the unavoidable absence of the President and the Hon. Treasurer. About fifty members and visitors were present. Messrs. Barrett and Bond were nominated scrutineers of the ballot, and the following candidates, approved by the Council, were duly elected as members :—

Dr. W. Macneile Dixon, LL.B., Professor of English Language and Literature, Birmingham University. (President-Elect.)

Mr. Walter Powell, Sub-Librarian, Public Libraries, Birmingham.

The Kensal Rise Public Library.

Mr. Eli Collins, Assistant Librarian, Patent Office Library.

Mr. Frank Searby, Solicitor and Honorary Secretary, Free Library Committee, Ilkeston.

Mr. William Ed. Simnett, Assistant Librarian, Institution of Civil Engineers, Westminster.

The CHAIRMAN called upon Mr. A. Cotgreave, librarian of the West Ham Public Libraries, Stratford, to read a paper, printed in full in another part of the present issue, on

Library Indicators : Pro and Con.

The CHAIRMAN said Mr. Cotgreave's exhaustive statement had been listened to with great interest. The subject was now open for discussion, and he would call upon Mr. DOUBLEDAY, who said he hoped he was not becoming a marked man. The opener of a discussion was in a some-what unfortunate position, and he preferred to have time for reflection, and to gather up thoughts from what other speakers said. His con-fidence in indicators was shown by the fact that he had adopted them in his library; but at the same time the keenest admirers of the indicator system must admit that indicators had their demerits. He considered that their chief demerit was the amount of space they occupied. Indicators must be placed in a good light and were bound to occupy much room. He knew a library in which a long series of indicators gradually overran what had been a fine open counter, and threatened to run out of the building, across the town and into the country. The way to arrest such rank growth was, he thought, to re-organise the lending library at intervals of years, and the collection would no doubt be the better for a periodical weeding out, especially of old science and fiction—possibly Mr. Cotgreave might claim that as an advantage for the indicator system. He could not agree with some of Mr. Cotgreave's arguments, particularly that relating to borrowers waiting at the counter. It was very poor fun for a person to stand awaiting his turn to be served. His opinion was that the smaller the indicator the better, and any contrivances for restricting their space was to be welcomed. In the main he was of opinion that the best means of introducing the books to the public was by means of the indicator in connection with an up-to-date card catalogue and a good printed catalogue. He hoped to hear other opinions, and trusted to pick up a few hints. Mr. Cotgreave had treated the subject in a broad-minded way, and he congratulated him upon his moderation. At the same time he thought the Council had made a huge mistake in arrang-ing for this and the previous meeting: they should have asked Mr. Jast to write upon the "Indicator System," and Mr. Cotgreave on "Open Access".

Mr. J. D. BROWN said: he took a very great interest in indicators, as one who had made some study of their powers and limitations. It cost a considerable mental effort to invent an indicator, but it brought out all the problems connected with the charging and registration of books in a very detailed and useful manner. He had invented several indi-cators, all of which were very good, and he felt that any one who tried to invent something new would find it very difficult to do so. He regarded the study of the indicator as a most stimulating mental exercise, coupled with which, it had the advantage of providing a useful experience in overcoming the practical difficulties connected with one important department of library management. He should strongly advise every librarian to try and invent a new indicator.

Mr. MASON said they were indebted to Mr. Cotgreave for his paper, although the subject of "Indicator *versus* Open Access" had been very well threshed out, and there was little new to be said. The indicator worked very well at his own library, and the question of space would not trouble him until it became urgent. Until he could give more space to open access than he could to indicators he thought he would stick to the latter. He thought the solution of the matter would be to use the indicator for fiction only.

The CHAIRMAN proposed that the hearty thanks of this meeting be accorded to Mr. Cotgreave for his admirable paper.

Mr. PLANT (Shoreditch) said: "I have much pleasure in seconding the vote of thanks to Mr. Cotgreave for his very interesting paper on such a practical subject. I agree with Messrs. Doubleday and Mason that the 'Cotgreave' Indicator occupies a great amount of counter space, and believe that in course of time it will be used in the larger libraries for fiction only. In many libraries, however, the method adopted for the numbering of the books is responsible to some extent for the great length of indicators which had to be provided. The system adopted at Shoreditch was to have a running number through all the classes, instead of numbering from one onwards in each of the various classes and providing unnecessary gaps in the indicators for anticipated additions. At the Shoreditch libraries there are no gaps; the last number entered in the indicator always clearly representing the total number of volumes located in the lending departments."

Library Association Notes.

Library of the Association.—The Council have decided to take immediate steps to re-organise the library of the Association, and have it made accessible to members. In the meantime, they will be glad to receive donations of money or books for the purpose of augmenting the existing collection. The library will be restricted to works relating to bibliography, the history and management of libraries, catalogues, and works of professional interest. Donations of money should be forwarded to the hon. treasurer, Mr. Henry R. Tedder, The Athenæum, Pall Mall, S.W., and gifts of books to Mr. J. D. Brown, Clerkenwell Public Library, Skinner Street, E.C., who has once more kindly consented to take charge of the Association's collection of books and make it available for the use of members of the Association.

Reprint of De Morgan's Paper.—Copies of the separate reprint, on hand-made paper, of Augustus De Morgan's paper, "On the Difficulty of Correct Description of Books," may now be had on application to the Assistant Secretary, at Whitcomb House, price one shilling *net*. Only a limited number of copies are for sale.

Correction.—In the report of the discussion on "Open Access" in the June number, Mr. Inkster is made to speak of 12,000 readers in one day: the number should have been 1,200.

Meeting at Nottingham, 5th June, 1902.

A meeting of the Library Association was held at Nottingham on Thursday, 5th June. The following members of the Association, and others, were present: Messrs. C. W. Sutton (Manchester), W. Crowther (Derby), F. S. Herne (Leicester), Harris (Birmingham), J. T. Radford (Nottingham), W. J. Willcock (Peterborough), and Kenning (Rugby), Mr. and Mrs. Brown (Wigan), Mr. and Mrs. Kirkby (Leicester), Mr. and Mrs. Dennis (Hucknall), Mr. E. A. Baker (Derby), Messrs. T. Dent, C. Gerring, Carlin, Glover, Pritchard, J. S. Kirk, W. A. Briscoe, and Miss Hill (Nottingham), Messrs. Miller (Buluwayo, Rhodesia), Andrews (Loughborough), Burkharett and Miss Harris (Rotherham), and Mr. McLean (Norwich).

Mr. J. Potter Briscoe, the city librarian, conducted the party to various places of interest in the city during the morning, including the Central Library, University College, Natural History Museum, Technical Schools, the Arboretum and the Church Cemetery Caverns. A visit was paid to Messrs. Cutts' Lace Factory, and the Bromley House and Mechanics' Institution Libraries.

In the afternoon the members assembled in the Exchange Hall, and were cordially welcomed by Alderman F. R. Radford, the Deputy Mayor of Nottingham. Mr. C. W. Sutton, M.A. (Manchester), having been elected to the chair, a paper was read by Mr. W. J. Willcock of Peterborough on "Library Lectures: a Retrospect and a Suggestion," in which he advocated short informal talks about books, such as had been introduced by Mr. Briscoe in Nottingham, and which had tended to popularise the library and spread the knowledge of its usefulness over a wide area. Mr. Briscoe, in course of discussion, said that the half-hour talks had been started about twelve years ago, and had been fairly well attended. He should like to see the system extended as much as possible, and hoped some day to have lectures instead of the half-hour talks.

A paper was then read by Mr. A. J. Caddie of Stoke on "The Reading-room in Connection with the Library," in which he observed that there was a great difference in the reading-room of to-day and that of thirty years ago. In his opinion there was too much pandering to what he would term the recreative side of reading—light literature.

A paper on "Reference Libraries in Small Towns" was read by Mr. H. Walker of Longton, who was of opinion that a small town could not support both a reference and a lending library, and that a choice must be made of either one or the other. In a residential district the reference library flourished, but in a manufacturing town a good lending library was more suitable, and productive of far better results. There was also great need for books on local industries. Mr. S. F. Kirk, of the Nottingham Reference Library, then read a paper entitled "The Library in Relation to the Elementary Teacher". Mr. Kirk stated that Nottingham was perhaps unique in having its Free Library and University College under one roof, and he had been able personally to note the value of the library to students. He was of opinion that reference libraries were of the greatest use to pupil teachers and young schoolmasters and schoolmistresses.

The subject of "Boy *versus* Girl Assistants in Public Libraries" was introduced by Mr. Harris of Birmingham, in which the difficulty of getting boy assistants owing to the low rate of remuneration was put forward.

During the discussion on the various papers, the Chairman referred to the desirability of library tables not being utilised so much for propagandist pamphlets, such as those issued by anti-vaccinators and advocates of obscure religions, which view was supported by Mr. Briscoe, who said that it was well realised that free libraries were good advertising mediums.

A comprehensive vote of thanks to the Mayor of Nottingham, Mr. Cutts, Mr. P. H. Stevenson, the secretary of the University College, Ald. F. R. Radford, the readers of the papers, and the Chairman having been proposed by Mr. Crowther, seconded by Mr. F. S. Herne and passed, the members proceeded to the Castle, where they were entertained to tea by Mr. Briscoe, and subsequently inspected the Art Galleries, the Castle Dungeons, and Mortimer's Hole.

Librarians of the Mersey District.

A successful meeting of the librarians of the Mersey District was held at Warrington on the 6th of June. The programme included a drive to Arley Hall and Great Budworth, Cheshire. Permission had been kindly granted for the party to ramble through the beautiful gardens at Arley, and this privilege was thoroughly appreciated. Tea was provided at the Cock Inn, Great Budworth, a hostel famous for its literary associations. The day was an ideal one for a drive, the weather not being too hot and the recent rains having effectively laid the dust. The return journey was through pretty country, the beauties of which were enhanced by the gorgeous rays of the setting sun. On arrival at Warrington Mr. Madeley was voted to the chair and heartily thanked for his work in organising a most enjoyable meeting and excursion. The resolution of the Council of the Library Association relative to the annual retirement of members of the Council was considered, and strong dissatisfaction expressed with the scheme therein suggested.

EDUCATION COMMITTEE.

PROFESSIONAL EXAMINATION, 28TH MAY, 1902.

Section 2.—Cataloguing, Classification and Shelf Arrangement.

CATALOGUING.

The following candidate has passed with merit:—
Mr. W. R. B. PRIDEAUX.
The following candidates have passed:—
Miss ELSIE BRAKE, B.A.
Mr. B. M. HEADICAR.
Mr. PERCY H. WOOD.

CLASSIFICATION AND SHELF ARRANGEMENT.

The following candidates have passed with honours:—
Miss ELSIE BRAKE, B.A.
Mr. B. M. HEADICAR.
The following candidates have passed with merit:—
Miss MABEL E. MORTON.
Mr. PERCY H. WOOD.
Miss ALICE JONES.
The following candidates have passed:—
Mr. W. F. RAPPLE.
Mr. JOHN WARNER.
Mr. W. R. B. PRIDEAUX.
Mr. J. D. STEWART.

The examiners note with pleasure a decided improvement in the quality of the papers on this subject.

(Signed)   JAMES DUFF BROWN.
L. STANLEY JAST.
FRANK J. BURGOYNE.

Note.—The candidates who have passed with honours have obtained full marks in their section. Those who have passed with merit have obtained over 75 per cent. of marks.

On behalf of the Education Committee,

(Signed)   HENRY D. ROBERTS,
Hon. Secretary.

ST. SAVIOUR'S PUBLIC LIBRARY,
44A SOUTHWARK BRIDGE ROAD, S.E.

COMMUNICATIONS.

THIS department of the RECORD, if properly appreciated, should prove of great practical value to our readers, affording them as it does a ready medium of inter-communication. We therefore invite our readers to make free use of these columns, for giving expression to views, criticisms and suggestions upon any subject that properly comes within the scope of librarianship and bibliography.

To the Editor of THE LIBRARY ASSOCIATION RECORD.

DEAR SIR,
    Herewith I beg to enclose you a cutting from *The Diamond Fields Advertiser* of to-day's date, descriptive of an old volume of Africana which has recently been presented to this library. Can you or any of your readers inform me if there is an earlier instance known of the regular issue of monthly lists of the additions to a public library than the one therein noticed by Mr. Jardine of the Cape Town Library in the years 1831-3?
    Personally, I am not aware of one, but I shall be glad to be corrected if I am wrong in attributing to Mr. Jardine, the enterprising and optimistic librarian of Cape Town from 1824 to 1841, the first issue of such lists? Elsewhere I have been at some pains to advance the claim of the "Dark Continent" to a far from backward place in the public library movement of the last century, and this additional evidence is at the least interesting.
                I am, yours faithfully,
                            BERTRAM L. DYER,
                                Librarian.

PUBLIC LIBRARY,
KIMBERLEY, 22*nd May*, 1902.

Literature at the Cape: Seventy Years Ago.

"Mr. Moses Cornwall, J.P., chairman of the Committee of the Kimberley Public Library, has presented to that institution an interesting old volume, bearing the Cape Town imprint, which forms a valuable addition to the collection of Africana which is gradually being accumulated in the Kimberley Reference Library.

"The volume is a slim quarto of some 416 pages, printed in three columns, dated 1832, and the second volume of *The Cape of Good Hope Literary Gazette*, which was commenced under the editorship of Mr. A. J. Jardine in 1830, and in spite of much flourishing of trumpets as to the possibilities of the Colony as a literary centre, came to an end in 1833.

"In the volume before us Mr. Jardine raises the shout of victory at the success of his first volume, and says that when he undertook the publication of the *Gazette* several friends smiled at what they were pleased to term his credulity in supposing the Colony ripe for a literary journal in the English language. Having made the experiment and witnessed the favourable results, he apprehends that some credit is due to him for thus rightly estimating the growing intelligence of 'this most interesting of the British Colonies'.

"The admirable success of the first volume and of the second, which we glean from the editor's farewell on the last page of the volume, was not continued in the third year of its existence, for, as we have stated, the *Gazette* disappeared in 1833, to re-appear in octavo form in 1847, under the editorship of a Mr. J. L. Fitzpatrick, and to vanish finally from human ken in 1848.

"Like many another literary journal which has been started in South Africa, our readers may say, for at the present moment there is not one periodical published in the whole of South Africa exclusively devoted to literary concerns, while the general monthly magazines have suffered from a heavy mortality, so that at the present but one, *The Veld*, attempts to appear with any regularity.

"The volume of the *Gazette* which is now before us has evidently been a treasured possession of its first owner, Mr. James Fitzpatrick, whose book-plate it still bears, for some of the original wrappers in which the *Gazette* was issued still remain at the end of the volume, the whole number having been originally bound, though the major portion of them has disappeared.

"These wrappers are of a very interesting character, for the editor of the *Gazette* was librarian of the South African Library, and on each of them that has remained in the volume appears a list of the month's additions to the shelves of that institution.

"In 1824 Thomas Pringle, the Laureate of South Africa, had resigned his appointment as librarian of the South African Library, in order, as Sir Walter Scott put it, 'to publish a Whig journal at the Cape of Good Hope,' and Mr. Jardine had been appointed as his successor. He held office till 1841, and during this period he was instrumental in popularising literature in Cape Town to an enormous extent. Twice were the constitutions of the South African Library remodelled, so as to enable the circulating library to be inaugurated, and the present library system of South Africa owes to Mr. Jardine its most distinctive feature—the local management of the libraries by committees elected by and from the subscribers who provide the main funds for the upkeep of the institutions. For it was during his librarianship that the wine tax, which formerly provided the main revenue of the South African Library, was repealed, and the system of annual subscriptions introduced, while the Governor and Council abolished the old and autocratic Trustees of the Public Library, and substituted for them a popularly elected committee. So great was the success of the new system that down to 1861 the Cape Town Library was mainly supported by the revenue derived from its circulating department, and not till 1862 did the Cape Government commence that series of handsome annual subsidies which have helped to make the Cape Town Library the largest library in South Africa, and which now, owing to the growth of the suburbs of Cape Town, each with its library, form the main portion of its income.

"The list of 'Additions to the South African Public Library,' which the enterprising and optimistic librarian printed on the back cover of his *Gazette*, is the earliest instance of a practice that is now fairly common—so far as its regularly monthly appearance in a periodical goes—and at the present moment it gives one a curious glimpse of the literary life of seventy years ago. The first feature that we note is that the 'periodicals' of October, 1831, were received at the Cape in February, 1832, and those of the succeeding months with regularity in March and April. Steamships have made the receipt of periodicals much more prompt in these days, and while 'The Family Library' is no more, the colonial editions of English books, appearing almost simultaneously with the English editions, and the general output of books from the Press now so great, that every library of size receives more than thirty new volumes in a month, yet it is not a little encouraging to find that in February, 1832, *The Mutineers of the Bounty* was received with six other works, while in April of that year thirty-one works were to hand, among them *Robert of Paris*, by the author of *Waverley*, *Eugene Aram*, by Hood, and *Newton Forster*.

"Turning from these lists of additions, there is other matter of interest on the wrappers of these old *Gazettes*. Education in England in 1832 we know to have been bad enough, but the following advertisement makes us wonder what Cape education was:—

"At Mr. Gray's Academy youths are carefully instructed in grammar, geography, the mathematics, and every other branch usually considered as forming part of an English school education. Terms: Rds. 12 per month. Two months' notice previous to the removal of a pupil. The rudiments of Latin and French, if required, without any addition.

"Surely for the rate of eighteen shillings a month—the equivalent of twelve rix-dollars—it was possible for English schoolmasters to include the rudiments of at least Latin as part of an English school education without any 'if'.

"The days of joint subscription to one or more home papers have passed away, in favour of those 'exchanges' which we now see advertised in the ladies' papers, but does not the following smack of the canny Scot:—

"Wanted, one or two partners as subscribers to the *Edinburgh Evening Post, Dumfries and Galloway Courier*, and *Atlas Newspapers*. N.B.—These newspapers are received at every first opportunity in the Colony.

"A sad reminiscence of the destruction of a town garden is the following advertisement:—

"Ornaments for a garden. The highest tender will be received by Saturday morning next, at 12 o'clock, for the purchase of the Javanese arbour and sundial fountain in the garden of the Public Library. The whole may be removed without injury.

"Turning to the literary pages of the *Gazette*, we learn that the Cape Town Library was located in the Commercial Exchange, and that there was a 'parlour garden' attached to it, and in 1832 it was decided to utilise the site of this garden for a Freemasons' Lodge. No less than eight and a half columns are given up to a description of the garden and its flowers, part poetical and part in prose, of which this passage is a fair sample:—

"The loss of a single town garden, however small, is a public loss. We fully agree with Professor Wilson that the 'man who loves not trees—to look at them—to lie under them—would make no bones of murdering'.

"There are many interesting notes as to the introduction of rare plants and trees to the Cape, which would interest the botanist.

"The literary contents of the magazine are of varied character, and the editor's quotations on the title-page could with almost equal appropriateness be placed on a South African literary journal in the year 1902, as they were in 1832 by Mr. Jardine.

" The first is from Robert Hall :—

" These are not the times in which it is safe for a country to repose in the lap of ignorance. If there ever were a season when public tranquillity was en- sured by the absence of knowledge, that season is past. Everything in the condition of mankind announces the approach of a great crisis, for which nothing can prepare us but the diffusion of knowledge, probity and the fear of the Lord.

" The second is from an anonymous writer in the *S.A. Quarterly Journal* for 1830.

" Men have done a great deal here, in preparing the means to sustain a populous community round the stone which used to receive the name of a pass- ing ship, and was left in solitude, but this community has not otherwise done much to develop the condition and resources of the strange territory it is placed in, and of those who have been investigating the teeming portions of nature's domain around us, all have been foreign to the land they illustrated.

" In the *Gazette* educational matters are discussed at some length, and the ' apparent intellectual deficiencies of the youth of this Colony are deplored, while the munificent donations for educational purposes of McGill to Montreal, and the establishment of the Guernsey College, are noted with a regret that ' the whole continent cannot present the establishment of any institution for the benefit of the people equally superb '.

" The notes on the early Cape newspapers are of great interest. The paper started by Pringle and Fairbairn in 1824 with the battle cry of ' the mass of the people must be barbarous if there is no printing,' comes in for criticism of a not ungenerous character, though the *Cape Town Gazette*, once a general newspaper till General Bourke, at the command of Lord Charles Somerset, ' commandered ' it and turned it into the official organ it still remains, is much praised.

" Castigation of the heaviest possible journalistic kind falls upon a paper called *De Zuid Afrikaan*, which ' viperous journal' is stated to deal only ' Profaneness, Hate, Fury and Disaffection throughout the land,' while it 'is evidently the production of besotted ignorance '.

" Much amusing sarcasm is poured out at the first appearance of the *Grahamstown Journal* :—

" The New Year has introduced to us a new paper from the chief seat of the British settlers, edited, published and printed by Mr. H. L. Muerant. The world is in a fair way of doing well. The *Cherokee Indian Free Press* is suc- ceeding to admiration. The *Bedouin Journal* takes vastly among the Arabs, and advocates the glorious principles of Whiggism, whilst on the other hand the *Wahabyan Sentinel*, a Tory, is greatly supported by the friends of good order, and the Dey of Algiers. A King's College is talked of. As for *De West Afrikaan*, of Ashantee, we take the following sample of its loyalty :—

> ' Hurrah for the brother of the sun,
> Hurrah for the father of the moon,
> Throughout all the world there is none
> Like Quashiboo—the only one
> Descended from the great Baboon—
> Baboon—African Baboon.'

" This African Laureate beats Southey hollow. But let us come nearer the contents of the *Grahamstown Journal*. Board and education at so much per annum, and *the children* to be prepared for the Universities of Oxford, Cambridge or Trinity College, Dublin, etc., etc.

" The allusion to and parody of Pringle are evident, while the refer- ence to baboons is to the Baviaans River, or River of Baboons, which flowed past the Glen-Lyden Settlement to the Great Fish River, and the

Gazette is not without other sarcastic references to the Laureate of South Africa, and the Aborigines Protection Society, of which he was long the secretary, though Mr. Jardine is outspoken in his condemnation of slavery.

"The loyal and patriotic address of the Cape Lutheran Community to Queen Adelaide is set forth, while the early troubles of the English Church in South Africa receive attention. At the time the Bishop of Calcutta appears to have included in his diocese the Cape, but his spiritual direction does not appear to have been unchallenged.

"Of new books reviewed in the *Gazette* there are not many which are of interest to-day, but Croker's edition of *Boswell's Life of Johnson* is praised, while 'the very best of Mr. Bulwer's productions' is said by Mr. Jardine to be *Eugene Aram*, of the real facts of the life of the hero of which novel a long account is given. Galt's *Lives of the Players*, and Babbage's *Economy of Machinery and Manufactures* are both favourably noticed, as is also *The Memoirs of the Duchess d'Abrantes*.

"These are but a few hasty gleanings from a volume that is full of interest to all who care to look into the records of the early days of Cape Colony, and there are many other items which would repay careful reading now, as early volumes such as this give actual representations of a state of society that has passed away for ever, and with each succeeding year will become more and more impossible to realise without the actual evidence of such books.

"It has been well said that the history of a country is not recorded in its public records one half so vividly as it is in its ephemeral literature, and it is on little half-forgotten volumes like this that the future historian will rely, rather than on official records, and one of the greatest uses of a public library is that it affords a place where these individually unimportant trifles, but collectively important materials for the history of a country, may be at once preserved and made accessible."

B. L. D.

To Publishers, Booksellers and Library Furnishers.

●●●●●●●●●●●●●●●●●●●●●●●●●●●●●●

THE attention of Publishers, Booksellers and Library Furnishers is called to the advantages of **The Library Association Record** as an effective advertising medium.

The Journal, which is published regularly each month, is the official organ of The Library Association, and circulates in no fewer than 600 libraries up and down the country, as well as amongst the more prominent book-lovers and collectors.

Furnishing, as it does, the transactions of The Library Association, with notices of forthcoming meetings, in addition to library notes and news from all parts of the world, it is eagerly looked for and scanned each month by librarians, being, in fact, their official medium of intercommunication.

Not only does the **Record** circulate in the United Kingdom, it has a much wider sphere of influence, having subscribers in most of the British Colonies, as well as in the principal Countries of Europe.

Our aim in making this announcement is to secure a representative set of advertisements which may serve as a Directory of Library Furnishers, whether in fixtures, stationery, books or other accessories. The advantages of such a medium must be quite obvious to all firms in any way catering for the library, enabling them, as it does, to keep themselves constantly before not only librarians but members of Library Committees and book-collectors.

No advertisement will be received which is not strictly in keeping with the character of the Journal.

◆ ◆ ◆

SCALE OF CHARGES.

	Page.	Half Page.	Quarter Page.
Back of Cover - - - -	£3 0 0	£2 0 0	£1 5 0
Inside Cover and Pages Facing			
Matter or Cover - - -	2 2 0	1 7 6	0 17 6
Any other Page- - - -	1 11 6	1 1 0	0 13 4

Less than Quarter Page, 4s. per Inch Single Column.

Reduction on a Series of	Three.	Six.	Twelve.
Insertions - - -	5 per cent.	10 per cent.	20 per cent.

Advertisements should be sent to the Assistant Secretary at the Offices of the Association, Whitcomb House, Whitcomb Street, Pall Mall East, S.W.; or to Mr. A. E. Bennetts, 176 Milkwood Road, London, S.E., not later than the 20th of each month.

(ix)

VOL. IV.   AUGUST—SEPTEMBER, 1902   NOS. 8-9

THE

Library Association Record

A MONTHLY MAGAZINE OF LIBRARIANSHIP AND BIBLIOGRAPHY

EDITED BY

HENRY GUPPY, M.A.

LIBRARIAN OF THE JOHN RYLANDS LIBRARY, MANCHESTER

London:

PUBLISHED BY THE LIBRARY ASSOCIATION

AT WHITCOMB HOUSE, WHITCOMB STREET

PALL MALL EAST, LONDON, S.W.

Price Two Shillings Net

(ii)

CONTENTS.

The Library Association Record,

AUGUST—SEPTEMBER, 1902.

SOME OF THE INSTITUTIONS OF BIRMINGHAM AND THE NEIGHBOURHOOD.

By ROBERT K. DENT, LIBRARIAN OF THE ASTON MANOR PUBLIC LIBRARY.

THE city which has been chosen as the meeting-place of the Library Association this year will doubtless seem to most of our visitors a place of quite modern growth, one that might have sprung up in the last fifty years. Yet this is far from being the case with Birmingham, and it only appears to be so from the fact that our ancestors built with stone of a very friable nature, so that their buildings were for the most part worn out a century or two ago. Birmingham was originally a Saxon settlement in a clearing of the great Forest of Arden, close to the little stream, the Rea or Rhea, and about a mile from the old Roman way known as the Icknield Way. Here the Beormings or sons of Beorm made their "ham" and thus gave the name to the place. For it must be remembered that "bromwycham" or Brummagen did not come into use until the seventeenth century, when careless spelling was the rule rather than the exception, and so through mere ignorance, and not as some would have us believe, through etymological derivation, the latter name arose.

Birmingham was made a market town by Henry II., and obtained a charter for an annual fair of four days' duration from Richard I. It was ruled by a Manorial Court, the lords of the manor taking the name of the town as their own. One of the De Berminghams was at the battle of

Evesham with Simon De Montfort, and another served in the Gascon campaign under Edward I., and was taken prisoner and carried in triumph to Paris. Four fine altar-tombs of members of the family may be seen in St. Martin's, the mother-church of Birmingham.

The ancient ecclesiastical and civic edifices of Birmingham have long passed away. The old Parish Church of St. Martin was founded about 1250, but there is good reason to believe an earlier church stood on the same site. When the original stonework became decayed the churchwardens of the time (1690) encased the building in an ugly covering of brickwork, and time after time further tasteless alterations were made, so that the only possible improvement was to entirely rebuild. This was done about thirty years ago, and the church is now a beautiful edifice in the style of its original date, Early English, and besides the tombs of the lords of Birmingham, above mentioned, has some fine modern stained-glass windows, and a sculptured reredos, representing the Holy Supper. Old St. Martin's was several times used as a place of sanctuary by criminals in the thirteenth and fourteenth centuries.

Besides St. Martin's, Birmingham had several ancient religious endowments. The Priory of St. Thomas the Apostle, founded in the fourteenth century, occupied a site in Bull Street, and had an extensive domain, including most of the land lying between that street and Dale End and Stafford Street and Steelhouse Lane. Two gilds—the Gild of the Holy Cross in New Street, and that of St. John the Baptist in Deritend—were also among the ancient possessions of the town, but these, with the Priory and the Chantries attached to the Parish Church, were seized during the Spoliation of the Religious House under Henry VIII. But from one of the gilds arose the Grammar School of Edward VI., to which reference is made on a subsequent page.

Of the principal churches now existing, the most important, next to St. Martin's, is St. Philip's, which will be a familiar object during the week to those who stay at the Grand or the Great Western Hotel. Standing in a fine open space, and on the highest ground in the city, it immediately attracts the attention of visitors. It was built in 1711-9, from designs by Thomas Archer, a pupil of Wren, and with its lofty tower and dome is a prominent object in all " prospects " of the town. It has four very fine stained-glass windows, designed by Sir Edward Burne-Jones, which ought to be seen by all visitors, and in the churchyard are several monuments of more than local interest. One of these is an obelisk to the memory of the late Colonel Burnaby; among others are the gravestones of Sarah Baskerville, whose name appears on the imprint of several books printed with the types of John Baskerville, her husband, whose " magnificent editions . . . went forth to astonish all the librarians of Europe ". On one of the pillars within the church is a tablet to the memory of Edmund Hector, whose name will be familar to all readers of Boswell, as the life-long friend of Johnson. Hector's house formerly stood in the Old Square, but was taken down during the formation of Corporation Street. The panelling of " Johnson's Sitting-room " now lines one of the rooms in Aston Hall which is devoted to memorials of Johnson.

Some of the newer churches are architecturally interesting, the best, perhaps, being St. Alban's, of which the late Mr. J. L. Pearson was the architect. The quaint old Chapel of St. John the Baptist, Deritend (although not the original Chapel of the Gild), is of interest, and the neighbourhood is one of the oldest parts of Birmingham. Close to the chapel is the Old Crown House, an edifice dating from the year 1400 or thereabouts, which is the " Mansion House of Timber " referred to in Leland's *Itinerary*, 1530. There are still several other low-browed timber houses in the same street, and it may be of interest to mention that John Rogers, the martyr, who assisted in the production of the second printed English Bible, known as Matthewe's Bible, was born in a house in Deritend, exactly opposite St. John's. A memorial bust of this brave old scholar and martyr was placed in the chapel about twenty years ago.

King Edward's School.

Arising out of the Gild of the Holy Cross, this is one of the most ancient institutions of Birmingham. The young king, or his advisers, restored to the town a portion of the revenues of the gild, on the petition of some of the townspeople, in 1552, for the foundation of a school "to be called the Free Grammar School of King Edward the Sixth". The old hall of the gild was first used as a schoolhouse, but like other ancient buildings it became worn out at the end of the seventeenth century, and the present Tudor building in New Street, by Barry, is the third used for this purpose, being erected in 1833. Among old Edwardians are proudly reckoned the late Archbishop Benson, Bishops Westcott and Lightfoot, and Sir Edward Burne-Jones. There are branch schools on this foundation at the Five Ways (Edgbaston), Aston, Camp Hill and Summer Hill. The privileges of this foundation are extended to girls as well as boys. Manchester visitors will recall the fact that their first bishop, Dr. J. Prince Lee, was formerly head master of the Birmingham school.

The Blue Coat School.

Occupying the eastern side of St. Philip's Churchyard, the Blue Coat School will doubtless attract the attention of visitors. It was founded in 1724, for the education and maintenance of about 250 boys and girls. Some of these may be often seen in the vicinity, in their quaint dress, exactly as represented in the two sculptured figures over the entrance. This landmark of old Birmingham will, however, soon pass away, for a new school building is about to be erected in a distant suburb, where the surroundings will be more conducive to the health of the children. The present school building dates from 1794.

Mason College and the Birmingham University.

The fine red brick building in Edmund Street, which has now become the home of the Birmingham University, arose out of the munificence of a Birmingham manufacturer, one of the pioneers of the steel-pen trade. Sir Josiah Mason

was one of those who love to see the fruits of their bene-
ficence in their lifetime; and after building and endowing
an orphanage and almshouses at Erdington, turned his
attention to the cherished project of his life, that of founding
a college wherein all classes might have "the means of
carrying on, in the capital of the Midlands, their scientific
studies as completely and thoroughly as they can be pro-
secuted in the great science schools of this country and the
continent". The "Mason Science College," as it was at
first called, was opened on the 1st of October, 1880. At
first the Deed of Foundation provided only for scientific
instruction and the teaching of modern languages, but
Faculties of Arts and Medicine and Surgery were afterwards
added, the latter being transferred from Queen's College.
In 1898 it became the Mason University College, and by
Act of Parliament in 1900 the property of the college was
transferred to the newly created University of Birmingham,
of which it is at present the headquarters. It comprises
Faculties of Science, Arts and Medicine. The Faculty of
Science includes Chairs of Mathematics, Physics, Chemistry,
Metallurgy, Zoology and Comparative Anatomy, Botany
and Vegetable Physiology, Geology and Physiography,
Engineering and Brewing. That of Arts consists of Greek
and Latin, English Language and Literature, French
Language and Literature, German Language and Litera-
ture, Mental and Moral Philosophy and Political Economy.
That of Medicine includes Anatomy, Physiology, Medicine,
Surgery, Pathology and Bacteriology, Materia Medica,
Therapeutics, Hygiene and Public Health, Midwifery,
Gynæcology, Forensic Medicine and Toxicology, Mental
Diseases, Operative Surgery, Ophthalmology and the various
branches of Dental Surgery. Recently a Chair of Commerce
has been established. The library, which contains 2,700
volumes, includes the Hensleigh Wedgwood Collection of
works on Philology.

Other Colleges, etc.

Queen's College, in Paradise Street, is now only the
shadow of its former self. It was founded by the late W.

Sands Cox, as a School of Medicine and Surgery, in 1828, but its scope was afterwards extended to include the Arts, being incorporated by Royal Charter in 1843. Its prosperity was hampered by many vicissitudes, and after the Departments of Medicine and Surgery were transferred to Mason College, it became chiefly a Theological Training College of the Church of England.

Wesleyan College, Handsworth.—One of the "Theological Institutions" of the Wesleyan Methodist Church, established in 1881.

Oscott College, situated at New Oscott, about five miles from the centre of the city, is a seminary of the Roman Catholic Church, situated on a commanding plateau, overlooking the valley which lies between it and Aston Manor. It was visited by the Association in 1887, and many of the members carried away pleasant memories of this beautifully situated edifice, and of the rich collections stored within its museum—pictures, church vestments and furniture, carvings in wood and ivory, choice missals and other illuminated manuscripts, and of the lovely chapel. If any members who were not present on that occasion care to visit this interesting institution, I shall be glad to try and arrange a small party to drive over to Oscott on the Saturday of the conference week.

Birmingham and Midland Institute.—This famous institution, the first stone of which was laid in 1855 by the late Prince Consort, belongs intimately to the history of modern Birmingham. Many of her foremost sons have either laboured in its formation and maintenance, or have received their best training within its walls. While on the one hand it contributes to the general culture and recreation of its members in its courses of high-class lectures and conversaziones, on the other it provides for the instruction of the people in its varied classes, in science, literature, languages and music. Among its past presidents it numbers nearly every famous contemporary in literature, science and art; Dickens, Kingsley, Huxley, Tyndall, Froude, Max Müller, Lowell, are among the names which instantly recur to the mind from the long list of presidents who have added lustre to the Institute; while the regular courses of lectures will compare with those of the Royal Institution and other similar bodies. Among the affiliated associations who have their home in the Institute is the Archæological Section, whose transactions form an important and valuable storehouse of Midland Antiquities.

Libraries.

Corporation Free Libraries.—The first Free Library was the predecessor of the present Constitution Hill Branch, the Act being adopted in 1860. The Central Library building, completing the Midland Institute block designed by Barry, was opened in 1865, the Reference Library, in the same building, being opened in October, 1866. Arising out of the Shakespeare Tercentenary celebration, a Shakespeare Memorial Library was formed, and was housed in the Central Library block, being opened in 1868. By 1868 the first group of branch libraries was completed, including Constitution Hill, Deritend, Gosta Green and Adderly Park, and a few years later the Reference Library was enriched by the gift of a collection of Cervantes literature, and the acquisition of a priceless collection of Warwickshire books and MSS., formed by Wm. Staunton, of Longbridge, and comprising several other valuable collections. But most of these treasures perished in the disastrous fire of January, 1879, the details of which will be well known to most librarians. Out of the ashes of the old building, however, has arisen a more perfectly equipped library, and a collection richer in many respects than that which was so tragically lost. Some priceless local manuscripts were lost for ever, but the valuable Gild Book of Knowle, and a portion of the Shakespeare collection escaped the fire. To these have been added local and Warwickshire collections of equal rarity, and, while all the special collections have been re-formed, the general library which has been built up is of far greater value than its predecessor. Since that time an outer circle of branch libraries has been established, including Bloomsbury (1892), Harbone (1892), Spring Hill (1893), Small Heath (1893-4), and Balsall Heath (1896), while the older branches have all been reorganised.   The total number of volumes in the libraries now exceeds 260,000.   The later branch library buildings are architecturally handsome ; a good typical example to visit would be that at Balsall Heath, reached by Moseley Road trams from the back of New Street Station.

The Birmingham Library, commonly known as the Old Library, was founded in 1779 by nineteen subscribers.   Since the last meeting of the Association in Birmingham the historic old building, which was the home of this institution for about a century, has been removed to make way for an arcade, but the library is now housed in a much more commodious building, specially erected for the purpose, in Margaret Street.   Subscribers have free access to the shelves, and a special feature of the place is the admirable suite of reading and conversation-rooms for subscribers and proprietors.   The motto which was inscribed over the old library—said to have been written by Dr. Samuel Parr, " Ad mercaturam bonarum artium profectus et tibi et omnibus ditesces," has been placed on the front of the new building, with a record of the foundation and removal of the library.   The collection now comprises about 80,000 volumes.

The *Birmingham Law Society* has a library of about 12,000 volumes, including a good collection of Reports of Celebrated Trials.   The library of the *Medical Institute* (Edmund Street) is also a valuable one, and contains many rare works on medicine, the total number of volumes being about 13,000.

The outlying districts of *Aston Manor, Handsworth* and *Smethwick* have all good libraries, and at each place visitors during the conference week will be very welcome. There are a few rarities in the *Aston Manor Reference Library,* the most important being a beautiful MS. Book of Hours of Flemish workmanship, with miniatures by Spierinck, *c.* 1498, in the original stamped leather binding.

Public Buildings.

A few words may be added in reference to some of the principal public buildings, other than those which have been noticed in the foregoing pages.   Principal among these is the *Town Hall,* which stands boldly at the head of New

Street and Colmore Row. It was built in 1832-4, and is modelled on the Corinthian example of the Temple of Jupiter Stator at Rome. Internally it consists chiefly of one apartment—a lofty 'and capacious hall, seating about 2,500 persons ; and as it is used for the Triennial Musical Festivals, which date from 1768, it has a fine organ, which at one time was held to be the largest and most powerful in the world. Organ recitals are given almost every week, by the city organist, Mr. C. W. Perkins. Upon the walls of the hall are a number of pictorial panels representing some of the leading events in the history of Birmingham. The *Council House*, which comprises within its walls the civic reception rooms, the council chamber, the Lord Mayor's parlour, and committee rooms and offices of the various municipal departments, was built in 1874-80, and is in the Renaissance style, with a frontage of 296 feet, and a dome which is a prominent object as seen from all the outlying districts around the city. In 1885 the *Art Gallery and Museum* portion of the building was completed, and this is approached by the portico facing Chamberlain Square. In its lofty turret is a public clock with chimes, the large bell, " Big Brum," being of rich tone and heard far and wide (as far away as Walsall and Sutton Coldfield on some occasions). The contents of the Galleries include a valuable collection of the works of modern artists, being especially rich in the works of the Pre-Raphaelite School, the works of David Cox (who, as is well known, was a native of Birmingham), and has a good number of examples of the British Water Colour School. The Museum has a gallery representative of the Italian architectural sculpture and metal work of the Renaissance, and an extensive collection of examples of art workmanship in every branch, including a large number of examples of Wedgwood ware. One feature which will interest the lovers of architecture is the series of careful drawings in water colour of some of the most beautiful of the old continental examples which are so rapidly passing to decay.

The *Society of Artists' Rooms*, in New Street (which members will have an opportunity of visiting on one of the evenings), occupy an almost unique place among provincial art exhibitions. In this handsome suite of rooms, which date from 1829, the Society has held annual exhibitions for over seventy years, and in later years there have been two shows in each year, at which not merely the works of the members and of local artists, but also those of many of the foremost painters of the day, may be seen.

Aston Hall, a fine old Jacobean mansion formerly belonging to the Holte family, is also used as a museum; but the most interesting exhibit is the hall itself, with its stately apartments, its fine ceilings and panelling, the superb great gallery and the grand old staircase; and I would venture to express the hope that no visitor will leave Birmingham without paying a visit to this stately old mansion. Steam trams from the Old Square pass the entrance to the park, but it is necessary that visitors should observe that the right trams have " Aston Cross " on the side and " Witton " on the front of the engine, or they will be set down at some distance from the hall. The museum includes a Natural History collection, pictures and other objects of art, and relics of the Holte family. One apartment has been fitted up as a Johnson Memorial Room.

The *Victoria Courts*, Corporation Street, is a very beautiful building in terra-cotta in the French Renaissance style, designed by Aston Webb and Ingress Bell. The great hall is a fine apartment, and the fitting-up of the Courts and the library will well repay inspection. There is a good deal of fine wood-carving about the building, and the modelled decoration in terra-cotta is also very rich.

There are many other interesting public buildings of which one would like to speak in detail, but to do so would run this paper to the length of a guide book. The *Parks* are worthy of a visit, more particularly *Cannon Hill*, which may be reached by the electric tram from Suffolk Street. Birmingham is a city of *arcades*, and these will attract our visitors. The Great Western and North Western (from Colmore Row to Corporation Street) are plain sailing, but the group of arcades between Union Street, High Street, and New Street are somewhat involved, so much so that for my own part I am never quite sure where I shall come out

when once the labyrinth is entered. The *theatres* are
numerous, but in the absence of the old "Royal" which
is now being rebuilt, the Prince of Wales's and the Grand
are the principal ; at the first named, Sir Henry Irving and
Miss Ellen Terry will appear during the conference week.
The Empire Music Hall (formerly Day's) is a handsome
structure, and will probably attract some of our more
frivolous friends. The *Botanical Gardens* at Edgbaston are
always charming and interesting, and one can only regret
that special arrangements have not been made to visit them.
As the football season will have begun, some members will
doubtless be tempted to pay a visit to the well-known enclosure of the Aston Villa team at Aston on the Saturday
afternoon. Those who visit Aston Hall may get a glimpse
of this great enclosure, which is said to accommodate 60,000
spectators.

BOOKS BROUGHT INTO RELATION WITH EACH OTHER AND MADE OPERATIVE.[1]

By Basil Anderton, B.A., Librarian of the Newcastle-on-Tyne Public Libraries.

BY way of introduction may I take a simple case to show how the bringing things into relation with one another increases their effectiveness to a quite wonderful extent? I refer to the elementary case of the letters of the alphabet. In the order in which we first learn them they are dull enough and meaningless enough. But begin to bring them into relation with one another, so as to form words, and the strength of their union begins to manifest itself. Take another step and bring words into relation, and you get a sentence. Bring sentences into relation and you get the elements of the magic of literature and of philosophy. For when your poet brings sentences into right combination he will give you a verse or a song.

> A gentle knight was pricking on the plaine,
> Ycladd in mightie armes and silver shielde,
> Wherein old dints of deepe woundes did remaine,
> The cruell markes of many a bloody fielde;
> Yet armes till that time did he never wield:
> His angry steede did chide his foming bitt,
> As much disdayning to the curbe to yield;
> Full jolly knight he seemd, and faire did sitt
> As one for knightly giusts and fierce encounters fitt.

When your logician does the like, he will give you a syllogism :—

> All A is B.
> All C is A.
> ∴ All C is B.

Advancing now to the next stage, when the poet brings the verses into coherent relation we get the canto, and after

---

[1] Read at a Meeting of the Northern Counties Library Association, 7th July, 1902.

the canto the complete poem, as in the *Faerie Queene*, or *Marmion*. And your philosopher, when he develops and expounds his syllogisms and brings his trains of reasoning and thought into due sequence, exhibits his philosophical system. So, too, with the historian, the novelist, or any other writer.

By means, then, of combining and classifying the letters, words, sentences and so forth, we are enabled to reach the production of books, and at this stage we get the elements with which librarians have to deal.

So much by way of introduction. Let us now consider books themselves. Let us, for the sake of illustration, suppose that the first book received into a library under our charge—say our personal library—is Bradley's *Latin Prose Composition*. When this has been carefully worked through, a fairly good Latin vocabulary will have been mastered, and the essentials of the grammar and syntax of the language will be understood. Of course some elementary groundwork in Latin is presupposed.

Next perhaps a copy of Virgil's *Æneid* will be added. A large number of the words and the chief constructions used by Virgil will be known—not all, however. The next thing needed will be a Latin dictionary, which will explain new words and illustrate, by quotations from other writers, new phrases and constructions. By patient work on these three books we shall acquire, assuming that the edition of Virgil has a just sufficient explanation of hexameter verse, a fruitful insight into Latin epic poetry.

But the music of Virgil's poetry will be more fully appreciated if we learn something of the early history and later development of Latin verse. We shall then see it in relation to the work of other poets and shall recognise its distinctive note. So, too, in regard to the matter of the *Æneid*. It will be illuminating to know the legends to which Virgil refers as they are recorded by other writers, and to see how far they formed part of the heritage of the Roman race. It will become necessary, if we are to grasp Virgil's true position and significance in Roman literature, to extend our studies and our books. We must consider the writings of his predecessors, of his contemporaries and of his successors. If poets, we must study their prosody. If prose writers, we must understand the beauties and intricacies of prose style. So we shall gradually feel our way onwards, bringing one after another into relation, and determining each writer's position in the range of Latin literature as a whole. We shall gather and read the historians (Livy, Cæsar, Tacitus), the satirists (Juvenal, Persius), the lyric poets (Horace, Catullus, etc.), the dramatists, the philosophers, and so forth. And gradually the whole literature and history of the Romans will be reconstructed and brought into a homogeneous whole.

But in reading this literature we are over and over again brought face to face with the fact that Latin literature owes an enormous debt to Greek literature. And in reading this history we shall see how intimate were the relations between Romans and Carthaginians, Romans and Gauls, Romans and Greeks, Romans and Britons. The relations were indeed those of growth on the one side and decay on the other; of conquest, and of submission; of life, and of death. And therefore no complete reconstruction will be possible for us without knowledge concerning the races with which Rome was brought into contact.

In regard to literature, Rome was most conspicuously influenced by Greece, and it is to Greek literature that the student who began with Latin literature will turn if he desires to go to the root of the matter. In bringing the Latin books into relation with each other, one development has been achieved. But when we study the Greek language and literature we shall begin to see how much the two races had in common, and at the same time how very different they were. Grammatical forms in the two languages will be found to be in many cases similar, in their origins often identical. Roman mythology again will be found to be closely related to Greek mythology; and it will be illuminating to compare the resemblances and the differences between the Greek Pallas Athene and the Latin Minerva, the Greek Aphrodite and the Latin Venus, the Greek Ares and the Latin Mars, the Greek Poseidon and the Latin Neptune. By observing the different ideas associated with these and other deities we shall gain insight into some of the radical differences between the Greek and the Roman genius, and shall recognise the greater freedom and joyousness and subtlety of the Greek mind as contrasted with the Roman.

Roman history, in like manner, will be found to be related more or less intimately to Greek history, and affected by it more or less profoundly. The war between the two races brought them of course into close contact with each other, and the Romans acquired, even if somewhat superficially, something of the higher culture attained by the art, the poetry and the philosophy of the vanquished nation. In course of time, too, many of the shifty, starveling Greeks established themselves in Rome and infected the simpler-minded Latins with the bad qualities of their shameless versatility.

And if this is true of the relations of old Greece and old Rome, it is no less true of the relations of old Rome and modern Italy. The body of traditions that formed so much of the character of the ancestors was carried on, influenced of course by later developments in religion and in history, into the language and the character of their posterity. He who knows Latin has made already a great step towards understanding the fundamentals of Italian. He who knows Roman mythology and has read the Roman poets will appreciate many a reference to them in their heir and rival Dante, and will wonder at and yet sympathise with the intimate blending of the old and the new in the Christian poet's scheme of things present and to come.

Nor can the language and history of Rome and Spain be dissociated, nor those of Rome and France, nor of Rome and England. The torch that illumines the human race is handed on, falteringly at times, but still inevitably, from one nation to another. Its light is of course modified by changing influences. It will be our business, as our studies progress, to observe the identities and to account for the differences in language, mythology, poetry and so on. As our views expand, we shall cease to regard Latin as a thing in one compartment of our mind, shut off and dissociated from Greek and Italian, from Spanish, French, English, German. We shall see the necessity that has driven men to institute the science of comparative philology, for example, of comparative mythology or of comparative philosophy; and which has enriched them with general ideas instead of ideas that are detached and unrelated.

I have confined myself to some of the questions suggested by studying language and literature. But in other fields of research similar necessities will be forced upon us. No student of anatomy, for instance, who has passed the elementary stages, would be content to investigate either a single animal, or the animals of a single district. He knows that much that is obscure in the structure of one animal is explained by the structure of another animal, which may perhaps be now found only in a remote country. Zoologists, too, and botanists find the like need of extending their observations and of comparing the fauna and the flora of all parts of the world. And what geologist could pass "beyond the veil" if he limited his horizon by the district or even the country in which he lived?

In the world of art, too, it were but a meagre equipment to know only the pictures or the sculpture or the architecture of England, and to shut off from one's ken the achievements of Greece, of Italy, of France.

Having now considered this matter from the internal, or student's, point of view, and sketched (though in mere outline) the tendency of his work, let us for a few minutes look at the question from the point of view of the outside observer. It is with this outside view that we, as librarians, are mainly concerned. In the first place, we cannot hope to acquire the internal view concerning the majority of the subjects with which we deal. In the second, we must yet so marshal our books and resources that they are readily accessible to students whose concern it is to acquire that internal view.

We have observed, then, from the experience I have above indicated, that students classify the results of their work, that they compare one writer with another, and get light on the views of one by studying those of another; and that this process of verification and sifting increases as knowledge expands. We shall therefore endeavour, since we desire to facilitate our readers' work as far as practicable, to group our books in such a way as to make this comparison as easy as possible. We must aim at finding the line of least resistance for the majority of students. Of course we cannot please everybody. We know that in nearly every science doctors disagree as to details; that it is a disputed question, for example, whether the lowest forms of life belong to the animal or the vegetable world; that physiology and psychology are in certain respects very closely in contact; that the limits of mind and matter are by many regarded as indefinable. But speaking broadly we know also that, for all ordinary purposes, and for the students with whom we are mainly concerned, certain general systems of classification are accepted within each science and art. And it is on the line of these generally received systems of arrangement (what we may call systems of notation, if you will) that we shall most profitably proceed.

We know that in the several sciences the establishment of a common system of arrangement has wonderfully increased facility of work by giving as it were a common language to scientists. It has thus become possible to record the body of acquired knowledge, and to save the vain repetitions of individual efforts. In spite of imperfections the old Linnean system of botanical arrangement, and the geological grouping (into quaternary, tertiary, secondary, primary, with the sub-divisions) have had this fundamental advantage. In music, too, the establishment of a common system of notation has enormously facilitated the study of the art and the comparison of achievements in various countries. In spite of certain defects this system has made co-ordination possible, and has supplied us moderns with a universal, even if a cumbrous, language—as those will admit who begin to study music as written say in the thirteenth or fourteenth century.

Probably, as I said before, in no branch of our work shall we be able fully to content every student. With the growth of knowledge the defects of classification seem to become inevitably recognised—naturally, because the bounds of knowledge are pushed back and changed. Yet although the ideal solution of the difficulty is in this matter, as in most others, unattainable, we may none the less hope to reach at least a working basis of agreement. We may hope to find a

28

scheme of arrangement for our books which, though in parts displeasing to ourselves and in parts a little jarring to our readers, has at least the following merits: that it is a scheme that covers nearly the whole field of our work, and that it is largely, and apparently increasingly, recognised and understood in the various countries and districts that maintain public libraries. This latter point alone is, I take it, of radical importance. Given the common "system of notation," it becomes admirably easy to compare the resources of one town with those of another, and to supplement the defects of the one by taking advantage of the wealth of the other. People travelling from one place to another are no longer compelled to master the different schemes of classification which this librarian or the other, for various reasons, chooses to adopt. They are no longer, in every town they reach, forced to master what may best be described as the intricacies of a fresh language. People writing to their friends or fellow-students in different districts can refer, secure from misunderstanding, to works in the class or subject they are investigating. Directness and ease in finding the class of books desired are thus attained; and the preliminary effort and futile labour often spent in the study of strange catalogues are, by the acceptance of a Volapük, done away. Moreover, to the librarian himself the acceptance of a common standard can bring great gain. He will often, in classing his own books, receive help and illumination from the catalogues of others who, from some special tendency or training, know more of one special subject than he does himself. Then again, when he comes to enrich his library in any given section, he will find very profitable suggestions in examining the catalogues of his more fortunately provided fellow-craftsmen.

When one thinks of the simplicity and ease secured all the world over in the matter of arithmetic by the general adoption of Arabic figures, and when one imagines the complication that would arise if some nations adopted the Arabic, others the cumbrous Roman notation, others the Greek, so that it were constantly necessary to interpret the one in terms of the other, one recognises very clearly the benefit that must arise from having a common language, a common notation, in the realm of books also. The influence of libraries is being increasingly established up and down the whole world. Let us then have some common system by means of which their work can be compared, classified and brought into relation. Then that work as a vast whole will be more likely to move forward homogeneously and in due co-ordination; we shall have found the " one touch of nature that makes the whole *book-world* kin ".

What system shall we adopt? That question, with the reasons for its definite answer, may perhaps form the subject of a second paper.

DEAN HONEYWOOD'S LIBRARY.[1]

By Canon F. R. Maddison, M.A., F.S.A., Librarian.

IN 1892 I had the honour of reading a paper to this Association on the subject of this library. As the paper was printed in the fourth volume of the magazine called *The Library* it would be needless for me to rewrite what is already in print. All I can do, therefore, is briefly to sketch the history of what is really Dean Honeywood's Library. He was the grandson of a remarkable woman whose portrait hangs on these walls, who lived to see 367 descendants: 16 her own children, 114 grandchildren, 228 great-grandchildren and 9 great-great-grandchildren. She was an intimate friend of Fox, the martyrologist, and her copy of his *Martyrs* is preserved in a family descended from her, as well as the Venetian glass goblet out of which she used to drink. Her grandson the Dean used to relate that he was present at a dinner given by her to a family party of 200 of her descendants.

The Dean was in exile during the Commonwealth, and this, which to him was a misfortune, proved the very reverse to the cathedral, for the splendid collection of books which he made and left to it was due to his enforced residence in the Low Countries where he had ample opportunities of picking up rare and valuable books. I shall be obliged in a measure to repeat myself if I attempt an enumeration of the literary treasures he bequeathed, but first of all we must remember that a library had existed since the earliest days of the cathedral. The *armarium* in which Haimo on being appointed Chancellor *circa* 1150 found certain MSS. was, so to speak, the cradle of our present library, and I am thankful

---

[1] Read before the members of the North Midland Library Association, 24th April, 1902.

to say that some of those MSS. still remain, notably the great Bible given by Nicholas, Canon and Archdeacon, *circa* 1106, and the " Homilies " of the Venerable Bede, which may be assigned to the end of the tenth century or the beginning of the eleventh. We cannot tell where the *armarium* or chest was kept which contained these treasures, but later on, no doubt, some sort of a library was built to receive the steady accretion of MSS. My reason for asserting this is that *circa* 1420 the *nova libraria* or *new* library is mentioned ; and the term *new* presupposes some older form of building though we cannot precisely say where it was. The new library, however, we can identify without difficulty. It is, of course, what is now a vestibule to Dean Honeywood's building. Everything about it points to the early part of the fifteenth century as the date of its erection.

Three MSS. are in existence which were specially given to this new library. One is in the British Museum having first found its way, no one knows how, into George III.'s library. It was given, according to the inscription on the fly-leaf, by Philip Repingdon, Bp. of Lincoln, 1405-23. Another we are fortunate enough still to possess ; the gift of Thomas Duffield, late Chancellor of Lincoln Cathedral, "to the new library," 1422. The third by an unhappy chance we missed recovering a few years ago. It was also the gift of Thomas Duffield, and was given like the preceding in 1422, and consisted of various tracts, most of them by Robert de Leicester, of the date of the fourteenth century, bound in the original oak boards. How it got into Sir Thomas Phillips' collection I cannot say, but it found its way into the market, and was sold at Sotheby's for £16. I had instructed the auctioneer to go up to £12, and had told him not to let us lose it for want of a few additional pounds ; but he let it go for £16, and all my efforts have been unable to trace it. Quaritch bought it for some one who wished to be nameless, and either would not or could not help me when I sought to find out who was the possessor. I fear the chance of recovering it will never come again.

I have spoken in my former paper of the chief treasures of this library, but I should like to mention one very valuable

little work, the value of which we did not know till within
the last few years. It is the Irish Catechism, printed in
Dublin in 1571, by Kerney or Kearney, in Irish, and is the
very earliest so printed. I believe only one copy besides
ours is known to exist, and is in Trinity College, Dublin.

We must all esteem it a fortunate circumstance that
Dibdin when he came on a foraging expedition after Caxtons
and Wynkyn de Wordes, and carried off the cream of our
collection, had no appetite for old English bibles and early
primers. We have a very valuable series of both still remaining. Two Caxtons survive, but I do not know whether
it was owing to the fact that they are imperfect that Dibdin
spared them. The larger of the two I had undervalued on
account of its imperfections, but a bibliomaniac on seeing
it said he would give £100 for it, so we may imagine what
it would be worth were it perfect as those were which Dibdin
carried off to Althorpe and which may be seen in the Rylands
Library at Manchester.

I may briefly glance at some of the treasures. The
original copy of Magna Charta, without the signatures
indeed, but endorsed "for Lincoln". Milton's *Lycidas*, as
it came out at Cambridge with a good many other elegies
on the death of Edward King his friend. The fine collection
of tracts and pamphlets collected by Honeywood. The
early Italian Madrigals. The splendid series of MSS.,
which sadly need a special catalogue. All these I have
described in my former papers and need only allude to.

At the present day the question has arisen, What are we
to do with the increasing number of books? Quite recently
the Rolls Series has been given to us, amounting to about
seventy volumes. The Dean and Chapter have just bought
the *Dictionary of National Biography*, which is about sixty
additional volumes. Where are they to be put? The book-
cases are filled, and we must allow space for works like the
Camden, Surtees, and Oxford Historical Societies, etc., which
increase at the rate of two volumes every year. We are at this
moment waiting for fresh book-cases which are being made
in London, and which will have to be placed all the way
down the room, spoiling the perspective and blocking up

space which is needful for its right proportions. I do not see any other alternative except building another library.

One word as to the *character* of the library. I contend that it is not a *circulating* one and was never intended to be one—it is a *reference* library. In these days of cheap editions it is unnecessary to buy books for it which any one with moderate means can acquire. What we ought in my opinion to do is to purchase works like the *Dictionary of National Biography*, which no ordinary clergyman or layman can afford to buy, and to give (as we do) facilities to those who desire to consult the rare and valuable books we possess.

The Diocesan Library supplies the cheaper books, but to fill this one with modern works which come out at a cheap rate is to my mind a degradation of the original library which Dean Honeywood collected. It is, in short, a library for *scholars*, and should supply what, as a rule, a scholar's resources are unable to supply.

LIBRARY LECTURES: A RETROSPECT AND SUGGESTION.[1]

By William J. Willcock, Librarian, Public Library, Peterborough.

WHEN asked to contribute a paper to this meeting I longed to discover some absolutely new idea which could be applied to library work. I went through the whole gamut of library economics from book-buying to open access, and found that everything had been well written and talked about.

A little further consideration led me to admit that the best results were not always obtained from startling innovation, but generally from some improvement or development of a system which had stood the test of time and had been proved of value.

Reasoning thus I decided to take for my subject library lectures: a subject by no means new, but about which not very much has been written or said.

Although this part of library work is not new there still remains a great deal of room for its development.

First of all I will review briefly some of the literature on the subject I have been able to come across. The first book consulted was Mr. J. J. Ogle's volume on *The Free Library* in the Library Series. In the chapter entitled " The Development of the Free Library," Mr. Ogle states that at the Annual Meeting of the Library Association at Manchester in 1879 Sir William Bailey called attention to the advisability of free lectures in connection with free libraries. In the same chapter Mr. Ogle also says " that free lectures are now [1897] an important part of the education obtainable at many free libraries in the United Kingdom ". I hope to show in this

---

[1] Read before the Library Association at Nottingham on 5th June, 1902.

paper that the latter statement will bear some slight modification. Throughout this history of the free library less than a dozen brief references are made to library lectures.

The next article I came across is in the *Library World* for 1899, under the heading of "Library Extension Work: Lectures". This consists of a series of questions set by the Editor about library lectures, together with extracts from letters on the subject from five librarians. Later on in the same year lengthy replies to the questions were published from Mr. R. K. Dent and Mr. H. D. Roberts.

All speak in favour of lectures. Some advocate paid lecturers, others do not. The Editorial promised that when a sufficient store of information was gathered together it would be tabulated and printed in the *Library World*. This has not yet been done. Probably because no other information has come to hand.

Next in order of date comes a brief article from the pen of Mr. Peter Cowell, of Liverpool, entitled "Free Public Library Lectures," published in the LIBRARY ASSOCIATION RECORD for 1899. In this article Mr. Cowell details his experience of library lectures during a period of twenty-five years. He strongly advocates lectures as valuable auxiliaries to the educational work of a library, favours the popular lecture rather than the erudite and dry-as-dust type, and suggests that it is desirable that the lecturer should mention the best books in the library on his subject during the course of the lecture.

Perhaps the most important contribution to the literature on the subject, and the only one which has elicited some practical discussion, is that of Dr. C. W. Kimmins, entitled "Lectures Under the Public Libraries Acts," read before the Library Association at the Annual Meeting at Bristol in 1900, and published in the LIBRARY ASSOCIATION RECORD in January, 1901. It is an ambitious paper and full of good suggestions. In it Dr. Kimmins says "that no public library could be efficient without a lecture-room ". Also "that the whole of the rate should not be devoted to purchasing and maintaining a collection of books ". A plea was also made for more liberality on the part of library committees.

The foregoing remarks, admirable and aspiring in tone as they are, could not be applied to any except large public libraries, and I doubt even then if such a scheme could be carried out efficiently on a penny rate without impoverishing some other useful portion of library work.

Dr. Kimmins' paper is a flight after the ideal. An ideal greatly desired, but which cannot be approached by hundreds of public libraries in the country for lack of sufficient funds.

Those librarians who took part in the discussion which followed the paper mostly represented large public libraries with fairly large incomes, therefore little or nothing was heard of the library lecture movement in the smaller towns. However, the paper is a valuable one, and has no doubt caused many of the librarians who heard it read to try what could be done on a smaller scale in their own libraries.

The great difficulty in writing upon a subject like this is the insufficiency of data to work upon. The foregoing is all the literature I could find. There may be more, and I should be pleased if any member would call my attention to it.

As I said before, the idea of lectures in connection with public libraries is not a new one. Let us admit that it is twenty-five years old, and then endeavour to see what progress it has made. From Greenwood's *Library Year Book* for 1901 I ascertain that up to July, 1901, there were 401 public libraries in the United Kingdom. One of the statistical abstracts in the same work states that out of this number only fifty-seven have inaugurated schemes for lectures. Not a large proportion by any means. This abstract merely consists of the names of the libraries where lectures are given. No information is given as to whether the lecturers are paid for their services or not, or whether the lectures are given in the reading-room, special lecture-room attached to the library, or in some place entirely apart from the library. Neither is there any mention made of the subjects of the lectures, their length, influence or results.

It will thus be seen that information regarding library lectures is far from being complete, and I should like to take this opportunity to suggest that the Executive of the Library Association should obtain officially as much information as possible and publish it in tabulated form in the *L.A. Year Book.*

Library reports are quite as reticent with regard to lectures. I have consulted many from libraries where lectures are given and obtained little information. They all report that lectures have been given, but most of them omit to mention anything further. However, in one report it was stated that eighteen lectures had been given during the winter season, and upon turning to the balance sheet I found an item of £40 for lecturers' fees, and another of £8 10s. for lantern and other expenses, close upon £2 14s. for each lecture. As the income of this particular library is over £2,000 per annum, perhaps a matter of £50 per annum for lectures may not be considered extravagant. But the same amount spent out of the income of the library of a town, say, of 30,000 inhabitants would be an extravagance. It would mean £50 less for new books, and in spite of Dr. Kimmins' dictum, " that the whole of the rate should not be devoted to purchasing and maintaining a collection of books," books after all, and not lectures, make the library. I do not wish to depreciate the value of lectures as adjuncts to library work. They certainly induce some people to visit the library who might not otherwise do so, call attention to a special book or class of books, and help to popularise the library in many directions.

Well then, if lectures form so valuable a part of library work, how is it that only fifty-seven out of the four hundred public libraries existing in the United Kingdom have taken steps to adopt them? Is it apathy, want of appreciation, or limited and narrow incomes? We shall endeavour to see.

Figures, they say, may prove anything, but as a rule they are capable of proving hard and incontrovertible facts. Sometimes facts and figures are hidden under an embellishment of words and phrases; or perhaps the writer upon a special subject advances an ideal theory and at the same time loses sight of the practical side. Let us be practical librarians first and idealists afterwards. Now to come to the hard bed-rock of fact. There are in the United Kingdom 161 public libraries with annual incomes varying

from £20 to £500, and fifty-one with incomes varying from
£600 to £1,200. Thus over one-third of our public libraries
have incomes of £500 and under, mostly under, and only
one-eighth have incomes of £1,200 and under; again mostly
under.

Surely these figures must make us pause when we talk
about paid lecturers, special lecture-rooms and a few other
things. Do these facts account for the small number of
libraries which have adopted lecture schemes? To a great
extent, yes. We may then safely admit that 161 public
libraries are absolutely unable to pay for lectures without
starving some other useful part of library work. In spite of
this there is a simple way out of the difficulty, but before
suggesting a solution I must say that I am working upon
the hypothesis that most of us admit that lectures in connection with the public library are beneficial, and that we
look upon them as a means of calling attention to the books
in the library, and not as substitutes for reading.

To illustrate my suggestion I may perhaps be permitted
to detail the working of the scheme of half-hour talks in
connection with the Peterborough Public Library. The
honour of introducing the informal " Half-hour Talk about
Books and Bookmen," belongs, I believe, to Mr. J. Potter
Briscoe,[1] who began them at Nottingham in 1890. Four
years later Peterborough followed Nottingham's example.

Now it is safe to say that in every town there is a goodly
proportion of intellectual people whose services may be
enlisted as talkers. In the case of Peterborough our talkers
are chiefly drawn from the professional classes. The City
Engineer is a specialist upon geological subjects, the City
Analyst a chemist and all-round scientist, the Master of the
School of Art an art specialist, one of the masters at the
Training College an authority upon local history and archæology, general history and biography, and a cathedral official
is well versed in the paths of literature.

In addition to these there are members of the medical,
clerical, scholastic, architectural and other professions always

---

[1 See Mr. Briscoe's paper read at the Belfast Meeting, and printed in *The
Library*, vol. vii., 1895, pp. 18-20.]

willing to give their services. Apart from the benefit the public derive from the generous work of these men, we succeed in getting the most influential men in the town to take a lively interest in the work of the library.

Having obtained our talkers the next thing is to advertise the talks. This is done by the means of small printed posters, copies of which are sent to the railway and other works, the College, School of Art, educational guilds and other institutions. Copies are also displayed outside the Guildhall and the Library, and the local papers call attention to each series of talks as arranged.

Next we come to the method of giving the talks. They are given in the reading-room every alternate Tuesday during the winter season. No chairman is appointed, therefore no time is lost over introduction or vote of thanks, consequently we get that informality which ought to characterise these talks or chats. The talkers are not strictly confined to the half-hour, but may, if they choose, take an extra ten minutes. It may be objected that the talks interrupt readers. To a certain extent this is true, but I have never had any complaint addressed to me by any one. The reader, if he choose, may listen to the talk or continue his reading.

In selecting subjects we try as far as possible to make them bear upon books in the library.

During the past two years the following are some of the talks calling attention to special books or classes of books : " Some English Essayists " (Addison, Steele, Lamb and Macaulay); " Poetry of Petrarch " (*The Sonnets*); " Aims and Methods of Some Modern Painters " (Ruskin's *Modern Painters*; " On the Origin of Surnames " (Bardsley's *English Surnames*); " Some Famous Letter Writers " (Chesterfield, Walpole and others); and " Some English Novels and Novelists " (special attention given to the eighteenth-century school).

I could mention dozens more of a similar nature, but I think these will be sufficient to show that a vast wealth of material for talks surrounds us in our libraries. Moreover, such talks are not extraneous to the work of the library, nor do they suggest the atmosphere of the collegiate or scientific lecture-room.

The only cost attached to the scheme is a slight one of 10s. per annum for poster printing. If a talker uses a lantern he supplies the same at his own cost. A screen which cost 35s. secondhand is kept at the library.

Now as to the influence and results of the talks. Of course it is always difficult to define material results of anything in the shape of lectures. However, the talks are always well attended and thoroughly appreciated. They undoubtedly tend to popularise the library and spread the knowledge of its educational usefulness over a wide area.

Such is our scheme at Peterborough, and I feel sure a similar one could be worked successfully in any town without much difficulty. We may not all have big incomes to adminstrate, but it lies within the power of every one of us to try what can be done on small means. If we have a love for our work, and in us the spirit of progress, much good may be done in a quiet way.

GESNER AND SAVIGNY.

BY P. EVANS LEWIN, OF THE WOOLWICH PUBLIC LIBRARIES.

"LE plus bel éloge qu'on puisse faire du chancelier Bacon est de regarder comme une émanation de son génie cet arbre encyclopédique où toutes les connaissances humaines sont suivies depuis leur germe radical jusqu'à leurs derniers rameaux. Ses compatriotes lui ont départi cet honneur, dont il jouit depuis deux siècles. Néanmoins Savigny a été son précurseur dans cette carrière. Bacon n'a donc joui jusqu'ici que d'une gloire usurpée. C'est donc en vain que l'Angleterre continuerait de réclamer en sa faveur un avantage de primauté qui nous appartient incontestablement." Thus writes Boulliot in his *Biographie Ardennaise*, enthusiastically claiming for his countryman, Christopher de Savigny, the honour of being the first to devise a tabulated system of classification.[1] But although Bacon as a classifier of knowledge must yield precedence to Savigny, yet the latter in his turn must give place to a man whose reputation as a savant was in his day second to none in Europe. There can be no question that Conrad Gesner, called the Pliny of Germany, and also "literarum miraculum" on account of his vast erudition,[2] was the father of systems of classification as we know them at the present day, and it is fit, therefore, that something should be done to put on record the debt which librarians owe to the real founder of classification. Although priority is here claimed for Gesner, it must be remembered that a scheme of classification was proposed eight years before Gesner issued his *Pandectarum sive Partitionum Universalium* by one Alexo Vanegas de Busto,[3] but the work of Vanegas gives the merest outlines of

---

[1] " Une liaison, chaîne, ou Arbre Encyclopédique " (Papillon).
[2] Dibdin calls him the first bibliographer.
[3] *Biographie Universelle. Nouvelle Biographie Générale.*

a scheme, whereas Gesner's work is the monumental record of a man whose vast erudition was the admiration of Europe.

Vanegas, who was born at Toledo, the "town of the great historic memory," where he kept a school of Latin and philosophy in the early part of the sixteenth century, was a man of great learning and friend of Gomez de Ciudad Real,[1] to whose poems[2] he contributes an introduction and notes. It is in a volume[3] issued in the year 1540 that he sketches a plan of classification, which is the first imperfect type of future efforts of this kind. The divisions, which are fourfold, are of value only to the historical student. The field of knowledge is divided into the following classes: Original—of the harmony between predestination and free will; Natural—of the philosophy of the visible world; Rational—of the function and the use of the reason; Revealed—of the authority of the scriptures.

As Toledo, the intellectual capital of Spain, was the birthplace of this proposed system, so Zürich, the intellectual capital of Switzerland, was the alma mater of what must be regarded as the first successful attempt at classification. It was in this beautiful town, the stronghold of Protestantism, that Conrad Gesner was born on the 26th of March, 1516. His father, Ours Gesner,[4] who was in very humble circumstances, being a worker in hides, was unable to give him the education he craved for. Moreover, Conrad was one of a large family, so that in his desire to obtain knowledge he was obliged to turn for help to his maternal uncle, John Friccius (Chaplain Frick), a Protestant minister of Zürich, who to his honour did everything in his power to foster the talents which he could not fail to discover in his young relative. But both father and uncle died, and Gesner, being thrown entirely on his own resources, at the early age of fifteen was reduced to great extremities, and is even said to

---

[1] Companion of Charles V. in his early studies.

[2] "De Militia Principis Burgundi," 1540.

[3] This book will be found in the British Museum, and is entitled *Primera parte de las diferecias de libros ꝗ ay eñl universo. Declaradas porel mæstro Alexio Vanegas. Nuevamente emendada y corregida porel mismo autor.* Impressa Toledo, 1546.

[4] Sir Wm. Jardine's Naturalists' Library, vol. xii.

have engaged himself as a servant at Strassburg.[1] But his passionate zeal for learning led him to travel, and in turn he studied at Bourges, Montpellier and Paris, in all of which places he remained for a considerable time. Having thus laid the foundations of a broader education than was then usual, he returned to Zürich, where he married at the early age of twenty years, and though in very poor circumstances never appears to have had the least occasion to regret this step. His whole day was occupied in teaching, but he employed the night hours in study, and in this way, though adding to the debt which posterity owes him, he too surely brought on that ill-health which led to his early death. He was in turn Professor of Greek at Lausanne and Professor of Physics and Natural History at Zürich, but in neither of these offices was he well paid, and he employed his spare time, partly from necessity and partly from a love of the work, in producing the three works for which he is so justly famous. Having written many works of a minor nature, he published in the year 1545 the first part of his *Bibliotheca Universalis*, to the Supplement of which book we are indebted for his scheme of classification. The title of this book, which is a catalogue of all the works in Latin, Greek and Hebrew, extant and not extant, published or yet unpublished, is *Bibliotheca Universalis sive Catalogus omnium scriptorum locupletissimus, in tribus linguis, Latina, Græca and Hebraica. . . .* Tiguri apud Christophorum Froschoverum mense Septembre anno MDXLV. Under each important name is to be found a vast amount of bibliographical information and criticism, and on page 180 Gesner gives his own autobiography.[2] The second part of this stupendous work was published in 1548 under the title of *Pandectarum sive Partitionum Universalium Conradi Gesneri Tigurini, Medici et Philosophiæ Professoris*, Libri XXI, and it is this which contains his celebrated scheme of classification. Of the twenty-one parts of the book only nineteen appeared in 1548, but the twenty-first, a theological encyclopædia, was

---

[1] Not, however, mentioned by Schmiedel, Gesner's ablest biographer.
[2] "Conradus Gesnerus Tigurinus" is the heading.

published in 1549.[1] The twentieth part, which was to contain the result of his medical labours, never appeared. It would be wearisome to give a list of the divisions and sub-divisions of this work, but the twenty-one main divisions may well be given, for they afford some insight into the scope and magnitude of this production. They are: (1) " De Grammatica et Philologia "; (2) " De Dialectica "; (3) " De Rhetorica "; (4) " De Poetica "; (5) " De Arithmetica "; (6) " De Geometria," etc.; (7) De Musica "; (8) " De Astronomia "; (9) " De Astrologia "; (10) " De Divinatione cum licita tum illicita, et Magia "; (11) " De Geographia "; (12) " De Historiis "; (13) " De Diversis Artibus Illiteratis, Mechanicis et aliis humanæ vitæ utilibus "; (14) " De Naturali Philosophia "; (15) " De Prima Philosophia seu Metaphysica "; (16) " De Morali Philosophia "; (17) " De Oeconomica Philosophia "; (18) " De Re Politica, id est Civili et Militari "; (19) " De Jurisprudentia "; (20) " De Re Medica "; (21) " De Theologia Christiana ".

These are again subdivided very considerably, the first, " De Grammatica," into sixty-three divisions, " De Poetica " into twenty-six divisions, " De Historiis " into fifteen divisions, and " De Theologia " (by far the most important part of the work) into seventy-nine divisions.

Gesner after producing this work did not rest upon his laurels. He was already well-known throughout Europe, and his correspondence was sought by all the leading men of letters. The *Bibliotheca Universalis* was followed by a work of perhaps a still more stupendous nature, issued between the years 1551 and 1587; his *Historia Animalium.* Complete copies of this work are scarce, but luckily the British Museum is well represented, for it possesses not only the first but other editions of Gesner's works. The *Historia Animalium,* which is noticed at length by Sir William Jardine, is adorned with fine wood engravings, many of them on a large scale, and the history itself is " mixed up with a great deal of quaint information and obsolete erudition, but when these are subtracted not a

---

[1] Bound with the other parts at the British Museum.

little sound natural history remains."[1] This work at once attracted wide attention, and it was translated into English in the year 1607, by Edward Topsell[2] under the following curious title: *The Historie of Foure-Footed Beastes, Describing the true and lively figure of every beast with a discourse of their severall names, conditions, kindes, vertues (both naturall and medicinall), countries of their breed, their love and hate to Mankinde and the wonderfull worke of God in their Creation, Preservation and Destruction.* Not a little information is to be gleaned from this quaint and scarce volume wherein the translator says: "I have followed D. Gesner as neer as I could. He was a Protestant Physitian (a rare thing to finde any Religion in a Physitian although Saint Luke, a Physitian, were a writer of the Gospell). His praises therefore shall remaine, and all living creatures shal witnesse for him at the last day."

In the production of this work Gesner travelled over the greater part of Europe, and he says in the translated preface: "I have put down also many proper observations, and have gathered togither many things, nowe and then by asking questions, without reproach of any man learned or unlearned, cittizens or strangers, Hunters, Fishers, Fawconers, Sheppheards, and all kind of men," and ends with these words: "For I hope (without offence be it spoken here) that this our labour or paines shall remaine to the world's end, not through the merit or desert of our learninge (which is but small), but through our dilegence which hath joined togither most dilegently and exactly, so many and great labours and stories, from a number of authors, as it were into one treasury or storehouse".

The English edition of this work, which closely follows that published at Zürich, is enriched with many quaint plates, some dealing with animals which certainly Gesner (or any one else) had never seen. One is "Of the Sphinga or Spinx, a kinde of Apes," another, "Of the Satyre, a most rare and seldome seene beast," and yet another, "Of the

---

[1] Jardine.
[2] "Chaplaine in the Church of Saint Buttolphe, Aldergate". See also *Dictionary of National Biography.*

Algopithecus ".   " Among the rest," he says, " is there a
beast called Pan, who in his head, face, horns, legs, and
loynes downwarde resembleth a Goat, but in his belly,
breast and armes, an Ape."   Topsell also translated Gesner's
Historie of Serpents, or the Second Booke of living Creatures,
which is also adorned with large plates.

Another very rare book translated from Gesner's works
is : *The Newe Iewell of Health, wherein is contayned the most
excellent Secretes of Phisicke and Philosophie, devided into fower
Bookes . . . treating very amplye of all Dystillations of Waters, of
Oyles, Balmes, Quintessences, . . . with the use and preparation
of Antimonie and potable Gold.   Faithfully corrected by George
Baker, Chirugian.*   London, 1576.   This is a black letter
volume of which perhaps the most curious part is the description of the potable gold, " the oyle of Golde which
cured certayne desperate disseases ".

The third great work to which Gesner devoted his life
was the preparation of a work on botany.   He made a large
collection of material towards this, but the work was never
completed owing to the complete failure of his health in the
year 1565.   While he was thus prostrated with illness he
was attacked by the plague, which then raged in Zürich, and
died on the 13th December, 1565, not having completed his
fiftieth year.   He desired to be carried into his museum, and
it was there he died in the arms of his wife, and surrounded
by the monuments of his labours.   His intense devotion to
science, and his almost incredible powers of acquisition, would
be seen from a mere catalouge of his works, many of which
are exceedingly rare.   It is impossible, however, to enumerate
them here.   The hard life which he led seems to have added
to the amiable qualities of his character rather than detracted
from them, and he is acknowledged to have been a man of
singularly pure and blameless conduct.   Zürich, which has
been the home of such men as Lavater the physiognomist,
the reformer Zwingli, Bodmer the poet, Orelli the philo-
logist, Horner the occulist, Hess, Pestallozi, Henry Meyer,
and a host of learned men, has never since produced a man
of the erudition of Gesner.

To claim for Savigny, as both Boulliot and Papillon [1] do, the production of the first tabulated scheme of classification is manifestly absurd, for Savigny's system was substantially the same as Gesner's. Christopher de Savigny, from whom Boulliot says in effect Bacon obtained his "small globe of the intellectual world," [2] is a man whose name was left in oblivion for nearly two hundred years. [3] Few works of biography speak of him, and this is the more remarkable as there can be no doubt that he was a man distinguished alike for his learning and for the position which he held as *Grand maitre de la garde-robe* in the household of Louis de Gonzague, duc de Nevers. Savigny himself tells us that he was brought up "par des précepteurs très-vertueux, très-doctes et très-savants personnages," and learnt Hebrew and Greek and the whole of the sciences then cultivated. His sole claim upon our attention, however, is as the author of a scheme of classification entitled *Tableaux accomplis de tous les arts liberaux, contenant brievement et clerement par singuliere methode de doctrine, une generale et sommaire partition des dicts arts, amassez et reduicts en ordre pour le soulagement et profit de la jeunesse.* Paris, 1587.

The classification, the scheme of which is contained in an atlas arranged on the "family-tree" principle, is divided in the following order: "Grammaire, rhétorique, dialectique, arithmétique, géométrie, optique, musique, cosmographie, astrologie, médecine, éthique, jurisprudence, histoire, théologie". The latter part was written, however, by the *avocat* Nicholas Bergeron, "homme très-docte et bien versé en sa profession," and the first author of "ces tables synchroniques qui présentent d'un seul coup d'œil la série des principaux évènements de l'histoire". [4] Savigny says, "Son bon amy et conseil M. Bergeron lui a presté la main à dresser les tableaux qu'il offre au public," and unlike many authors does not grudge his friend the recognition of the assistance he rendered in the production of the work. The following curious *jeu*

[1] See also *Les Bibliothèques Françoises*, par Grudé de la Croix du Main.
[2] *The Advancement of Learning.*
[3] Boulliot, "Personne ne nous fournit de détails sur sa vie".
[4] Grudé de la Croix du Main.

d'esprit occurs under the heading médecine: "Il ne faut jamais donner aucun médicament purgatif à ceux qui sont en bonne disposition".

The *Tableaux accomplis*, which is adorned with some very beautiful woodcuts, is of great rarity. Boulliot mentions but four copies, amongst them being the one in the British Museum. The frontispiece,[1] which bears the liberal motto for the age—

> Tost ou tard, pres ou loing,
> A le fort du foible besiong,

is elaborately decorated. The third page contains a fine woodcut with portraits of Louis de Gonzague and Savigny, and is followed by this dedication: "A Treshault Trespuissant, Tresmagnanime et Tresillustre Prince Monseigneur Ludovic de Gonzague, duc de Niernois et de Rhetelois, etc.," and then comes the *Partition*[2] proper which is a kind of pedigree of the arts and sciences in the form of the old family-tree bound together by the symbol of a chain.

This work, which is on an extensive scale, is divided into various subdivisions: thus "Grammaire" has 78 parts, "Poésie" 92, "Optique" 37, and "Astrologie" 100. Papillon (b. 1698) was unable to see the first edition,[3] but gives a description of the later one in his *Traité historique de la gravure en bois*. At an early date the *Tableaux accomplis* was translated into Portuguese by Manoel Pinto Villalobos[4] under the title of *Enciclopedia*, and wrongly attributed to Bergeron, but the work does not otherwise seem to have gained much attention.

It will thus be seen that Savigny, who died about the year 1608, although a forerunner of Bacon, was the third who proposed a scheme of classification, and in this connection it is worthy of remark that Toledo, the intellectual capital of Spain, produced the first system, that proposed by Alexo Vanegas de Busto; Zürich, the intellectual centre

[1] Attributed to the celebrated painter Jean Cousin, Brunet's *Manuel du Libraire.*

[2] It is worth noticing that the word partition is always used in these old systems when speaking of classification. The latter word was first used by Burke in the year 1790.

[3] Boulliot.   [4] *Nouvelle Biographie Générale.*

of Switzerland, the second; Paris, the third; and London, the fourth. The subject is one well worthy of study, and a vast amount of information on early systems of classification remains to be gleaned at the British Museum and elsewhere. It may not be without interest to mention here that the first bibliographical system as distinguished from a classification of knowledge was produced by Florianus Treflerus, a Bavarian Benedictine, in a book entitled *Methodus Exhibens per Varios Indices et Classes subinde quorumlibet librorum, cujuslibet Bibliothecæ, brevĕ, facilem, imitabilem ordinationem.* This little book, which, according to Peignot's *Dictionnaire de Bibliologie*, 1802, was printed in the year 1560 at Augsbourg, although it bears no date, is to be found in the British Museum, and contains a contemporary note stating it to be the gift of the author to a certain abbot "as a perpetual memorial". This treatise of Treflerus was already numbered amongst books of great rarity almost 250 years ago. Both Zoller and Albert (in common with Ziegelbauer) appear never to have seen the book itself, but describe it on the authority of an elaborate notice by Struve in the Jena periodical *Bibliotheca Antiqua* for January, 1706.[1] That Treflerus had studied Gesner is shown by a reference to him on page 28, but the classification, which has seventeen divisions (probably corresponding to the number of the book presses), is, according to Peignot, " plus que médiocre ".[2]

In conclusion it is a singular circumstance that Zürich, which saw the production of the first great scheme of classification, is, more than 350 years later, perhaps directly owing to Gesner's influence as a Zoologist, the place whence another great bibliographical undertaking is now being issued, *viz.*, Dr. Field's *Concilium Bibliographicum.*

---

[1] See Edward Edwards' *Memoirs of Libraries.*

[2] Peignot, article " Système Bibliographique," which describes very liberally several French systems.

CAUSERIE.

Mr. Carnegie and Lord Acton's Library.—Mr. Carnegie, who does nothing by halves, says a writer in the *Manchester Guardian*, has surprised the world afresh by presenting the late Lord Acton's library to Mr. John Morley, M.P. To a scholar no gift could be more interesting, though its size might well embarrass the most successful author, for the library contains between 60,000 and 80,000 volumes—almost as many, that is, as are in the John Rylands Library. Indeed it is no secret that the late Lord Acton, who not only collected but read and annotated this vast array of books, found late in life that he could not afford to keep them. Mr. Carnegie then bought the library as it stood, and allowed it to remain in Lord Acton's possession until his death. The Empress Catherine of Russia did as much for Diderot, when he had to sell his library to provide a marriage portion for his daughter. But Mr. Carnegie has improved upon the great Empress's example, for she carried off Diderot's library after his death to Russia, while Mr. Carnegie transfers his purchase to the keeping of a fellow-scholar of Lord Acton's, so that it may remain in England, perhaps to be added in the near future to the collections of one of our universities. But something like an older parallel Diderot himself has supplied us with in his article in the *Encyclopædia* on "Libraries," or, to speak more correctly, two parallels. The most ancient is that of the gift by the Roman Senate to the family of Regulus of the books found in Carthage after the taking of it. A library was a national gift and the most honourable they could bestow. That of a later date is to be found in Tiraboschi, who relates that Nicholas Niccoli left his library at his death to the public, but his debts being greater than his effects, Cosmo De Medici secured the bequest by paying the debts, and increased the number of books by Greek, Hebrew and other MSS., for which he likewise built a splendid resting-place. Lord Acton, the most learned man of his time, will thus have his literary monument after all, for the vast range of his knowledge and interests is nowhere so well represented as in his books. In a sympathetic notice of him which appeared lately in the New York *Nation*, the writer, to show that Lord Acton's learning was encyclopædic, stated that few American scholars knew as much as he did about the United States Constitution, though ecclesiastical controversy and the history of European thought were supposed to monopolise his attention. The pity is that a man of such attainments wrote so little, though his influence upon and his encouragement of younger scholars counted for much in the progress of English historical scholarship during the last half-century. However, we must console ourselves with the fact that though the master workman is gone his tools remain, and are sure to be worthily used by their new owner. Lately, perhaps, Mr. Morley's eminence as a statesman has somewhat obscured his high reputation as a historian and biographer, but Mr. Carnegie's happy tribute to his scholarship will remind even the most forgetful people of the services rendered to literature by the author of *Voltaire* and *Diderot*, *Cobden* and *Cromwell*, and many other fascinating volumes. We can only wish Mr. Morley long life to enjoy the pleasures of using the Acton Library. The library is rich in many departments, especially in all the literature of the Council of Trent, of the Bartholomew Massacre, of the Inquisition; in Jesuitica; in Expurgatorial Indexes; in the Annals of the Popes; in the story of Protestantism in France. Among other treasures is a unique collection of Italian, Latin and other printed letters; also of rare material for French local history, and Italian provincial history, if provincial be here the right word. It is rich in memoirs, in General European history in most branches, and in the whole literature of political science.

The Exportation of Rare Books to America.—A correspondent

of *The Times* writes with reference to the library acquired recently by Mr. Pierpont Morgan :—

"Can nothing be done to stem the continuous and wholesale exportation of rare early printed and other books and illuminated MSS. to the United States of America? The 'drain' has been going on for over half a century; within recent years it has reached huge proportions; and now we have the mournful privilege of chronicling the most important single transaction which has occurred—or, perhaps, is likely to occur—in connection with this subject. The significance of the transaction will be at once recognised when it is stated that the library which Messrs. Sotheby, Wilkinson & Hodge have just sold by private treaty to an American gentleman (who does not wish his name disclosed) includes thirty-two examples of Caxton's press, and that the price paid is only a little less than that at which Mrs. Rylands acquired the Spencer Library which consisted of several thousand volumes. The library was for the most part formed by the late William Morris. Soon after Morris's death in 1896, the whole of his splendid collection of early printed books and MSS. was purchased *en bloc* by a well-known collector, whom the Ashburnham and other sales of the five or six succeeding years enabled to make very considerable additions to a library already distinguished by its choice and rare character. The library, as it now stands, comprises only about 700 articles, but every one of these is of the highest interest and value.

"What, it naturally may be asked, was the object of forming this library, and for what reason was it, so soon after its completion, placed in the market? Both questions admit of a ready answer. The owner's object, apart from the intellectual joys of the bibliophile, was to form a collection of books which should exemplify the origin and development of the early illustrated book, starting from the illuminated manuscript, through the block books and onwards to the finished typographical specimen; so that there are scarcely any books in this collection of a later date than 1500. As to the second of the two questions, change of residence and occupation in other matters rendered it necessary for the owner to part company with the treasures which he has brought together with so much enterprise within such a very brief space of time. He has made the most of opportunities which cannot reasonably be expected to occur again. His greatest *coup* was made when, as we have said, he purchased *en bloc* the whole of William Morris's fine library. From this he selected only the very choicest articles, both manuscript and printed book, and placed the remainder, which did not help his collection, under the hammer at Sotheby's. This sale took place on 5th December, 1898, and five following days, and produced a total of close on £11,000. Articles describing William Morris's Library at the time of his death and the selection sold in 1898 appeared in *The Times* of 7th November, 1896, and November, 1898. Fine as were the books sold in 1898, they appear third-rate by the side of those which were retained by the owner. At the Ashburnham sales, 1897-8, his agents carried off a very considerable percentage of the prizes which came within the limits of his requirements. Apart from, and in addition to, these two primary sources, he has been a fearless purchaser whenever anything important came into the market; and for years past he has been scouring the Continent in the search after illuminated MSS.

"With these few preliminary remarks, we may pass on to consider the chief features of the 700 odd volumes which constitute the library. To start with there are no fewer than 111 illuminated MSS., French, English, German, Dutch, Italian, etc. Those of English origin, thirteen in number, will naturally be of most interest to English readers; and these are additionally attractive from the fact that, with four exceptions, they were in the Morris Library. The more important include the 'Huntingfield Psalter,' formerly the property of Roger de Huntingfield, with sixty-eight miniatures on thirty-four leaves folio, executed about the year 1150; the 'Worksop Priory Bestiary,' said to be the finest of its kind in existence, with 106 splendid miniatures, executed about the year 1170, and presented to Worksop Priory seventeen years afterwards; the 'Nottingham Psalter,' dating from about 1220, with fine illuminations in the calendar, and initials throughout; the 'Clare Psalter,' *circa* 1270, with the arms of Clare, Plantagenet, Warren and Gifford incorporated at the beginning: the 'Edindon Bible,' formerly in the monastery of Edindon or Hedington, executed about the year 1270, with a great number of extremely delicate miniatures of the English school; the 'Tiptoft Missal,' executed in 1332, at the time of the alliance between John Fitz Roger or Clavering and Hawse de Tibetot (Tiptoft), the arms of both families occur frequently, with 616 full-page illuminated borders containing miniatures—one of the very finest MSS. of its kind in existence; the 'Gloucester Abbey Hymn Book and Horæ,' written at the Abbey of St. Peter, Gloucester, about the year 1430; the 'Sheldon Missal,' executed in 1440, and formerly the property of Sir John Sheldon, Lord Mayor of London, with 176 illuminations; and the 'Kildare Book of Hours,' with seventy-five full-page and other illuminations, formerly the property of the old Fitzgerald family, Earls of Kildare.

"It would require several columns to describe with anything like adequacy the various MSS. of Continental workmanship. But a few of the chief examples may be indicated. Of the Italian, special mention may be made of the 'Evangeliarum' of Pope Eugenius IV., illuminated with fifty miniatures by John de Monterchio, and presented by Peter, Bishop of Padua, to the Pope on his presiding at the Council of Basilicons in 1436—this MS. is of the finest artistic interest; and of the 'Morosini Missal,' executed for the family of that name, whose arms are incorporated in the illuminations; a fifteenth-century MS., with three full-page and sixteen smaller miniatures; the Italian Horæ and Offices include several very choice examples. The Flemish MSS. are chiefly Psalters of the thirteenth century—one of the finest, executed for a lady named Katherine, contains eighteen full-page miniatures and twenty smaller ones; while the 'Liège Psalter' is adorned with four full-page miniatures and 300 smaller examples.

"The French MSS. are nearly seventy in number, and where all are fine it is exceedingly difficult to make a selection for special notice. Some of the more splendid examples were in the famous Firman-Didot collection, notably the 'Limoges Gospels,' with thirty full-page miniatures, executed about the year 1150, and formerly the property of the Abbey of St. Martial at Limoges; the 'Angoulême Bible,' dating from about 1225, and formerly the property of the Frères Mineurs d'Engolismen; the 'St. Lousis Psalter,' *circa* 1250, with sixteen full-page and twenty-one smaller miniatures, a superb MS., which belonged to Gerald, Bishop of Cambray, in 1374; a fine MS. of 'Le Roman de la Rose' executed about the year 1370, with fourteen pictures in *grisaille;* Marie Stuart's 'Book of Hours,' bound for her at her marriage in 1558; a fifteenth-century MS., with twenty large and thirty-four small miniatures. The Psalters are especially fine, the 'Beauvais Psalter,' executed about 1260, with ten full-page miniatures and numerous other smaller illuminations being one of the finest; the Horæ are not only numerous, but include several with interesting pedigrees—that, for instance, which once belonged to Anne and Françoise de Saligny; another which was presented to Louis XI.; another executed at the order of Louis le Batard de Bourbon, as a present to his son Charles de Roussilon, and afterwards the property of Louis XIII.; one which belonged to King James II., and so forth. Linking together the illuminated MS. and the printed book, come the block books which are so excessively rare, but of which this library contains several of the most interesting and important.

"But the crowning interest of the whole library, so far as English collectors are concerned, lies in the magnificent series of Caxtons. When William Blades published the revised edition of his work on Caxton in 1877, he described ninety-nine works by Caxton; of these thirty-eight were known by a single copy or fragments only. There were eighty-one in the British Museum, of which twenty-five were duplicates, thus reducing the number to fifty-six, of which three are mere fragments. The Spencer Caxtons (now in the John Rylands Library), although numerically fewer than those in the National Library, make a more complete collection and embrace fifty-seven separate works. The University Library at Cambridge possesses forty-one different (or including duplicates fifty-two) examples, the Bodleian coming next with twenty-eight, and the Chatsworth Library of the Duke of Devonshire with twenty-five. It will be seen, therefore, that this collection of thirty-two Caxtons ranks as the fourth largest in existence; and it is probably the most numerous series which has occurred in one library since John Ratcliffe's sale at Christie's in 1776, when forty-eight Caxtons realised the total of £236 5s. 6d., which to-day would scarcely purchase a few leaves from Caxton's press! The series leads off appropriately enough with *Corydale: Les Quatre Derrenieres Choses,* which is believed to be one of Caxton's earliest works, printed by him at Bruges, *circa* 1474; the only other copy known is in the British Museum, and this was discovered by Mr. Winter Jones, bound up with another work, when recataloguing a portion of the old Royal Library. Following this come the Ashburnham copy of the first book printed in the English language, Le Fevre's *Recuyell of the Historyes of Troyes, circa* 1474, and a copy of the later edition, *circa* 1477, of the same work. The other Caxtons include the Hardwicke example of *The Game and Playe of Chesse,* 1474-5; *The Dictes and Sayings of the Philosophers,* 1477, one of five perfect copies known; *A Boke of the Hoole Lyf of Jason, circa* 1477, the finest of the three perfect examples, acquired at the Ashburnham sale for £2,100; *The Booke named Corydale, or the Fowr Last Thinges,* 1478; two imperfect copies of the first edition of Chaucer 1478; three of Higden's *Polychronicon,* 1482, each wanting a good many leaves; *The Booke callyd Caton,* 1483; *The Booke of the Ordre of Chivalry of Knyghthode,* 1483, an excessively rare Caxton, only four other copies being known; one of three perfect copies of Lydgate's *The Lyf of our Lady,* 1484, *The Proffytable Boke for Mannes Soule . . . which boke is called the chastysing of Goddes chyldren* 1490-01, the Perkins copy of the first book printed in England with a title-page; and *A Boke of Divers Truytful, Ghoostly Matters,* &c., 1490, one of five copies. There are eight Caxtons with illustrations, starting with the earliest of all, *The Mirrour of the World,* 1481.

"The early Oxford Press is represented by three books, one being the celebrated *Sancti Ieronimi Exposicio in Simbolum Apostolorum* with the error in the date of 1468 for 1478, which caused so much bibliographical discussion during the early part of the last century. This is the first book printed at Oxford, and of it only about nine copies are known. The second Oxford book is an edition of Richard Rolle de Hampole, *Explanationes Notabiles Devotissimi*, etc., 1481-6, the only one of four copies not in a public library—this was purchased at the Inglis sale in 1900 for £300; and J. Lathbury, *Liber moralium super trenis Jhereime Prophete*, 1482, with illustrations. The presses of the other early English printers are well represented. Many of these are almost as rare as Caxtons. Wynkyn de Worde, Pynson, the mysterious St. Albans printer, and Lettou being represented by over forty books.

"The section which comprises books printed in Germany, the Low Countries, etc., forms a highly representative one, numbering as it does over 200 articles, nearly all of which were in William Morris's library. Two specimens of Peter Schoeffer's press are printed on vellum. All these books are very rare, many excessively so, and in one or two instances they are unique; whilst a number have bibliographical and other notes in Morris's own handwriting. The early Italian printed books number over 160, ten of which are upon vellum, whilst those of French presses number about 120, twenty-nine (chiefly Books of Hours) being printed on vellum.

"A fully annotated and descriptive catalogue alone would do justice to this library, but the few foregoing facts will serve to indicate some of the principal features. It was formed, as we have already stated, with a well-defined object, and it is reasonably complete within those limits. The formation of another such collection scarcely comes within the range of the possible—even granted half a century and an unlimited amount of money to attempt such a task. It is, therefore, for these and for other reasons little short of a public calamity for the collection to pass out of this country; but, unfortunately, in these matters there is no such element as sentiment—the man with the biggest purse gets the prize. If English collectors will not avail themselves of such unique opportunities, it is, at all events, comforting to reflect that, as in the present instance, the collection is in the custody of an English-speaking nation."

The Muratori Archives to be made Accessible to Scholars.—

The heirs of the famous historian Muratori, the author of the *Scriptores Rerum Italicarum*, who are living at Modena in extreme poverty, lately announced their intention to offer for sale the valuable "Muratori Archives" in the possession of the family. These consist of the manuscripts and prodigious collections used by that scholar in the preparation of his great work. The Municipal Council of Modena, the Directors of the Biblioteca Estense, and a Deputazione di Storia Patria, thereupon applied to the Italian Government for aid to purchase the entire collection, pointing out the danger of any dispersal of its contents and the loss to Italy by the sale of the whole or any fragments of it to foreign libraries or collectors. Thanks to the instant energy of the present Italian Minister of Education any such catastrophe has been averted. A grant of 45,000 lire has been made to the city of Modena for the purchase of the archives, on condition that they are placed in the Biblioteca Estense and made accessible to scholars. The city is to repay the State in ten yearly instalments.

The Leonine Reference Library in the Vatican.—

A correspondent of the *Kölnische Volkszeitung* sends an account of this recently created addition to the treasures of the Vatican Library, for which the members of the Roman Historical Institute especially thanked Pope Leo XIII. when lately received by him. The Vatican Archives and Library consist almost entirely of MSS., which the liberal policy of the reigning Pontiff has thrown widely open to the researches of students. But in these days of critical study, it is absolutely necessary in order to deal satisfactorily with MS. material, to have also to hand a great number of printed works of reference. Neither the Vatican nor the other libraries of Rome offered this convenience. Since the Italian Government took over the public libraries in 1870 little or nothing has been done to supply new books in foreign languages, or on subjects not connected with Italy. A like want was felt of the large and costly collections, such as memoirs of academies, the publications of various archives, etc. The munificence of Leo XIII. has now supplied such a reference library on a most ample scale and in highly artistic surroundings.

The northern suite of apartments whose windows look into the Cortile della Stamperia have been utilised for the housing of those printed books which were formerly kept in the Borgia apartments, and whose removal from the latter has permitted the splendid frescoes of Pinturicchio to be restored and thrown open to the public. This collection of older books is itself of great value. In addition to the old Heidelberg or Palatina Library, it contains also the valuable library of Cardinal Angelo Mai, and several other collections. Under the direction of Father Ehrle large quantities of books are continually coming in, which have hitherto for want of room been scattered. Thus the Holy Office and the Index Congregations have restored the volumes they held belonging to the Palatina Library. At present, therefore, this collection in the four large northern apartments may safely be reckoned as the most complete of all Roman libraries for printed books of an early date from the very invention of printing onwards. It is being busily arranged and catalogued, and soon will form a model library. The new Reference Library is, however, quite a new creation. It occupies the southern portion of the apartments. A winding staircase leads up to the working room of the library, whilst on the other side the Reference Library communicates immediately by doors with the working rooms of the Archives. The Reference Library is freely open to all who are working in either the Vatican Library or Archives.

The books are arranged in tall book-cases chiefly according to countries. One of the largest collections is that of Baden, a gift of the Grand Duke Frederick to the Holy Father. All the volumes of this collection are uniformly bound in brown leather, and bear the arms of Baden. A similar very fine collection relates to Bohemia. German books, as might be expected, occupy a very large proportion of the total space.

Attached to this apartment is a second one in which are arranged all the encyclopædias, the complete collections of the Fathers and the Councils, lexicons, and liturgical, exegetical, epigraphical and legal books. At the opposite end, also in an adjoining room, are the works relating to the various religious orders and to the history of individual dioceses. The total number of volumes is very considerable, and constantly growing, as Father Ehrle, the indefatigable Prefect, is ever adding to it by new acquisitions. The Leonine Reference Library is thus becoming a truly international consulting library, and as such will very soon rank as the first in the world. It would be desirable that the various Governments should follow the good example given by some few in contributing copies of their various national collections to this central library, which is one more monument to the princely munificence of Leo XIII. in the cause of learning.

The Manuscripts of the Royal Library of Brussels.

—It was in the fifteenth century that Philip the Good, Duke of Burgundy, the most enlightened and esteemed sovereign of his time, whose Court was the most brilliant in all Europe, formed the collection of books which was long, under the name of the *Bibliothèque de Bourgogne*, one of the most famous libraries in the world. The collection now forms practically the MS. department of the Royal Library so familiar to English tourists in Brussels. But since its incorporation into that important national institution, the collection has steadily increased. The number of MSS. has grown from 18,000 in 1842 to a total of 24,984 at the present day. Still it is true that the chief treasures of this collection belong to the ancient Burgundian library. It was a happy inspiration of the Belgian Government to appoint a few years ago the learned Bollandist, Father Joseph van den Gheyn, S.J., to the responsible post of Keeper of MSS. at the Bibliothèque Royale. Father van den Gheyn is one of the most distinguished scholars that Belgium can boast. He first became known as an Orientalist devoted to the study of the Aryan languages and especially to ethnography. He made himself a considerable name by his writings on Indian philology, on the tribes of Central Asia, and especially on the vexed question of the origin of the Aryan peoples. For some time he was Professor of Sanskrit in the Catholic Institute of Paris. Then he was elected to the enviable position of one of the Bollandists, whose house and library are situated in Brussels. He has done good work by his publication of various texts in connection with the labours of that learned congregation. Thus his early brilliant career and his consequent familiarity with so many Eastern languages and with MS. research fittingly prepared him for the important post he now occupies.

Father van den Gheyn soon signalised his tenure of this post by arranging an admirable museum of the chief MS. treasures of his library, beautifully arranged and displayed in glass cases in one of the large rooms on the ground floor, which will be found well worth a visit by the tourist. But more than this, he set himself to the heavy task of compiling an entirely new and complete catalogue of the entire library of MSS., a work involving immense labour and varied learning. The old three-volumed catalogue of Marchal, issued in 1842, has long been out of date. Since then special portions of the collection have been studied and catalogued by individual writers, *e.g.*, the Irish MSS. by Dr. Todd in the *Proceedings of the Royal Irish Academy*, vol. iii., pp. 447-502 (1847). Similiar partial work has been done in the *Monumenta Germaniae Historica* and the *Archiv* of Pertz. The present undertaking of Father van den Gheyn will occupy at least twelve goodly volumes, the first of which has lately appeared (*Catalogue des Manuscrits de la Bibliothèque royale de Belgique*, tome i., *Ecriture sainte et Liturgie*, pp. xv and 592, Bruxelles, Lamertin). The Belgian Minister of the Interior and of Education accorded the necessary funds for the publication, which he has encouraged in every way. This first volume, devoted entirely to Holy Scripture and Liturgy, deals with 1414 MSS. out of the total of nearly 25,000. It is a model of what such a catalogue should be. Each individual MS. is most carefully described in all its details, its contents fully tabulated, its date, country and history indicated or discussed. There are several entries of some interest to English readers, but above all the celebrated " Peterborough Psalter " (No. 593), one of the greatest treasures of the library. This magnificent codex is a masterpiece of illumination and calligraphy. It is written entirely in letters of gold, azure and vermilion, without any black ink. All the initial letters are ornamented, and there are a great many superb headpieces, whilst many pages are richly bordered with arabesques, garlands of flowers, birds and grotesque figures. Folios 92 and 93 are covered with splendid miniatures, forming altogether 109 pictures representing scenes in the Old and New Testament, with explanatory verses in blue and red. It has been definitely proved by M. Delisle, of the National Library of Paris, who is probably the greatest living authority on these subjects, that this superb thirteenth-century work was executed in the Abbey of Peterborough, a Benedictine house. From England it passed into the possession of Kings Charles V. and Charles VI. of France, and thence into that of the Dukes of Burgundy, which accounts for its presence in the old *Bibliothèque de Bourgogne.*

A Leaf Stolen from the Sinai Palimpsest.—The June number of *The Expository Times* has what is described as a remarkable communication from Mrs. Lewis, Phil.Dr. (Halle), LL.D. (St. Andrews). The article describes the disappearance of a leaf from the Syriac Palimpsest of the Four Gospels on Mount Sinai. Mrs. Lewis missed it whilst she was in the Convent Library in February of this year, but the monks had previously noticed its disappearance. It is f. 101, which contains part of the story of Mary, slave of Tertullus. Mrs. Lewis continues: "I was informed that a party of several scholars had worked for some time at that MS. during the course of last summer; and it is safe to suppose that a fair number of passing travellers have been permitted not only to look at it, but also to handle it. My surmise is that one of these latter, wishing to make an addition to his own collection of Oriental curios, has slipped the leaf betwixt the pages of a book in the fond belief that it would never be missed. The manuscript is kept in a box of mahogany, lined with cedar-wood, which I presented to the Convent in 1893, for its safe custody. This box has two lids, the inner one being of glass, so that the manuscript might be displayed to visitors without its having to bear the touch of their fingers. It is further protected from dust by a silken cover, made for it by the late Mrs. Bensly, and the monks are very careful to put it neatly into this; for any want of dexterity in so doing would take something from the crumbling margins. Except for the loss of a leaf, the manuscript has suffered in no way since I last saw it in 1897; indeed, as the years roll on, its pages have tended to become cleaner. But most of the binding had disappeared before 1895, the cord which held the quires together having given way even earlier. Many quires and several leaves are, therefore, quite loose; thus the latter offer a too ready temptation to the spoiler. But who has done this deed? Who has found it in his heart to mutilate one of the most ancient of Gospel manuscripts, a codex eccentric in its readings, if you will, but unique in the light which it has shed on some of our Lord's sayings, and in the interest which its text has awakened amongst biblical scholars? It is not only the monks who have been robbed, it is the Christian world, which has surely a right of heritage in those sacred records which enshrine the earliest forms of the Gospel story. For 1,200 years that codex has remained unaltered, intact so far as its later script—the lives of holy women—is concerned, and for 1,600 years its 142 leaves of the Gospel writing have held together, preserved to us, we may well believe, by something more than mere chance. The theft has certainly not been the act of a scholar. This we may know from the fact that f. 100 has several rents near the top, as if its neighbour had been roughly and hurriedly torn off. F. 102 is quite detached from it, and now naturally begins the eleventh quire, as will be seen from Dr. Rendel Harris's Table A in the edition of 1894. The thief has evidently been restrained by no scruple about injuring the context; we therefore judge that he was unable to read the Syriac text, and was probably a thoughtless visitor, eager to acquire a specimen of something either for himself or for the library of his University. Even if we allow that there may have been an excuse for such conduct in the old days, when the manuscript treasures of Eastern monasteries were hidden from the view of scholars, it is surely now a great breach of faith and honour towards the hospitable monks of Mount Sinai, who have spent both thought and money in the rearrangement of their books and who receive every European visitor with a kindness and a simple trustfulness which should place him on his honour." The article is accompanied by a facsimile of the stolen leaf, and Mrs. Lewis states that if the possessor of it, or any one who may recognise the leaf from the photographs, will send it by post, carefully protected between two pieces of cardboard, either to her at "Castlebrae, Cambridge," or to the editor or the publishers of *The Expository Times*, they will undertake to replace it in the codex. It is added that no questions will be asked, nor any attempt made to acquire information which is not voluntarily given.

Reproduction of the Bodleian Manuscripts.—The librarian of the Bodleian Library, Oxford, who has just issued a first list of the photographic reproductions of the important palæographic MSS. which the library possesses, appeals for the support of other libraries in this highly useful undertaking. He makes a special appeal in connection with the palæographical collotypes which are not likely to be purchased largely by the general public. They are prepared only for palæographers, and are not accompanied by transcripts for beginners in the study of MSS. Each, however, will have an adequate account at the foot of the page embodying the results of original examination of the MS. in question. Very few of the important MSS. in the Bodleian have as yet been exemplified elsewhere. It is hoped that all will be included in the series here announced, if adequate support is given by other libraries. One feature of the reproductions is that, in the case of a MS. written by more than one contemporaneous scribe, an attempt will be made to represent every hand which can be clearly distinguished. And where the hand of a single scribe alters so much that the end of the MS. seems to have been written by another person, specimens of his earlier and later style will be given. The librarian hopes also to collotype specimens of bindings employed by different monasteries, as well as of pages illustrating their writing, ornamentation, shelf-marks and inscriptions of ownership.

An "Unique" Caxton.—In the 1850's, at a small auction of books held in Ghent, M. Ferdinand Van der Haeghen, the late librarian of the University Library in that old-world city, bought a small early printed volume, whose type, unknown to him, attracted his attention. Five or six years thereafter, M. Campbell, engaged at the time in collecting materials for his *Annales Typographiques*, was M. Van der Haeghen's guest, and the little book was shown to him. The particular form of the black-letter used was unfamiliar to him too, and seeing that it was not a product of any of the Netherland presses, he laid it aside. Later, while the librarian was arranging and identifying various early examples printed at Ghent, a number of volumes that puzzled him were placed together. When, about 1875, these books were sent to the Royal Library at The Hague, in order that there, with more extensive material at hand, the printers and places of printing might be discovered, one after another was identified, until finally a single work remained. This was a *Commemoratio Lamentacionis sive Compassionis Beatæ Mariæ* in small 4to, twenty-four lines to a page, without headlines or pagination, but consisting of sixty-two pages, signed by the sheet, and not by the leaf. On the title-page appears a woodcut of the Virgin enthroned, the dead Christ on her knee. The book was compared with early examples of German, Italian, French and Netherlandish printing, but in vain. Finally, M. Campbell turned to Blades's *Life of Caxton*, and by identifying the type with that known as No. 5, added another to the known works of our great printer. The *Commemoratio*, a late production of Caxton's press *c.* 1490, agrees typographically with the *Festum Transfigurationis D. N., Iesu Christi*, of which the unique copy now in the British Museum fetched £200 in 1862. The paper used in each case is the smallest of the three sizes employed by Caxton, the full sheet measuring about 18 ins. by 12 ins., so that an uncut 4to should be about 8¾ ins. by 5¾ ins. This volume proves to be unique, and hence has been chosen as the first to be facsimiled by the Lancashire Bibliographical Society, one of whose aims is thus to reproduce unique examples of important early printed books. The *Commemoratio* is one among a small group of interesting liturgical books known as *Nova Festa*, intended as supplements to the Breviary and Missal, printed towards the end of the fifteenth century. The volume under consideration consists of three parts—the Breviary Services for a Commemoration of the Compassio B.V.M., on one particular day of the year; a Mass corresponding; and the Breviary Services for the Compassio when adapted for a festival with octave instead of for a Commemoration. Although the Mass as here printed is found in the *Sarum Missal*, Rouen, 1497, the full service appears to have been in the nature of an unsuccessful experiment.

The Rights of a Public Library over its own Books.—A

writer in the *Manchester Guardian* has raised an interesting question as to the rights of a public library over its own books. It will be remembered that the Northampton Free Library recently sold a number of books, once the property of that ill-fated minor poet, John Clare, which had been presented to the library by a municipal subscription at the time of his death. Some of these volumes, which included first editions of Keats, Lamb and Tennyson, made valuable by the autographs of their authors, were lately discovered in a locked cupboard, where the illiterate or thrifty librarian, who received them thirty-six years ago, had carefully packed them away. The Northampton Library Committee decided that these books were too valuable to be retained as "curiosities," and disposed of them at a well-known auction room; one volume, the first edition of the *Essays of Elia*, containing Lamb's autograph, brought no less than £88. The Library Committee proposes to spend the proceeds of the sale, amounting to several hundred pounds, in books for the reference library. The question now raised is whether they were justified in so doing on ethical and literary as well as on legal grounds. No one will doubt that the Committee acted with the best intentions, and it may reasonably be argued that the books in question, having been locked up in a cupboard ever since they came into the Free Library's keeping, will be no great loss to Northampton. But, to compare small things with great, we need only try to imagine what an uproar would be caused if Magdalen College proposed to sell the manuscript of Pepys's *Diary* in order to purchase works of reference, or the John Rylands Library wished to "trade away" one of its Caxtons for the latest atlases and encyclopædias, to see that a point of wider interest than the literary taste of Northampton has been raised. As the writer already mentioned well puts it, "it is to be hoped that this strictly utilitarian policy will not be followed by other Free Library Committees, for it will at once arrest the flow of private generosity which brought these valuable books into the possession of ungrateful Northampton". There are higher considerations than even reference libraries, and it would be hard to say how many sets of Larousse and Stieler and the *Encyclopædia Britannica* would really counterbalance the distinction given to a provincial library by the possession of books which had once been in Lamb's hands and were dignified by his autograph.

Free Libraries for the Blind.

—Viscount Midleton, writing as President of the Home Teaching Society for the Blind with reference to the suggestion to commemorate the Coronation by the establishment of a free circulating library for the blind, explains that his organisation has already fourteen such libraries in as many districts in London, and that the four or five hundred volumes belonging to each of them are distributed on loan, gratuitously, at the homes of the blind by the teachers of the institution. Books are exchanged by them once a fortnight, and, after passing round one district, are brought back to the Central Office at 53 Victoria Street, Westminster, and passed on to another district. Constant variety is thus secured, and there is no danger of such a book as *The Pickwick Papers*—which costs £2 9s. and makes fourteen volumes even of interpointed Braille type—lying idle at Poplar when it is wanted at Chelsea. People who really know the blind are aware that most of those who enjoy books the best are precisely those who would have the greatest difficulty in going, or sending, to a distance to exchange them. He proceeds: "Instead, therefore, of endowing a large new library, or of presenting embossed books to municipal libraries where they could be comparatively little used, would it not be better to contribute to the funds of the Home Teaching Society? It combines the advantages of a centre for exchange and a complete organisation for the free distribution of books in every metropolitan borough, and far out into the suburbs. Want of money alone limits the extent of its work." Subscriptions should be sent to Miss E. Bainbrigge, the secretary of the society, 53 Victoria Street, Westminster.

Village Libraries and Popular Education.

—We are pleased to notice that in connection with the University Extension Meeting at Cambridge this year, the subject of village libraries was introduced and discussed. As we have already pointed out in these pages the rural districts, not only in this country but also in Ireland, call for more earnest consideration in the matter of provision for intellectual improvement than they have received hitherto. We have advocated the travelling library which has been worked with such marked success in the United States and Australia, and also in certain parts of our own country, under the auspices of the " Union of Institutes ". Lady Verney has done very much to help forward the movement by demonstrating what may be done by means of grouping small villages, and we venture to hope that many ladies in the country may be stimulated by her successful experiments to follow her example.

Prof. T. M'Kenny Hughes, who presided at the discussion at Cambridge, said that this was not a suggestion of effort in the direction of small parochial benevolence. Among the many philanthropic schemes in which Lady Verney, who would open the discussion, had taken an active part this was not one of the least important, whether they regarded it as a proposal for the improvement of the domestic and social life of our rural population, or whether they looked upon it as a means of checking to some extent the depletion of our agricultural districts and the congestion of our towns. This last point of view was one which they had frequently brought before them in their Chamber of Agriculture. Where were our agriculturists to look for the labour necessary for the work of the farm if all the most energetic, most quick-witted and resourceful of the village lads sought employment elsewhere? Who could blame them when by higher education their eyes had been opened and facilities of travel had brought them into contact with those who had, as they would say, bettered themselves, for seeking larger opportunities for themselves? Even our country girls now scorned domestic service if they could get the greater freedom of employment in some commercial establishment. We wanted working men's and women's clubs suited to the conditions of the people, with simple amusements for some and opportunities of intellectual improvement for others.

Lady Verney said that the object of her paper was not to state a theory, but the actual experience of a group of Buckinghamshire villages. They lived in the village of Middle Claydon, which has under 250 inhabitants. Nine years ago the ratepayers by vote adopted the Free Libraries Act, and as soon as the Parish Council came into being they took over the little library. She emphasised the great success of the public library, which was on the rates, as contrasted with private voluntary libraries which failed from want of freshness of supply. Groups of villages round were gradually adopting the plan in consequence of seeing what Middle Claydon had done. Supposing a village adopted the Act, they had great liberty as to how the money should be spent. They might have just a circulating library, with a box of books kept in a private house by leave of the Parish Council, or they might spend the money in the hire of a room for newspapers. As to those villages which had a reading-room, if they would adopt the Act it would bring fresh light into their reading-room. It was important to note that the rate was not indefinite, but was strictly limited to 1d. in the £.

Rural Libraries in Ireland.—Mr. John P. Boland has an interesting article in the *New Ireland Review*, which deals with the need for the establishment of rural libraries in Ireland. The writer points out that the facilities existing in this country for the promoting of libraries are very far from being equal to those which exist across the Channel. Parish Councils in England are enabled to provide for the needs of the population in this respect, but in Ireland the districts which have power to adopt the Libraries Act are wholly urban. Comparatively few, however, of these districts have availed of the powers they possess. But in extenuation of this apathy it is pointed out that it would be extremely difficult to equip and maintain a library in a town with the limited sum which the levying of 1d. rate would produce, and the employment of the borrowing powers, conferred by the Acts, raises still wider issues. Mr. Boland pays a tribute to the intellectual awakening which has been accomplished by the Gaelic League with its 400 branches, each an active centre for the acquisition of knowledge pertaining to Ireland. He points out that "unfortunately the means of gratifying this desire for extended knowledge is anything but equal to the demand. The village library is, with few exceptions here and there due to individual generosity and enterprise, practically non-existent, and public libraries in the towns are the exception rather than the rule. This deficiency in the case of rural districts calls for legislative action, in that of the towns for a public-spirited determination on the part of the citizens to keep pace with, if not to move in advance of, the tendencies and needs of the time. The need for such action is all the greater in a country such as Ireland from which tens of thousands of the young and strong flee every year, where there is but little to brighten the lives of the people, and where, moreover, in the absence of facilities for reading useful books, our young people are forced to fall back on the cheap, ephemeral and, too often, degrading literature that finds its way over from England. In order to check these baneful tendencies and, at the same time, to provide a substitute in the form of useful and ennobling literature, the extension of free public libraries throughout the country is urgently called for ". Discussing the desirability of legislative changes being effected which would place the rural District Councils of this country in a similar position to that occupied by the English Parish Councils, Mr. Boland deals with the efforts that have been made to secure for rural areas in Ireland the privileges conferred by the English Acts. He points out that the Local Government Act of 1898 has removed many of the difficulties which formerly stood in the way of the application of the English statutes to this country. Of course the adoption of the Libraries Acts being purely optional, and the ratepayers, especially in sparsley populated localities, being averse to incurring a charge which might conceivably benefit only the inhabitants of the principal centres of population, the suggested powers, were they applicable, might not be put in force in many cases. To meet the needs of such rural districts Mr. Boland makes a suggestion which may be worth considering by those interested in the subject. He says: "The school-house may be regarded as the chief intellectual centre of the Irish country district. It is natural under these circumstances that its further utilisation for library purposes would naturally commend itself as both reasonable and suitable. The premises are admirably adapted for forming a storing place for books, and, in view of the advantage to the population of the district, the consent of those in whom the schools are vested would be readily secured. The success which has already attended the formation of school libraries is a sufficient guarantee of the practicability of this initial part of the system which is here outlined. The schoolmaster, by reason of his training, and of the respect which his position ensures, is well fitted for the responsible post of custodian of the books which would be allotted to his particular school. An obvious advantage which would be conferred by the utilisation of the school premises consists in the employment of the school children as carriers. To put the people under the necessity of calling in person for the books at the close of school hours, the time for collection and distribution that naturally suggests itself, would not, in practice, be found to work satisfactorily. No labourer, least of all the small farmer, could spare the time from his work. But, under proper safeguards, the children could readily act as carriers for their parents." Mr. Dillon recently introduced a Bill (the text of which was printed in our last issue) which is intended to bring about the reforms desired in this connection. It proposes to enable rural District Councils to adopt the principal Act for the rural districts, and to apply the provisions of the Public Libraries (Ireland) Act of 1894. It also contains a clause enabling the library authority to enter into agreements with the managers of any school for the use of such school as a library, and for the care of the books and the management of the library, upon such terms as may be mutually agreed upon by such library authority and school managers.

Billiards in the Public Library.—We must confess to a feeling of surprise—by no means agreeable—upon reading a suggestion made by Mr. Hew Morrison to the Library Committee of Montrose on the occasion of his visit to that town to confer with the members of the committee as to the establishment of the Free Library, towards which Mr. Carnegie has generously contributed £7,500. Mr. Morrison remarked "that it had been said by some parties that the upkeep of a building costing £7,000 might prove too great a burden on a town like Montrose. In regard to that he might be permitted to make one or two suggestions. First of all he would say that the building should have a public character—that was to say, it should be a building of somewhat elaborate design, and one which would readily attract the passers-by. Then in regard to meeting the expense of upkeep, he would advise the committee not only to have a good newsroom in connection with it, but they should also have a large recreation-hall, which might be used for lectures, from which a small revenue might be derived. He was not a billiard player himself, and he was not there specially to advocate billiard playing, still they might have a part of the recreation-room set apart for billiard playing, for which a charge could be made. Free libraries in different parts of the country had introduced billiards, which had not only met the cost of the tables, etc., but had left a balance to be applied to the general purposes of the libraries, while they had been the means of keeping young people out of the public-house or from other temptations. He laid special stress on the importance of having a large, well-ventilated newsroom, because that was where they would begin the education of the great mass of the people. When they began to count up their readers of books they would likely meet with some discouragement in the fact that readers were not attracted as they expected but-by-and, by they would find, as the young people read the newspapers and magazines in the newsroom, that the reading of books would increase. Then in Montrose there should be a good circulating library. He was not so strong upon the reference library point, because the number of people in Montrose requiring to consult books of reference would be rather limited. As a Library Committee they should put in books which they considered would be for the general weal of the people, and if they provided such works he had no doubt they would be read."

Quite apart from the wisdom of suggesting the introduction of billiards into the public library building, which to our way of thinking is contrary to the spirit of the Act, we venture to think that to resort to such an expedient for the raising of funds to be applied to the general purposes of the library would create difficulties with the rating authorities. The danger which Mr. Morrison touches upon so lightly is a very real one. The cost of maintenance should be one of the first considerations, should indeed determine the style of the building to be erected. There are instances, fortunately they are few, where the upkeep of a too costly structure swallows up the whole of the income, leaving nothing for additions to the shelves. There should be no need to adopt such expedients as Mr. Morrison suggests. We are in accord with him in reference to the lecture-room, for this is part of the legitimate equipment of a public library, but we cannot agree with him as to the reference library, this is surely a libel upon the people of Montrose.

A Woman Librarian in Germany.—The following paragraph, which appeared recently in *The Queen*, will be of interest to many, if not to all, of our readers : " The recent appointment of Fräulein Barbara Reuz—Dr.Phil.—to an assistant librarianship in the Munich State Library, writes a correspondent in Munich, raised quite a storm in the Bavarian capital. Her opponents based their objections on the grounds (1) that her studies had been carried on mainly out of Germany; (2) that younger librarians are more desirable—Dr. Reuz has reached the not very venerable age of thirty-eight ; (3) that she lacks the necessary qualifications. Dr. Reuz's reply, published in the leading Bavarian papers, is both dignified and moderate in tone, and should be interesting to all women who have the progress of their fellow-women at heart.

" To the first two objections she replies that as such a course of study as she wished to pursue was not open to her at any German University, she was forced to seek it elsewhere ; and that until fewer difficulties are placed in the way of German women-students, younger candidates for posts requiring a high standard of culture will not be forthcoming. In answer to the third objection, she simply enumerates the subjects in which she passed examinations at the University of Rome, in six of which she obtained the highest possible marks: (1) Theoretical philo-sophy (logic-metaphysics); (2) mathematical geography; (3) Italian and Latin grammar; (4) philology; (5) Italian literature; (6) pedagogy; (7) ancient history; (8) comparative grammar of the Classic and Sanskrit languages; (9) modern history; (10) history of philosophy; (11) Latin literature; (12) Greek literature; (13) moral philosophy; (14) experi-mental physiology. A somewhat convincing reply, certainly! When she adds that she passed further stiff examinations in Greek and various scientific subjects in the United States, where she held several University posts, one begins to wonder who *is* qualified for her present appointment if *she* is not; as, moreover, she herself points out the difficulty of her examinations was not exactly lessened by the fact that they were all held in Italian or English. The objection as to age seems specially absurd; an efficient librarian must possess an amount of all-round culture, impossible for a very young person of either sex. One cannot help wondering whether it would ever have been raised had the new librarian been a man."

Books and Other Printed Matter Published in Scotland before 1700.

—The Edinburgh Bibliographical Society is at present engaged upon a work of considerable importance to all interested in the history of Scottish printing. Six years ago the society resolved to begin the compilation of a bibliographical catalogue of books, etc., published in Scotland before 1700. The direction of the work was undertaken by Mr. H. G. Aldis, now of the University Library, Cam-bridge, in whose hands materials have accumulated to such an extent that the title-slips now number about 3,500. In order to facilitate further progress and to enable contributors to know what titles are still unre-corded or defective, it has been decided to issue a preliminary handlist of one-line titles, which it is hoped will soon be in the hands of the printer. This handlist will consist of about 150 quarto pages, and will contain the titles arranged in chronological order, followed by a list of the printers and booksellers, and an index of authors, etc. The main object in printing the list is that copies may be distributed to biblio-graphers and others who have opportunities of furthering the completion of the bibliography, and who may be willing to send in additional in-formation. But beyond the particular purpose it is intended to serve, the list will form a very useful record of Scottish printing of the period dealt with. At present, as a writer in the *Glasgow Herald* points out, there is no formal history of printing in Scotland during the seventeenth century. Dickson and Edmond's admirable history comes down only to 1600, and a knowledge of what was being done by Scottish printers during the next hundred years can only be picked up slowly and labori-ously, from such books as Watson's preface, or Mr. Edmond's volume on the Aberdeen printers, or a recondite work with the unpromising title of Lee's *Memorial for the Bible Societies of Scotland*. Despite a few works printed at Stirling and St. Andrews, and possibly by John Scott, at Dundee, in the sixteenth century, it was only in the next century that printing was generally practised outside Edinburgh; and it is therefore to be hoped that the material for history available in this list of titles will be placed at the disposal of that portion of the public which is interested in the matters that pertain to the annals of printing.

Sidney Lee on National Biography.

—In connection with the University Extension Meeting at Cambridge, Mr. Sidney Lee lectured

on the 8th August on "National Biography". After showing how
national biography, properly organised, was the most permanent form
of national memorial, and best satisfied the commemorative instinct
of a nation, the lecturer distinguished, in the first place, the aims of
biography from those of history, and, in the second, the concise
methods essential to the proper conduct of national biography from
the more discursive methods that ordinarily characterised individual'
biography. National biography should only notice men and women
who could be justly credited with some serious distinctive achievement, but it should notice all such. Statistics indicated that, in the
United Kingdom as at present constituted, only one in every 4,000
persons who reached adult life was likely to deserve the attention of
the national biographer. Mr. Lee described various early efforts in
the field of national biography in this country, and spoke in conclusion
of the last and most elaborate effort known to the United Kingdom, or,
in fact, to the world, the *Dictionary of National Biography*, with the
production of which he had been closely identified. That large undertaking was due to the public spirit of the eminent publisher, the late
George Smith, who died last year when the work was practically
complete, and it was gratifying to know that in the crypt of St. Paul's
Cathedral—at the heart of the busy capital of the empire, where Mr.
Smith was born, and where the work of his life was mainly done—his
friends had been permitted by the Dean and Chapter to place a tablet
to the memory of him "to whom," in the words of the inscription,
"English literature owes the *Dictionary of National Biography*".
Men of letters, especially those who had been personally associated
with him, also rejoiced that Sir Leslie Stephen, the first editor of the
Dictionary, had received from the King, on the occasion of the Coronation, the honour of a Knight Commandership of the Bath; it was the
first time that that distinction had been conferred on a member of the
profession of letters. The task of producing the *Dictionary of National
Biography* in sixty-six volumes, the last forty of which had been edited
by the lecturer, was not light. Every quarter-day, without any break
during nearly sixteen years, had witnessed the publication of one of
those volumes, each of which contained on the average at least 50,000
statements of fact or date. Possibly more perfect results might have
been attained had the work been done more slowly, but Mr. Lee
believed that the public had substantially gained by the regular and
rapid rate of production. The *Dictionary* was the only work of like
magnitude that had reached the letter Z within an equally moderate
period of time. As a whole it recorded, in thirty million words—as
small a space as was possible—some three million facts and dates.
The inevitable risk of error was great. No editor could thoroughly
test for himself at first hand every one of the facts and dates that found
a place in the *Dictionary*, even if his life were to be prolonged through
five centuries, and he devoted to the task all the working days of 500
years. Nearly half the persons commemorated in the *Dictionary* had,
moreover, been accorded by it biographic honours for the first time;
many of the biographies were thus pioneer biographies, and future
explorers might be expected to supplement and correct them. Such
gains to knowledge would be welcomed by none more warmly than by
the pioneers themselves. The editor of the *Dictionary*, owing partly
to the frankness of his many hundred correspondents, knew more than
other people about his errors, both of commission and omission. Mr.
Lee stated that, in the interests of exact scholarship, he was preparing
for publication a list of all the genuine *errata* that had been brought to
his notice. He believed that the number, of such *errata*, when it was
compared with the aggregate number of facts and dates in the *Dic-*

tionary, would offer the best of all testimonies to the general value and accuracy of the work. The *Dictionary* could fairly claim to have brought together a greater mass of accurate information respecting the past achievements of the British and Irish race than had been put at the disposal of the English-speaking peoples in any previous literary undertaking. Such a work of reference might be justly held to serve the national and the beneficial purpose of helping the present and future generations to realise more thoroughly than would be otherwise possible the character of their ancestors' collective achievement, of which they now enjoyed the fruits.

When is a Writer " Great " ?—What does one mean when one speaks of a writer or a book as "great"? No critical epithet is so vaguely used, or perhaps so often abused. It is true that there are some writers—Homer, Dante, Shakespeare, Molière—as to whom there is no doubt at all; they are "great" in every sense—even in the slangy American sense—of the word. But when we come to think of writers like Catullus or Shelley or Musset the question of their "greatness" is more open to argument, and we must allow, with Goldsmith's critic, that there is a good deal to be said on both sides. There is, then, much that is helpful in such a classification as Prof. W. P. Trent, of Columbia University, has endeavoured to make in an interesting article which he contributes to the *International Monthly*. There is much suggestion and helpfulness in such a table as a writer in the *Academy* has constructed from this article, which is well worth quoting here :—

"Great writers: Homer, Sophocles, Virgil, Goethe, Dante, Shakespeare, Milton, Molière, Cervantes, etc.; to this class Prof. Trent is inclined to add Balzac and Hugo. Writers of great power but not universal in their genius : Pindar, Lucretius, Petrarch, Tasso, Ariosto, Montaigne, Chaucer, Spenser, Schiller, Heine, Rabelais, Gibbon, etc. Writers whom one cannot call supreme, although one would as little think of calling them minor : Catullus, Horace, Leopardi, Marlowe, Ben Jonson, Keats, Browning, Byron, Lamb, Dryden, Pope, Gray, Burns, Coleridge, Tennyson, Wordsworth, Shelley, Landor, Hawthorne, etc."
Of course Prof. Trent only presents this as a tentative list, on which every critic is at liberty to make his own modifications. He adds, very justly, that any such list is subject to personal qualification or alteration.

"And we must always remember that any scheme of classification is bad if it tends to make our judgments hard and fast, if it induces us to think that we can stick a pin through a writer and ticket him as an entomologist does an insect. But if we use such a scheme intelligently it may prove useful, if only by stimulating us to candid objections, for candid objections imply honest thought, and honest thought on such a noble subject as literature cannot but be beneficial."

Girls' Books.—Many of our readers are interested in the " Juvenile Department " of the public library, and for their benefit we reprint a letter to the editor, which appeared in the *Saturday Review* of the 14th June last, upon the subject of "Girls' Books". The letter is full of sound reasoning and will well repay careful perusal by any of our readers who may be interested in this side of library work :—

"ILKLEY, *5th June.*

" SIR,

"The influence of a child's reading upon the child's development of intellect and character is so great that few topics of educational discussion can interest parents more than the composition of a children's library. But at the onset I would fain protest against any division of the library into separate parts for boys and girls. Most of your correspondents, I rejoice, are agreed on the essential oneness in boy and girl nature. The boys may more often choose one book, and the girls another, but let both have the same range of thought. Thus a closer community of feeling and interest is cultivated, the gain of which is felt in sympathetic interests shared in later life. I also dislike the term 'girls' books'. At once the imagination of the writer is cramped, and the perspective of life shortened, when characters are limited to so small a platform. Why have 'girls' books' and not 'grandmothers' books'? Why classify any one section of humanity and write down or up to them according to the genius of the writer?

"From the biography of all great women, we know that one and all date their love of literature from the time they were thrown at a very early age into well-chosen libraries, and allowed to read and ponder over the literary masterpieces of the world. Rather let us use the term literature, and let there be continuity from the first book of the little one to the books of the adult. Our first principle must be in the library 'there should be no book in it that has not a good reason for being there'. So wrote one of our leading educationists many years ago. We must protect our children from books that may be a cause of evil by the negative results which they produce until the child's taste is formed. I would first introduce the child mind to the folk-lore of all nations. Our fathers were nursed on this literature, and our knowledge of all nations is extended, and our sympathies are widened. Andrew Lang's Fairy Books, Andersen's Fairy Tales, Celtic Fairy Tales, Irish Fairy Tales, Æsop's Fables, Indian Fairy Tales, are all enjoyed by very small children. I would not omit here *The King of the Golden River*, by Ruskin, which is a classic that ought to be in every nursery. Also Mr. Edward Lear's *Book of Nonsense*. All children understand distinctly the value of pure nonsense, and claim, as against the namby-pamby rubbish which is mostly tendered to them, the right to become foolish at times. If only parents, who are not quite sure of what is good style, would judge each book on the assumption that childhood must be treated with the respect due to it, and a book must be written in simple and forcible language, not in the pigeon style and dialect so common in the present day 'boys' books' and 'girls' books,' they would give their children a real love and enthusiasm for the highest and best in literature.

"I would gradually introduce the young readers to the delights of heroic romance. Church's *Stories from the Greek Tragedians, Froissart* by Henry Newbolt are much enjoyed by boys and girls of ten. One boy, who went away to school at that age, somewhat startled his master by writing out a tale from Froissart, when asked to give an account of his favourite book. *The Boy's Odyssey*, Walter Perry; *Heroes*, Kingsley; *Tanglewood Tales*, Hawthorne; *Hiawatha* and *The Golden Legend*, Long-fellow; *Lays of Ancient Rome*, Macaulay, can be placed in our ideal library. As several of your correspondents have pointed out, tales of adventure and travel are a necessity to the boy and girl mind. Ballantyne, Mayne Reid, Fenimore Cooper and Stevenson have written books which will be familar to many readers.

"In the corner devoted to historic novels, tales, etc., I would place Walter Scott's novels. Many editions are unfortunately printed in small type, and after speaking to several children who ought to have read them through, I have found that this was the reason they rather avoided them. So I would recommend parents and teachers to buy larger and clearer typed editions of the Waverley novels. Henty's books many children know and love. Stevenson's *Kidnapped*, Besant's *For Faith and Freedom*, and all historic ballads go on the third shelf. *Tom Brown* is a classic and claims a place by prescriptive right. So likewise do Lewis Carroll's books and Kingsley's *Water Babies*. The two latter are instances of perfect art in prose. *The Rose and the Ring* belongs to all ages; but no library can be considered perfect that does not contain a copy. Thackeray's *Esmond, The Virginians* and *The Newcomes* ought to be read very early in the teens.

"If we would save our children from being neurotic and from nerve-storms—alas so common—in old age, let us see to it that they are fed from a very early age on healthy, pure-toned, wholesome literature.

"Yours truly,
"EMELINE PETRIE STEINTHAL."

How to Begin a New Life.—In a recent number of the *Spectator* Sir M. E. Grant Duff, a close friend of the late Lord Acton, writes a letter giving some interesting glimpses of the great scholar, and concludes his reminiscences with a valuable disclosure. "If I had the power," Sir Grant Duff writes, "I would place upon his (Lord Acton's) monument the words which he wrote as a preface to a list of ninety-eight books he drew up, and about which he still hoped to read a paper at Cambridge, when he wrote to me on the subject last autumn." Here are the words, as quoted by Sir M. E. Grant Duff:—

"This list is submitted with a view to assisting an English youth, whose education is finished, who knows common things, and is not training for a profession, to perfect his mind and open windows in every direction; to raise him to the level of his age, so that he may know the (twenty or thirty) forces that have made our world what it is, and still reign over it; to guard him against surprises and against the constant sources of errors within; to supply him both with the strongest stimulants and the surest guides; to give force and fulness and clearness and sincerity and independence and elevation and generosity and serenity to his mind, that he may know the method and law of the process by which error is conquered and truth is won, discerning knowledge from probability and prejudice from belief; that he may learn to master what he rejects as fully as what he adopts; that he may understand the origin as well as the strength and vitality of systems and the better motive of men who are wrong; to steel him against the charm of literary beauty and talent, so that each book thoroughly taken in shall be the beginning of a new life, and shall make a new man of him."

Naturally one wonders what was the list that Lord Acton drew up? It was probably compiled in the early eighties, and Sir Grant Duff has little doubt but that Lord Acton would, had he been able to deliver his Cambridge lecture, have slightly revised and added to a list nearly twenty years old. The list will not be published until the family of Lord Acton has been consulted and given its consent—consent which we hope will not be withheld.

Book-shelves.—The words are commonplace enough; but to the lover of books, and to those sportsmen who are book-hunters, they are suggestive of a world of romance. The humblest book-lover knows how keen is the pleasure of shelving his treasures. The owner of a large library can classify his volumes. His shelves will be allotted in due proportion to the different headings under which his books are grouped; but it is your owner of a small library—of any number of volumes, say, between a hundred and two or three thousand—who gets the most pleasure out of his shelves. He attempts little classification, but arranges his books to suit his eye and his sense of what is becoming. He lingers over the arrangement of each shelf, while the odd collocations and companionships which result are not without a suggestion of humour.

It was no wonder that Dominie Sampson fairly shouted with rapture when he was turned loose among Colonel Mannering's books and shelves. What greater pleasure could a bookman have than fell to the Dominie's lot—stacks of empty shelves round the room, and on the floor piles and piles of books and cases of books, all to be examined and sorted and tasted, and finally arranged in due order on the waiting shelves. Just as to a tourist of properly constituted mind the chief attraction of a carefully planned route is found in the many opportunities of departing therefrom, so to the Dominie, or any other man whose business it is to reduce a chaos of books to the stately order of the shelves, the chief pleasure lies in the discoveries of this and that unknown or unremembered volume which are continually interrupting the work in hand. We cannot share the good Sampson's aversion to volumes of poems, plays and belles-lettres generally, which " he tossed indignantly aside, with the implied censure of ' pshaw ' or ' frivolous ' " ; but every lover of books can appreciate the loving care with which the Dominie entered the title of each work in his catalogue, and then placed the volume on the destined shelf with all the reverence, says Scott, " which I have seen a lady pay to a jar of old china ". Sir Walter was a bookman himself, and knew thoroughly the pitfalls which beset the progress of the uncouth librarian's task; and so he goes on to show how Sampson, opening a volume when half-way up the library steps, would remain there, absorbed in his book, till a servant came and pulled him by the skirts to assure him that dinner waited. Peace to the Dominie! He was a good book-lover.

The book-shelves that have long remained undisturbed hold many secrets. Occasionally, when some long neglected library is overhauled by a diligent and keen-scented hunter, or more often, alas, when the contents of the shelves are transferred to the auction room, surprising discoveries are made. Now and then a duplicate is found of some work long supposed to be unique; or books previously known only by name, or even not known at all, are brought to light. During the last fifty years many famous libraries have been overhauled, and not a few discoveries have been made; yet it is tolerably certain that there are rare books and pamphlets still lurking in the recesses of dusty shelves in the libraries of old country halls and mansions, of the very existence of which their respective owners are quite unaware. Some day, however, their time will come, and bibliographers will have a field-day.

LIBRARY NOTES AND NEWS.

UNITED KINGDOM.

BARRY: *Mr. Carnegie's Offer of £8,000 Accepted and Site Selected.*—A special meeting of the Barry Urban District Council was held recently to consider a resolution from the Public Libraries Committee in connection with Mr. Carnegie's gift of £8,000 to the town of Barry for the purpose of erecting a public library. It was resolved that the generous offer of Mr. Carnegie be accepted, and a committee was appointed to select a suitable site on the Council's land off Holton Road and Tynewydd Road, in the centre of the town, and to invite plans for the erection of the building.

BIRMINGHAM PUBLIC LIBRARIES: *A Successful Year's Work.*—The report of the Birmingham Free Libraries Committee for the past year has just been issued, and in view of the fact that the Association will for a second time hold its Annual Meeting at Birmingham during the present month, it possesses an additional interest for our readers. Great as has been the growth of many of the public institutions of the town, the history of few, if any, show a more rapid and sustained development than that of the Free Libraries. Whether one turns to the statistics relating to the Reference Library or the Lending Library in Mr. Capel Shaw's exhaustive report one finds the same evidence of continual expansion. When the Reference Library was opened in 1886 it possessed the comparative modest collection of 16,195 volumes, and during the year there were 11,468 issues of these books. At the present time the number of volumes in the Reference Library is 164,319, and last year the issues reached a total of 395,582. The Public Libraries Act was adopted in Birmingham in 1860. The following year the Lending Library was opened, the number of volumes on the shelves then being 6,288, the number of issues during the first year being 108,057. Now the various public lending libraries in the city comprise no fewer than 107,829 volumes, and last year the issues attained the enormous aggregate of 936,733, the total issues from all the libraries for the twelve months being 1,332,315, or a daily average of 4,177, compared with an issue of 1,260,000, or a daily average of 3,965 volumes in the previous year. Of the total number of 272,166 volumes in all the libraries, no fewer than 86,796 were devoted to history, biography, voyages and travels, prose fiction coming next in the numerical order with 49,317 volumes. The only other section which at all approximates to this number is that of arts, sciences, natural history and patents, which has a total of 42,160. The figures relating to the other denominations are theology, moral philosophy and ecclesiastical history, 16,409; law, politics, commerce and education, 12,558; poetry and drama, 18,993; magazines and periodicals, 10,708; juvenile literature, 9,456; embossed books for the blind, 470; foreign literature, 697; music, 1,972; and miscellaneous, including dictionaries and cyclopædias, 22,612. The novel still continues to be the popular form of literature, and altogether last year there were 652,116 issues of works of prose fiction. How this number compares with those of previous years, however, is apparently not shown. The next class of book in most demand was that denominated as juvenile literature, of which there were 130,862 issues. It is gratifying to see that the call

for works of history, biography, voyages and travels was so great as to
require the issue of no fewer than 127,933 volumes. The totals of the
other issues are returned by the chief librarian as follows: Theology,
moral philosophy and ecclesiastical history, 20,226; law, politics, commerce and education, 8,742; arts, sciences and natural history, 88,178;
poetry and drama, 14,818; magazines and periodicals, 29,329; miscellaneous, including dictionaries and cyclopædias, 42,548; books for the
blind, 333; foreign literature, 1,771; and music, 12,895. At the Reference
Library there was a great demand for current periodicals, the number
of issues of this class of literature totalling up to 158,471. It is also not
without interest to note that there were 44,093 issues of works relating
to patents. The Reference Library was first opened on Sundays in
April, 1872, and the Boys' Room in February, 1901, and that this is not
inappreciated is evidenced from the fact that, whereas the ordinary
daily issues during the year was 1,105, the Sunday average during the
same period was 1,127. Some interesting data concerning the reading
age is furnished by a table, showing the ages of the borrowers at the
Lending Libraries who qualified in 1900-1 and 1901-2. From these
figures it appears that of the 30,888 borrowers who qualified during the
time stated 7,040 were under 14 years of age; 9,026 between 14 and 20
years; 4,385, 21 to 25; 2,896, 26 to 30; 1,573, 31 to 35; 1,409, 36 to 40;
781, 41 to 45; 666, 46 to 50; 410, 51 to 55; 382, 56 to 60; 437 over 60.
But as 1,883 of the qualifying borrowers failed to state their age—no
doubt lady borrowers—the data is not so complete as one could have
wished.

BIRMINGHAM: *Mr. Carnegie gives £3,000 towards another Suburban
Library.*—Mr. Carnegie has given £3,000 towards the establishment of
a library for Moseley and King's Heath, suburbs of Birmingham. The
gift is subject to the usual conditions.

BRANKSOME: *Mr. Carnegie Offers £2,000 for the Erection of a
Public Library.*—At a meeting of the Branksome Urban District
Council on the 9th July, it was announced that Mr. Carnegie had
offered to furnish £2,000 to erect a Free Public Library building for
Branksome, providing that the Free Libraries Act be adopted, the
maximum assessment levied, and that a suitable site be given, the cost
of which shall not be a charge on the library revenue under the Act.
It was resolved that the best thanks of the Council be tendered to Mr.
Carnegie for his munificent offer, and that he be assured the Council
would exert their utmost endeavours in order to carry out his conditions.

BRISTOL: *The Report of the Libraries Committee.*—The report of
the Libraries Committee for the year ended the 31st March last contains much interesting information with regard to the work of the
public libraries in Bristol. It is stated that the consent of the Ecclesiastical Commissioners has been obtained for acquiring from the Dean
and Chapter the site adjoining the Norman Arch in College Green for
the new Stuckey-Lean Central Library, that site—the one originally
proposed by the committee—having been accepted by the Council.
A detailed report of the departmental requirements of the building
has been prepared by the city librarian, and the committee will
shortly be in a position to invite architects to submit plans. The
building and equipment will be entirely provided under the bequest
of the late Mr. Vincent Stuckey-Lean. The maintenance of the
library, however, is a question that has seriously to be considered,
the income from a 1d. rate already being exhausted in the maintenance of the existing libraries established under the Acts. A resolution of the joint Libraries and Museums Committee, recommending
the increase of the library rate by a ½d. for public library purposes,
and an increase of a ½d. for the maintenance of an art gallery,

was approved by the Council, but when the question was submitted to a town's meeting, a poll was demanded. This was about the time when the Docks Committee were proceeding with their new Docks Bill, and at the wish of the latter body the Libraries and Museums Committee consented to a postponement of the poll for library and art gallery purposes.

To show the increasing popularity of the libraries, the committee mention that during the year there was an aggregate issue of 588,194 volumes, compared with a total of 445,839 volumes issued during 1899. The number of readers in reading and newsrooms, according to a computation based on a census taken, reached close upon two and a half millions. In connection with this very large circulation of books and attendance of readers, it is specially gratifying to report that not a single volume has been lost to the libraries during the year, while the behaviour of the large crowds daily frequenting the newsrooms has been most satisfactory. The additions to the various libraries during the year amounted to 6,613 volumes, of which 4,949 were purchased, 1,291 were presented, and 373 were added from surplus stock. Of this number, 946 volumes were added to replace copies worn out in service. The "Vincent Stuckey-Lean" collection now in the hands of the city librarian, prior to its permanent location in the new Central Library, has been classified and catalogued, and the catalogue will shortly be published in book form. The stock of books in the public libraries (not including the Museum Library) is 114,867 volumes. The number of volumes re-bound and repaired was 4,895, of which 4,469 were done exclusively by the library binding staff. A large number of worn-out and discarded books—about 1,500 volumes—have been handed over to the Board of Guardians, the Medical Officer of Health and the City and County Asylum.

With the object of informing the scientific student and the artisan population what books relating to local trades and industries are obtainable at the various libraries a series of handlists has been printed, and it is gratifying to know that the effort made in this way to increase the usefulness of the public libraries has been much appreciated. Continued success attended the opening of the North District Library in Cheltenham Road. There are 5,293 registered borrowers on the list, and the issue of books has frequently amounted to over one thousand volumes a day. The Redland Library is now being re-classified and re-catalogued. The committee have had under consideration the pressing need of extended space at this branch, but with the limited sum at present available for maintenance they are unable to recommend the necessary expenditure. At the Bedminster Library an extension of the indicator in the lending department to provide for an additional 2,000 volumes has been made to meet the growing wants of borrowers. Here, again, the question of increased accommodation has pressed itself upon the committee. The reading-room is frequently crowded with readers to its utmost capacity, and sooner or later it will be absolutely necessary to extend the building. With reference to the provision for branch library accommodation in the Somerset Ward, although a site was secured some time ago for the purpose, the committee are unable at present to proceed with the erection of a library, as the amount of their income under the 1d. rate is barely sufficient for the nine existing libraries.

BUCKLEY: *The Battle of the Sites.*—It will be remembered that a few months ago Mr. Carnegie made an offer of a sum of money, amounting to about £1,600 towards the erection of a free library at Buckley. At the same time Mr. Herbert Gladstone offered £500, the Rev. Harry

Drew (vicar of Buckley), £100, Mrs. Drew, £100 ; and Mr. and Mrs. Drew also offered to be responsible for collecting another £100. A site was also offered in the vicinity of Buckley Church. Since then another offer of a site has been made by Mr. Griffiths, of Chester, this site being in a central position, adjoining the present Council offices. The first-mentioned site is much nearer Hawarden, and is, along with some of the smaller gifts proposed, conditional to the erection of a recreation-room and assembly hall as well as a free library. Mr. Carnegie's offer has been accepted, but the other gifts and the offered sites are in abeyance, pending the decision of the Urban Council as to which site it will be most advisable to accept. There is some divergence of opinion, and "the battle of the sites" will probably form a leading feature of the Urban Council's discussions in the near future.

CHELMSFORD: *Site Secured for the Public Library, etc.*—The Corporation have approved the draft contract for the purchase of a site for the erection of a public library and reading-room, museum and science and art school at the cost of £1,100. Fifteen members of the Corporation voted for the scheme and four against.

CORK: *Mr. Carnegie Promises £1,000 for a Public Library.*—On Saturday, the 2nd August, at the presentation of an address from the Municipality of Cork to the Christian Brothers of that city, on the occasion of the centenary of the foundation of the Order, the Lord Mayor, in reply to the toast of his health, announced that in answer to his appeal Mr. Andrew Carnegie had promised to give £1,000 to Cork for the establishment of a public library for that city. The announcement was received with great enthusiasm.

CRICCIETH (CARNARVON): *Mr. Carnegie Offers £800 towards a Public Library.*—Mr. Carnegie has offered to make a grant of £800 towards building and fitting up a public library in Criccieth, Carnarvonshire, provided the Free Libraries Act is adopted, and £700 subscribed locally and invested as a maintenance fund. The offer has been accepted.

CRIEFF: *Gift to the Taylor's Trust Free Library.*—Under the will of the late Rev. Dr. James Rankin, of Muthill, for some time one of the leading writers in the Church of Scotland, and who possessed one of the finest libraries in the county, there has been bequeathed to the Taylor's Trust Free Library, Crieff, the greater portion of his library, consisting of works on theology, church history, hymnology, parochial antiquities, and works on kindred subjects. These, it is expressly stated in the will, which has just been recorded in the books of Council and Session, shall be specially "set apart as the nucleus of a solid library".

DALTON-IN-FURNESS: *Mr. Carnegie Offers £3,500 for a Public Library.*—Mr. Carnegie has offered to give £3,500 for the erection of a public free library at Dalton-in-Furness, on condition that the town provides a site, and the Free Libraries Act be fully carried out. In consequence of the announcement of this offer a special meeting of the Dalton-in-Furness Co-operators was held on Saturday, the 19th July, to consider the handing over of their library of 4,000 volumes to the town. Mr. James Dickinson, president of the society, who secured the gift, moved that the library should be given over to the town, and, after discussion, the resolution was carried unanimously, not one dissentient voice being raised. The Co-operative Library has cost the members £4,000.

EASTBOURNE: *Mr. Carnegie Offers £10,000 for a Public Library.*—Mr. Carnegie has offered the sum of £10,000 to the Eastbourne Public Libraries Committee on condition (*a*) that the town provide a site for the new building, (*b*) and that the existing rate of ½d. be increased to ¾d.

The former condition has already been complied with, his Grace the Duke of Devonshire, K.G., having presented a valuable central site (as a memento of his past mayoralty) to the town, on which to erect a free library and technical institute. The committee are recommending the Council at their next meeting to raise the rate to ¾d., and to accept a tender for the erection of the new building—the plans for which have already been passed—at a cost of £50,000.

EDINBURGH : *Efforts to get Established a National Reference Library.*—An effort is apparently to be made again to get established in Edinburgh a national reference library. At a meeting of the Annual Committee of the Convention of Royal Burghs, held in Edinburgh the other day, the question was discussed, and eventually it was agreed that the Faculty of Advocates should be communicated with, with the view of securing their concurrence in a petition to the Government on the subject. The nationalisation of the Faculty Library has often been suggested, and probably may come in time, although whether the advocates, who have, on admission, to pay handsomely towards the library funds, will welcome such a step is quite another matter.

FENTON : *Mr. Carnegie Offers £5,000 for a Public Library.*—Mr. J. S. Goddard, chairman of the Fenton Urban District Council, having had his attention attracted to Mr. Carnegie's benefactions to various towns for free library purposes, wrote to Mr. Carnegie calling his attention to the position of Fenton, which, though a progressive town, does not possess such a desirable institution. Having been supplied with full particulars of the case, Mr. Carnegie has informed Mr. Goddard that if the town adopts the Free Libraries Act, and provides a suitable site for the building, he will be glad to furnish £5,000 to erect a free public library for Fenton. A stipulation is that the cost of the site will not be a charge on the revenue from the 1d. rate. Mr. W. M. Baker, of Hasfield Court, Gloucester, the representative of an old Fenton family and a large property owner in the township, has generously presented a site for the free library in a central situation at the rear of the Town Hall, which was erected by him and leased to the Council. Mr. Goddard has opened a fund for the raising of the money required for the proper equipment of the library. The generosity of Mr. Carnegie and Mr. Baker is very highly appreciated, and the inhabitants recognise their indebtedness to Mr. Goddard for his action in the matter.

FLINT : *Grant in Aid of the Free Library Movement by Mr. Carnegie.* —Mr. Carnegie has agreed to make a grant not exceeding £200 in aid of the free library movement at Flint. He has declined a similar application from Holywell.

GATESHEAD : *The Work of the Public Library.*—The annual report of the committee states that 76,908 volumes have been issued as against 68,354 for the previous year. The stock of books has been augmented by the addition of 785 volumes, the total stock being 13,816 volumes. The number of borrowers' tickets in force is 3,392. There are 1,650 books in the juvenile section, and 15,454 have been issued as against 10,920 last year. A grant of £90 was made by the Town Council for the purchase of technical books. A portrait in oils of the chairman (Ald. Armour) was presented to that gentleman by the members of the Library Committee and Town Council at their last meeting as a mark of their appreciation of him personally and of his services on the Library and School of Art Committees since their institution. In accepting the portrait Ald. Armour said he would like to be permitted to offer it to the Library Committee with a view to it being placed in the library. The Committee cordially agreed to carry out the wish as expressed by the chairman.

GLASGOW: *Opening of the Gorbals Branch Library.*—In the early part of last year, by direction of the Town Council, a scheme was drawn up showing the number, approximate positions and cost of a system of public libraries for the whole city of Glasgow. The scheme, which was generally approved, provided for the erection of eight district libraries and five reading-rooms; but this plan was subsequently extended through the munificence of Mr. Carnegie, whose gift of £100,000 enabled the Corporation to increase the number of libraries to fourteen, divided into three grades—five of the establishments being ranked as first grade, six as second grade and three as third grade. The distinction in grades is based upon cost, the first class being allocated £8,500 for building and furnishing and £1,500 for the purchase of the first stock of books; the second £7,000 and £1,200; and the third £5,000 and £900 each respectively. The first grade or largest of the libraries will be placed in the most densely populated districts, and the smaller ones in parts of the city where the population is not so heavy. These branches will each embrace a lending department as well as an open collection of reference books, accommodation for women, and a juvenile section for boys and girls. Here it may be mentioned that the different institutions are not intended to be in their contents mere replicas one of another, but to a large extent complementary, so as to form in the aggregate a complete library, to be ultimately placed at the general service by a central exchange system. The first of the branch libraries to be opened is that at Gorbals, which is housed in the upper floors of the Corporation Bath buildings in Main Street. The collection already in the building numbers about 11,000 volumes, but up till now only the reading-room has been in use. On Monday, the 11th August, the lending department was inaugurated. The catalogue of the contents which has been made available for public use is a volume of about 450 pages, issued at the price of fourpence in paper cover or eightpence in cloth—a model of what such a catalogue should be. We offer Mr. Barrett our warmest congratulations upon the success which has attended the inauguration of the first of the branch libraries.

GRAYS: *Mr. Carnegie Offers £3,000 for a Public Library.*—Mr. Carnegie has offered £3,000 for the erection of a public library at Grays, provided a site be given; and with commendable public spirit, Mr. Charles Seabrooke, J.P., and Mr. Astley, the joint owners of a plot of land opposite the Fire Station, have offered the ground for the purpose. In addition fourteen persons have promised donations amounting to £100, so that it is reasonable to expect that in the near future Grays will have a well-equipped public library for the use of the inhabitants.

HARTLEPOOL: *Mr. Carnegie Offers £5,000 for the Erection of a Public Library.*—At a recent meeting of the Hartlepool Town Council a letter was read from Mr. Andrew Carnegie offering £5,000 for the erection of a public free library in that town, the only condition being that the town provide the site for the building without encroaching upon the 1d. rate. The offer was accepted with thanks, on the motion of Ald. Murray, chairman of the Library Committee. For five or six years past a library has been carried on in temporary premises in Middlegate and Vollum's Chare, but the committee being anxious to provide an institution which would meet more fully the requirements of the town, the chairman approached Mr. Carnegie who promptly responded with the above-mentioned handsome offer.

HAWORTH: *Mr. Carnegie Contributes £1,500 Towards the Building of a Free Library.*—Mr. Carnegie has made a gift of £1,500 towards the building of a free library for Haworth (the home of the Brontës).

This will make possible the carrying out of a proposal which has been under contemplation for several years past. The offer is made subject to conditions, one of which is that the district shall raise £100 a year for the maintenance of the library, and the other that the cost of the site for the library building shall not be charged against the maintenance fund—in other words, that the cost of the site shall be cleared at first, if it should prove necessary to purchase a site. The scheme, as before stated, has been in hand for several years, and was first begun because of the suspension of the former Mechanics' Institute, a committee then being selected, representing various interests, to put the scheme into form. The Haworth District Council adopted the Free Libraries Act, and the amount from the 1d. rate which they thus became entitled to levy has accumulated during the past three years, and the new rate for the fourth year was laid a month ago. This rate brings in about £70 a year, so that, including the new rate, there is about £280 in hand from that source. In addition there is an offer from the Mechanics' Institute of £500 on the laying of the foundation-stone, and another of £50 from the Haworth Co-operative Society, and sums in hand from various sources of £45, so that the total available capital, including the proceeds of the rate, is about £875. It is not considered that there will be any special difficulty in securing consent to this money being utilised as an endowment for the library, in order that the interest may be added to the sum realised by the public rate, so that the initial condition of Mr. Carnegie's offer of the raising of an annual sum of £100 may be met in that manner. In the absence of a response from Mr. Carnegie when first approached, the committee have not been in any haste to push forward the scheme, though they have recently had under consideration offers of sites, and had decided to take certain preliminary steps, such as inspection, towards making a purchase. A meeting of the Library Committee of the District Council was held recently at which a resolution was adopted thanking Mr. Carnegie for his generous offer, and stating that the committee had taken steps to obtain such financial support as would make up the annual income of the library to £100, in accordance with his conditions, and that they were considering certain offers which have been made of sites.

HECKMONDWIKE: *Steps to be taken towards the Adoption of the Library Act.*—At a meeting of the Heckmondwike District Council on the 21st July, the chairman, Mr. T. Redfearn, reported the receipt of a letter from a prominent individual in the town, inquiring whether the Council intended doing anything towards securing its quota of Mr. Carnegie's offer to spend part of his fortune in assisting free libraries, provided the local authority were prepared to levy the maximum rate of 1d. in the £. There were few towns the same size, the chairman went on to say, which possessed more advantages in the shape of public works than Heckmondwike, and he strongly advocated that something should be done towards the adoption of the Act referred to. He suggested that the site at the junction of Shaver Hill and Oldfield Lane, which was centrally situated, and belonged to the town, might be utilised for the building, and that the money required, which had been variously estimated at from £3,000 to £5,000, could be borrowed with the sanction of the Local Government Board. The idea met with the general approval of the Council, but the question was eventually adjourned until the next meeting.

HOLYWELL: *Effort to Establish a Free Library.*—An effort is being made to establish a free library at Holywell, and the Coronation Celebration Committee intend to devote the balance of the festivities fund—some fifteen guineas—to this object. The Urban Council having adopted the Free Libraries Act, made an application to Mr. Carnegie for assistance, which was backed by Mr. Herbert Lewis, M.P., but unfortunately without success. The library will be housed in the large upper room of the new Town Hall.

LARNE: *Mr. Carnegie Offers £2,500 for a Public Library.*—At a specially convened meeting of Larne Council on the 1st July, a letter was read from Mr. Andrew Carnegie offering a sum of £2,500 for a free public library building for the town of Larne, provided the Urban Council undertake to collect or otherwise guarantee an endowment fund of £125 per annum. The clerk was directed to write thanking Mr. Carnegie and to intimate that the Council would do their utmost to comply with the terms of the proposed gift.

LIVERPOOL PUBLIC LIBRARIES: *Erection of a New Branch Library.*—A new branch library has been erected to supersede the old library at the lower end of Upper Parliament Street. The building which stands on a site at the corner of Windsor Street and Upper Parliament Street, includes both library and newsroom. The principal front elevation and main entrance are in Windsor Street. The structure has been erected from designs of Mr. Thomas Shelmerdine, the Corporation architect and surveyor. From the entrance in Windsor Street a vestibule is reached. Leading from the main central hall on the right is the ladies' reading-room, 56 feet 6 inches by 30 feet. On the left is the general or men's reading-room, 66 feet by 30 feet. In the central building are the lending department and book-store. There are upwards of 25,000 volumes of books in this library. From the vestibule there is a staircase by which access is obtained to the basement, in which is situated the boys' reading-room, 47 feet by 30 feet. In addition to the public accommodition there is a mezzanine or gallery floor, which provides accommodation for books, for the repair of books, and for the staff. On the ground floor is the librarian's room, and on the first floor the assistant's common-room. The entire building is of fireproof construction. The main walls are of red wire-cut Ruabon bricks and Cefnstone dressings, and the roof is covered with Cumberland green slates. The building is English Renaissance in style. The contract price for the building was upwards of £12,100.

LLANDUDNO: *Gift of a Free Library by an Anonymous Donor.*—A correspondent of the *Manchester Guardian* understands that Lord Mostyn, the chairman of the Llandudno Urban District Council, has received a letter from a local gentleman, who, however, desires that his name should not be disclosed, offering to the Council debenture stock of the value of £6,000 as a Coronation commemoration gift, provided the money is devoted to the provision of a free library to be taken over and managed by the Council.

LONDON: **BRITISH MUSEUM**: *Return for the Year* 1901.—From a return which has just been issued relating to the British Museum it appears that the grand total number of visits to the museum in the year 1901 was 718,614. This is an increase of more than 29,000 on the total of the year 1900, which was 689,249; and that total again was an increase of more than 25,000 on that of the previous year. This gratifying augmentation of upwards of 54,000 visits during the past two years has carried the total of last year above the average of the years 1880-3, when the removal of the natural history collections to Cromwell Road was accomplished and entailed a serious diminution of the numbers, the total for 1884 being only 468,873. It is also satisfactory that the number of visits on Sunday afternoons has steadily increased year by year, the total for 1901 being 48,895, as against 43,892 in 1900. In the several departments other than the reading-room there has been a further increase in the number of visits of students, the total last year being 57,943, as against 56,043 in 1900. The departments of prints and drawings and of coins and medals have been more frequented; but there has been a decline in the number of students drawing in the sculpture galleries.

Improved electric alarm circuits have been installed both within and without the building. The condition of the wooden floors in the public galleries has called for serious attention, the former system of scouring with water and cleansing fluids having caused the surfaces to decay very considerably. Several of the floors have now been refaced, and are treated with polish, washing with water being thus superseded. This system will be extended to the wooden flooring throughout the building.

The works added to the collection of printed books during the past year have, as far as possible, been placed on the shelves of the library according to the system of classification adopted in the museum. The press-marks, indicating their respective localities, have been marked on the inside and affixed to the back of each volume; also on the titles. The total number of these press-marks amounts to 76,294; in addition to which 39,428 press-marks have been altered in consequence of changes and re-arrangements carried out in the library; 31,018 labels have been affixed to books and volumes of newspapers, and 96,196 obliterated labels have been renewed. The process of attaching third-marks to the books in the new library, with the view of accelerating their delivery to readers, has been continued; 13,410 books have been thus marked during the year, and the corresponding alterations, amounting to 53,655, have been carried out in the general and hand catalogues; 2,717 volumes of country newspapers have also been numbered, and 3,064 index-slips have been written for London and country newspapers. The number of stamps impressed upon articles received has been 314,114; 4,441 presses of books and newspapers have been dusted in the course of the year.

As regards the work of cataloguing, 47,978 titles have been written (the term "title" applying equally to a main title and to a cross reference). Of these, 30,024 were written for the general catalogue, 2,244 for the map catalogue and 15,710 for the music catalogue; 31,581 titles and 769 index-slips for the general catalogue, 1,469 for the map catalogue, and 17,068 for the music catalogue, having been prepared for printing during the year; 32,215 title-slips and 1,060 index-slips for the general catalogue, and 1,469 title-slips for the map catalogue have been printed. 32,207 title-slips and 1,175 index-slips have been incorporated into each of the three copies of the general catalogue. This incorporation has rendered it necessary in order to maintain as far as possible the alphabetical arrangement, to remove and re-insert 36,451 title-slips in each copy, and to add to each copy 445 new leaves. The number of new entries made in the hand catalogue of "Academies" was 313; in that of "Periodical Publications," 370; in that of "Maps and Charts," 1,112; in that of music, 3,046; and in the hand catalogues of London and country newspapers, 603 and 2,461 respectively. 2,244 titles have been written for the map catalogue and 2,209 title-slips have been incorporated into each of three copies of it. This incorporation has rendered it necessary to remove and re-insert 3,210 title-slips in each copy, and to add to each copy seventeen new leaves. 15,710 titles have been written for the music catalogue, and 13,792 title-slips have been incorporated into each of two copies of it. This incorporation has rendered it necessary to remove and re-insert 25,008 title-slips in each copy, and to add to each copy 305 new leaves. For the shelf catalogue, in which the title-slips, mounted on cards, are arranged in order of press-marks, 37,340 have been so mounted, and 131,700 have been incorporated in their proper order. The additions and alterations in each of the three interleaved copies of the catalogue of books of reference in the reading-room, which are requisite in order to record the changes in this collection by the addition of new works and the substitution of new for earlier editions, have been made; they number 44 in each copy. Additions have been made also to the collection of books in the galleries of the reading-room by the incorporation of new works of interest and importance, and by the substitution of new for earlier editions. The number of such editions to each of the two interleaved copies of the catalogue of this collection is 101.

The number of volumes and sets of pamphlets bound during the year was 10,168, including 3,362 volumes of newspapers. Besides this the following binding has been done in the library itself: 7,388 volumes have been repaired; 112 broadsides, etc., have been inserted in guard books; 4,197 volumes of reports, parts of periodicals, etc., have been formed in a light style of binding; 37,393 numbers of colonial newspapers have been folded into 490 parcels, and 373 parcels have been tied up and labelled. The number of volumes returned to the General Library from use in the reading-room was 778,059, to the King's Library 24,714, to the Grenville Library 1,192, to the Map Room 3,624, to the presses in which books are kept from day to day for the use of readers 574,799, and to the Oriental department 142, making a total amount of 1,382,530 volumes supplied to readers during the year. The number of readers was 200,035, giving an average of over 664 daily, the room having been open 301 days; with an average of almost seven volumes daily for each reader, not reckoning those volumes taken from the shelves of the reading-room by the readers themselves. In the newspaper-room the number of readers during the year was 25,511, giving a daily average of over 84. The number of volumes replaced after use was 41,020, not reckoning those, chiefly Parliamentary papers, taken from the shelves of the newspaper-room by the readers themselves.

42,855 volumes and pamphlets (including 53 atlases and 1,505 books of music) have been added to the library in the course of the year. Of these 21,766 were presented, 12,723 were received under the provisions of the Copyright Act, 430 by colonial copyright, 558 by international exchange, and 7,378 by purchase. 60,956 parts of volumes (or separate numbers of periodical publications and of works in progress) have also been added to the library, of which 3,471 were presented. 34,639 received under the provisions of the Copyright Act, 183 by colonial copyright, 545 by international exchange, and 22,118 by purchase. 1,385 maps in 10,974 sheets have been added to the collection in the course of the year, of which 507 maps in 827 sheets were presented; 606 maps in 9,260 sheets were received under the provisions of the Copyright Act, 16 maps in 19 sheets by colonial copyright, and 256 maps in 868 sheets acquired by purchase. 8,511 musical publications have been added to the collection of which 8,063 have been received under the provisions of the Copyright Act, 257 by colonial copyright. and 191 acquired by purchase.

The number of newspapers published in the United Kingdom received under the provisions of the Copyright Act during the past year has been 3,170, comprising 208,582 single numbers published in London and its suburbs; 1,563 in other parts of England and Wales and in the Channel Islands; 270 in Scotland and 224 in Ireland; 8 sets containing 1,029 numbers have been received by colonial copyright; 222 sets containing 29,311 numbers of colonial and foreign newspapers have been presented, and 76 sets containing 12 volumes and 14,899 numbers of current colonial and foreign newspapers have been purchased.

3,002 articles have been received in the department not included in the foregoing paragraphs, consisting of broadsides, Parliamentary papers and other miscellaneous items. The addition of this number to those already given produces a total of 115,204 articles, exclusive ot newspapers, received in the department in the course of the year.

LONDON: BATTERSEA: *Steps to be Taken to Increase the Library Rate.*—The Battersea Borough Council decided at their last meeting to take the necessary steps to procure power to increase the local library rate from 1d. to 2d. It was stated as a reason for this that three new branch libraries were urgently needed, and that the proceeds of the present rate were insufficient to enable the Council properly to remunerate their employees. In connection with this matter Mr. Sherwood Ramsey, the chairman of the Library Committee, has been for some time past in communication with Mr. Carnegie, and has just received a letter from his secretary as follows: " Mr. Carnegie will be glad to furnish £15,000 required to erect three branch library buildings if sites are furnished and proposed legislation is effected to enable Battersea to levy a tax for maintenance of the libraries, as you state that those existing require all of the proceeds of the 1d. rate to support them." This offer will, it is thought, enable the Council to meet the necessary outlay with the proceeds of an additional ½d. rate. The Mayor of Battersea (Mr. Howarth Barnes) is a little doubtful whether the offer can be accepted owing to its stringent conditions.

LONDON: FINSBURY: *£13,000 Offered by Mr. Carnegie for the Extension of the Public Library System.*—At a meeting of the Finsbury Borough Council held on the 17th July, the Rev. John E. Wakerley, chairman of the Public Libraries Committee, announced the receipt of a letter from Mr. Andrew Carnegie offering £13,000 for the extension of the public library system in Finsbury, with special reference to the St. Luke's, St. Sepulchre's and Charterhouse districts. This offer was made conditionally that free sites were obtained, and that the Public Library Acts were adopted throughout the borough, with a maximum of a 1d. rate. The gift, with the condition attached, was cordially accepted.

LONDON: HAMMERSMITH: *Mr. Carnegie Offers £10,000 for the Erection of a Central Library.*—At a meeting of the Borough Council held on the 16th July, a letter from Mr. Carnegie's secretary was read to the following effect: " Mr. Carnegie understands that the Free Libraries Act is operative over the whole of the borough, and that the maximum assessment is levied. If a site be provided, the cost not being a burden on the proceeds of the 1d. rate, Mr. Carnegie will be glad to furnish the ten thousand pounds sterling (£10,000), estimated as needed to erect a central free public library building for Hammersmith." It was resolved that the grateful thanks of the Council be conveyed to Mr. Carnegie for his generous offer, and that the letter be referred to the Libraries Committee and the Finance Committee for consideration and report.

It is proposed to erect the new building in the neighbourhood of the Broadway, and judging by the use that has been made of the temporary reading-room which was opened in January last, there is no doubt that it will be greatly appreciated.

LONDON: LAMBETH: *Mr. Carnegie Offers £12,500 for the Erection of Branch Libraries.*—The Libraries Committee of the Lambeth Borough Council report that in the course of the year 1901 an application was made to Mr. Andrew Carnegie for assistance in the establishment of a library for the inhabitants of Herne Hill and Tulse Hill. Mr. Carnegie refused the application, on the ground that he was only making gifts to his native country (Scotland), and his adopted country (America). Finding, however, at the commencement of the present year that Mr. Carnegie was making exceptions to his rule in favour of certain towns and districts in England, the chief librarian renewed the application on behalf of Lambeth, and this time with a successful result. After some preliminary correspondence the following letter has now been received from Mr. Carnegie: "It gives me great pleasure to say that I shall be glad to supply the £12,500, which you say is needed to complete your library system by erecting a branch library for the district of Tulse Hill and Herne Hill. When you have acquired the site and are ready to proceed with building, cash payments will be arranged. Hearty congratulations.—Very truly yours, ANDREW CARNEGIE."

LONDON: PADDINGTON: *Mr. Carnegie Offers £15,000 for the Erection of Two Public Libraries.*—The Mayor of Paddington (Sir John Aird, M.P.) has received an offer from Mr. Andrew Carnegie of £15,000 for the erection of two free public library buildings in Paddington on condition that the Borough Council supply the sites and agree to levy the maximum 1d. rate under the Public Libraries Act, for the purchase of books and general maintenance of the libraries. Several attempts have been made to secure a free public library or libraries for Paddington, but the poles are no longer necessary and the Borough Council may, if they think fit, directly adopt the Libraries Act. Mr. Carnegie's proposal will be submitted to them in due course.

LONDON: RICHMOND: *The Year's Work.*—According to the last report of the Committee of the Richmond Public Library, the total issues during the last twelve months were 96,030, representing a daily average of 397, as against 100,053 issues and a daily average of 412 during the preceding twelve months. The decline last year was mainly in works of fiction; the returns show an increased demand for the more solid classes of literature. There was added to the library 1,616 volumes, of which 435 were placed on the reference shelves.

LONDON: WANDSWORTH: *Bazaar in Aid of the Public Library.*—So small is the sum raised by the library rate that many Councils find it hard to develop them as they would like. Were it not for the Carnegies and the Passmore Edwardses, who have borne the cost of so many of the fabrics, the number of public libraries, erected and proposed, would have been about half what it is now, so insignificant is the sum available in the hands of the Borough Councils, which are confined to a 1d. rate. A novel plan for assisting these useful institutions on voluntary lines has been tried in Wandsworth with so much success that we may expect it to be adopted in other districts. A number of ladies in the borough formed themselves into a committee on their own account, and conducted a bazaar to raise funds to help to swell the library bookshelves. As a result over 500 new books were purchased.

LONDON: WESTMINSTER: *The Year's Work* (1901-2).—Evidence of the popularity of the public libraries in the city of Westminster is furnished by the Public Libraries Committee of Westminster in their report to the City Council for the year 1901-2, which gives details of the work in the five libraries of Buckingham Palace Road and South Audley Street (St. George, Hanover Square), Great Smith Street, Westminster, and Trevor Square, Knightsbridge (St. Margaret and St. John), and St. Martin's Public Library, St. Martin's Lane. The Public Libraries Act being now in force throughout the city, the expenses of carrying out those Acts are allocable rateably over the whole area which forms one library district. In the year under review 4,144 volumes have been acquired, the stock of books in the several libraries now numbering 102,140. From the lending departments 277,970 books were issued, and 157,472 were consulted in the reference libraries, making a total of 435,442. Periodical counts show estimated total attendances of 2,702,000 readers who have visited the libraries during the twelve months. The Committee note with satisfaction the testimony of the librarians to the educational effect of the libraries and their increasing influence in raising the standard of reading.

LONDON: WOOLWICH: *Mr. Carnegie Offers £14,000 towards the Building of two Branch Libraries.*—As a result of an appeal made by the chairman and the librarian of the Woolwich Public Library, Mr. Andrew Carnegie has signified his willingness to assist the borough to extend the benefits of the Public Libraries Act to Plumstead and Eltham in a letter dated 11th July, 1902, which reads as follows: "Mr. Carnegie notes that the Free Libraries Act is operative over the whole borough, and that you have £5,000 towards the erection of buildings at Plumstead and Eltham, out of £19,000 required. On conditions (*a*) that maximum rate of 1d. will continue to be levied, and (*b*) that sites for the buildings will be provided and not be a burden on the proceeds of the library rate, Mr. Carnegie will take pleasure in furnishing the £14,000 additional needed to erect free public buildings at Plumstead and Eltham."

LONDONDERRY: *Mr. Carnegie Offers £8,000 for the Provision of a Library.*—£8,000 has been offered to Londonderry by Mr. Carnegie for the provision of a library, and the Corporation have appointed a committee to arrange the details.

LOWESTOFT: *Mr. Carnegie Promises £6,000 for a Public Library.*—Mr. Carnegie has promised to give £6,000 for the purpose of building a free library for Lowestoft. The offer is conditional on the Town Council providing a site and adopting the Free Libraries Act.

MANCHESTER: PUBLIC LIBRARIES: *Proposed New Branch Libraries.*—The Free Libraries Committee of the Manchester Corporation have adopted a resolution tendering to Dr. Dreyfus (one of the representatives of the Bradford Ward) their thanks for his generous offer of a plot of land at Clayton for the erection of a new library. It appears to them, after an inspection of the site, that the population in the locality is not sufficiently large to justify them in providing a new library at the present time. They suggest that, if agreeable to Dr. Dreyfus, his proposed gift of ten acres of land be made to the Parks Committee with the proviso that if the Libraries Committee deem it desirable at any future time to erect a library they shall have the option of selecting for this purpose any portion of the plot not exceeding one acre in extent. The committee have also resolved that in accordance with the resolution of the Council on the 2nd October, 1901, they have further considered the suggestion for the erection of a reading-room on the plot of land in Butler Street, Ancoats, and have also visited the site, but having regard to the proximity of Rochdale Road and Ancoats branches, to the more urgent requirements of other districts of the city, and to the limited resources at the disposal of the committee, they regret they cannot see their way to adopt the suggestion.

MANSFIELD: *An Offer of £3,500 from Mr. Carnegie for a Free Library.*—Mr. A. B. Markham, M.P. for the Mansfield Division, has received a letter from Mr. Andrew Carnegie offering to furnish £3,500 for the purpose of erecting a free public library for Mansfield on the following conditions: (*a*) That the Public Libraries Act be adopted, and the maximum assessment levied; (*b*) that a suitable site be provided at a cost which shall not be a burden to the 1d. rate. Mr. Markham has communicated the contents of the letter to Mr. I. H. Wallace, chairman of the Public Libraries Committee, and says he has no doubt the town will be glad to accept Mr. Carnegie's generous offer, and intimates that if any help is required he will be pleased to assist. He further trusts that the townspeople will place on record their appreciation of Mr. Carnegie's kindness.

NEWPORT (ISLE OF WIGHT): *Foundation-stone of Institute and Library Laid.*—On Wednesday, the 26th July, the long looked for ceremony of foundation-stone laying of the Isle of Wight Technical Institute and Public Library took place, under conditions which were a happy augury for the future of this very necessary educational institution which is being provided through the munificence of Sir Charles Seely, Bart., coupled with the wise and commendable endeavour of the County Council and its excellent Technical Education Committee, to enable the Island to keep abreast of the times on this vitally important direction. Mrs. Godfrey Baring and Miss Seely, upon whom the "masonic" ceremony devolved, acquitted themselves very capably and gracefully, and sentiments appropriate to the occasion were admirably expressed by the chairman of the County Council (Mr. Godfrey Baring), the chairman of the County Technical Education Committee (Ald. Robey F. Eldridge), Sir Charles Seely, Ald. James Thomas, Ald. George Fellows, and Mr. G. F. Ingram. There was a very felicitous passage in the speech of Sir Charles Seely, the munificent founder and donor of the Free Library. Referring to the union of the two institutions as symbolised by the ceremony in which the names of "Baring" and "Seely" had been joined, he gave expression to the earnest hope that the "marriage" might be a very happy one and that the Technical Institute and the Free Library would spend a very long and prosperous life together. That they will do so we have every confidence.

NOTTINGHAM: *Valuable Gift to the Public Library.*—The Public Reference Library has been enriched through the generosity of Dr. Waterhouse, a former resident of Nottingham. The gift consists of about eight hundred volumes of works on "Comparative Philology," "Linguistics" and "Topography," the result of nearly forty years' collecting. These works are in about a hundred and eighty languages and dialects. The city librarian reported this valuable gift to the Town Council, who accorded a special vote of thanks to the donor.

WAKEFIELD: *Mr. Carnegie Offers £8,000 towards a Free Library.*—The Mayor of Wakefield recently received an intimation from Mr. Carnegie to the effect that he would give £8,000 towards a free library for Wakefield. The chief magistrate at once called a meeting, and the offer was gladly accepted. For several years an agitation for a free library has been in progress in Wakefield.

SOUTH AFRICA.

KIMBERLEY: *Attempts to Popularise the Kimberley Public Library.*—A special general meeting of the subscribers of the Kimberley Public Library was held in the latter part of the month of June to consider the proposed alterations in the rules, the effect of which will be to give subscribers the full privilege of the library, and one book for home reading, for an annual subscription of £1, while for families desirous of having more than one book at a time, yearly subscriptions of £2 or £3 will give three books and three admissions, or five books and five admissions to the rooms, respectively. It was hoped that the advantages offered would induce an increased number of young men to join the library. At the end of last year there were 350 subscribers, while at the end of May of the present year the number was 375. The chairman sincerely trusted that at the close of the present year they would have at least 450 or 500 subscribers. It was, he was sure, the sincere wish of the committee to make the library a real power for good in the community, and he trusted that the step about to be taken would assist in no small measure in accomplishing that object. The proposed alterations of the rules were adopted, and it is sincerely hoped that the library may enter upon a larger sphere of usefulness.

UNITED STATES.

NEW YORK: *The Carter Brown Library.*—An interesting article appears in the New York *Tribune* on the Carter Brown Library in that city. This library was recently given to the Brown University, together with $650,000 in cash for its maintenance, under the will of the late Mr. J. N. Brown. It has taken about seventy-five years to assemble this almost priceless collection of books. As a conservative estimate places the value of the books at $500,000, the entire gift amounts to $1,150,000. There are about 15,000 volumes, and that many of them are rare and some unique is proved by the fact that it takes four large catalogue volumes to describe them. These books are almost exclusively Americana, dealing with the period previous to 1800. The oldest book on America is the *Letter of Christopher Columbus to Rafael Sanchez*, written on board the caravel while returning from his first voyage. Published at Barcelona, May, 1493. This book was written in Spanish, but translated and printed in Latin, as were most of the books at that time. The library contains copies of five different editions of this letter, the others being reprinted at Rome, Paris and Basle. All are in Latin, and each cost a moderate fortune to acquire. The rarest book in the library is the *Dutch Vespucius*, being the celebrated letter of Americus Vespucius, describing his third voyage to America in the year 1501. This was written in Italian, and translated into Latin, and from Latin into Dutch. It was printed at Antwerp about 1507, and no other copy of this issue is known to exist. It was procured by Mr. Brown in 1871, from an Amsterdam bookseller. It came from an insignificant library sold the year previously at Antwerp, and was bound up with three other pieces, all printed there in the first ten years of the sixteenth century. The book is illustrated with rude woodcuts descriptive of the natives whom Vespucius encountered on the mainland of America. It consists of only sixteen small pages, and is probably the most valuable bit of Americana—certainly for its size—in the world. A recent addition is a copy of the famous edition of Ptolemy's geography, printed at Ulm in 1482, in which is the first engraved map of the world, as known at that time ever printed. The library contains the original editions of all the books of the sixteenth century explorers. A unique book is the original manuscript of Champlain's voyage to the West Indies from 1599 to 1602, illustrated with maps and drawings in colours. The ink used in making this priceless volume is as bright to-day as it was 300 years ago. The collection is especially rich in the early Mexican and South American publications. In an altar book printed in Mexico in the sixteenth century the printing and illustrations compare favourably with the best of modern work. Colonial history contributes thousands of volumes to the library. There is one of the best collections of books in the Indian language extant, among these being several copies of Eliot's Bible and his primer. The Revolutionary period is thoroughly covered. All the early books about Rhode Island and the other New England colonies are found here, including a full set of the writings of Roger Williams, and of Cotton Mather. It is perhaps needless to say that these are all in the original editions.

OBITUARY.

WALL (Charles).—Mr. Charles Wall, editor of the *Wigan Observer*, died 8th June, aged 51. He was a member of the firm of Messrs. Wall & Sons, Printers and Newspaper Proprietors, of Wigan, and was an Honorary Member of the Library Committee of the Wigan Corporation. He took a very active interest in public library work, and was always ready to assist its progress by his advice in committee and by his pen as a journalist. He had been a member of the Library Association since 1881.

BIRCH (A. J.).—It is with much regret that we have to record the death of Mr. A. J. Birch, librarian of the Great Western Railway Mechanics' Institution, Swindon, which took place on 17th June, after a short illness. Mr. Birch had been librarian at Swindon since 1876, and for five years prior to that date he had acted as assistant to Mr. Scarse at the Birmingham Old Library. He was one of the original members of the Association and a regular attendant at the Annual Meetings. Although a man of retiring disposition, he had won the respect of all who knew him by his aimable and courteous manners, and his well-known figure will be greatly missed at future meetings.

OFFICIAL GAZETTE.

Bailey (Ernest).—The librarianship of the South Shields Public Library, rendered vacant by the retirement of Mr. Thomas Pyke, has been conferred upon Mr. Ernest Bailey, the sub-librarian, who entered the service in November, 1894, as junior assistant. The promotion of Mr. Bailey was unanimously agreed to by the Library Committee.

Craigie (James), librarian of the Arbroath Public Library, has been appointed librarian of the Sandeman Public Library, Perth, in succession to Mr. John Minto. Mr. Craigie is forty-eight years of age. When the Public Libraries Act was adopted for the city of Brechin in 1892, he was appointed librarian there, but before beginning his duties he had the privilege of four months' training to library work in the Edinburgh Public Library. In the Brechin Library, which opened with 8,000 volumes, the books were all classified and arranged and the catalogue compiled and edited by Mr. Craigie. He also drew up the bye-laws, organised all the arrangements for working the library, and acted as clerk and treasurer to the committee. He was transferred to his present position on the adoption of the Act for the Burgh of Arbroath in 1897, and there he had to do work, or superintend the execution of work, similar to that which he performed in Brechin.

Errington (Alfred), assistant in the South Shields Public Library, has been appointed sub-librarian in succession to Mr. Ernest Bailey, who becomes librarian. Mr. Errington was previously engaged in the Subscription Library at Sunderland.

Pyke (Thomas).—Mr. Thomas Pyke, secretary and librarian of the South Shields Public Library, has resigned his post after fifteen years' service. Mr. Pyke is a native of South Shields, and has been connected with the Public Library and its predecessors, the Mechanics' Institution and the Working Men's Institute, in various capacities for more than half a century. He took an active interest in public affairs, was a prominent non-conformist, and an ardent volunteer, rising to the rank of major in the 3rd Durham Artillery. Mr. Pyke will carry with him into his retirement the good wishes of a host of friends, who trust that he may enjoy his well-earned leisure for many years to come.

NOTES AND QUERIES ON PUBLIC LIBRARY LAW.

UNDER this heading we continue from time to time to publish questions on the operation of the Public Libraries Acts which have been submitted to the Hon. Solicitor of the Association, together with the answers he has given.

All questions should be addressed to the Hon. Solicitor, H. W. FOVARGUE, Esq., Town Hall, Eastbourne, who will send his replies direct to correspondents, on the distinct understanding that both question and answer are to be published in the THE LIBRARY ASSOCIATION RECORD.

Gifts of Sites for Libraries by Local Authorities.

Question.—Will you kindly let me have any precedents you happen to know of for building sites being given by the Council, or other local authority, for the purpose of erecting libraries. Also your opinion as to the legality of such gifts. We have just received a munificent offer from Mr. Carnegie on condition that sites are provided, and we propose asking the Council to provide the site for one of our libraries. I think there are precedents, but I am unable to trace the authority in the Libraries Acts, or rather our Town Clerk questions the application of paragraph 23 in 55 & 56 Vict., cap. 53.

Answer.—Assuming that your Council has land vested in them, they may, under sect. 23 of the Public Libraries Act, 1892, with the sanction of the Local Government Board, appropriate the same for the purposes of the Public Libraries Act. This section was not repealed by the London Government Act, 1899—all the powers of the Vestry or District Board were transferred to the New Borough Councils by sect. 4 of that Act. I am assuming that the Act is in force in your borough.

Sect. 12 of the Public Libraries Act, 1892, gives a similar power to a library authority of an Urban District. Upon that section I find I made the following note: "If an authority, with the consent of the Local Government Board, appropriates land for the purposes of the Act, they are not *required* to charge the 1d. rate with any rent or purchase money". I cannot add to this statement. It applies equally to sect. 23. Possibly the Local Government Board, if asked, would tell you if they would require any charge to be made upon the library rate assuming this course is adopted.

I am sorry to say I know of no precedents of building sites being given by Councils. As this will appear in the LIBRARY ASSOCIATION RECORD, doubtless some of the members of the Association may be able to give the desired information.

Exemption from Rates and Taxes.

Question.—We have just received the welcome news that Mr. Carnegie will provide us with £5,000 for a new building if the town finds the site. There is plenty of room to build a library in the grounds adjoining our present quarters, and we are applying to the Council—in whom the land is vested—for the gift of a site.

It is most likely that we shall get it, but one individual Councillor has no love for libraries and he is using some very trivial arguments to prejudice the Council: one is that we shall not be able to pay the rates and taxes of the building. I shall be exceedingly glad if you will tell me what method to adopt to secure exemption from rates and taxes. I understand that many libraries have obtained a certificate of exemption, and I am anxious to be in possession of any particulars which will enable us to say that we are exempted from the payment of rates and taxes.

Answer.—The library will be exempt from property tax, that is made clear by the case of Manchester *v.* Macadam. It will be exempt from rates if you obtain the certificate of the Registrar of Friendly Societies as provided by the Scientific Societies Exemption Act, 1843. To enable you to obtain this certificate the institution would have to be supported either wholly or in part by annual contributions, not necessarily of money. You will find the Act in *Chambers' Law Relating to Public Libraries*, page 250, and the matter is discussed at page 139 of the same volume.

Legality of Charges for Establishment Expenses.

Question.—Our Borough Council is about to debit the Libraries Fund with an annual charge of £45 for "establishment expenses". Is this a legal charge, or has the Council power to impose it? It is made to cover cost of printing our portion of the minutes of the Council, etc., and, presumably, cost of services rendered by the Borough Accountant, Town Clerk and others.

This is the only library I have been connected with, and the first time in my experience of nearly thirty years where such a charge has been imposed.

Answer.—Like you I have never heard of any Borough Council charging a Library Committee with any portion of the establishment expenses, but I cannot say that it is an illegal charge. It must, however, not include any proportion of the cost of collecting the rate, and I should think that it would be exceedingly difficult to arrive at the amount.

Establishment of a Public Library.

Questions.—(1) Can the Council rent a room or building for library purposes and charge the same to the general district rate (not the 1d. rate) under sect. 12 of the Public Libraries Act, 1892, or any other rate?

(2) Can the Public Libraries Act be rescinded by the Council after adoption, and if so, how is it to be done?

(3) Can the Public Libraries Act be adopted and a library established as a Free Public Library under the Act without any rate whatever being levied?

(4) Can the library rate on an Urban District be levied with and as part of the poor rate instead of being collected on the general district rate assessment?

(5) Can any portion of the loss to library income through differ-ential rating on agricultural land be claimed under the Agricultural Rates Act, 1896 and 1901 ?

(6) Is it possible to provide out of the general district rate funds for library purposes without stating same in demand note or charging same to library rate?

Answers.—(1) The Council can hire a room or building under sect. 11 of the Public Libraries Act, 1892, and in an Urban District the rent would be charged upon the general district rate.   See sect. 18 (1) (*b*).

(2) I know of no power enabling the rescission of the adoption of the Public Libraries Act.

(3) Although the Act may be adopted, there is no obligation on the Council to levy a rate, except that they would be obliged to raise a rate to cover the cost of any building they had provided and hired.   Probably where the Acts are adopted in consideration of a gift, the party making the gift might be able to compel the Council to maintain the library.

(4) No. See sect. 18 (1) (*b*).

(5) Land is assessed for general district rate purposes at one-fourth the estimated annual value.   The loss in this respect is not due to the Agricultural Rates Act, but to the fact that the Legislature has provided that in an Urban District the rate is to be levied as part of the general district rate and not the poor rate.   If the latter rate had been fixed the land would be assessed in full, but under the Agricultural Rates Act a portion only would be charged on the tenants, the balance being re-couped by the Government.

(6) Sect. 11 of the Local Goverment Act, 1894, does not apply to an Urban District Council but only to a Parish Council.   The latter Council is obliged on the demand note to state the proportion levied for the carrying out of the Public Libraries Act.   I think there is no obligation on the District Council to show the libra:y rate separately, though this is desirable.   They are, however, subject to the provisions of the Act limiting the amount to be expended in any one year.

RECORD OF BIBLIOGRAPHY AND LIBRARY LITERATURE.

CUMULATIVE LIST OF BIBLIOGRAPHIES.

BIBLIOGRAPHY OF BIBLIOGRAPHIES.

BIBLIOGRAPHY OF BIBLIOGRAPHIES.—INSTITUT INTERNATIONAL DE BIBLIOGRAPHIE. Répertoire annuel des travaux de bibliographie, 1898, 1899. [Par H. La Fontaine.] Bruxelles : *Siège de l'Institut.* 2 vols. 8vo.

Excellently printed, indexed and arranged. The two volumes comprise 1,057 entries.

BIBLIOGRAPHIES OF PARTICULAR SUBJECTS.

AIR AND GAS ENGINES.—SCHÖTTLER (R.). Die Gasmaschine. Braunschweig : *Gieritz.* 2 parts in 8vo.

Pp. 370-89 : Bibliography.

ALCOHOLISM.—SCHMIDT (P.). Bibliographie des Alkoholismus der letzten 20 Jahre (1800-1900). Theil i. Deutsche Litteratur. Dresden : *Böhmert*, 1901. 8vo, pp. iv, 70.

ANTHROPOLOGY.—*See also* PERU : ANTHROPOLOGY.

ARCHITECTURE : FRENCH ECCLESIASTICAL.—ENLART (C. D. L.). Manuel d'archéologie française depuis les temps mérovingiens jusqu'à la Renaissance. I. Architecture : 1. Architecture religieuse. Paris : *Picard*, 1902. 8vo.

This very complete manual of French Ecclesiastical Architecture (816 pp. with 405 illus.) has at the end of each chapter a classified bibliography of the matters dealt with therein.

ARMY-WORM.—*See* WORMS.

ART : GENERAL.—ANNOTATED BIBLIOGRAPHY OF FINE ART : painting, sculpture, architecture, arts of decoration and illustration, by R. Sturgis ; music, by H. E. Krehbiel. Edited by G. Iles. Boston : *Library Bureau*, 1897. 8vo, pp. 96.

One of the American Library Association annotated lists.

ART: GENERAL.—JELLINEK (A. L.). Internationale Biblio-
graphie der Kunstwissenschaft. Herausgegeben von A. L.
Jellinek. Erster Jahrgang, 1902; 1 Heft, April, 1902.
Berlin: *B. Behr's Verlag,* 1902. 8vo.
A classified list, to appear bimonthly, of current art literature.

———— **EARLY CHRISTIAN.**—LOWRIE (W.). Christian art
and archæology, being a handbook to the monuments of the
early Church. New York and London: *Macmillan,* 1901.
8vo.
Pp. 415-26: Select bibliography (classified and with useful notes as to the
scope and value of the works included).

———— **INDUSTRIAL.**—*See* INDUSTRIAL ARTS.

———— **ITALIAN RENAISSANCE.**—JOSEPH (D.). Bibliographie de l'histoire de l'art de la première Renaissance
(trecento et quattrocento) en Italie. Abrégé par D. J.
Bruxelles: *Veuve F. Larcier,* 1898. 8vo, pp. 68.

AZO-DYE-STUFFS.—JAUBERT (G. F.). "L'industrie des
matières colorantes azoïques." (*Encyclopédie scientifique des
Aide-mémoire.*) Paris: G. *Villars* [1899].
Pp. 160: A tabulated review of the literature, patents, properties and applications of the Azo-dye stuffs.

BEE-KEEPING.—APICULTEUR (L'). Tables (1856-96). I.,
Table des auteurs; II., Table des matières; III., Table des
planches et gravures. Chartres: *Garnier,* 1900. 8vo, pp.
228.

BIOGRAPHY: ENGLISH.—BOASE (Frederic). Modern English biography since 1850, with an index of the most interesting
matter. Truro: *Netherton & Worth,* 1892-1901. 3 vols.,
4to.
Mr. Boase's work possesses a bibliographical as well as a biographical value,
special attention having been paid to the recording of portraits, pseudonyms,
etc. A subject-index of "interesting facts" is appended to each volnme.

BOOKBINDING.—HARMS (Bernhard). Zur Entwickelungs-
geschichte der deutschen Buchbinderei in der zweiten Hälfte
des 19 Jahrhunderts. Tübingen: *Mohr,* 1902. La. 8vo.
Pp. 170-84: Anhang; Zur Geschichte der Buchbindereilitteratur [und
Bibliographie].

BYZANTINE HISTORY.—KRUMBACHER (C.). "Geschichte
der byzantinischen Litteratur von Justinian bis zum Ende
des oströmischen Reiches, 527-1453." 2te Auflage. (*Hand-
buch der klassischen Altertums Wissenschaft,* herausgegeben
von Dr. I. v. Müller. Bd. ix. Abt. 1.) München, 1897.
8vo.
Pp. 1068-1144: General bibliography of Byzantine history.

CANADA: GEOLOGY.—Geological Survey of Canada. General index to the reports of progress, 1863-84. Compiled by D. B. Dowling. Ottawa, 1900. 8vo, pp. 475.

CEMENTS: ARMOURED.—Christophe (Paul). Le béton armé. Paris: *Béranger*, 1902. 8vo.

Pp. 727-39: Bibliography.

CERAMICS: GREEK VASES.—Huddilston (J. H.). Lessons from Greek pottery, to which is added a bibliography of Greek ceramics. New York and London: *Macmillan*, 1902. 8vo.

The classified bibliography extends from p. 103 to p. 140.

CHANTILLY.—" Bibliographie (Château de Chantilly)." In *Revue de l'Art ancien et moderne*, vol. iii., No. 4, pp. 390-2. Paris, 1898. 4to.

In a special number entirely devoted to Chantilly.

CHEMISTRY.—Chemisches Centralblatt. General-Register Folge V., Jahrg., 1897-1901. Bearbeitet von R. Arendt. Berlin, 1902. 8vo, pp. 1297.

——— **THEORETICAL AND PHYSICAL.**—Zeitschrift für physikalische Chemie. Namen-und Sach-Register zu den Bänden 1-24 von T. Paul. Leipzig, 1900, etc. 8vo. *In progress.*

COMMERCE.—Great Britain: Consular Service. Index to [Consular] reports, 1898-9. London, 1902. 8vo.

Prepared by the Commercial Intelligence Branch of the Board of Trade. To be published annually.

COTTON.—Deschamps (Louis). Le coton. Paris: *Michelet* [1885]. La. 8vo.

Pp. 223-39: Bibliography.

DYEING.—Georgievics (G. von). "Lehrbuch der Farben-Chemie." (*Lehrbuch der chemischen Technologie der Gerpinstfasern*, i.) 2te Auflage. Leipzig: *Denticke*, 1902. 8vo.

Pp. 352-436: Bibliography and German patent lists; forming a supplement to G. Schultz's *Chemie des Steinkohlenthadis.*

——— *See also* Azo-Dye-stuffs.

ELECTRICITY.—Institution of Electrical Engineers. Index to the journal, vols. xxi.-xxx., 1892-1901. Compiled by W. G. McMillan. London, 1901. Pp. 138.

Consists as before of two alphabets, (*a*) of transactions and original communications, (*b*) of abstracts. The latter were discontinued in 1898, their publication being transferred to *Science Abstracts.*

ELECTROLYSIS.—*See* Water (Electrolysis).

ENGINEERING.—ANNALES DES PONTS ET CHAUSSÉES. Tables générales, vii. série, 1891-1900. Paris: *Dunod*, 1901. 8vo, pp. viii, 239; +957.

—— **SANITARY.**—*See* SANITARY ENGINEERING.

ENTOMOLOGY (NORTH AMERICA).—HOWARD (Leland Ossian). The insect book: a popular account of North American insects, exclusive of butterflies, moths and beetles. New York: *Doubleday, Page & Co.*, 1901. Pp. 28+429.
Pp. 12: Bibliography.

FINANCE.—LA REVUE DES SERVICES FINANCIERS. Table générale alphabétique et chronologique des matières (années 1884-99). Paris: *Berger-Levrault*, 1901. 8vo, double col., 198 pp.

FRENCH POETRY. — LACHÈVRE (F.). Bibliographie des recueils collectifs de poésies publiés de 1597 à 1700, donnant: 1° la description et le contenu des recueils; 2° les pièces de chaque auteur classées dans l'ordre alphabétique du premier vers, précédées d'une notice bio-bibliographique, etc.; 3° une table générale des pièces anonymes ou signées d'initiales (titre et premier vers), avec l'indication des noms des auteurs pour celles qui ont pu leur être attribuées; 4° la reproduction des pièces qui n'ont pas été relevées par les derniers éditeurs des poètes figurant dans les recueils collectifs; 5° une table des noms cités dans le texte et le premier vers des pièces des recueils collectifs, etc.; par Frédéric Lachèvre. T. 1ᵉʳ (1597-1635): Recueils des Du Petit Val, des Bonfons, des Du Breuil, de Mathieu Guillemot, de Toussainct du Bray, etc., et Pièces non relevées par les éditeurs de Bertaut, de Brach, Agrippa d'Aubigné, Desportes, Des Yveteaux, Du Perron, Maynard, Racan, N. Rapin, Saint-Gelais, Théophile. Paris: *Leclerc*, 1901. 4to, pp. xii, 414.

GAS ENGINES.—*See also* AIR AND GAS ENGINES.

GAS MANUFACTURE, ETC.—SHELTON (F. H.). "A Gas Association Library." (List of books on illuminating gas.) In *Progressive Age*, 15th June, 1901. Pp. 260-3.

GEOLOGY.—*See also* CANADA (Geology). *See also* PHILIPPINE ISLANDS (Geology).

HYGIENE AND SANITARY ENGINEERING.—SANITARY INSTITUTE. General index to the transactions and journals, vols. i.-xxi., including three volumes of miscellaneous papers, 1876-1900. London: *Stanford* [1901]. 8vo, pp. 232.

INDEXES: ANALYTICAL LITERARY.—FLETCHER (W. I.), and BOWKER (R. R.). The annual literary index, 1900. New York: Office of *The Publishers' Weekly*, 1901. Col. 8+pp. 258. 4to.

INDUSTRIAL ARTS.—BERLIN: *Königliche Museen.* Hauptwerke der Bibliothek des Kunstgewerbe-Museums. Berlin: *Spemann*, 1896. 8vo.

    I. Möbel und Holzarbeiten, iv and 38 pp. 1896.
      2 ed., iv and 28 pp. 1901.
    II. Dekorative Malerei, iv and 26 pp. 1896.
      2 ed., iv and 28 pp. 1902.
    III. Dekorative Plastik, iv and 30 pp. 1896.
    IV. Ornament, iv and 32 pp. 1896.
      2 ed., iv and 28 pp. 1900.
    V. Metall, iv and 24 pp. 1897.
    VI. Buchgewerbe, iv and 30 pp. 1898.

A series of classified lists of the more important works on each subject in the library of the Kgl. Kunstgewerbe-museum.

———— DRESDEN: *Kgl. Kunstgewerbeschule.* Katalog der Bibliothek. Dresden: *W. Hoffmann*, 1896-7. 8vo.

    I. Figuren, flach und plastisch, iv and 72 pp. 1896.
    II. Thiere, Pflanzen, Landschaften, flach und plastisch, iv and 48 pp. 1896.
    III. Baukunst, iv and 70 pp. 1896.
    IV. Bildhauerei, iv and 44 pp. 1896.
    V. Malerei und Decorations-Malerei, iv and 60 pp. 1896.
    VI. Arbeiten in Thon, Glas, Edelstein, iv and 56 pp. 1896.
    VII. Arbeiten in Metall, iv and 83 pp. 1896.
    VIII. Arbeiten in Holz, Elfenbein, etc., iv and 74 pp. 1896.
    IX. Textil-Arbeiten, iv and 63 pp. 1896.
    X. Druckausstattung und graphische Künste-Lederarbeiten, iv and 54 pp. 1896.
    XI. Hilfswissenschaften (Politische, Cultur- und Literatur-Geschichte, Mythologie, Trachten- und Wappenkunde), iv and 60 pp. 1896.
    XII. Geschichte u. Theorie von Kunst u. Gewerbe, iv and 79 pp. 1896.

XIII. Bildungswesen für Kunst und Gewerbe (Schulen, Sammlungen, Ausstellungen, Vereine, Innungen), iv and 57 pp. 1896.

XIV. Zeichen-Unterricht, Stilisiren, Farbenlehre, Geometrie, etc., iv and 31 pp. 1896.

Alphabetisches Sach-Verzeichniss und Katalog-Eintheilung, 14 pp. 1897.

Nachtrag I. (für 1896), 39 pp. 1897.

A series of classified and indexed class-lists.

IRON AND STEEL METALLURGY.—*See* METALLURGY.

ITALIAN RENAISSANCE ART.—*See* ART (Italian Renaissance).

LYONS.—BAUDRIER (J.). Bibliographie lyonnaise. Recherches sur les imprimeurs, libraires, relieurs et fondeurs de lettres de Lyon au xvie siècle, 4e série. Avec 175 reproductions en fac-similé. Lyon—Paris: *Picard*, 1899. 8vo, pp. 427.

MECHANICS.—*See also* MINING, MECHANICS AND METALLURGY.

METALLURGY: IRON AND STEEL.—IRON AND STEEL INSTITUTE JOURNAL. General index, vols. xxxvi.-lviii., 1890-1900. With a history of the Iron and Steel Institute by B. H. Brough. London, 1902. 8vo, pp. 511.

———— *See also* MINING, MECHANICS AND METALLURGY.

METEOROLOGY.—SCIENTIFIC ROLL and magazine of systematised notes. Conducted by A. Ramsay. Climate, vol. i.; Part I., General; Part II., Aqueous vapour; Part III., Baric conditions. London: *O'Driscoll, Lennox & Co.,* 1882-99. 2 vols. 8vo.

MILITARY SCIENCE.—MÉMORIAL DE L'OFFICIER DU GÉNIE. Table des matières (1re série, Nos. 1-15, années 1803-48). Par M. Augoyat. Paris, 1848. 8vo, pp. 76.

MILK.—ROTHSCHILD (Henri de). Bibliographia lactaria. Premier supplément (année 1900) à la Bibliographie générale des travaux parus sur le lait et sur l'allaitement jusqu'en 1899. Paris: *Doin*, 1901. Pp. vi, 98.

MINING, MECHANICS, METALLURGY.—NORTH OF ENGLAND INSTITUTE OF MINING AND MECHANICAL ENGINEERS. Subject-matter index of mining, mechanical and metallurgical literature for 1900. Edited by M. W. Brown. Newcastle-upon-Tyne, 1902. 8vo, pp. xxiv, 197. Price 42s.

Entries are registered in class order according to a minutely divided scheme of classification which deserves, but does not possess, an index. A list of some 500 periodicals analysed shows the scope of the undertaking. A bad feature of the scheme is the substitution of a number for the abbreviated title of the work indexed.

MONTPELLIER: DIOCESE.—Bonnet (E.). "Bibliographie du diocèse de Montpellier." In *Mélanges de littérature et d'histoire religieuses*, publiés à l'occasion du jubilé épiscopal de Mgr. de Cabriers, évêque de Montpellier, 1874-99, vol. iii., pp. 305-435. Paris: *Picard*, 1899. 8vo.

MUSEUMS: FRENCH.—France: *Ministère de l'Instruction publique.* Annuaire des Musées scientifiques et archéologiques des départements, 1900. Paris: *Leroux*, 1900. 8vo, pp. iv and 436.
List of museums, with summary of contents, and list of publications.

——— **ETC.: GERMAN.**—Berlin: *Königliche Museen.* Kunsthandbuch für Deutschland. Verzeichnis der Behörden, Sammlungen, Lehranstalten und Vereine für Kunst, Kunstgewerbe und Altertumskunde. 5 Aufl. Berlin: *Spemann*, 1897. 8vo, pp. vi and 676.
A classified list of public and private collections, art academies and schools, art and antiquarian societies, with lists of their publications.

PERIODICAL LITERATURE.—Fletcher (W. I.), and Poole (Mary). Poole's index to periodical literature. Abriged ed. to the end of 1899. Boston: *Houghton, Mifflin & Co.*, 1901. 8vo, pp. 843.

——— ——— **SCIENTIFIC AND TECHNICAL.**—Repertorium der technischen Journal-Literatur. Hrsg. im Kais.-Patentamt, Jahrg., 1900. Berlin: *Heymann*, 1901. La. 8vo, 4 pp. + 1039 col.

——— ——— [Analytical Author-index.] *Royal Society of London.* Catalogue of scientific papers (1800-83). Supplementary volume. Vol. xii. London: *Clay*, 1902. 4to, pp. 32 + 807.
The preface contains the welcome information that the period 1884-1900 is in hand, also a class-index to the first twelve volumes. With the year 1901 the Royal Society ceases its independent action, continuing the publication of author- and class-lists on behalf of the "International Council".

——— ——— [Analytical Author- and Subject-index.] International catalogue of scientific literature. First annual issue [1901]. D, Chemistry; Part I., pp. xiv, 468. M, Botany; Part I., pp. xix, 378. London: *Harrison*. 2 parts. 8vo.

PERU: ANTHROPOLOGY.—Dorsey (G. A.). A bibliography of the anthropology of Peru. 206 pp. Chicago: *Field Columbian Museum*, 1898. 8vo.
Publication 23 (Anthropological series, vol. iii., No. 2) of the Field Columbian Museum.

PHILIPPINE ISLANDS: GEOLOGY.—"List of books and papers on Philippine geology." In *U.S. Geological Survey*, Report xxi., Part III., pp. 594-605.

PHOTOGRAPHY.—*See also* SURVEYING (Photographic).

PHYSICS.—PHYSIKALISCH-TECHNISCHE REICHSANSTALT, *Berlin*. Verzeichnis der Veröffentlichungen, 1887-1900. Berlin: *Springer*, 1901. 4to, pp. 53.

POETRY.—*See also* FRENCH POETRY.

POLITICAL SCIENCE.—DUNNING (W. A.). A history of political theories, ancient and mediæval. New York, 1902. 8vo, pp. xxv, 360.
Pp. 327-45; Bibliography.

—— *Political Science Quarterly.* Index, vols. i.-xv. Part I., Original communications; II., Abstracts; III., Record of political events; IV., Name-index of contributors. London: *Ginn & Co.*, 1902. 8vo, pp. 89.

PRINTING: LYONS.—*See* LYONS: BAUDRIER (J.). Bibliographie lyonnaise, etc.

PSYCHOLOGY.—"Bibliographie der psycho-physiologischen Literatur des J. 1900, m. Unterstützg. v. Prof. H. C. Warren zusammengestellt v. Leo Hirschlaff." [From the *Zeitschr. f. Psychologie u. Physiologie d. Sinnesorgane.*] Leipzig: *Barth*, 1902. La. 8vo, pp. 305-490.

RENAISSANCE ART (ITALIAN).—*See* ART (Italian Renaissance).

SANITARY ENGINEERING.—*See also* HYGIENE AND SANITARY ENGINEERING.

SCIENCE: APPLIED.—*School of Mines Quarterly.* Contents and index, vols. xi.-xx., Nov., 1889-July, 1899. New York: *Columbia University*, 1900. 8vo, pp. 82.

SPONTANEOUS COMBUSTION.—BONELLI (M.). Sulla combustione spontanea dei foraggi. Verona: *Franchini*, 1900. 8vo.
Pp. 65-72: Bibliography.

STARCH: CHEMISTRY AND PHYSIOLOGY.—MEYER (Arthur). Untersuchungen über die Stärkekörner. Jena: *Fischer*, 1895. La. 8vo.
Pp. 311-8: Bibliography.

SURVEYING: PHOTOGRAPHIC.—PAGANINI (P.). Foto grammetria. Milano: *Hoepli*, 1901. 16mo.
Pp. 275-88: Analytical bibliography.

TEXTILE FABRICS (CHEMICAL TECHNOLOGY).—GARCON (Jules). Répertoire général; ou dictionnaire méthodique de bibliographie des industries tinctoriales et des industries annexes depuis les origines jusqu' à la fin de 1896. Technologie et chimie. Paris: *Gauthier Villars*, 1900-1. 3 vols. La. 8vo.
Vol. i. contains a bibliographical introduction and name-index to works entered in the general subject alphabet, which forms vol. ii.-iii.

ULTRAMARINE. — HOFFMANN (Reinhold). Ultramarin. Braunschweig: *Vieweg*, 1902. 8vo.
Pp. 143-54: Bibliography.

VASES (GREEK).—*See* CERAMICS.

WATER: ELECTROLYSIS.—ENGELHARDT (Viktor). "Die Elektrolyses der Wassers." (*Monographien über angewandte Elektro-Chemie*, Band i.) Halle a S.: *Knapp*, 1902. 8vo.
Contains a bibliography of the earlier workers from A.D. 1789-1879; pp. 3-6.

WORMS.—CHITTENDEN (F. H.). "The fall army-worm and variegated cut-worm." *In U.S. Dept. of Agriculture*, 1901: Div. of Entomology, Bulletin 29.
Pp. 40-5: Chronological list.

BIBLIOGRAPHIES OF PARTICULAR PERSONS.

APIAN (Pierre).—VAN ORTROY (F.). Bibliographie de l'œuvre de Pierre Apian. Besançon, 1902. 8vo.
Extrait du Bibliographe moderne (mars-octobre, 1901).

BUONNARROTTI (Michel Angelo).—MONTAIGLON (A. de C. de). "Essai de Bibliographie Michelangelesque." In *Gazette des Beaux Arts*, 2nd series, vol. xiii., pp. 301-12. Paris, 1876. 4to.
Founded on the bibliography of Michel Angelo by L. Passerini.

KEENE (Charles).—PENNELL (J.). The work of Charles Keene. To which is added a bibliography of the books Keene illustrated by W. H. Chesson. London: *Fisher Unwin*, 1897. 4to.
Pp. 277-89: List of books illustrated by Charles Keene.

LEECH (John).—CHAMBERS (C. E. S.). A list of works containing illustrations by John Leech. Edinburgh: *Brown*, 1892. 8vo, pp. 24.

MORRIS (William).—Forman (H. B.). The books of William Morris described, with some account of his doings in literature and in the allied crafts. London: *Hollings*, 1897. 8vo, pp. 224.

NAPOLEON. — Kircheisen (F.). Bibliographie Napoléons. Berlin: *Mittler & Sohn.* 8vo, pp. viii, 188.

OSSIAN.—Tombo (Rudolf), *jr.* Ossian in Germany: bibliography, general survey, Ossian's influence upon Klopstock and the bards. (Columbia University Germanic studies, vol. i., No. 2.) New York: *Macmillan*, 1901. 8vo, pp. 6+157.

PARMENTIER (Antoine Auguste).—Balland (A.). La chimie alimentaire dans l'œuvre de Parmentier. Paris, 1902. 8vo. Pp. 377-437: Contains a bibliography of the writings of Parmentier (165 entries) and of his life.

RUSKIN (John).—Jameson (M. E.). A bibliographical contribution to the study of John Ruskin. Cambridge: *Riverside Press*, 1901. 12mo, 154 pp.

WHISTLER (J. A. McN.).—Albany: *University of the State of New York.* State Library Bulletin, Bibliography No. 1, May, 1895. Guide to the study of J. A. McN. Whistler, compiled by W. G. Forsyth and J. Le R. Harrison, Albany, 1895. 4to, pp. 12.

REVIEWS.

THE LITERATURE OF AMERICAN HISTORY: A Bibliographical Guide; in which the scope, character and comparative worth of books in selected lists are set forth in brief notes by critics of authority. Edited for the American Library Association by J. N. Larned. Boston: Published for the American Library Association by Houghton, Mifflin & Co., 1902. $6 (30s.).

We have been looking forward to the publication of this book with high expectations, and our hope that it would be a proud and notable landmark in the history of annotation has been amply fulfilled. In mere size and extent we have here a bibliographical work that has no predecessor to compare with it since Mr. Swan Sonnenschein's two volumes, *The Best Books* and *A Reader's Guide*, appeared in 1891 and 1895; whilst if we place it beside the previous works that have aimed to furnish readers with comparative estimates of the intrinsic value of books, these are seen to be mere experiments. The present work is the first comprehensive survey, on these lines, of an important branch of human knowledge.

To "appraise" a guide dealing with the character and merits of 4,145 separate books is a task that could only be done satisfactorily after it had been worked with constantly for a long period. Only a historian of equal attainments could reasonably venture to "evaluate" the annotations of such a distinguished body of scholars as have collaborated here. It will perhaps be years before the work will be finally appraised, before its defects will have been revealed, and its excellences fully discovered, by the continual references of students and scholars. For this volume of 600 pages contains the learning and the judgment which hitherto have had to be sought for in a whole library of carefully selected books. I shall merely attempt now to give an external description of the book, with some explanation of the methods adopted to provide readers with the most efficient guidance.

The contributors number forty, about half of whom are professors in the leading American universities, and the remainder, journalists, military experts and others, including, it is interesting to note, seven librarians. "Each department has been given to the best available specialist," Mr. Iles assures us, and the endeavour to give the general reader benefits on a par with those enjoyed by young men and women at the colleges and universities has been well realised. The preface puts the case for such a book admirably :—

"Only those who have to do with the work of public libraries know how much there is of the desire for substantial knowledge among people who can satisfy it nowhere if not at those libraries, and how much such readers are misled towards books which are obsolete, or shoddy-made, or otherwise unprofitable, missing the ones that would instruct them most and inspire them best. All that librarians can do to light the way of the seeker to the worthiest literature is generally being done, with anxious and inventive zeal ; but the utmost they are able to accomplish in their catalogues, without help from special students in a thousand different regions of knowledge, answers to the need of common students scarcely more than a railway map for travellers as compared with a *Baedeker Guide.*"

The first chapter, preceding the bibliography proper, is "a syllabus of existing materials for original study of American history," by the late Paul Leicester Ford. This includes a survey of the historical societies and their papers. Then, in 442 pages, we have the annotated lists, arranged in five main classes : America at large (48 pp.), the United States (289 pp.), the United States by sections (37 pp.), Canada (46 pp.), and Spanish and Portugese America and the West Indies (22 pp.). Prof. Edward Channing adds a valuable appendix containing select lists of books for (1) a good school library, (2) a town library, and (3) a good working library. A most elaborate and exhaustive index to subjects, authors and titles, occupies 100 pages. As I do not propose to criticise the notes, but only to explain their object, I will quote only one specimen as a typical entry :—

Adams, John. Works; with life, notes and illustrations by Charles Francis Adams. Boston: Little. 1850-6. 10 v.

The famous grandson of John Adams was well fitted to collect and order the vast mass of documents, the memorials of the long life-work of the second President. His cool judicial portrayal shows no trace of a tendency to exaggerate the merits of his subject: there is a marked abstention from filial partiality or family glorification. While many of the documents are invaluable, the world now and hereafter will probably most prize the letters and the diary. The character of John Adams is revealed in these in a most attractive light,— as frankly artless almost as Sewall, as abrupt and prejudiced as Dr. Johnson,— testy, full of foibles, self-conscious, but brave and honest to the very core; a brain of the finest power and a heart of oak.—J. K. H.

The word history is interpreted in a wide sense, and the book includes works on Geography and Physiography, Archæology and Anthropology, Discovery and Exploration. And as to the principle of selection adopted and the extent to which "appraisal" is exercised, let me quote the preface again :—

"At the outset, those who consult this work should understand that it is intended to be neither an exhaustive bibliography of American history, nor merely a selection of the best books in that department of literature, nor does it name merely curious books. The selective aim in its preparation has been to embrace the books of every character, good, bad and indifferent, concerning which it seems to be important that readers of various classes should be told what their merit or demerit is. This takes in text-books for school children, as well as source-books for historians and treatises for statesmen; and it includes a considerable class of popular writings from past generations which have disappeared from the book stores, but which survive on the shelves of public libraries, where lingering echoes of an old undeserved reputation help to carry them into unwary hands."

This important paragraph sets forth in clear and unmistakable language the principles that Mr. George Iles and his collaborators have insisted upon as the proper basis for a comprehensive series of guide-books to the various branches of literature and science, such a series as the present work might fittingly inaugurate. Mr. Iles has by lecture and printed article eloquently and convincingly enunciated these principles, and the thousands of dollars which he has generously devoted to the production of the guides will be an even more convincing argument to many. But this paragraph definitely raises the whole question at issue between the advocates and the opponents of evaluation. Is it the proper function of a bibliographical guide to judge, approve or condemn, in this fashion, the books submitted to it by the public? At all events would it not be better to condemn by exclusion such books as the colla-borators in this work have gone out of their way to stigmatise as rubbish? The answer to the latter question is that the book is addressed, not merely to historians, nor merely to students, but to a very wide public, a public including all classes of readers. As every librarian is aware, rubbishy books are an active and mischievous nuisance, that requires active measures to get rid of it. Merely to keep silence about certain books will abate not a jot of their popularity, at least that may be argued from the case of a notorious author whom the critics are in a conspiracy never to mention. And I think the book itself is the most complete refutation of the arguments against appraisal. Imagine what sort of a guide it would have been had the authors confined themselves to descriptive analysis, no matter how full, of the books to be surveyed. It would be worse than offering a map to a man in a fog and denying him the use of a compass. It would be as if a man asked you to point out to him the chief medical or legal authority on some special case, and you put into his hands the London Directory. To quote Mr. Iles again: "A merchant or banker, when he has taken an inventory of his assets, is not content with a mere enumeration of them; he deems a bare list as of no worth whatever until each item has been carefully valued. So I take it, the trustees of literature will enter upon a doubled usefulness when they can set before the public not catalogues merely, but also a judicious discrimination of the more from the less valuable stores in their keeping."

My only complaint against the mode of discrimination adopted is that it is not sufficiently clear and graphic to be used easily and readily as a text-book by uninstructed readers. Had the books been arranged in three classes, elementary books, books for students, and advanced works for historians; and had the most valuable and helpful books been distinguished by an asterisk, its practical usefulness would have been well-nigh doubled.

The system of collaboration adopted combines most of the advantages of signed reviews by scholars of weight with the judicial spirit of a bench of critics. In a private letter to me, Mr. Iles observed.

" By grace of fortune the ablest of our staff have passed upon the most important books; the notes of such a scholar as Prof. Osgood, of Columbia, will never, in my judgment, be excelled, however far appraisal may be carried. Pray observe, as a fine example of the judicial spirit, the Division which offers a selection of the literature of the Civil War, 1861-5. Mark the fairness with which the contributor, General J. D. Cox, presents the best authors on both sides, and how, while a convinced Northener, he speaks only with respect of the Southern cause and its heroes.

"I had an instructive experience with the Canadian part. For thirty years I lived in Canada, and most of my friends are there. It was therefore with regret that I saw last September how inadequate were the Canadian galleys. Fortunately I was then in Montreal and at once went to an intimate friend, Wm. McLennan, a scholar of mark in the field of Canadian history. He consented to remake the whole part. His work is really admirable : he more than doubled the number of titles ; he filled gaps ; he gave unity to the whole ; he wrote an excellent introduction. Here, then is something worth noting : It is most desirable to have each part of a Bibliography under the editorship of a specialist broad enough to give it completeness within its appointed limits, and sufficiently respected to be able to ask for and receive the rewriting of a note, which, in its first form is unsatisfactory."

This glimpse of the thought and anxiety, the industry and unselfish devotion that have gone to the making of this book will enable us to form an initial estimate of its real cost. And a word may be said in conclusion as to the mere vulgar question of finances. Mr. Iles gave $10,000 towards the expenses of this bibliography, and the Editor gave his services free. I presume that the contributors likewise received nothing like an adequate remuneration for their services. Mr. Iles tells me that "the sale of ' Guides' is so limited that the only method is that of private gift for the purpose "; and adds—

" Indeed, my own wish, and I believe it to be shared by my fellow-members of the Publishing Board, is that our Guides may *never* pay. If they ever do pay, the field will immediately tempt the makers of "guides" [to become] secretly or openly, the creatures of publishers. After all, the truth about books will sell more volumes than anything else than the truth, always suspected for what it is by the clear-headed men and women who really control or direct large purchases."

To the two deaths that the preface laments among the forty contributors must now be added that of Paul Leicester Ford, one of the most brilliant and one of the best known on this side of the Atlantic, a death that occurred in dreadfully tragic circumstances only a month or two ago.

ERNEST A. BAKER.

THE AMERICAN LIBRARY ASSOCIATION INDEX. AN INDEX TO GENERAL LITERATURE : biographical, historical and literary essays and sketches, reports and publications of boards and societies dealing with education, health, labour, charities and corrections, etc., etc. By William I. Fletcher. With the co-operation of many librarians. Second edition greatly enlarged and brought down to 1st January, 1900. Boston and New York: Houghton, Mifflin & Co., 1900. 8vo, pp. iv, 679. $10 (£2).

We live in an age of widening interests. The rapid advance in all directions of the iron roads, with their forerunners, the telegraph wires, the steadily increasing rate of ocean travel, the multiplication of cheap books and papers which vie in giving the latest information on every current topic—all of these features of modern life have tended to bring distant countries nearer together and to make them more intimately acquainted with one another than neighbouring towns were a few generations ago. Travels, whether they be made in person, or by proxy through the medium of the printed page, immensely extend the mental horizon. Personages and places famous in history, objects of art and archæology all are thus brought under our notice. But it is not alone in the realm of history that this enlargement of the mental vision is observable. The researches of science are every day revealing new objects for admiration and inquiry. There is little cause to wonder that the subjects which excite men's interests are continually on the increase.

The librarian, however, is not so immediately concerned with the circumstances which have enlarged the field of human inquiry as with the provision of the necessary equipment for the workers in it. His duty and privilege it is, when the catalogue fails to supply the requisite information, to give the necessary direction to the student. Fortunate is he if the subject on which he is consulted happens to be one for which, if personal knowledge fail him, he can refer to some copious index or bibliography. Often he is not so fortunate. Some apparently simple request for information leads to a prolonged but fruitless search. At such times he is wont more than ever to regret his inability, through lack of the needful time, to analyse the numerous volumes which he is well aware call for such treatment, or, as the best substitute for his own work, he longs for some ready-made index to general literature.

There lies before us one of these literary time-savers, *viz.,* the much enlarged second edition of *The American Library Association Index to General Literature,* prepared by William I. Fletcher, the librarian of Amherst College, with the assistance of other members of the American Library Association. It is a volume that calls for unqualified praise, alike for comprehensiveness and accuracy. The following classes of works have been indexed: (1) Essays, biographical, historical and literary; (2) Books of travel and history, to a limited extent only on account of the immense number, and others in which individual persons, places, events or topics are treated with any fullness; (3) Reports and publications of boards and societies dealing with education, hygiene, labour, charities, etc.; (4) Miscellaneous books which for various reasons it might seem desirable to include.

No foreign books are included in the *Index,* and the selection of English ones has wisely been limited to those likely to be found in most American libraries, and, we may add, in English ones. The limitation in the number of entries in the class of history and travel is amply compensated for by the character of them, only the titles of the best works on any place being given. Even with these limitations of scope the *Index* extends to 645 pp., royal 8vo.

We have already not infrequently consulted with profit the pages of this most valuable work. To give some idea of the variety of subjects on which references are found, we propose to open one or two pages at random and to select some of the topics that present themselves. Opening at p. 270 we find references (to mention but a few out of over fifty subjects) to the Baptists of Hertfordshire, Hever Castle, hexameter verse, Peter Heylyn, Thomas Heywood, hibernation of animals, hides and leather in Europe in 1896, hieratic papyri, etc. Turning to p. 589 we make another selection: Treaty obligations, H. Beerbohm Tree, tree-worship, S. P. Tregelles, Bishop Trelawny, Baron Trenck, battle of Trenton, holy coat of Treves, the little Trianon and

La Malmaison, trichiniæ, etc. Surely a sufficiently varied assortment of subjects !

The list of works indexed, which follows the index, occupies thirty-three pages. The titles are given in the most abbreviated form, so that the number of works analysed can be seen to be very large. Roughly we should estimate the number at nearly 3,000, many of them being works in several volumes. The labour involved in the construction of an index of so comprehensive a character will be appreciated by all who have any practical experience in the matter. To men in the literary and journalistic profession it will be a work of the greatest service, and many, we are sure, will add a copy to their private collections. To librarians it is an indispensable work of reference, and we advise every one who has not yet purchased a copy for the shelves of his library to do so without further delay.

THE NEW BRITISH ACADEMY.—The British Academy, which was incorporated by Royal Charter dated the 8th August, is a sister to the Royal Society, representing the students of history, philology, philosophy, economics and law, as the Royal Society represents the students of the natural sciences. The grant is "for the promotion of historical, philosophical and philological studies". Forty-nine gentlemen are named in the charter as first Fellows of the new Academy. The list includes Lord Rosebery, Mr. Balfour, Lord Dillon, Lord Reay, Mr. Bryce, Mr. Lecky, Mr. John Morley, Sir W. R. Anson, Sir C. P. Ilbert, Sir E. Maunde Thompson, Sir R. C. Jebb, Sir Frederick Pollock, Sir Leslie Stephen, Dr. Monro, Dr. A. W. Ward, Dr. Caird, Professors Bywater, Butcher, Cowell, Maitland, Rhys and Skeat, Dr. J. A. H. Murray, and other scholars of distinction. For a student to be elected one of its members will be to receive the country's acknowledgment of the value of his work, and even if this hall-mark of distinction is not prized by the man himself, it will at least be useful for the unlearned public to be thus shown where it may be safe to place its trust, and not least of all will this comparative security be of value to the Government of the day when, as in the appointment, say, of an economist upon a Royal Commission, it has at once to appraise the ability of a man of science and to satisfy the public of the wisdom of its choice.

MR. CARNEGIE AND BIBLIOGRAPHY.—The proposal made by Dr. Emil Reich in his letter to *The Times* some time since for "a selective bibliography for free public libraries," like many other useful proposals appears to have been anticipated, as Mr. Charles W. Sutton has pointed out in his communication to *The Times* of the 16th August, where he says: " I do not know whether Dr. Emil Reich will feel pleased that he has been forestalled in his admirable suggestion, but he will be encouraged to learn that Mr. Carnegie has already responded with noble generosity to a similar proposition which has been made in America. In March last Dr. Billings, the eminent director of the New York Public Library, made to Mr. Carnegie the suggestion that he should give to the American Library Association a special fund, the income of which should be applied to the preparation and publication of such reading lists, indexes and other bibliographical and library aids as would be specially useful in the circulating libraries of that country. The main part of the income would be expended in employing competent persons to prepare the lists, indexes, etc., and to read proofs. The cost of paper and printing would be met by sales to the libraries. It was represented that such a gift would be wisely administered by the Publication Committee of the American Library Association, and that the results would be of great value in promoting the circulation of the best books. In response to this suggestion, Mr. Carnegie sent Dr. Billings a cheque for $100,000 as a donation for the purpose named, and the responsibility of spending the money has been undertaken by the American Library Association."

In a further letter which appeared on the 22nd August, Dr. Emil Reich returns to the advocacy of his project for a selective bibliography, and explains that what Mr. Carnegie is doing by the agency of Dr. J. S. Billings, however good, does not forestall his suggestion. What he wants is not lists, even critical lists of current literature, but an organised survey by from three to five experts of the thirty or forty departments of serious literature ending with the close of the nineteenth century. In this way, by a system which he is ready to explain in detail, " authoritative lists of really useful works might be drawn up, graded according to the needs of small, large, and very large public libraries, and of a character so substantial, of a value so abiding, as have hitherto never been either proposed or realised ". Such lists would be of great use to students, but would obviously need supplementing and revising from time to time. The difficulties of the task which Dr. Reich proposes are immense. Out of the hundreds of editions of the *Complete Angler*, who can select the absolutely best ? Of the very considerable literature that has grown up around the *Imitatio Christi*, who could pick out the editions and the criticisms that should be found in a small, a large, and a very large library ? In some departments of knowledge the progress of research renders obsolete in a few years even excellent books. Yet these may, and often do, retain value as historical documents. But that all the hundreds and thousands of difficulties can be overcome or evaded we do not doubt. Even if the selective bibliography did not reach the standard of perfection that Dr. Reich desires, the result would be a great gain to the serious student. In the vast forest of the literature of facts it is often difficult to see the wood for the trees, and also the trees for the wood ; and a sensible and trustworthy guide would be welcome.

NOTEWORTHY BOOKS.

(Compiled by GUTHRIE VINE, M.A.)

The classification of each work according to Dewey's System of Decimal Classification is given in square brackets.

ÆSCHYLUS. Prometheus Bound ; rendered into English verse by E. R. Bevan. [882.1] 4to. *Bevan.* 5s. *net.*

ÆSOP. Three hundred of Æsop's fables, literally translated from the Greek by G. Fyler Townsend. With illustrations by Harrison Weir. [888.6] 8vo. 256 pp. *Routledge.* 3s. 6d.

ALBEE (E.). The history of English utilitarianism. [171.5] 8vo. 444 pp. *Sonnenschein.* 10s. 6d.

ALBERT (E.). Diagnosis of surgical diseases. [616.07] 8vo. *Hirschfeld.* 18s. *net.*

BAESSLER (A.). Ancient Peruvian art : contributions to the archæology of the Empire of the Incas. Translated by A. H. Keane. Part I. [913.85] Fol. *Asher.* £1 10s. *net.*

BATESON (W.). Mendel's principles of heredity : a defence by W. Bateson. With a translation of Mendel's original papers on hybridisation. [575.1] 8vo. xiv, 212 pp. *Clay.* 4s. *net.*

BEECH (F.). The dyeing of woollen fabrics. [667.2] 8vo. 246 pp. *Scott, Greenwood & Co.* 7s. 6d. *net.*

BERKELEY (George), *Bishop of Cloyne.* The works of G. Berkeley, formerly Bishop of Cloyne. With prefaces, annotations, appendices and an account of his life by A. C. Fraser. [192.3] 8vo. 4 vols. *Clarendon Press.* 24s.

BOWDOIN (W. G.). James M'Neil Whistler : the man and his work. [927.5] 8vo. 78 pp. *Delamore Press.* 3s. 6d. *net.*

BRÉAL (A.). Rembrandt : a critical essay. [759.9] 12mo. 192 pp. *Duckworth.* 2s. *net.*

BRENAN (G.). A history of the house of Percy from the earliest times down to the present century. Edited by W. A. Lindsay. [929.2] 8vo. 2 vols. *Freemantle.* £2 2s. *net.*

BRIERLEY (J.). Ourselves and the universe : studies in life and religion. [204] 8vo. 348 pp. *J. Clarke.* 6s.

BUSLEY (C.). The marine steam engine ; its construction, etc. Vol. i. [621.12] 4to. *Grevel.* £2.

CAFFIN (C. H.). Photography as a fine art. [770] 4to. *Gay & Bird.* 15s. *net.*

CHARPENTIER (P.). Timber : a study of wood in all its aspects, commercial and botanical, showing its different applications and uses. Translated from the French. [674] 8vo. 438 pp. *Scott, Greenwood & Co.* 12s. 6d. *net.*

CHITTENDEN (H. M.). The American fur trade of the Far West: a history of the pioneer trading posts and early fur companies of the Missouri Valley and the Rocky Mountains, and of the overland commerce with Santa Fé. [978] 8vo. 3 vols. *New York.* £2 10s. *net.*

CICERO (M. T.). Epistulæ ad familiares. Edited by L. C. Purser. (*Oxford Classical Texts.*) [876.1] 8vo. *Frowde.* 3s.

COBB (S. H.). The rise of religious liberty in America. [277.8] 8vo. *Macmillan.* 17s. *net.*

CRANE (W.). Bases of design. [740] 8vo. 400 pp. *Bell.* 6s. *net.*

CROSSING (W.). Ancient stone crosses of Dartmoor, etc. Revised edition. [913.42] 8vo. *J. G. Commin.* 7s. 6d. *net.*

DALE (L.). Problems of English constitutional history. [842.42] 8vo. 522 pp. *Longmans.* 6s.

DALMAN (G.). The words of Jesus; considered in the light of post-Biblical Jewish writings and the Aramaic language. Authorised English version by D. M. Kay. [226] 8vo. 364 pp. *T. & T. Clark.* 7s. 6d. *net.*

DAVITT (Michael). The Boer fight for freedom. [968] 8vo. *Funk & Wagnalls.* 6s.

ELLIS (George). Modern practical joinery: a treatise on the practice of joiner's work by hand and machine for the use of apprentices, workmen and builders. [694] 4to. *Batsford.* 12s. 6d. *net.*

FERSEN (*Count* Axel). The diary and correspondence of Count A. Fersen, Grand-Marshal of Sweden, relating to the court of France. Translated by K. P. Wormeley. [944.041] 8vo. 366 pp. *Heinemann.* 21s. *net.*

FYFE (H. C.). Submarine warfare, past, present and future. With a chapter on the probable future of submarine boat construction by Sir E. J. Reid. [623.9] 8vo. 360 pp. *Richards.* 7s. 6d. *net.*

GAIRDNER (J.). The English church in the sixteenth century from the accession of Henry VIII. to the death of Mary. [274.2] 8vo. 446 pp. *Macmillan.* 7s. 6d.

GRADLE (H.). Diseases of nose, pharynx and ear. [616.21] 8vo. 548 pp. *Saunders.* 15s. *net.*

GREEN (E.). Bibliotheca Somersetensis: a catalogue of books, etc., connected with the county of Somerset. [015.4288] 4to. 3 vols. *Taunton, Barnicott.* £3 3s. *net.*

GRIMBLE (A.). The salmon rivers of Scotland. Illustrated by Archibald Thorburn and others. [799] 4to. 412 pp. *Paul.* 21s. *net.*

GULIAN (K. H.). An elementary modern Armenian grammar. [491.54] 8vo. 204 pp. *Low.* 3s.

HATTON (R. G.). Design: an exposition of the principles and practice of the making of patterns. [745] 8vo. 190 pp. *Chapman.* 5s. *net.*

HAYWARD (J. W.). Protoplasm: its origin, varieties and functions. [576.2] 8vo. 52 pp. *Simpkin.* 1s. 6d. *net.*

HEMPEL (W.). Methods of gas analysis. Translated from the third German edition and considerably enlarged by L. M. Dennis. [545.7] 8vo. 510 pp. *Macmillan.* 10s. *net.*

HOLBORN (A.). The Pentateuch in the light of to-day: a simple introduction to the Pentateuch on the lines of the higher criticism. [222.1] 8vo. 124 pp. *T. & T. Clark.* 2s. *net.*

HUEFFER (F. M.). Rossetti : a critical essay on his art. [**759.2**] 12mo. 208 pp. *Duckworth.* 2s. *net.*

HURRELL (John W.). Measured drawings of old oak English furniture, also of some remains of architectural woodwork, plasterwork, metalwork, glazing, etc. (110 plates.) [**684**; refer from **729**] 4to. *Batsford.* £2 2s. *net.*

JEKYLL (Gertude), and MAWLEY (E.). Roses for English gardens. (*Country Life Library.*) [**716.2**] 8vo. 182 pp. *Newnes.* 12s. 6d. *net.*

JENNINGS (A. S.). Paint and colour mixing : a practical handbook for painters and all who have to mix colours. [**667.6**] 8vo. 98 pp. *Spon.* 5s. *net.*

JORDAN (D. S.), and EVERMANN (B. W.). American food and game fishes ; a popular account of all species found in America north of the equator. [**597**] 8vo. *Hutchinson.* 21s. *net.*

JOURDAIN (E. F.). A study in the symbolism of the Divina Commedia. [**851.15**] 8vo. 78 pp. *Norland Press.* 2s. *net.*

KEELING (Elsa d'Esterre). Sir Joshua Reynolds. With a portrait and 20 plates after Reynolds. (*Makers of British Art.*) [**927.5**] 8vo. 244 pp. *W. Scott.* 3s. 6d. *net.*

KENNY (C. S.). Outlines of criminal law ; based on lectures delivered in Cambridge University. [**343**] 8vo. 550 pp. *Clay.* 10s.

KIRKBY (William). The evolution of artificial mineral waters. With views of Jewsbury & Brown's mineral water manufactory, Manchester, and other illustrations. [**668.6**] 8vo. x, 155 pp. *Manchester, Jewsbury & Brown.*

KOVALEVSKY (M.). Russian political institutions : the growth and development of these institutions from the beginnings of Russian history to the present time. [**354.47**] 8vo. *Chicago.* 7s. 6d. *net.*

LADD (G. T.). The philosophy of conduct : a treatise of the facts, principles and ideals of ethics. [**171**] 8vo. *New York.* 18s. *net.*

LARNED (J. N.). A guide to the literature of American history. [**016.973**] 8vo. *Boston.* £1 10s.

LEHNER (S.). Ink manufacture, including writing, copying, lithographic, marking, stamping and laundry inks. Translated from the German fifth edition by Arthur Morris and Herbert Robson. [**667.4**] 8vo. 162 pp. *Scott, Greenwood & Co.* 5s. *net.*

LESPINASSE (Claire Françoise). Letters of C. F. Lespinasse. With notes on her life and character by D'Alembert Marmontel, comte de Guibert, etc., and an introduction by E. A. Sainte-Beuve. Translated by P. Wormeley. [**846.5**] 8vo. 348 pp. *Heinemann.* 21s. *net.*

LIADAIN. Liadain and Curithir. An Irish ninth-century love story ; edited and translated by Kuno Meyer. [**891.6**] 8vo. *Nutt.* 1s. 3d. *net.*

LINN (W. A.). Story of the Mormons from the date of their origin to 1901. [**298**] 8vo. *Macmillan.* 17s. *net.*

LUTZOW, *Count.* The story of Prague. Illustrated by N. Ericksen. (*Mediæval Towns.*) [**943.71**] 12mo. 232 pp. *Dent.* 3s. 6d. *net.*

MACGREGOR (J. G.). An elementary treatise on kinematics and dynamics. [**531**] 8vo. 558 pp. *Macmillan.* 10s. 6d.

MALDEN (H. E.). Trinity Hall ; or, the college of scholars of the Holy Trinity of Norwich in the University of Cambridge. [**878.42**] 8vo. 298 pp. *F. E. Robinson.* 5s. *net.*

Manson (J. A.). Sir Edwin Landseer. (*Makers of British Art.*) [927.5] 8vo. 236 pp. *W. Scott.* 3s. 6d.

Mellor (J. W.). Higher mathematics; for students of chemistry and physics; with special reference to practical work. [510.2] 8vo. 566 pp. *Longmans.* 12s. 6d. *net.*

Miall (L. C.). Injurious and useful insects: an introduction to the study of economic entomology. [591.6] 8vo. 264 pp. *Bell.* 3s. 6d.

Miller (W.). Mediæval Rome: from Hildebrand to Clement VIII., 1073-1600. (*Story of the Nations.*) [945] 8vo. 394 pp. *Unwin.* 5s.

Mueller (E. B. I.). Lord Milner and South Africa. [968] 8vo. 784 pp. *Heinemann.* 15s. *net.*

Naylor (W.). Trades waste: its treatment and utilisation. With special reference to the prevention of river pollution. [628.541] 8vo. 284 pp. *Griffin.* 21s. *net.*

Neilson (Robert M.). The steam turbine. [621.12] 8vo. *Longmans.* 7s. 6d. *net.*

Newell (F. H.). Irrigation in the United States. [626.8] 12mo. *New York.* 10s. 6d.

Norman (H.). All the Russias: travels and studies in contemporary European Russia, Finland, Siberia, Caucasus and Central Asia. [914.7] 8vo. 492 pp. *Heinemann.* 18s. *net.*

Oesterley (W. O. E.). Studies in the Greek and Latin versions of the book of Amos. [224.6] 8vo. 120 pp. *Clay.* 4s. *net.*

Oman (C.). Seven Roman statesmen of the later republic: the Gracchi, Sulla, Crassus, Cato, Pompey, Cæsar. [937.05] 8vo. 356 pp. *E. Arnold.* 6s.

Paulsen (F.). Immanuel Kant: his life and doctrine. Translated from the revised German edition by J. E. Creighton and A. Lefevre. [193.2] 8vo. 440 pp. *J. C. Nimmo.* 10s. 6d. *net.*

Pike (Zebulon Montgomery). Expeditions of Z. M. Pike to the head waters of the Mississippi river, the interior parts of Louisiana, Mexico and Texas, 1805 to 1807. Edited by Dr. Elliott Cones. [917.8] 8vo. 3 vols. *New York.* £2 10s. *net.*

Plummer (C.). The life and times of Alfred the Great. Ford lectures for 1901. [942.01] 8vo. 244 pp. *Frowde.* 5s. *net.*

Pollard (A. F.). Henry VIII. Illustrated from contemporary works of art. [942.052] 4to. 310 pp. *Gonpil.* £3 3s. *net.*

Poole (S. L.). The story of Cairo. (*Mediæval Towns.*) [962.1] 12mo. 360 pp. *Dent.* 4s. 6d. *net.*

Poore (G. V.). The earth in relation to the preservation and destruction of contagia: Milroy lectures, 1899. With other papers on sanitation. [614.7] 8vo. 268 pp. *Longmans.* 5s.

Psenosiris. The epistle of Psenosiris: an original document from the Diocletian persecution (Papyrus 713 Brit. Mus.). Edited and explained by Adolf Deissmann. [272.1] 8vo. x, 66 pp. *Black.* 2s. 6d. *net.*

Robinson (J. Armitage). The study of the gospels. (*Handbooks for the Clergy.*) [226] 8vo. *Longmans.* 2s. 6d. *net.*

Rouse (William H. D.). Greek votive offerings: an essay in the history of Greek religion. [292] 8vo. 480 pp. *Clay.* 15s. *net.*

Sabatier (A.). Outlines of a philosophy of religion based on psychology and history. [201] 8vo. 364 pp. *Hodder & Stoughton.* 7s. 6d.

SEDGWICK (W. T.). Principles of sanitary science and the public health. [614] 8vo. *Stock.* 12s. 6d. *net.*

SHARP (G.). Birds in the garden : studies with a camera. With 100 illustrations. [598.2] 8vo. 122 pp. *Dent.* 7s. 6d. *net.*

SIBERIAN RAILWAY. A guide to the great Siberian railway. English translation by Miss Kúkol-Yasnopólsky, revised by J. Marshall. [915.7] 8vo. *Stanford.* 18s. *net.*

STAPLETON (A.). Memorials of the Huguenots in America, with special reference to their emigration to Pennsylvania. [277.8] 8vo. *Philadelphia.* 7s. 6d.

STEVENS (W. J.). Investment and speculation in British railways. [882.6] 8vo. 268 pp. *E. Wilson.* 4s. *net.*

STURT (H.). Personal idealism : philosophical essays by eight members of Oxford University. [141] 8vo. 404 pp. *Macmillan.* 10s. *net.*

STYAN (K. E.). A short history of sepulchral cross slabs, with reference to other emblems found thereon. [718; refer from 246] 8vo. *Bemrose.* 7s. 6d. *net.*

TEMPLE (*Sir* Richard). The progress of India, Japan and China in the nineteenth century. [950] 8vo. *W. & R. Chambers.* 5s. *net.*

TENNANT (F. R.). The origin and propagation of sin. The Hulsean lectures in 1901-2. [288.2] 8vo. 248 pp. *Clay.* 3s. 6d. *net.*

THOMSON (David Croal). The Barbizon school of painters : Corot, Rousseau, Diaz, Millet, Daubigny, etc. With 130 illustrations. [759.4] 4to. *Simpkin.* £2 2s.

TUCKERMAN (Alfred). Index to the literature of the spectroscope, 1887-1900. (*Smithsonian Miscel. Col.*) [016.53584] 8vo. 374 pp. *Wesley.* 7s. *net.*

VIGNAUD (H.). Toscanelli and Columbus : the letter and chart of Toscanelli on the route to the Indies by way of the West sent in 1474 to the Portuguese Fernam Martins and later on to Christopher Columbus : a critical study on the authenticity and value of these documents and the sources of the cosmographical ideas of Columbus, followed by the various texts of the letter, with translations, annotations, several facsimiles and a map. [973.1] 8vo. 386 pp. *Sands.* 10s. 6d. *net.*

WAITE (Arthur Edward). The doctrine and literature of the Kabalah. [181.8] 8vo. *Theosophical Publishing Society.* 7s. 6d. *net.*

WILLINGTON (J. R.). Dark pages of English history : a short account of the penal laws against Catholics from Henry VIII. to George IV. [282.42] 8vo. 184 pp. *Art and Book Co.* 2s. 6d. *net.*

YOUNG (Keith). Delhi, 1857 : the siege, assault and capture as given in the diary and correspondence of Col. K. Young. Edited by Gen. Sir H. W. Norman and Miss K. Young. With a memoir and introduction by Sir H. W. Norman. [954.5] 8vo. 398 pp. *Chambers.* 21s. *net.*

LIBRARY ASSOCIATION: PROCEEDINGS AND NOTICES.

Meeting at Wigan, 16th July, 1902.

A MEETING of the Library Association was held at Wigan on Wednesday, 16th July. About fifty members and friends were present during the day.

At eleven o'clock the visitors assembled in the reference department of the Wigan Free Library, where they were heartily welcomed by the Mayor (Alderman R. E. Kellett, J.P.). Councillor J. T. Gee (vice-chairman of the Wigan Library Committee) having been elected chairman for the day, the company inspected the library and proceeded to the new Technical College in Library Street, Mr. C. M. Percy, F.G.S., acting as cicerone. After inspecting the college building, now nearing completion, the members, at the invitation of the Mayor, visited Standish, driving (by kind permission of Lord Crawford) through the Haigh Plantations. At Standish the members were met by the Rev. C. W. N. Hutton, M.A. (the rector), and Mr. J. M. Ainscough, J.P. (church-warden), and conducted over the ancient church. After inspecting the parish registers and old communion plate, the party visited the Market Cross and the stocks, returning to Wigan soon after two o'clock.

On arriving at Wigan the members were entertained to luncheon at the Royal Hotel at the invitation of Mr. Henry Flint, of Wigan, a member of the Association. The Mayor presided, and proposed the health of the King in a loyal and patriotic speech, after which "God Save the King" was sung. Councillor Plummer (Manchester) then proposed the health of Mr. Flint.

After luncheon the members proceeded to the library, where a meeting was held in the reference-room under the chairmanship of Councillor Gee.

The first paper was read by Mr. J. P. Edmond, librarian to Lord Crawford, dealing with Capital Letters in printing and cataloguing, and was discussed by Mr. Folkard (Wigan) and Mr. Sutton (Manchester), the latter moving that the paper should be printed in the RECORD. Replying to the discussion, Mr. Edmond contended that what was wanted was a systematic use and treatment of capitals, and gave instances to enforce his argument. There was no better guide, in his opinion, than the authorised version of the English Bible.

Mr. C. W. SUTTON, M.A. (Manchester), then opened a discussion on the employment of women assistants in libraries. He thought it was obvious that the profession was as suitable for women as for men, but that there were few inducements for them to take up the work; it was an employment full of drudgery, ill paid, involving long hours, scanty leisure, and few prizes, the restricted means of the governing bodies making it impossible for them to offer salaries commensurate with the services demanded. Committees and librarians were obliged to take such boys and girls as would come for the meagre salaries offered, and it was remarkable how in course of time the former qualified themselves and proved efficient librarians: the girls must show their merit to be equal to that of men. He had some hopes that librarianship and bibliography might be introduced into the curriculum of the Manchester School of Technology. In the branch libraries at Manchester they had now close upon a hundred women assistants, some of whom had risen to be branch librarians, with salaries from £60 to £95 a year; they proved steady, regular and reliable assistants, doing what they were told to do with intelligence and obedience, but he was inclined to think women were too unambitious.

Councillor PLUMMER (Manchester) deplored the listlessness of women assistants, and thought that there was the opportunity, if the disposition was manifest, for women to attain to a higher sphere in library work.

Mr. COWELL (Liverpool) said women did not take library work seriously, because they never lost the idea of marriage. No doubt that was the reason the women assistants at Liverpool preferred to contract out of the Superannuation Scheme, because they did not expect to remain in the service of the Corporation until they were eligible for pensions.

Mr. FOLKARD (Wigan) said the experiment had been tried in Wigan, and he thought that in the reference department and in cataloguing and book-keeping the work of women was equally good with that of men.

Councillor GEE agreed that women were better adapted for reference and cataloguing work than for the lending library, but contended that while girls could get better salaries as teachers there was no encouragement for them to take up library work.

Some interesting particulars and statistics having been given by Mr. G. L. Campbell (Wigan) relating to the Boys' Reading Room and Library presented to the town by Sir Francis Powell, M.P. for Wigan, Mr. Folkard spoke a few words on the subject of the Wigan Reference Library catalogue now in course of publication, and stated the progress made with this important work, which has reached the letter M, and numbers about 2,300 printed pages.

Votes of thanks were then passed to the Mayor and Corporation of Wigan for the use of the library, to the various gentlemen who had read papers, to the Chairman, and to the Rev. C. W. N. Hutton, Mr. Ainscough and Mr. C. M. Percy for their services during the day.

At the close of the proceedings the members were entertained to tea by the Mayor.

Meeting at Richmond, 17th July, 1902.

A very successful meeting of the Library Association took place at Richmond, Surrey, on 17th July, when about a hundred members and friends visited the borough. The visitors assembled at the Richmond Library soon after two o'clock, and after inspecting the library proceeded to the Town Hall by way of the Green and through the historic archway of the Old Palace. At the Town Hall they were received in the Council Chamber by the Mayor (Alderman Alfred Aldin, J.P.), attended by the Town Clerk and Macebearer, and Councillor Clifford Edgar, chairman of the Library Committee.

The Mayor having been voted to the chair, welcomed the Association to Richmond on behalf of the Burgesses and Town Council.

The Honorary Secretary then read the minutes of the Fifth Monthly Meeting and the Meeting at Nottingham, which were confirmed and signed by the Chairman, and Messrs. Davis and Doubleday having been nominated scrutineers of the ballot, the following candidates, approved by the Council, were duly elected as members:—

Mr. William Andrews, Hull Subscription Library, Royal Institution, Hull.

Mr. Frederick Vallance James, Librarian and Curator, Museum and Public Library, Maidstone.

Mr. W. Addis Miller, M.A., Assistant, University Library, Edinburgh.

Mr. William Wall, Journalist, Upper Dicconson Street, Wigan.

Mr. A. A. BARKAS, librarian of the Richmond Public Library, then read the paper of the evening: "A Richmond Fifteenth-century Library," which we hope to print in another issue.

Following this paper Mr. Barkas added some notes on the Richmond Free Library.

Mr. DOUBLEDAY (Hampstead) and Mr. NORRIS MATHEWS (Bristol) spoke in terms of eulogy of the interesting papers read by Mr. Barkas, and Alderman Burt, speaking as a private visitor, complimented Mr. Barkas for his invaluable help to readers when in any literary difficulty. Mr. BEER, librarian of the Public Libraries of New Orleans, also added a few remarks, and a formal vote of thanks was passed to Mr. Barkas.

The HON. SECRETARY proposed a vote of thanks to the Mayor for his kindness and courtesy in receiving them, which was seconded by Mr. NORRIS MATHEWS, who wished that all meetings of the Association could be held under such pleasant conditions. Thanks were also tendered, on the motion of Mr. CECIL DAVIS, to the Chairman and Committee of the Public Library for the excellent arrangements made for the meeting.

Mr. CLIFFORD EDGAR having responded, the visitors adjourned to the Mayor's parlour, and after partaking of afternoon tea, kindly provided by the Mayor, proceeded by way of the river side and the Terrace Gardens to Doughty House, where at six o'clock they were received by Sir Frederick and Lady Cook in the galleries, and inspected the celebrated art treasures collected there. The visitors were entertained with music by pupils from the Royal College of Music, Miss Laurence contributing "Hear ye, Israel," from Mendelssohn's "Elijah".

On leaving Doughty House the members proceeded to the Star and Garter Hotel, where Councillor Edgar entertained about 140 ladies and gentlemen to dinner. The guests were received by Councillor and Mrs. Edgar in the Princes Hall, and before dinner the entire party were photographed on the terrace of the hotel. The chair was taken by Mr. Clifford Edgar, supported by the Mayor. In proposing the "King," the CHAIRMAN said there was a special meaning to their toast of the King's health that night, and they would all earnestly pray that His Majesty who was on the high road to recovery might be spared to his people for many years. The Chairman then gave "The Library Association" which, he said, could look back upon twenty-five years of valuable and important work, and had received the honour of a royal charter. The Association promoted the adoption of the Free Libraries Acts, efficiency of library administration, status of librarianship, bibliographical work, and in addition conducted examinations. It was not inappropriate that the Association, which was entering upon its second quarter century, should visit Richmond this Coronation year, when the Richmond Library had attained its majority. It was, with one exception, the first library established under the Public Libraries Acts in the London area, and they were justly proud of its influence, and did not fear comparison with any other. He was glad to welcome the members of the Association to that home of hospitality, the windows of which commanded a view which was difficult to equal and impossible to surpass. Thanks to the efforts of the London County Council and the exertions of many public spirited men, including His Worship the Mayor of Richmond and Alderman Burt, a member of the Free Library Committee, the danger which threatened that view had been averted. He had little doubt that the members of the Library Association if they dined there in fifty years' time would still look upon the same glorious view.

Mr. H. R. TEDDER (hon. treasurer), in responding to the toast, was glad to say that the membership of the Association was steadily progressing, and the members were most grateful to the Chairman for the splendid entertainment they had enjoyed. On behalf of the members. of the Association he warmly thanked the Chairman for the kind welcome he had extended to them that day.

Mr. L. INKSTER (hon. secretary) then proposed the " Borough of Richmond," referring to the age of the town, but the infancy of the borough.   He congratulated the authorities on the success of their working class dwellings and of their public library, and thought the whole country, he might almost say the Empire, was indebted to Richmond for the effort made in saving the view from the Hill. Chiefly, as members of the Association, were they indebted to the borough, as represented by the Mayor, for the kindly welcome they had received.

The MAYOR, in returning thanks, referred to the saving of the Richmond Hill view, and said it was an achievement of which he was specially proud, as it had taken place during his year of office.

Mr. CHARLES WELCH proposed the last toast, that of their host and Chairman. They knew that Mr. Edgar enjoyed many distinctions, but they knew him that evening as their very generous host. He had displayed unbounded liberality, and Mrs. Edgar had charmingly assisted him in the reception.

Mr. CLIFFORD EDGAR, who was enthusiastically received, thanked the company on behalf of himself and Mrs. Edgar for the cordiality with which they had received the toast. It was a great pleasure to him to have been the instrument of bringing them together, and he desired to acknowledge the great assistance he had received from Mr. Barkas.

An excellent musical programme was provided and carried out in its entirety during the evening.

Official Notes.

Library Association Classes.—The council have arranged with the Governors of the London School of Economics for classes in

I. Elementary Bibliography ;

II. Cataloguing, Classification and Shelf Arrangement,

to be held at the London School of Economics, Passmore Edwards Hall, Clare Market, W.C., during the session which begins in the autumn of the present year.

The lecturers on these subjects will be nominated by the Council, the classes will be open to all comers, and the Council will continue to hold the professional examinations and to grant certificates.

The classes will be under the management of a Committee composed in equal proportions of members of the Governing Body of the School of Economics and the Council of the Library Association.

Each course will consist of ten lectures, and the Council of the Library Association will pay half the fees of students approved by them.

Annual Meeting, 1902.—The following notice has been circulated amongst the members of the Association:—

> " Whitcomb House, Whitcomb Street,
> " Pall Mall East, S.W.,
> " 18*th July*, 1902.

" Dear Sir (or Madam),

"Your attendance is requested at the Twenty-fifth Annual Meeting of this Association, which will be held at Birmingham, by invitation of the Free Libraries Committee of the Birmingham City Council, the Council of the Birmingham University, and the Committee of the Birmingham Old Library, on 23rd, 24th, 25th and 26th September, for the transaction of the annual business of the Association, and of such other business as may be lawfully dealt with. The Meeting will begin, in the Council Chamber, Council House, Birmingham, on Tuesday, 23rd September, at 10 A.M.

"BUSINESS.

" 1. Installation of the President.

" 2. The Scrutineers' Certificate as to the result of the Election for Officers and Council will be read.

" 3. Vote of Thanks to the Retiring President (G. K. Fortescue, Esq.).

" 4. The Candidates proposed since the last Monthly Meeting, and approved by the Council, will be balloted for.

" *The Council will (under the provisions of Bye-law* 16) *admit as Local Members, those Subscribers of One Guinea and upwards, who may desire to attend the Meeting and Receptions.*

" 5. The President will deliver the Annual Address.

" 6. Papers and Discussions.

" 7. Notices of Motion for the Annual Business Meeting, as follows:—

"(*a*) By the Council.

" ' That the following Addition be made to Bye-law No. 5:—

" ' Provided that at each Annual Election of Council, two London Members and three Country Members shall be disqualified for nomination at the Annual Election in the following year, but shall become eligible again at the Election in the succeeding year. The Members so disqualified shall be those who receive the least number of votes.'

"(*b*) By Mr. Bernard Kettle.

" ' To ammend the Addition to Bye-law No. 5, submitted by the Council, as follows :—

" ' That all words after " Provided that " be struck out, and that the following words be substituted, *viz.* :—

" ' The 32 Councillors be elected for four years, one-fourth '(in the proportion of three London and five Country Members) retiring annually by rotation, who shall not be eligible for nomination either as Councillors or Vice-Presidents for one year. For the purposes of bringing this new procedure into operation, Councillors elected in 1903 shall retire as follows: The fourth then polling the highest number of votes shall retire in 1907; the next fourth in 1906; the next fourth in 1905; and the remaining fourth in 1904.'

"A complete programme of the Proceedings, and the arrangements made by the Local Committee, will be issued at a later date.

"I am, dear Sir (or Madam),

"Yours faithfully,

"LAWRENCE INKSTER,

"*Hon. Secretary.*"

Important.

Members who propose to attend the Annual Meeting at Birmingham are requested to notify Mr. W. S. Pritchett, the Council House, Birmingham, without delay.

Education Committee Notices.—The next professional examination of the Library Association will be held in January, 1903, at centres to suit the convenience of candidates. Full particulars may be obtained from the Hon. Secretary of the Education Committee. Copies of the syllabus and questions set at recent examinations may also be seen in the *Library Association Year Book*, the 1902 issue of which is now ready. It has been issued to members and associates, but non-members may obtain copies from the Assistant Secretary, price one shilling *net*.

The next series of classes will commence on 15th October at 3.30 P.M., and will be held at the London School of Economics, Clare Market, E.C. A course of ten lectures on "Elementary Bibliography" will be given by Mr. J. D. Brown, and also on Wednesdays during the Michaelmas term a course of lectures on "Bibliographies of Special Subjects" will be given by various specialists. The Association will pay half the fees of any students nominated by one of its members. Further particulars of these lectures may be had on application to the Hon. Secretary of the Education Committee, or to the Director of the London School of Economics.

An account of the relations of the Association with the London School of Economics as to the above lectures will be found in the report of the Education Committee, contained in the report of the Council to be presented to the forthcoming Annual Meeting.

Northern Counties Library Association.

The Quarterly Meeting of the above Association was held on the 7th July, at the Alexandra Hotel, Harrogate, by invitation of the Mayor and the Library Committee.

About forty members and visitors were present, including the president, Mr. Basil Anderton, B.A.

The proceedings opened with a hearty welcome from the Mayor (Alderman Simpson, J.P.).

A meeting of the Executive Committee was held during the morning, at which various modifications in the Rules of the Association as to the method of electing the committee were agreed upon. It was also decided that in order to improve the financial position of the Association, the subscription from the new year be as follows: Chief Librarians, 5s.; Branch Librarians and Senior Assistants, 2s. 6d.; other Assistants, 1s. per annum.

It was resolved upon the motion of Mr. R. K. Hill seconded by Mr. Wm. Andrews—

"That the grateful thanks of the Association be accorded to Mr. Andrew Carnegie for the splendid gifts to Library and Educational Authorities in general, and particularly for the timely aid rendered at Keighley, Workington, Hartlepool, Dalton-in-Furness, Cockermouth, and Aspatria, which towns are within the district of the Northern Counties Library Association".

33*

The following papers were read and provoked considerable discussion:—

1. "The Inter-relations of Books." By the President. (This paper is printed in full in another part of the present issue.)

2. "Juvenile Reading and the Selection of Books for Juveniles." By Mr. Alf. Errington of the South Shields Public Library.

3. Essay on "Prepare an Estimate of Expenditure for an Established Public Library whose income is £750 *net* per annum, showing what proportion of the money to be spent on books would be devoted to history, literature, fiction and science". By Mr. D. W. Herdman of the Newcastle-on-Tyne Public Libraries. (First prize winner in the competition.)

4. "The Literary and Historical Side of Harrogate." By Mr. G. W. Byers, librarian, Harrogate.

Visits were afterwards paid to the Public Library, the Winter Gardens, where afternoon tea was provided, to the Royal Baths and in the evening to the Royal Spa Concert Rooms.

Votes of thanks to the Mayor, to the other gentlemen who by their kind hospitality had contributed to the success of the meeting, and to the Harrogate librarian (Mr. Byers), brought a most interesting and enjoyable meeting to a close.

We notice that every public library in the six northern counties, north of Hull, Huddersfield and Preston, with the exception of Sowerby Bridge, Stockton and Thornaby-on-Tees, is now affiliated to the Northern Counties Library Association, which has a roll of about eighty-three members.

COMMUNICATIONS.

THIS department of the RECORD, if properly appreciated, should prove of great practical value to our readers, affording them as it does a ready medium of inter-communication. We therefore invite our readers to make free use of these columns for giving expression to views, criticisms and suggestions upon any subject that properly comes within the scope of librarianship and bibliography.

To the Editor of THE LIBRARY ASSOCIATION RECORD.

Re Rating of Public Libraries.

SIR,

The question of as to how to get exempt from local rates has often been asked, and answered by the Hon. Solicitor to the Library Association. We at Hyde have accepted his advice, and have for three years refused to pay any rates, on the grounds of having complied with the Registrar's conditions, and have been granted a certificate of exemption, which is as follows: "It is hereby certified that this (*Hyde Public Free Library*) Society is entitled to the benefit of the Act, 6 & 7 Vict., cap. 36, intituled, 'An Act to exempt from County, Borough, Parochial and other Local Rates, Lands and Buildings Occupied by Scientific or Literary Societies'".

We have presented this certificate to the Assessment Committee, and have on three different occasions been before them, and pleaded to all intents and purposes for them to accept the certificate, or otherwise put us on a nominal assessment.

We have quoted the judges' statements as regards the Manchester case, reported in *The Library*, vol. viii., pp. 401-9, also the exemption of the Royal College of Music; besides these we have stated that independent of the Registrar's certificate, we ought to be exempt on the grounds of "none beneficial occupation," as was granted to the "L.C.C. *v.* Lambeth," in which the Council were held not rateable for Brockwell Park under "none beneficial occupation". With all this and other evidence of what we have to contend with out of a small income, together with a list of public libraries exempt from all rates and taxes, which were copied from Greenwood's *Year Book*, we could make no impression. The Assessment Committee have had Counsel's opinion, which, as we were aware, stated that the Committee were not bound to accept the Registrar's certificate. Here, then, is the English law! The Registrar states, if you comply with certain conditions and pay a registering fee of one guinea, I will grant you a certificate of exemption. This, as I have previously stated, we did. We get the certificate and hand it to the Assessment Committee who will not accept it.

What is our next course? We are informed that we must appeal to Quarter Sessions, and still refuse to pay. But when a library is some

£400 in debt, besides having to pay yearly instalments of principal and interest of over £60 out of an income of £500, the question is, where is the money to come from? Should the money be forthcoming we might meet at Quarter Sessions with the same obstinate and unsympathetic spirit as the local Assessment Committee, and lose our case and perhaps be involved in all the costs. What is wanted to settle this most annoying and vexed question is that an Act of Parliament should be passed, so that all public libraries shall be exempt, and not the poor struggling library, rated up to the hilt, having to pay, as is the case here, and only a distance of a few miles away a wealthy library totally exempt. Failing an Act of Parliament, if those libraries who have to pay rates would combine together as regards costs, and take a case to Quarter Sessions, or if need be further, something might be done in this direction, or at any rate to know exactly where we stand as regards the certificate of exemption.

Could not the Library Association take this matter up, and, if possible, rouse some enthusiasm in the country, so that instead of one poor library having to find all the money to fight the question, it could be more universally divided.

I shall be pleased to hear of any other course that can be taken, or of any other library that has been to Quarter Session and the result.

It is a question that ought to be kept to the front in library legislature, and in my opinion none are so capable as the Library Association to keep it there and at the same time to give it every assistance.

Any librarian similarly situated might correspond with me, and also bring the matter before his chairman's notice, so that if there is any possibility whatever of public libraries being relieved from this monstrous burden, we may each take our part in seeing that it is done.

I am,
Yours truly,
JOHN CHORTON,
Librarian.

BOROUGH OF HYDE PUBLIC FREE LIBRARY,
26th August, 1902.

To Publishers, Booksellers and Library Furnishers.

•••••••••••••••••••••••••••••••••

THE attention of Publishers, Booksellers and Library Furnishers is called to the advantages of **The Library Association Record** as an effective advertising medium.

The Journal, which is published regularly each month, is the official organ of The Library Association, and circulates in no fewer than 600 libraries up and down the country, as well as amongst the more prominent book-lovers and collectors.

Furnishing, as it does, the transactions of The Library Association, with notices of forthcoming meetings, in addition to library notes and news from all parts of the world, it is eagerly looked for and scanned each month by librarians, being, in fact, their official medium of intercommunication.

Not only does the **Record** circulate in the United Kingdom, it has a much wider sphere of influence, having subscribers in most of the British Colonies, as well as in the principal Countries of Europe.

Our aim in making this announcement is to secure a representative set of advertisements which may serve as a Directory of Library Furnishers, whether in fixtures, stationery, books or other accessories. The advantages of such a medium must be quite obvious to all firms in any way catering for the library, enabling them, as it does, to keep themselves constantly before not only librarians but members of Library Committees and book-collectors.

No advertisement will be received which is not strictly in keeping with the character of the Journal.

◆ ◆ ◆

SCALE OF CHARGES.

	Page.	Half Page.	Quarter Page.
Back of Cover - - - -	£3 0 0	£2 0 0	£1 5 0
Inside Cover and Pages Facing			
Matter or Cover - - -	2 2 0	1 7 6	0 17 6
Any other Page- - - -	1 11 6	1 1 0	0 13 4

Less than Quarter Page, 4s. per Inch Single Column.

Reduction on a Series of	Three.	Six.	Twelve.
Insertions - - -	5 per cent.	10 per cent.	20 per cent.

Advertisements should be sent to the Assistant Secretary at the Offices of the Association, Whitcomb House, Whitcomb Street, Pall Mall East, S.W.; or to Mr. A. E. Bennetts, 176 Milkwood Road, London, S.E., not later than the 20th of each month.

JOHN & ED. BUMPUS, Ltd.,

350 OXFORD STREET,

LONDON, W.

New and Second-hand Booksellers.

THE LARGEST RETAIL BOOKSELLERS IN THE KINGDOM.

LIBRARIANS of Public Libraries are solicited to apply for Tenders for the supply of New Books.

Messrs. BUMPUS have almost invariably been successful in obtaining orders for the supply of Public Libraries when Tenders have been submitted to open competition.

A LARGE STOCK OF

SECOND-HAND BOOKS

Always on hand, from the marked prices of which a Liberal Discount is allowed to Public Libraries.

CATALOGUES ISSUED.

"REMAINDERS" sold at a small percentage upon cost price.

Printed for the Proprietors (THE LIBRARY ASSOCIATION) by
THE ABERDEEN UNIVERSITY PRESS LIMITED.

FOR NOTICE OF NEXT MEETING, SEE PAGE 566

VOL. IV.   OCTOBER—NOVEMBER, 1902   Nos. 10-11

THE

Library Association Record

A MONTHLY MAGAZINE OF LIBRARIANSHIP AND BIBLIOGRAPHY

THE LIBRARY ASSOCIATION

EDITED BY

HENRY GUPPY, M.A.

LIBRARIAN OF THE JOHN RYLANDS LIBRARY, MANCHESTER

London:

PUBLISHED BY THE LIBRARY ASSOCIATION

AT WHITCOMB HOUSE, WHITCOMB STREET

PALL MALL EAST, LONDON, S.W.

Price Two Shillings Net

CONTENTS.

The Library Association Record,

OCTOBER—NOVEMBER, 1902.

THE WORLD OF BOOKS.

BEING THE PRESIDENTIAL ADDRESS OF PROFESSOR W. MACNEILE DIXON, LITT.D., LL.B., TO THE LIBRARY ASSOCIATION AT BIRMINGHAM, 23RD SEPTEMBER, 1902.

WERE it not forbidden by your courtesy, gentlemen, you would naturally ask for an explanation of my presence before you on so important an occasion; you would naturally inquire how so distinguished an office, dignified by the great names associated with it in the past, should to-day have fallen to my lot. I see myself surrounded by men of wider experience, of maturer scholarship, whose lives have been given to the public service in a sphere of work wherein I am no more than an amateur. I am conscious that I have not earned the right to address you from this chair. But I have the good fortune to be connected with the University of Birmingham, and this city, desiring to do honour to the youngest of its public institutions, conceived that a young and undistinguished member of its University staff would most appropriately represent so new and unproven a foundation. Birmingham desired to do honour to its University, and your Association with the greatest good-will accepted the city's nomination to your Presidential chair. To my fellow-citizens and to you, gentlemen, my thanks are due; I can assure you that I am a most grateful recipient of so high and unexpected an honour. It is therefore with no little degree of pride that I join with my Lord Mayor in bidding you a warm welcome to Birmingham ; a city which has always taken the liveliest interest in the objects of your Association ; on a former occasion had the honour of receiving it, and still numbers among its leaders of thought one of your ex-Presidents, Mr. G. J. Johnson ; a city whose name is written large in the history of Liberalism, and is hardly less famous throughout the world to-day than the capital itself, since to it the people of England owe an unshaken pillar of their Empire.

While, however, it is with pride and pleasure that I find myself before you in so honourable a capacity, I feel that it would be highly impolitic, not to say presumptuous in me, to address to you any remarks upon the technical side of the work of your society, and I trust therefore that I shall have your pardon if I consult not your interests, but my own safety, and attempt to escape into a more abstract region of thought.

Of collections of books in general I suppose the broadest and most salient characteristic is that they induce a retrospect ; we turn with them to face the past, and they offer us a view of things through other men's eyes, eyes for the most part that have long since closed upon terrestrial affairs.   In a library the secular intervals are bridged by a single shelf and the generations of men meet under one roof.   We find ourselves in a parliament of man.   And if it were possible to discover, as in some measure, indeed, it may be possible, if it were possible, it could not fail to be interesting and important to know what advice this great oracle, as I may call it, of human experience, wise with the wisdom of ages, would offer to men to-day ; what it would declare to be the things in life that are truly of consequence, that really matter. The well-advised oracle of Apollo on a certain occasion pronounced Socrates to be the wisest of men, the same Socrates whom the Athenians accused of impiety, and who suffered death at their hands.   Later opinion is, on the whole, against the Athenians, and considers that they were not wiser than the oracle ; and, if discoverable, it would be important to know whether the judgment of our disinterested tribunal of authors would coincide with that of the present day, whether the wisest men, in the opinion of this oracle, would be found among those whom the modern world has selected to honour and to follow, or among those less conspicuous whom it holds of little or no account. To a question of this kind, however, no categorical answer can be given, and in times like these, which feel in a high degree the pressure of the present and the future, in which the authority of the past tends to relax, even if an answer were obtainable, it would probably not accord with our superior mental temper to take counsel with the dead.

Rather than consult the old books of navigation, men look to living men to be their pilots in dealing with the winds and currents of modern life. Nothing is perhaps more natural and inevitable than that it should be so. In the conduct of human affairs, books can never take the place of men, nor precept that of practice. Yet here and there a student of history will at least be conscious that upon the wisdom of the past governments laws and social systems are founded, that the spirits of the dead rule us from their urns, and will tell himself that no man is truly civilised until he knows not only what he is, but how he comes to be what he is. Such a student will be aware that as memory serves the individual and enables him to profit by the varied experiences of his life, so the records of the past, the written or printed things, serve the body politic and social. In the libraries we have access to the memory of the race. And I think it may be safely declared that a memory of this kind is indispensable to society, engaged as it is upon the eternal process of reconstruction that makes for progress. For upon the material offered to them in their environment men are hourly engaged in arranging and manipulating things that the external world of facts may be brought into harmony with the inner world of their feelings and desires. Innumerable difficulties, indeed, beset us in the attempt to subdue the environment to our wishes. The external world is so exasperatingly intractable, and unhappily, the individual, in his effort to bring his own surroundings into harmony with his mental and emotional requirements, runs counter to his companions engaged upon the same project. We do not always succeed in working together. As Phocion remarked on one occasion, "How many generals we have here, and how few soldiers". Yet I suppose we may believe that organised society makes steady, if lingering, progress, and that we are at birth immersed in a social order, corresponding to something like the best that men have hitherto thought and known. By universal consent, at least, the task of the social unit is to maintain the good he has inherited and continue the work of reconstruction, to carry on the building of the city of the soul.

But it is a sombre reflection, with which some philosophers have broken their intellectual rest, that the gains of civilisation have been paid for in large and irrecoverable losses. Just as the bright world of the child, once dimmed, never again swims into the ken of his maturer eye, so with the larger world,

Storm worn since Being began with the wind and thunder of things.

One misses in its middle age some of the gifts and graces of its youth ; one misses the touch of wisdom or of beauty, the type of character, the gracious custom or noble institution that charms us in the landscape of the past. Only a superstitious worshipper of our materialistic times would claim for them an insolent superiority over all times that have gone, a superiority from first to last, and would assert that we have swept into our intellectual granaries the wealth of all the harvests of the years. Who will assure us even that we are to-day richer in all good things than our ancestors who built the cathedrals, or those more remote who gave us the song of Arthur, and the high simplicities and courtesies of the Round Table ? Who will calculate for us the pressure in the spiritual or intellectual barometer of our epoch, and declare that it has risen uninterruptedly since the dawn of history ? Because the development of the human mind does not seem to be continuous, because the flower of one age's achievement seems invariably to close before that of another expands, and to crave like Phidias or paint like Raphael seems to be difficult while we trade like Mr. Morgan; because of this, not to keep the past in remembrance is to limit one's vision to a particular case, a single type of excellence. We need to press the past into the service of the present, to have some acquaintance with the achievements of the previous tenants of earth, useless, indeed, we are willing to sacrifice much of the advantage of our position in time, and permit, to the impoverishment of life, all that was lovely and inspiring and of good report in the career of the younger world to be buried with its dead. Why not rather summon the genius of each departed age, and require that it should

> Speak from its lips of immemorial speech
> If but one word to each ?

The libraries serve them to put us in mind of our intellectual and moral obligations, to remind us that, like the coral island of Pacific seas, the pillars of our world rest upon the labours of others. They remind us of this, and they preserve for us the fragments of an incommunicable past, which, however we choose to regard it, remains the proud and inexorable critic of our modern doings, inquiring of us what we can offer the days to come which shall take its place unabashed beside the great illuminated pages in human history, the page that holds the art and wisdom of Greece, the order and equity of Rome, the passionate loyalties of the Middle Ages.

If you consider it, the library appears to be the natural home of the idealist, for he can hardly fail to observe the singular unanimity with which the books of the world uphold the highest ethical and spiritual standards ; he can hardly fail to observe the gratifying fact that the authors are of the same way of thinking as himself, that they dwell with peculiar satisfaction upon heroic names and high and difficult achievements. Nothing is more interesting than to observe how rarely the sordid or ignoble view of things finds its way into print. Bad people seem, on the whole, reluctant to write books, or they practice the art of concealing their wickedness and appearing to be good. In the streets and bazaars, undoubtedly, it is sometimes whispered that high standards of conduct are impossible of attainment, that magnanimity is not business, and that the enthusiasms and passions of the sage and of the poet are webs of gossamer. There it may appear that the battle is to the strong, and that the idealist is betrayed by fables. But these things are only whispered, they are not often proclaimed on the housetops, and the books are indisputably on the other side. In them, for some reason, it is seldom asserted that the gods are asleep or on a journey, in them the cause of virtue and heroism is the wise man's cause, in them it is always worth while "to stand or fall by the noblest hypothesis". The world being in proportion inferior to the soul, as Bacon says, there is agreeable to the spirit of man a more ample greatness, a more exact goodness than can be found in things, and the imagination is often a safer guide to reality than the fact.

It would appear then that the books which are the registers of human conviction maintain, in effect, that the word reality is much abused, that the world of mental, emotional and spiritual facts, of art and religion and poetry is the true world, and its rival, with all its attractions and pomps and splendours, but the fierce vexation of a dream. The authors appear to be engaged in a veritable conspiracy on behalf of idealism. So determined an attitude, however noble in itself, might strain the faith of the average man, were it not that he secretly nourishes a preference for the ideal, and would like to be a hero or a saint himself, if to be a hero or a saint were only easy, were only compatible with a safe and pleasant life. The beautiful in conduct is difficult, and its pursuit sometimes dangerous, but every one of us is aware that death, the great destroyer of the material illusion, has in all ages failed to vanquish the spirits of some men, and that to these even the practical world does homage. It ranks the hero, it is even inclined to rank the saint, above the tradesman. You are to be congratulated, gentlemen, that your business in life appears to place you, in the language of the philosophers, on the side of the real as opposed to the apparent, on the side of the protest made by humanity against the encroachment of

the merely material life, which consists of the appearances
or show of things. Unlike the politician and the members
of most professions, you are beyond the reach of the satirist
and the cynic. It need not surprise us, therefore, to find
that a faith in books is a part of any man's creed, it need
not surprise us that in the libraries many men should dis-
cern a hope for the world. The magnificent liberality of
Mr. Carnegie, a liberality to which it would be difficult to
find a parallel in history, proves him to be in possession of
this hope, and Mr. Carnegie, at least, is as much a man of
affairs as he is a man of ideas. Against him the practical
world is not likely to bring a railing accusation.

It must, indeed, be admitted that books have the defects
of their qualities; they are rarely accused of materialising
the mind, but they fall short of what is sometimes expected
of them. Most of us are impatiently awaiting a book which
shall tell us how to become meritoriously distinguished
without effort, or a book which shall tell us how a large
fortune may be easily and rapidly acquired, and we have
been so far obliged to put up with something less than this.
And it seems probable that we shall have to content ourselves with less dazzling advantages, simply the companion-
ship of nobler spirits than our own, the larger outlook upon
the world of those who have been the guests of great men.

But I may be told that " He who would bring home the
wealth of the Indies must carry out the wealth of the
Indies," that it is not every one who profits by his reading.
I shall very likely be told that it is an age of readers indeed,
but an age of readers who perversely decline to study the
" hundred best," and fasten greedily upon the ten thousand
worst books, that the majority is entirely given over to
domestic tragedy and honey-sweet romance. I suppose I
must frankly admit my sympathy with the multitude. Yet
" Even when the bird walks we see that it has wings ". This
passion for romance, to what is it due, what is its significance? It tells us, I think, that not the abstract, but the
concrete, remains the paramount interest with men, not
philosophies and distillations of the intellect, not theories of
things, but life itself. " Men taste well," it has been said,

"knowledges that are drenched in flesh and blood." The passion for romance tells us that the life of a modern manufacturing or commercial community imprisons the spirit, and the balance needs readjustment. Harassed by the intolerable tyranny of circumscribed horizons, the incurable monotony of the daily round, the common task, the prisoners would escape their toils. And since the interest of reading depends entirely upon finding in a book something that answers to individual necessities, to demand beauties and heroisms in one's emotional and intellectual diet is at least to have one's foot on the road that leads to their mountain home. Fortunately for us, the world has not yet grown old, still

> Tears waken tears, and honour honour brings
> And mortal hearts are moved by mortal things.

And I may acknowledge my personal indebtedness to all those writers who help to keep it young; to the poet, for example, who, despite his occasionally strident rhetoric, can transmute the telegraph, the steamship, the railway, and even the weather office into the fine gold of romance :—

> I sent a message to my dear—
>   A thousand leagues and more to Her—
> The dumb sea-levels thrilled to hear
>   And lost Atlantis bore to Her.
> Behind my message hard I came,
>   And nigh had found a grave for me;
> But that I launched of steel and flame
>   Did war against the wave for me.
> Uprose the deep in gale on gale,
>   To bid me change my mind again—
> He broke his teeth along my rail,
>   And, roaring, swung behind again.
>
> I stayed the sun at noon to tell
>   My way across the waste of it;
> I read the storm before it fell
>   And made the better haste of it.
> Afar I hailed the land at night—
>   The towers I built had heard of me—
> And ere my rocket reached its height,
>   Had flashed my Love the word of me.
> Earth sold her chosen men of strength,
>   They lived and strove and died for me,
> To drive my road a nation's length,
>   And toss the miles aside for me.

Shorn of romance the spirit of man might well at times despair, but he possesses in it a kind of *elixir vitæ*, it bids for him defiance to the narrow limits of his fate, often it is his guide to the true significance of things. It enables him to step from the dusty pavement in the dull and soulless street to the little chamber on the wall; from the meaningless cries and bustle to the window that overlooks the gleaming hills and the wide and silent plain, where winds the wizard stream. There, undisturbed by touch of things soiled by ignoble use, he can hold converse with winds and waters, and many a travelling star. There he becomes the willing bondman of the enchanter's flute, and keeps step to magical airs. Let the fickle jade, Fortune, fling her outrageous shafts.

> Still at the worst of the worst, books and a chamber remain.

I must, indeed, admit that the good readers, those who resort to books for other ends than to fleet the time carelessly, those who make more than a passing acquaintance with their contents, that good readers are in the minority, and only the good reader has the key to all the rooms of the palace. It is told of a visitor to Laconia that he could not accommodate his palate to the Spartan fare, and that in particular the broth, which formed the staple of the city's diet, failed to arouse his appetite. "To make this broth relish," said his host, "you should first have bathed yourself in the river Eurotas." In the realm of intellect the conditions are similar; a Spartan discipline brings the relish for the Spartan fare. Some men, indeed, seem to be born freedmen of the guild of mind, but for most of us the taste for the abstruser paths of knowledge comes only after long apprenticeship. "To make this broth relish you should first have bathed yourself in the river Eurotas."

I am not prepared, gentlemen, to defend the thesis that the libraries contain nothing that can be spared. Man is a loquacious animal, and the preserved verbosity of centuries may be surmised to contain some vain repetitions and lifeless redundances not a few. Much printed matter has been produced merely that the author might "Keep his mutton-twirling at his fire," much by the men and women, who pick up their little knowledge from reviews, and minister to his " Majesty the Public " by misinforming him in an agreeable fashion ; much has come from minds afflicted with an ardour of self-revelation, which

> forced them, as it were, in spite
> Of nature and their stars, to write.

I fear also that the Universities are occasionally responsible for

> The mighty Scholiast, whose unwearied pains
> Makes Horace dull, and humbles Milton's strains.

Nor, indeed, is it at times easy to disagree with the cynic who remarked that the faculty of speech was bestowed upon man for the purpose of enabling him to conceal his ideas. But he that can discriminate, as the Indian proverb says, is the Father of his Father; and for the rest, to borrow a saying from Plutarch, "I forgive the many for the sake of the few, the living for the dead".

I have now, perhaps, gentlemen, sufficiently laboured a point, which you, at all events, are not likely to dispute, that the libraries of the world are one of its most valuable assets, an asset I may add, not of lessening, but of increasing value. If, as appears to some of our prophets inevitable, the world becomes duller as it becomes older, it may even chance that the books we write and house for them may afford some compensation to our successors. For books must gain rather than lose in importance. As human documents and as a means of communicating ideas they can hardly fail to play day by day a larger part in human history. And since it offers a peaceful market for the ideas of all races, races which in other spheres seem likely for generations to be engaged in perpetual strife, the library may justly be regarded as a kind of international University. Only here can the untravelled student learn to understand his neighbours in the wide world of men, only here can he embark for the country of the past, that lost continent, for which from no other port can he set sail. Here racial pre--

judices are extinguished, here meet the " Merchants of
light " with the friendly wares from the four corners of the
world. Here at a trifling expense in time and attention one
may purchase from the East something of Eastern dignity
and composure of mind ; from the Greek something of his
balanced judgment, his sense of proportion and dislike of
needless emphasis ; from the Roman his largeness of view,
his magnanimity, his resolute temper ; from the Latin peoples
their eager sympathies, their allegiance to the beautiful ;
from the Teuton his endurance, his purposefulness ; from
the Celt his hatred of tyranny, his inspiring, his inextinguish-
able spirituality ; from the younger races their mental buoy-
ancy and belief in the future of mankind. An international
University, an international chamber of commerce for ideas,
such the library already is, and such it must in still larger
measure become.

And if you will permit me to deviate for a moment into
another, but adjoining region of ideas, I may state my entire
conviction that it is by their zeal for ideas, for knowledge,
measured by benefactions and endowments, public and private,
to such institutions as represent ideas and knowledge—poly-
technics, universities, libraries—that the progressive nations
of the world to-day are known. The governing nations of
the future will be the nations who to-day love ideas, who
believe in knowledge, and are willing to pay a high price for
it. Such is my conviction. I wish I could give expression
to a conviction equally strong, that among the progressive
peoples might be numbered our own, the people of this
country. But it is one thing to love knowledge, to believe
in ideas, and to be prepared to pay a high price for them ;
it is quite another thing reluctantly to admit their value
and attempt to buy them cheap.

But as I am merely an academic person I dare not tres-
pass upon the ground sacred to the magnificent operations
of the practical man, and I shall venture only one remark.
The clue to most of the successful undertakings the world
has known lies in a word, " It is no use running, one must
start betimes ".

In conclusion, gentlemen, I may say that education in an

international University of the kind of which I have spoken,
leads to glimpses of what that distinguished countryman of
ours who was for so long resident in Birmingham, Cardinal
Newman, called " The master view of things ". I do not
propose here to discuss what the master view of things may
require of us as active members of a social order, what it
may expect from some of us in the way of a contribution
towards the progress of the community. The mass of mankind seem vastly more concerned with what they can get
out of the world than what they can give to it, and it might
be incautious, it might even give rise to a social revolution
to inquire whether the master view of things would not
debar a man of honesty and honour from drawing out, in
wealth let us say, a sum in excess of the value to the community of his labour or thought. Waiving, however, this
interesting but dangerous question, I may ask, will the books
assist us in selecting among the things we may obtain in
exchange for the work we do, will they assist us in deciding,
as we cannot have everything, what is best worth our having?
There is little doubt in my own mind that such assistance
they can and do render, and that the master view of things,
of which they afford us glimpses, will declare on the whole
that it is better to understand the world than to possess it ;
that, subject as we are to the shock of mortal circumstance,
it will be best for us to get as quickly as possible on good
relations with reality. The mind accustomed to move
among realities, as opposed to appearances, will remain at
home, however far from the comforts of a world of sense the
future of his lot may fling him. And however fair that
world, of which we are the transient possessors, we are in
truth imprisoned by its celestial and terrestrial splendours :—

Man, whom Fate, his victor, magnanimous, clement in triumph,
Holds as a captive King, mewed in a palace divine ;
Wide its leagues of pleasance and ample of purview its windows,
Airily laughs in its courts laughter of fountains at play :
Naught, when the harpers are harping, untimely reminds him of durance ;
None as he sits at the feast whispers captivity's name ;
But would he parley with silence, withdraw for a while unattended,
Forth to the beckoning world 'scape for an hour and be free,
Lo, his adventurous fancy, coercing at once and provoking,

Rise the unscalable walls, built with a word at the prime;
Lo, immobile as statues, with pitiless faces of iron,
Armed at each obstinate gate stand the impassable guards.

Our spiritual freedom alone is left to us, for like our earliest ancestors we are still outside Eden. And the sentinels stand before the doors of man's house, the sworded Seraphim, Space and Time, whose flaming blades turn every way and keep the gates of the garden and the mystery of God.

THE BIRMINGHAM FREE LIBRARIES.[1]

BY A. CAPEL SHAW, CHIEF LIBRARIAN, FREE LIBRARIES, BIRMINGHAM.

IT seems to be the usual thing for the public librarian of a city honoured by a visit from the Library Association to prepare a paper on the free libraries under his control. Such a paper is one of the standing dishes prepared for the entertainment of an audience supposed above all things to be hungry after information. It may indeed be considered to be the joint of our intellectual banquet, both on account of its greater solidity and its closer resemblance to our every-day fare, and it may possibly be owing to these two qualities that there seems a general disposition to take these papers as read.

Far be it from me to hint that librarians do not want to hear about libraries, but I must confess that on several occasions when the announcement has been made, that owing to lack of time the paper on the local libraries would be taken as read, the assembled librarians have borne their disappointment in a touching spirit of resignation.

It is now exactly fifty years since the first attempt to establish a free library in Birmingham was made. Fifty years ago, the exact date being 6th February, 1852, Mr. Councillor Boyce introduced the subject in the Town Council, and moved that at the next meeting the Council should take it into consideration and decide as to the advisability of introducing the Act into the borough.

If you come to think of it, this was perhaps the most important and far-reaching thing that was brought before the Council on that day, or for many days before and after that event. No doubt to some of the assembled Councillors

---

[1] Read at the Annual Meeting of the Library Association, Birmingham, 23rd September, 1902.

it was a novel and perhaps undesirable proposal; to others a trifling and unimportant matter; to the discerning few a proposal fraught with immense possibilities.

Let us honour the memory of Mr. Councillor Boyce; by his proposal he has built for himself an enduring memorial. He was not successful in his effort, but that does not detract from his title to our gratitude. He first cast to earth the seed which ultimately sprang up and brought forth the noble libraries which adorn our city to-day. To the honour of the Town Council be it said that they did not reject his proposal, but by resolution requested the Mayor, Mr. Henry Hawkes, to take the necessary steps to ascertain from the burgesses whether the Public Libraries Act should be adopted in Birmingham or not.

The friends of the movement immediately set to work. On the 21st March a meeting was held at the Public Office and a sub-committee elected to canvas the town and endeavour to secure the necessary majority.

That they did their work well, and spared no efforts to secure the two-thirds majority of the votes recorded, which was required by the Act of 1850, we can readily believe. The names of the members forming this sub-committee are sufficient to assure us of this, but against stupidity even the gods are said to fight in vain.

The poll was taken on 7th April, 534 votes being recorded for, and 363 against the [adoption of the Act. The votes in favour were thus twenty-five short of the two-thirds majority required, and the proposal was lost.

Of the members of the sub-committee whose efforts for the time being ended in failure, some have passed away, and some by the increasing infirmities of age are no longer capable of active work on behalf of the libraries they loved so well, but I am glad to say that one member of that early committee is still with us, and still actively engaged in promoting the interests of the Birmingham Free Libraries. I refer to the present chairman of our Management sub-Committee, Mr. William Harris. He has lived to see that first defeat redeemed by triumphant victory. During all these years his interest in the libraries has never failed, his labours on their behalf have been untiring, and to-day, not-withstanding the flight of time, he presides over the deliberations of the Management sub-Committee with the zeal and energy of youth, combined with the wisdom gained by life-long experience.

After this unfortunate defeat the matter remained in abeyance for some time.

According to the provisions of the Act two years at least must pass before the question could again be brought before the burgesses. The two years passed away, but the promoters of the movement did not feel that the time was ripe for action. Unwilling to risk another defeat they possessed their souls in patience, and devoted themselves to forming such a body of public opinion as should ensure success on the next occasion. Not indeed until seven years had passed away was any further action taken in the matter. Then on 16th August, 1859, the subject was again brought before the Town Council by Mr. E. C. Osborne, who moved a resolution requesting the Mayor, Mr. Thomas Lloyd, to convene a public meeting of the burgesses to determine whether the Act should be adopted or not.

An amendment to this resolution, suggesting the appointment of a committee to consider the subject and report to the Council previous to a meeting of the burgesses, was moved and adopted. The report of this committee, strongly recommending the adoption of the Act, was presented to the Council on the 3rd January, 1860, and approved.

A meeting of the burgesses was held in the Town Hall on 21st February, 1860, at which a resolution for the adoption of the Act was carried by an overwhelming majority, and Birmingham thus fell into line with Manchester, Liverpool and other towns which had already adopted the Act.

The preliminary difficulties having thus been overcome, a committee, consisting of eight members of the Council and eight non-Councillors, was elected to carry into effect the provisions of the Act. The committee recommended that the scheme as a whole should comprise a central reference library, with reading and newsrooms, and four district lending libraries with newsrooms attached. Their recommendations being approved by the Council on the 15th May, 1860, the committee began immediately to carry them out, and so energetically was the work proceeded with that the first district library was opened in Constitution Hill on 3rd April, 1861, by the Mayor, Mr. Arthur Ryland.

The first librarian was Mr. Edward Lings, who was appointed 1st December, 1860.

For some years the library at Constitution Hill was the only portion of the scheme that was carried out. This, however, was not due to any diminution of interest or lack of zeal on the part of the committee. In their first annual report, published in 1862, while referring to the extraordinary success that had attended the opening of the library at Constitution Hill, they expressed their regret that they had been unable to open either of the other three branch libraries, and gave as a reason the difficulty of obtaining suitable sites.

Even when these difficulties were overcome and suitable sites had been found, some considerable time had to elapse before they could come into the possession of the Free Libraries Committee.

Meanwhile, the number of libraries was increased in an unexpected way by the acceptance of an offer of the Right Hon. C. B. Adderley, M.P., to grant to the Council a lease of Adderley Park at Saltley, with the library and museum thereon for a term of 999 years at an annual rental of 5s. This library was opened to the public on 11th January, 1864.

The next work taken in hand by the committee was the erection of the Central Reference Library, with which was to be united the Lending Library and Newsroom for the Central and Western Districts. A site for these libraries had been found on a piece of land which had been conveyed in 1854 to the Midland Institute by the Corporation, for the Institute building, which was originally intended to include an art gallery. This part of the plan, however, having been deferred, the Institute Council now offered to return the unused land to the Corporation for the purposes of a library and art gallery.

The site was in many respects an admirable one, very central and of considerable size, and the offer was gladly accepted, as also was a condition that the library buildings should be entrusted to Mr. E. M. Barry, the architect of the Institute, in order that they might harmonise with his original plan. This condition, however, it was found impossible to carry out except at a greater cost than the committee were prepared to recommend. They therefore recommended that some other architect should be employed. Competitive designs were invited, and those of Mr. William Martin were approved. Fresh tenders were obtained, and finally in October, 1862, the tender of Messrs. Branson & Murray for £8,600 was accepted.

A strike amongst the stonemasons much delayed the progress of the work, but on 6th September, 1865, the Central Lending Library and the Art Gallery were opened on the occasion of the meeting of the British Association in Birmingham, and the first issue of books was made on 19th September, the rooms having in the interval been used by the British Association.

The Reference Library was not yet completed, but meanwhile the selection of books went on steadily, the work being entrusted in the main to Mr. Jacob Phillips, the chairman of the committee, Mr. Samuel Timmins and Mr. J. D. Mullins, who had been appointed chief librarian on 30th May, 1865.

Twelve months after the opening of the Central Lending *viz.*, on 26th October, 1866, the Reference Library was opened, and on the same memorable day the branch library at Deritend was opened, and the foundation-stone of the library at Gosta Green was laid. When this library was opened in 1868 the entire original scheme of the Free Libraries Committee was completed.

An addition of special interest was made to the Reference Library two years after its opening, *viz.*, the Shakespeare Memorial Library.

As early as 1858 the question of establishing a Shakespeare Library in Birmingham had been raised by Mr. Timmins, and again in 1861 by Mr. George Dawson. In

1863 a committee was formed for the purpose of establishing such a library, and at their request a room was obtained in the Central Library building. On 23rd April, 1864, the tercentenary of Shakespeare's birth, the Mayor, Mr. W. Holliday, entertained the Memorial Committee and a number of other gentlemen at breakfast, and on this occasion a large collection of editions of Shakespeare's works, and of literature relating to them, was presented to the Mayor on behalf of the Corporation, together with about £450 in money to be spent by the Memorial Committee in the purchase of books.

The conditions on which the presentation was made were :—

1. That a special room, to be called " The Shakespeare Memorial Library " and to be exclusively used for that purpose, should be appropriated to the collection.

2. That the library should be placed under the same regulations as the Free Reference Library.

3. That the library be maintained and augumented by the Free Libraries Committee, and all works of the same class purchased by them, or by the Shakespeare Memorial Library Committee, be placed and arranged in the Shakespeare Memorial Library.

The room that had been set apart for the purpose was completely fitted and stored with the books early in 1868, and on the 23rd April in that year the Memorial Library was opened by the Mayor, Mr. Thomas Avery.

At the date of opening the Memorial Library consisted of 1,239 volumes. It was increased every year by purchases and gifts until the collection reached a total of 7,000 volumes, when it was entirely destroyed in the disastrous fire of 11th January, 1879.

The history of the free libraries from the completion of the original scheme to the fire in 1879 was one of continual progress, chequered at times by the lack of funds which prevented the committee from buying books to such an extent as was necessary to keep the libraries in a satisfactory condition. In 1870, in their annual report, the Library Committee complained seriously of the want of funds. The 1d.

rate yielded only £4,500, and of this amount £2,000 was required for the interest on loans and the repayment of the principal, leaving only £2,500 for the current expenses of six libraries and newsrooms, and the Art Gallery. This difficulty, however, was not peculiar to Birmingham; it is felt, I believe, in all places where the rate is limited to 1d.

Experience has shown over and over again that the 1d. rate is not sufficient to bear the expenses of interest on loans and repayment of principal, and at the same time to maintain the libraries in that state of efficiency which is desirable and which the people expect. So serious was the pressure in Birmingham in 1870, that the committee could only spend £125 in the purchase of new books for the five lending libraries, with the result that there was a considerable decrease in the issues compared with the preceding year.

Happily this state of things as far as Birmingham is concerned has long since passed away. I have referred to it and emphasise it more especially in the interest of those libraries which are still limited to the 1d. rate. From the experience of Birmingham it is evident that when buildings, maintenance and books have to be provided out of the 1d. rate, something must suffer. As the debts in the shape of interest and sinking fund must be paid, it becomes a question of starving the libraries or starving the librarians. There may be a difference of opinion as to which of these two courses it is better to adopt. There are no doubt librarians who are ambitious of a martyr's crown, and who would glory in being starved in so good a cause as that of the free libraries which are under their control, but I cannot truthfully say that my own ambition lies in that direction. Better by far is the removal of the 1d. limit, which is the method adopted in Birmingham. By a clause in the Birmingham Corporation Consolidation Act of 1883, the limit of the library rate to 1d. in the £ was removed. Henceforth the committee were able to provide in a suitable manner for the maintenance of the libraries, without being hampered by the consideration that they must not exceed the limit of the rate allotted them.

It might be thought by some that in thus fixing no limit

to the rate for free libraries, the people of Birmingham were embarking on a career of reckless expenditure. This, however, has not proved to be the case. The confidence placed in the committee has been amply justified, for up till the present time the expenditure on all the libraries has never been much above 1½d. in the £.

It may be interesting to other librarians to learn how the finances are arranged in Birmingham. At the close of the financial year, the committee prepare an estimate of their anticipated expenditure for the forthcoming year. This estimate is based on the actual expenditure for the year just ended, and takes into account any additional expense for work required during the coming year. They also prepare an estimate of income derived from fines, sale of catalogues, etc. These estimates are forwarded to the Finance Committee of the Council, and embodied in their estimate of income and expenditure for the new financial year for the whole of the Corporation, which is submitted to the Council, and in accordance with which the borough rate is levied. If the estimate is approved by the City Council, an amount equal to the sum required is transferred from the Borough Fund to the Free Libraries Account.

The amount in the £ varies from year to year, as it depends on the proportion that the sum required by the Free Libraries Committee bears to the total amount required for the city. For the year ending 31st March, 1902, the amount received from the rate was in round figures, £16,700, which was equal to a rate of 1·47d. in the £.

Thus at a cost amounting to about 1½d. in the £ the eleven libraries now in existence are maintained in a high state of efficiency, the interest on the capital expenditure is paid, and a certain amount (about £1,700 or £1,800) is devoted to the repayment of the loans which were obtained for building and furnishing the various libraries.

In 1872 an important change was made in the administration of the libraries. In order to render the Central Libraries more generally available, the committee asked for power to open them on Sundays. This proposal excited great opposition among the religious bodies in the town, and a deputation from the Lord's Day Defence Association asked permission to attend the Council meeting on 2nd January, 1872, and to speak against the proposal of the Free Libraries Committee. Although such a course was very undesirable and would form a bad precedent, the public feeling was so strongly excited that it was thought better to allow the deputation to attend the meeting. They presented memorials against Sunday opening from twenty-two chapels, and from seven other bodies engaged in religious work.

At the Council meeting in March, 1872, Mr. Alderman Jesse Collings, who was then chairman of the Free Libraries Committee, presented a number of memorials in favour of Sunday opening. Finally at the Council meeting on the 2nd April, 1872, Alderman Collings moved and Alderman Osborne seconded the approval of the committee's report. An amendment rejecting the report was moved and seconded, but was defeated by twenty-five votes to seventeen. The motion for opening the Reference Library and Art Gallery on Sundays was then carried without a division.

The Reference Library and Art Gallery were accordingly opened on Sunday the 28th April, 1872, and from that time until the present no attempt has been made to reverse this arrangement, and Sunday opening in Birmingham has taken its place among the things which exist, and concerning which no question is ever raised.

In 1875 the Reference Library was enriched by the acquisition of the unique and exceedingly interesting Staunton collection of books, manuscripts, etc., illustrative of the history and antiquities of Warwickshire. The price of this famous collection was £2,285; and towards this sum about £1,700 was raised by a special committee, the deficiency being paid out of the library funds. Unfortunately the library did not long retain possession of its new treasure, for this unique and practically irreplaceable collection was almost entirely destroyed in the great fire of 1879. Only a few of the items were saved, among them, however, being the beautifully written and richly illuminated "Registerium Gilde Sancte Anne de Knolle 1412-35". This choice MS.

volume owed its preservation to the fact that it was kept locked up in an iron safe. In this way it passed safely through the fire, and in due time became No. 1 of the reconstructed Reference Library.

Year by year the library continued to grow in extent and usefulness until it began to be seriously hampered by the second of the two troubles with which libraries and librarians have always to contend. I have already referred to the first, namely, lack of funds, and the second, namely, want of space now threatened to be equally troublesome.

As far back as 1872 the need for extension had become manifest, and negotiations to obtain the necessary space were entered into with the Midland Institute Council. Plans were prepared for carrying out the alterations at a cost of £11,000 and the approval of the Town Council obtained, but nothing at that time was done, progress being stopped by a scheme for the reconstruction of the Midland Institute, which necessarily affected the Central Libraries.

In 1875 the matter was again considered, and revised plans prepared, but it was not until 1878 that any steps were actually taken in the matter. The plans were again revised and submitted to the Town Council in February, 1878. The revised plans provided for an Art Gallery and an Industrial Museum, and for the enlargement of the existing Reference and Lending Libraries at an estimated cost of £22,000. The report was adopted, and the Committee authorised to proceed with the work, which they accordingly did. For some few months the work went on, and good progress was being made when suddenly it was interrupted by an overwhelming catastrophe. On Saturday, 11th January, 1879, about 1.30 P.M., the officials and readers in the Reference Library were startled by a cry of fire. The cry came from the outside of a wooden partition reaching from the ground floor to the top of the building, which had been erected as a temporary wall during the operations for the extension of the buildings. In the neighbourhood of this partition there was a cupboard through which the main gas-pipes and taps for the service of the Reference Library had been brought. These pipes had been packed round with shavings by one of the gas-men to protect them from the frost. When the alarm of fire was given smoke was seen to be proceeding from this cupboard. Immediately a chain of men was formed, and buckets of water, filled from a large butt placed at the entrance door of the Reference Library, were passed rapidly from hand to hand and emptied into the cupboard, and by this means all fire which at the time was visible in the library was extinguished. Immediately afterwards, however, the fire reappeared above the book-cases under the gallery in the same part of the room. By this time the firemen had arrived with the hose and began to play on the fire in the Reference Library. The steam fire engine was unfortunately delayed a few minutes owing to the absence of the driver, but about 2.10 the hose from the steam engine began to play at the back of the partition, and played continuously till late at night. The slight delay in getting the steam engine to work was not regarded at the time as in any way affecting the progress of the fire. The wooden partition afforded such fuel for the flames, and the draught in consequence was so great that nothing probably could have saved the library. In fact all hope of saving the Reference Library was abandoned before two o'clock, in consequence of the intensity of the heat and the denseness of the smoke. The Lending Library being on the ground floor, and not so early attacked by the flames, was more accessible, and a considerable portion of its contents was rescued before the progress of the fire rendered access to the room impossible. When night fell upon the scene a black and smoking heap was all that was left of the Reference Library which had been gathered together with so much care and judgment. Only 1,000 volumes out of the 50,000 it contained were saved, the rest were wholly destroyed. Of the Lending Library about 15,000 out of 17,000 were saved.

This great calamity was met in the true spirit of Englishmen. The Free Libraries Committee lost no time, but met on the Monday after the fire. Their first business was to pass a resolution, declaring it to be a public duty at once to repair the loss, and asking for a subscription of not less than £10,000 in aid of the insurance fund. At the same meeting the committee instructed a sub-committee to confer with the architects as to the plans for a new building. At the request of the committee, the Mayor, Mr. Alderman Collings, called a public meeting of persons willing to contribute to the restoration fund. This meeting was held on Friday, 17th January, and was very largely attended. A resolution, moved by Mr. Joseph Chamberlain, M.P., and seconded by the Rev. A. R. Vardy, head master of King Edward's School, declared that "under the heavy calamity which has befallen Birmingham by the loss of the Reference Library, our first duty is to take immediate measures for the restoration of the library, on a scale of completeness worthy of the town".

A committee to raise a fund in aid was appointed, with the Mayor as chairman. A large amount was subscribed in the room, and at the close of the year the fund amounted to more than £14,000, and was ultimately raised to £15,197.

This fund has been of great service to the library, as it enabled the committee to purchase valuable books which otherwise they might have been unable to obtain. About £5,000 of this fund still remains, and the interest of this sum, which amounts to about £200 a year, is devoted to the purchase of such costly works as the library ought to possess, but which it might be undesirable to pay for out of the rate. In this way a copy of Gould's works, at a cost of £550, was obtained, and other costly works have been purchased, without causing any addition to the estimate submitted to the Council.

In addition to this voluntary fund, a sum of £25,000 was received from the insurance companies with whom the libraries were insured.

The Free Libraries Committee were greatly cheered and encouraged by the sympathy shown throughout the country, and in literary circles abroad, sympathy which it may be said did not end in words, but found expression in many valuable gifts of books towards the restoration of the library.

It is impossible here to detail all the donors, but they included Her Majesty Queen Victoria, the chief public departments, libraries, institutions, societies, publishers and booksellers.

The work of restoration was carried on with characteristic energy, and meanwhile a suite of rooms at the Council House was placed at the disposal of the committee by the Council for immediate use. On the 10th June a newsroom was opened for the use of the public, and on the 12th September the Central Lending Library and the Reference Library were opened in their temporary home.

The plans for the new building were approved by the Council in May, 1879, and the work was completed in about three years. The new Reference and Lending Libraries, together with the Newsroom in Ratcliff Place, were opened on Thursday, 1st June, 1882. This was a great day in the history of the Birmingham Free Libraries. A large and representative gathering from all parts of the country assembled to do honour to the occasion. The opening address was delivered by the Right Hon. John Bright, M.P., and in the evening a banquet in commemoration of the event was given by the Mayor, after which speeches were delivered by the Mayor, Lord Norton, Mr. Bright, Mr. Chamberlain, Mr. R. W. Dale, Alderman Collings, Sir Philip Cunliffe Owen, Alderman Baker, Mayor of Manchester, Sir Henry Parkes, Prime Minister of New South Wales (formerly a Birmingham man), and Mr. E. B. Nicholson of the Bodleian Library. Inaugurated under these favourable auspices, the new Central Libraries started on a renewed career of prosperity which has known no diminution until the present time. The period of stress and toil was over, henceforward the history of the libraries is one of steady growth and development.

The lease of the building which had hitherto been used for the Constitution Hill Library expired in March, 1881. As it was impossible to renew the lease it became necessary to erect a new building. A suitable site in the immediate neighbourhood was obtained, the work was pushed on as rapidly as possible, and the new library was opened on 1st July, 1883.

After the passing of the Birmingham Corporation Consolidation Act in 1883, the Museum and School of Art, which had hitherto been under the control of the Free Libraries Committee, were separated from the Free Libraries, and placed under the control of a separate committee and thus started on a new and independent career.

In June, 1885, a scheme for erecting three additional branch libraries was put before the Council, but the question was deferred until the School of Art and the Art Gallery were completed, and their permanent demands on the rate ascertained.

In 1889 the Free Libraries Committee put in a claim for a share in the new revenue expected to accrue from the operation of the Local Government Act, 1888. They received authority from the Council to purchase sites, obtain plans and estimates, and enter into contracts for new branch libraries at Bloomsbury, Small Heath and Spring Hill. The work had hardly been begun when the scheme was enlarged, in accordance with the pledges made to the districts which were added to the city in 1891. Two of these districts, Balsall Heath and Harborne, made it a condition of joining the city that free libraries should be provided in the district; the third, Saltley, stipulated that the branch library at Adderley Park, already in existence, should be enlarged and reorganised. The enlarged scheme thus included the provision of five new branch libraries, and the reorganisation of one of the existing branches. The work was pushed on rapidly, and the new libraries opened on the following dates: Bloomsbury, June, 1892; Harborne, August, 1892; Spring Hill, January, 1893; Adderley Park enlarged, October, 1893; Small Heath, December, 1893; and Balsall Heath, April, 1896. In addition, in 1896 the library at Gosta Green was enlarged by the inclusion of a passage and sub-room in the newsroom, and in 1898 the library at Deritend was almost doubled, by extending the building on a piece of land belonging to the committee, which adjoined the library. Thus at the end of 1898 all the six libraries included in the original scheme had been greatly enlarged, and in some cases rebuilt, and five entirely new libraries had been provided.

The year 1887 was marked in a special way by the

visit of the Library Association to Birmingham, under the presidency of Mr. Alderman Johnson, chairman of the Free Libraries Committee. The meetings were in every way successful, and one of the practical results in Birmingham was the adoption by the committee of a suggestion, made in a paper read before the Association, to allow the readers to have free access to Dictionaries, Encyclopædias, Gazetteers and other similar books of reference. A beginning was made with a case that would contain between two and three hundred volumes of large size. This proved so successful and was so much appreciated that it was soon found necessary to increase the number of such books, and three rows of shelves, which could be reached without a ladder, on one side of the wing of the Reference Library, and which would contain about 800 volumes, were devoted to this purpose. At the suggestion of the late Mr. Fulford the principle was extended to the branch libraries, a case containing two or three hundred similar books of reference, accessible to all comers, being placed in each of the branches. It is perhaps not altogether out of place to say that neither at the Reference nor Branch Libraries is any record kept of the use of these books. They are not included in the tables of issue, which are therefore not so large by many hundreds a day as they would be if the issues of these books were included. What the tables of statistics lose is however far more than compensated for by the increased facilities thus afforded to the public of consulting such books without loss of time.

In November, 1893, the Free Libraries Committee suffered a great, but fortunately only temporary, loss by the election of their chairman, Mr. Alderman G. J. Johnson, as Mayor of the city. This election rendered it necessary for him to resign the chairmanship of the committee, which he had held continuously since the year 1880. It is impossible to over-estimate the value of his services to the free libraries during his chairmanship of fourteen years. The fact that he was re-elected year after year for so long a period, is in itself evidence of the value placed on those services by his colleagues on the committee. His unfailing courtesy, wise judgment, extensive knowledge and liberal spirit eminently qualified him for the post, which he held to the satisfaction of all. In all the events which marked the history of the Birmingham Free Libraries during those years he took a leading part; he might indeed appropriate the words of Æneas before Dido, and say, " Et quorum pars magna fui ".

The next chairman, Mr. Alderman Fallows, held the office for only one year, as he too at the end of that time became Mayor of the city.

Mr. Fallows was succeeded by Mr. Councillor Charles Green, whose name will always be held in the highest esteem by the staff, on account of the interest he took in their welfare, and the successful effort he made to improve their position by the institution of a scale of salaries and wages. The proposed scale, which was submitted to the City Council in March, 1896, received their approval at the same meeting, and came into operation on 1st April, 1896. The chief provisions of the scale, which applies to male assistants only, are as follows :—

Junior assistants of fourteen years of age to begin at 6s. a week, rising yearly by 2s. a week till they reach the age of twenty-one.

Assistants over twenty-one years of age to be paid a minimum wage of 25s. a week.

Librarians of the branch lending libraries to be paid a minimum wage of 30s. a week, rising by instalments to a maximum of 50s. a week.

Senior assistants at the branches over twenty-one years of age to be paid a minimum wage of 25s. a week, rising to a maximum of 30s. a week.

The scale as far as the junior assistants is concerned is automatic, the rise to which their age entitles them being given at the end of the first full week after their birthdays. In the case of the senior assistants and librarians, the scale, although not absolutely, is practically automatic, as they receive an annual increase until they reach the maximum for the position they hold. The operation of the scale has therefore greatly benefited the officials who come within its scope, and they of course form the great majority of the staff. To what an extent they have benefited may be seen by a comparison of the wages account for the year ending 31st March, 1896, amounting to £3,973, with that for the year ending 31st March, 1902, when it amounted to £5,642, an increase of no less than £1,669 a year, of which increase about £1,200 is due directly to the operation of the scale.

In 1897, on the suggestion of Mr. William Harris, the committee made the experiment of providing the branch libraries with catalogues to be sold at one penny, advertisements being for the first time allowed in order to lessen the cost. It was found that when the price of the catalogue was fixed at such a sum as would cover the cost of production, the edition lasted much too long, and long before it was sold out ceased to represent the contents of the library. As a matter of fact editions at the higher price were very seldom entirely disposed of, and in this way involved the library in considerable loss, with the extra disadvantage to the public that there was no current catalogue of the library available for sale. By fixing the price at one penny the first loss is considerable, but about three times as many copies of the catalogue are sold, so that a new edition is required every two or three years. In this way not only are the catalogues kept more nearly up to date, but a much larger proportion of the borrowers buy them, and so become better acquainted with the contents of the libraries.

The year 1898 was marked by the resignation of Mr. J. D. Mullins, who had been in failing heath for some years, and who retired on 30th June, 1898, in accordance with the provisions of the Birmingham Superannuation Scheme. The following quotation from the annual report for that year will serve to show the esteem in which he was held by the Free Libraries Committee :—

During the year the library has suffered a great loss by the resignation of the chief librarian, J. D. Mullins.

Mr. Mullins was appointed chief librarian on the 13th May, 1865, and it is difficult to over-estimate the benefits which the free libraries have derived from his careful and judicious choice of books, and his selection of efficient assistants.

Even since his health began to fail, his wide and accurate knowledge and his long experience of library work, induced the committee to urge upon him to continue his services as long as possible.

He retired with the sincere thanks of the committee for his long and most useful services to the city.

Later in the same year Mr. Samuel Timmins was obliged
to sever his long connection with the Birmingham Free
Libraries in consequence of failing health. He was among
the earliest promoters of the scheme for establishing free
libraries in Birmingham, having been a member of the sub-
committee appointed in 1852 to canvas the town, and secure
the necessary majority in favour of the Act, and from that
time onward until the date of his resignation his devotion
to their interest never flagged. Especially in the formation
of the Reference Library, both before and after the fire, his
services were of the greatest value. Endowed with a passionate love of books, and having acquired an extensive
knowledge of literature, he filled for many years the office
of chairman of the Book sub-Committee, both to the satisfaction of the committee and the great advantage of the
library. He was also a liberal donor, having presented to
the library from first to last more than a thousand volumes,
many of them being rare and curious books. His devotion
to the libraries is commemorated by a bust which stands
in a prominent position in the Reference Library. His
resignation was accepted with regret, and the following resolution was passed by the City Council :—

> Resolved,—That in receiving the announcement of the retirement of
> Mr. Samuel Timmins from the Free Libraries Committee, of
> which he has been a member since its first constitution in 1860,
> the Council desire to thank him for the unfailing interest he
> has taken in the free libraries as evidenced not only by the
> unstinted service and valuable counsel given by him during so
> long a period, but by the many contributions which he has
> made from his own books to the contents of the Reference
> Library.

In 1899, in order to give the public a better opportunity
of seeing some of the more valuable illustrated works contained in the Reference Library, a large show-case was
provided in which such books are displayed under glass.
This case forms a fine addition to the room, and is much
appreciated by the public, many of whom, until its existence,
had no notion of the beautiful and costly books provided for
their use by the Free Libraries Committee. With the same
view of making the people generally, better acquainted with

the contents of the libraries, the committee sanctioned the publication of occasional lists, showing what books on special subjects are contained not only in the Reference Library but also in the Lending Libraries.   Lists of books on China and British South Africa have already been issued, and a third list on trade books is now in the printer's hands.   An edition of 10,000 copies of each list is issued and distributed gratuitously at the various libraries, and among the large factories and workshops in the town.

During the late autumn of 1900 and early in 1901 the issue on Sundays began to show signs of a very remarkable increase which seems to have been due to the following cause :—

To save the wear and tear on the bound volumes of *Graphic*, *Illustrated London News* and other pictorial papers, the plan was devised of stitching into cheap board wrappers with a cloth back the duplicate copies of these papers from the branch libraries, which had hitherto been either wasted or sent to the workhouse and other similar institutions, These were issued to the boys who came to the Reference Library on Sundays instead of the bound volumes.   Either because the supply of such papers was thereby very largely increased, or for some other wholly unexplained reason, the boys began to come in ever-increasing numbers.   They finally became so numerous that they almost monopolised the library to the great discomfort of the regular readers, and in February, 1901, the committee sanctioned opening the wing of the Central Lending Library on Sunday for their accommodation. This has proved a very great success, and here on Sunday evenings may be seen a rather extraordinary spectacle, every chair occupied and rows of boys sitting on the floor in every available spot, each occupied in looking at the pictures in the papers that are so abundantly provided for them. It is not contended that they are doing much reading, as a rule probably they are not reading at all; they are of a class who are more interested in the illustrations than in the printed page, but even though this be the case the work that is being done is by no means to be despised.

How very considerable the increase in the issue is may

be seen by comparing the figures for 1899-1900 and 1901-2. The average issue on Sundays in 1899-1900 was 416, while in the year 1901-2 the average was 1,127.

During the year 1900-1 the Reference Library was enriched by the addition of a well-selected and valuable library containing about 7,000 volumes, bequeathed by the late H. Payton Badley, Esq. When these came to be catalogued it was found that there would be about 2,000 duplicates of works already in the Reference Library. In order to keep the Badley Library intact, it was decided to remove the duplicates from the Reference Library and use them as the foundation of a reference library in one of the branches. This was accordingly done, and the youngest of the Birmingham branch libraries, which differs from the other branches inasmuch as it is a reference library only, was opened on Monday, 22nd September, by the Lord Mayor of Birmingham, Alderman J. H. Lloyd, and is thus associated in a very interesting way with the visit of the Library Association to Birmingham.

I have thus brought the history of the Birmingham Free Libraries down to date, but I feel that my paper will be somewhat incomplete if I do not give a brief account of the way in which these twelve libraries are managed and the work carried on.

To begin with, all the libraries are under the direction and control of the chief librarian, who is responsible to the committee for their condition and management. They are, however, almost entirely independent of each other, and almost as much separate institutions as if they existed in different towns. Each library possesses its own staff, its own stock of books and newspapers, and its own list of borrowers. The borrowers' tickets are not transferable, and with one exception can only be used for the library at which they are taken out. The exception is in the case of books other than fiction at the Central Lending Library. Borrowers at the branches can obtain a transfer ticket which enables them to take out any book other than fiction that is in the Central Lending Library and not at their branch, their ordinary ticket being meanwhile suspended.

As the books are thus available for the whole town the committee are able to place in the Central Lending Library somewhat more expensive books on history, biography, travel and science, and a much larger collection of books in foreign languages than they would otherwise feel justified in doing. In addition duly qualified persons can become borrowers at any or all of the lending libraries at the same time, by obtaining separate vouchers at each place. It is thus possible for a borrower to obtain ten books at once, if he is desirous of so doing, and no one can reasonably say that the facilities for borrowing books are unduly restricted.

The accounts of all the libraries are kept quite distinct. An estimate of the amount required for each head of expense such as books, binding, wages, gas, etc., is prepared for every library, and the expenditure for any library is based on the estimate for that library, and as far as possible kept within it. There is a librarian at every library, and a staff of assistants, ranging from one at Adderley Park to eight in the Central Lending. The librarian has the general oversight of the library under his charge. It is his duty to suggest the books required for addition and replacement, to select the books that require binding, to catalogue the books when received, and to prepare the accounts. In the earlier history of the libraries this work was all done under the direct supervision of the chief librarian, who himself checked the work of the librarians in all details, the books being sent to the Reference Library for this purpose. In June, 1882, partly to save sending these heavy parcels weekly to the Reference Library and partly to save the chief librarian's time, who was much occupied with the reconstruction of the Reference Library, the committee authorised the delegation of this work to an assistant. It was accordingly performed by the sub-librarian, who paid a weekly visit to each of the lending libraries to check the additions, replacements, binding and other work of the department, and to report to the chief librarian thereon. The work remained in his hands for more than ten years until owing to the increase in the number of the libraries it began to absorb too much of his time, and in December, 1892, an officer was specially appointed to take charge of this work. He did not for some few years devote his whole time to the work, but as the new libraries were opened one after another this finally became necessary, and an Inspector of Lending Libraries was appointed who was instructed to devote his whole time to the duties of his office, reporting daily to the chief librarian the result of his visits, and monthly to the Management sub-Committee, and in this way a most effective oversight of the libraries has been obtained.

Until last June the system of issue in use in all the lending libraries was the old ledger system. This involved keeping a register in which the numbers of both the book and borrowers' ticket were entered at the time of issue, marking off the books when returned, and keeping a Posting Book, in which the date of issue was posted to the number of the book issued. An indicator was in use at the Central Lending Library, but it was only used to show whether the books were in or out, and did none of the other work which an indicator is supposed to perform. In June last an experiment was made at the Balsall Heath Branch by the introduction of the Cotgreave Indicator, the ledger system being there abandoned. So far it appears to be satisfactory, but it is too early yet to say how it will compare with the system that has been in force for so many years, and is still retained in all our other lending libraries.

The method of obtaining the books required for addition and replacement in the lending libraries is as follows :—

In the estimate for the year a certain sum is apportioned to each library for the purchase of books. This sum varies according to the size and importance of the library, and ranges from £40 a year for the Adderley Park Branch to £300 a year for the Central Lending Library. The librarian of each library prepares week by week a rough list of books for addition which is submitted to the Inspector on his next visit. If they seem to him desirable the books are entered in the Suggestion Book, together with the price and other particulars. Books suggested for replacement are also submitted to the Inspector, and if approved are entered in the Suggestion Book in the same way. About the third week in each month the Suggestion Book is made up, and the net cost of the suggestions shown. This amount should not exceed the monthly proportion of the sum allotted to the library for the year. The Suggestion Books are all examined by the chief librarian, and are then submitted to the Lending Libraries Book sub-Committee, who recommend the purchase of such of them as they think desirable. The books are ordered after they have been approved by the Free Libraries Committee, and are dealt with week by week at the various libraries as they come from the booksellers. It is a part of the Inspector's duty to see that all books are supplied at the prices ordered, that they are properly entered in the Receiving Book, catalogued, cut and stamped, and in the case of replacements, that the old copies are either destroyed or marked in such a way as shall prevent them from getting into circulation again. When they are thus marked many of the worn-out copies are given to the workhouse, the Working Boys' Home and other similar institutions. At the workhouse, for example, there is a considerable library made up of the discarded copies from the Birmingham Free Libraries. Among the happy inmates of that luxurious retreat there is, or was, a bookbinder, who had charge of these books, and he told me that he was often able to make one complete and tolerably clean copy out of two or three worn-out, and perhaps incomplete copies that were sent to him from the libraries. The books are all stoved and purified as far as possible before they are circulated in the workhouse.

With regard to the purification of books it may not be out of place to mention here the course that is adopted in Birmingham in the case of books coming from infected houses. When the Sanitary Inspector visits any of the houses where there are contagious diseases he is instructed by the Health Department to ascertain whether there are any books in the house belonging to the Birmingham Free Libraries. If there are he takes possession of them and notifies the fact to the library. The books are then either destroyed by the Health Department, or returned to the library from which they were taken out, for identification, where they are burnt. They never go into circulation again, even if the borrower states that they have not been handled by, or been in the same room as the patient.

Books for the Reference Library are ordered by the Book sub-Committee, which meets once a month for that purpose. Suggestions for additions are made by members of the committee, the chief librarian and staff, and by the public. The Proposal Books containing these various suggestions are submitted to the committee, and every suggestion is separately considered and voted on. The amount included in the estimate for the Reference Library is £700 a year, and this sum is spent in the purchase of the ordinary works which are necessary to keep the library in a living condition. In addition the interest of the Book Fund, amounting to about £200 a year, can be used for the purchase of luxuries in the shape of rare and costly books.

The work done in the Reference Library is of a most multifarious character. It includes not only the work proper to the Reference Library itself, but all the general work that relates to all the libraries. Here the general statistics are tabulated and kept, here the accounts of all the libraries are finally checked and ledgered, here the committee work is prepared and the minutes of the various sub-committees entered, and here too the great bulk of the correspondence relating to all the libraries is dealt with. Without a well-organised system it would be practically impossible to get through the work, and as it is the work in the Reference Library is never ended. The careful organisation of the work made by my predecessor Mr. Mullins and embodied in the Routine Books is of great practical value. I know the system is not universally approved, and has even been the subject of a certain amount of ridicule, but I believe most thoroughly that no large library or collection of libraries, such as we have here, can be carried on successfully without a well-defined system, and the embodiment of that system in a book instead of in the failing memories of individual librarians, seems to me the only satisfactory way. The Daily Routine Book in the Reference Library includes more than a hundred items, some of which may perhaps be open to the criticism of dealing with the infinitely little.

It is, however, with respect to these apparently trifling matters that a Routine Book is most necessary. Are we not told on very high authority that it is the little foxes which spoil the grapes, and do we not know that a man would often be more seriously annoyed to find that he had no button on his shirt than to find he had no shirt to wear. Even therefore though the Routine Book does provide for such small matters as the sharpening of pencils for the counters, I contend that it is justified by the fact that the pencils are sharpened, and are not in the condition of those in a great public department into which I had occasion to go the other day, where out of the many pencils provided there was not a single one fit for use. A similar though less extensive Routine Book is in use in all the lending libraries, and long experience has convinced me that without some such system many of the things which require to be done daily would be left undone. They would either be forgotten altogether, or postponed to that more convenient season, which never comes. With the Routine Book before them there is no excuse for forgetting the work, and as part of the Inspector's duty is to see that the Routine Book is properly filled up, postponement of duty becomes a luxury which it is not wise for the librarian to indulge in too often. No doubt libraries can be and sometimes are carried on without any such helps to exact and careful management, and no doubt they muddle through; but should we be satisfied with merely muddling through; is it not better to have what after all is a great business carried on in a business-like and satisfactory manner? The carrying out of the instructions in the Routine Book is not left to chance. In the Reference Library an officer is appointed daily to see to this work, and is held responsible for getting the work done. In the Lending Libraries the librarian in charge is responsible. In this way the work is kept current, and it will seldom if ever happen that the month before last copy of the *Contemporary Review* is still in the cover on the table, while no one knows where the current number has been put, or that there are no readers' tickets or vouchers on the counter available for use, and that intending readers have to wait while a parcel is fetched from the store-room. Such a system may perhaps not be absolutely necessary in a small library where one or two officers only are concerned in the administration, but in a large library without some such system the work would, I feel sure, be likely to get hopelessly in arrear.

Time does not permit me to go more fully into detail as to the methods of work in the Birmingham Free Libraries, nor perhaps is such detail necessary in the case of an audience composed chiefly of librarians. They presumably are more or less acquainted with all the existing methods of library work and management, and require only an outline of the scheme to enable them to fill in the detail for themselves.

Such an outline I have attempted to present, and while I should not like to claim perfection for the Birmingham system, or even to say that there are no better methods in existence, this much may safely be said, that by means of this system the libraries here are on the whole well organised and equipped, and have reached a fairly high standard of efficiency and success.

In closing, however, I cannot refrain from saying, that I am not wholly satisfied with the success already attained. It is true the libraries have increased in number from one in 1861 to twelve in 1902, that the number of volumes in the libraries has increased from 6,288 to 272,000, and the issue from 108,000 to 1,332,000. These figures no doubt show a fairly satisfactory growth, but, like Oliver Twist, I crave for more. There is room for more libraries, for there are two or three districts which are still a considerable distance from any of the existing libraries, and there is room for a large increase in the use made of the books.

The total number of borrowers in the Lending Libraries is 30,000, but the population of the city is in round figures 530,000. We get the 30,000, but where are the 500,000? The issue is a little over a million and a quarter. It sounds large, but after all it is not three books a year for every member of the population. The same thing is no doubt true of the other library centres, but it does not seem to me that either the borrowers or the issue is proportionate to the population. Here as elsewhere there must be an immense number of people to whom the libraries are an unknown land, and I ask how can these people be made acquainted with the treasures that are waiting for them, how can they be induced to make fuller use of their libraries? In the discussion which follows my paper I hope some suggestions may be made which will indicate how this may be done. Personally, I shall not feel quite satisfied until our borrowers are 100,000, and our issue at least 10,000 a day.

It only remains for me to acknowledge the debt I owe to Dr. Langford's *History of the Birmingham Free Libraries* and the *History of the Corporation of Birmingham,* by Messrs. Bunce and Vince. As a matter of fact the earlier portion of my paper is little more than an abridgment of Mr. Bunce's account of the Libraries contained in Vol. II. of the History of the Corporation.

PROCEEDINGS OF
THE TWENTY-FIFTH ANNUAL MEETING OF THE LIBRARY ASSOCIATION.

HELD AT BIRMINGHAM, 23RD, 24TH, 25TH AND 26TH SEPTEMBER, 1902.

TUESDAY, 23RD SEPTEMBER.

First Session.

The proceedings of the Twenty-Fifth Annual Meeting of the Library Association were opened at Birmingham on the morning of Tuesday, the 23rd of September, in the Council Chamber of the Council House.

At 9.45 the members of the Association were welcomed by the Right Honourable the Lord Mayor of Birmingham (Alderman J. H. Lloyd), who was supported by Prof. W. Macneile Dixon, Litt.D., LL.B (president-elect), Dr. Richard Garnett, C.B., Councillor Haines, chairman of the Birmingham Free Libraries Committee, Mr. Henry R. Tedder (hon. treasurer), and Mr. Lawrence Inkster (hon. secretary).

A number of well-known local gentlemen were present, including Mr. J. G. Johnson (chairman of the Reception Committee), Mr. A. Capel Shaw, Mr. C. E. Scarse, Mr. W. S. Pritchett (local secretary); with members and delegates from all parts of the United Kingdom to the number of nearly three hundred. The assembly was graced by the presence of a number of ladies, including the assistant secretary, Mrs. K. Reilly.

Welcome by the Lord Mayor.

The LORD MAYOR in opening the proceedings said that he had been asked, in the absence of the retiring President, to occupy the chair until the new President took his seat. He had very great pleasure, on behalf of the Corporation and citizens of Birmingham, in welcoming the Association to the city. They could not show antiquities dating back many hundreds or thousands of years. They could not show any very beautiful ancient buildings in the city itself; neither could they show any of those marvels of great age which have belonged to other places visited by the Association in the past, such as Plymouth, Bristol and London. In coming to Birmingham they had come to a modern town, so modern that the recent coronation was the first the Corporation had had the honour of seeing. Notwithstanding the absence of antiquity he wished to give them a most hearty welcome, and to co-operate with them in every way to ensure the success of the visit. The work of the Association was one in which the Corporation took a deep interest, not only in theory but in practice. During the last forty years in which the town had grown up, the subject of libraries had been well kept before them. It was about forty years since the little library at Constitution

Hill was first opened, while it was in 1859 that the Public Libraries Act was adopted.   In 1865 the Central Lending Library was begun, and now in addition to the Central Lending and Reference Libraries Birmingham had nine branch lending libraries, and one branch reference library at Harborne, which was opened on Monday.   Altogether there were twelve libraries in connection with the Corporation, upon which about £17,000 was annually spent, £16,000 coming directly from the rates.   The Reference Library issued 395,000 books a year, and the Lending Libraries 936,000, making a total issue of about 1,332,000.   The total number of their books was about half a million.   His Lordship thought these few points would give some little idea of the work performed by the Free Library Committee on behalf of the Corporation of the city.   He believed that the branch libraries were thoroughly appreciated, and he trusted that the visit of the members of the Library Association to Birmingham would help to keep the libraries of the country abreast of the times in every possible way.   There was a great deal to be done in the way of keeping the better class of books before the people, and in providing facilities for the public to get access to the books they desired.   Concluding, his Lordship said, he had very great pleasure in heartily welcoming the Library Association, and hoped that at the end of their stay the members would feel that they had spent a pleasant and profitable time in Birmingham.

The HON. SECRETARY (Mr. Lawrence Inkster) then read the scrutineers' certificate as to the result of the ballot for officers and Council for the ensuing year, which was as follows:—

PRESIDENT.

Prof. W. Macneile Dixon, Litt.D., LL.B., Birmingham University.

VICE-PRESIDENTS.

Sir William H. Bailey, a Governor of the John Rylands Library, Manchester.
Francis T. Barrett, City Librarian, Glasgow.
J. Potter Briscoe, City Librarian, Nottingham.
Peter Cowell, Librarian of the Public Libraries, Liverpool.
Alderman Francis Fox, Public Libraries Committee, Bristol.
J. W. Knapman, Librarian of the Pharmaceutical Society of Great Britain.
T. G. Law, Librarian of the Signet Library, Edinburgh.
T. W. Lyster, Librarian of the National Library of Ireland, Dublin.
Thomas Mason, Librarian of St. Martin's Public Library, City of Westminster.
Councillor H. Plummer, Chairman, Manchester Public Libraries Committee.
C. W. Sutton, Librarian of the Public Libraries, Manchester.
W. H. K. Wright, Librarian of the Public Library, Plymouth.

HON. TREASURER.

Henry R. Tedder, Secretary and Librarian of the Athenæum, Pall Mall.

HON. SECRETARY.

Lawrence Inkster, Librarian of the Public Libraries, Battersea.

HON. SOLICITOR.

H. W. Fovargue, Town Clerk, Eastbourne.
All the above have been elected without a contest.

LONDON COUNCILLORS.

Elected.	*No. of Votes.*
1. F. J. Burgoyne	185
2. W. E. Doubleday	180
3. F. T. Barrett	172
4. J. D. Brown	159
5. H. Bond	139
6. C. T. Davis	137
7. A. W. Pollard	133
8. J. R. Boosé	132
9. E. Wyndham Hulme	131
10. T. Aldred	127
11. W. C. Plant	122
12. H. D. Roberts	122

Not Elected.

13. E. G. Rees	120

COUNTRY COUNCILLORS.

Elected.	*No. of Votes.*
1. Henry Guppy	155
2. W. Crowther	150
3. R. K. Dent	150
4. J. Ballinger	145
5. L. S. Jast	143
6. Butler Wood	142
7. A. Lancaster	141
8. B. Anderton	140
9. J. P. Edmond	140
10 C. Madeley	139
11. J. J. Ogle	137
12. G. T. Shaw	137
13 H. T. Folkard	136
14. E. R. N. Mathews	135
15. W. E. A. Axon	132
16. T. W. Hand	131
17. Alderman W. H. Brittain	123
18. G. H. Elliott	123
19. C. V. Kirkby	121
20. G. L. Campbell	113

Not Elected.

21. T. Johnston	111

Installation of New President.

The LORD MAYOR then introduced the PRESIDENT, who took the chair, amid applause.

Sir WILLIAM H. BAILEY said that before they congratulated the President upon his election, he wished to move a vote of thanks to the Lord Mayor of Birmingham for the very handsome manner in which they had been received that morning. He spoke of the excellent libraries in the city, and particularly mentioned the Shakespeare Library, which he unhesitatingly described as the greatest and best Shakespearean library in the world. Birmingham was not an ancient city, but it had a splendid reputation in the world of letters, as in the world of invention. Most of the great inventions have had a home in Birmingham—gas-lighting, steam engines and the earlier labours of Stephenson. In the world of thought and history the city occupied a very dignified position, although it could not boast the antiquity of Salford, which was mentioned in Domesday Book, and of which Edward the Confessor was Lord of the Manor. He then moved that the best thanks of the Association be given to the Lord Mayor for his kind reception on their second visit to Birmingham.

Alderman SOUTHERN, J.P. (Manchester), seconding the resolution, said that the welcome which the Association received wherever it went testified, he thought, to the high esteem in which the public library movement was held in all the great centres of population in the kingdom. He was pleased that they had had an opportunity of coming to Birmingham, which, if not an ancient city, had the advantage of being very modern and up-to-date. He thought the meeting promised to be an exceedingly successful one, from the large number of delegates who were present, the interesting nature of the papers before them, and also from the recreative side.

The vote of thanks, which the President put to the meeting, was carried with acclamation, and the Lord Mayor returned thanks.

The HON. SECRETARY read the names of the following candidates for election, who had been approved by the Council. The usual ballot having been suspended, they were unanimously elected to membership of the Association :—

Dr. H. W. Syers, M.R.C.P., 75 Wimpole Street, London, W.

Mr. S. A. Grundy-Newman, Solicitor, Littleton Place, Walsall.

Mr. John Ross, Librarian of the Public Library, Pietermaritzburg, Natal.

Widnes Public Library.

Councillor Hugh Ross, Member of the Wigan Library Committee, Wallgate, Wigan.

Mr. George Henry Brown, 137 Scholes, Wigan.

Devonport Public Library (Mr. Alderman Thomas Bowen, Riversdale, St. Budeaux, Devonport).

Mr. Robert Halliwell, J.P., Honorary Member of the Wigan Library Committee, Rodney Street, Wigan.

Mr. Thurston Cocker, Wigan.

Mr. John Walls, Chairman of the Public Libraries Committee, Bristol.

Thanks to the Retiring President.

Dr. RICHARD GARNETT, C.B., said he rose with great pleasure to propose a resolution to which they would agree with great unanimity. It gave him very great pleasure to move a vote of thanks to the late president, Mr. G. K. Fortescue. He had had ample opportunities of appreciating Mr. Fortescue, both as a librarian and in connection with literature. The amount of personal labour which Mr. Fortescue took upon himself with the British Museum catalogue would hardly be credited by those who were not cognisant of it. He would say nothing more of his merit as a librarian. They would all remember with what extreme energy he threw himself into the work at the Plymouth meeting, what a desire he showed that everything should proceed in the best way possible, the great attention he paid to the business and to every indivi-dual member. Mr. Fortescue had infused a spirit of energy and goodwill into our proceedings. He had very great pleasure in proposing that a vote of thanks be accorded to Mr. Fortescue for his able services as President of the Association during the past year.

Mr. HENRY R. TEDDER (hon. treasurer) said he had very much

pleasure in briefly but very cordially seconding the vote of thanks to the retiring President. He had had many occasions during the past year of seeing the great interest taken by Mr. Fortescue in the affairs of the Association, and he could assure them that he fully deserved both offici-ally and unofficially the very grateful thanks of the Association. The President having put the motion to the meeting, it was carried unanimously.

President's Address.

Prof. W. MACNEILE DIXON then delivered his presidential address, which will be found on pages 479-491.

Mr. T. W. LYSTER (National Library, Ireland), said he had the honour and pleasure to move that the thanks of the Association be offered to the President for his eloquent and beautiful address, which he thought was one of the most admirable which had ever been heard by the Association. He felt it was quite impossible to speak with justice upon it immediately after hearing it. The President had delivered just such an address as was required. He had taken them out of their everyday life of detail, out of the immediate present, and to their great spiritual profit, he had carried them on beyond and above the practical affairs of the hour and day. The President had spoken heartfelt truths valuable to them all, and he moved that the best thanks of the Associa-tion be offered to him.

Mr. FRANCIS T. BARRETT (Glasgow) seconded the resolution, and said they had listened to an address not only witty and wise but eloquent and philosophical. It had come to many of them who were tied too much to the drudgery of daily work—immersed in detail—as a breath from the heights—invigorating, lofty and inspiriting. The President had done the Association a very great service by his address.

The vote having been put to the meeting by the Lord Mayor, was carried with acclamation, and the President, after warmly thanking the Lord Mayor, his old friend Mr. Lyster and Mr. Barrett, called upon:

Mr. A. CAPEL SHAW, Librarian, Birmingham Public Libraries, to read his paper on

The Birmingham Free Libraries,

in which he traced their history from fifty years ago, when the proposal to establish a free library in Birmingham was first introduced by Mr. Councillor Boyce, down to the opening of the Reference Library at Harborne on Monday. Mr. Shaw then proceeded to describe the manner in which the libraries are managed and the work carried on, and said that while he did not claim perfection for the Birmingham system, or even say that there were no better methods in existence, it might safely be said that by means of the system the libraries were, on the whole, well organised and equipped, and had reached a fairly high standard of efficiency and success. There was room for more libraries, for there were two or three districts which were a considerable distance from any of those in existence, and there was room for a large increase in the use made of the books. The total number of borrowers in the lending libraries was 30,000, but the population of the city was, in round figures, 530,000. He should not be satisfied until the borrowers numbered 100,000, with an issue of at least 10,000 a day.

Publishers and Publishing.

Mr. WALTER POWELL, Sub-Librarian, Birmingham Public Libraries, read an interesting paper on " Publishers and Publishing," the special object of which was to call attention to unnecessary irregularities which were frequently found when books were collated, and also to the many books which were so padded, either by the use of thick paper or large type, as to form volumes two or three times larger than was necessary, apparently with the object of justifying an unreasonable price. In the first place much of the paper used nowadays was very poor, but the question had been taken up by the Society of Arts, and a committee had reported upon the subject; it was sincerely to be hoped that good results would come of this. If books intended for permanent preservation were carefully collated when received various vagaries of the publisher came to light. Some publishers, for instance, left the first leaf—not page—blank, yet calculated it in the pagination. While the book remained in the publisher's case it was easy to see that the blank leaf was part of the sheet, and, therefore, it might be presumed to count in the pagination. If the book were re-bound, however, ninety-nine binders out of every hundred would carefully remove the blank leaf, and thus unconsciously render the work imperfect. The possibility of this could be removed by the simple expedient of not including blank leaves in the pagination. Another stupid departure was to have only one pagination, and there was the much more frequent omission of lists of contents, lists of maps or plates, or of index. The new volumes of the *Encyclopædia Britannica* contained a number of plates of which there were no lists. Another point in connection with the beginning of books was the undated title-page. He supposed the title-page was often left undated from commercial considerations, as it was no doubt easier to sell a book which was ten years old if the purchaser thought it was new. But there were innumerable cases of books without dates for which no satisfactory reasons could be given; indeed, the evil was so widespread that he was afraid there would be no improvement until His Majesty's Government ranged the crime with murder and high treason, and made it a capital offence. Passing lightly over several "barbarous methods" adopted for holding sheets together, Mr. Powell proceeded to enter a protest against recent ideas as to lettering the backs of books, and said there appeared to be a tendency to indulge in extremely ornamental backs, in which the title was so carefully interweaved and hidden that it would sometimes seem that the words "Puzzle, find the title," had been printed on the back. A most important ground for complaining of publishers was the dishing-up of old wares as new matter. He gave three instances in corroboration of his statement. Mr. Powell next contended that the modern craze for "series" was being much overdone, and pointed out that some publishers appeared to have a positive passion for beginning fresh series in the publications of various learned societies.

Dr. R. GARNETT, C.B., regretted that for many years past the excellent plan of introducing the water-mark date in publications had been discontinued. That was a matter of great importance to students of history and literary matter in general, because it enabled them to fix the date. Thirty years ago the insertion of the date in the water-mark was almost a matter of course, but now it was hardly ever given. He had communicated with the Papermakers' Association on the subject, who said that though they entirely agreed with him, they found that the makers would not give the date for fear that in doing so they would show that the paper they were selling was not quite new. Those engaged in historical researches would suffer a good deal in future from the absence of date. As to indexing, he could say a good word for the publishers, and he had reason to think some few important books would never have had any circulation but for the publishers.

Mr. A. J. CADDIE (Stoke-on-Trent) pointed out that the absence of date was not always the fault of the publishers. Frequently it was the writer's fault. For example, the printed copy of Mr. Powell's paper did not include anything to show where it was read or the date. That was a striking example of the necessity shown.

Mr. W. E. DOUBLEDAY (Hampstead) suggested that military authors should be asked to give some indication of their rank in the army and also to give their initials.

Mr. C. CHIVERS (Bath) thought the paper very valuable, but could hardly imagine the publishers indulging in unnecessary over-stitching; the process was too costly; he had never met with such a case.

Mr. H. M. GILBERT (Southampton) suggested that the Association should extract from the paper three or four recommendations and try to get publishers to carry them out.

Mr. S. MARTIN (Hammersmith) complained of sub-titles being used as first titles. It was a foolish practice which ought to be pointed out to the publishers. Another very questionable practice was that of dating books for the following year, which was very misleading. For instance a book issued in October was dated for the next year. That was misleading and really false, and publishers' attention should be called to the fact. He regretted to say it was done by some of the best publishers. In another case one eminent novelist, whose book was actually written by his lady assistant, put his own name to it. He thought that a very improper practice.

Sir WM. BAILEY cited an instance where an edition of *The Works of John Keats* only contained one-third of his works. He thought that was obtaining money by false pretences, and as one of the purchasers he thought he had a good ground of action. Yet that was done by a respectable firm of publishers in London, and he thought he should " paddle his own canoe " by proceeding against them. The paper was a valuable one, and they were indebted to the writer for calling attention to many things that required publicity.

Mr. H. GUPPY (Manchester) urged the extreme importance of collation. It was necessary and in most cases not a difficult matter in regard to modern books with pagination, but how much more necessary was it when they got back to the older books where there was no pagination, and in some cases neither foliation nor signatures. The difficulty was often very great and only to be overcome by a careful collation by water-marks such as Dr. Garnett had referred to. In order to emphasise the necessity for proper collation the speaker cited a case which had come under his notice quite recently of a work which had at first sight all the appearance of completeness. But when it came to be analysed or collated it was found to want at the beginning twelve preliminary leaves, although the signatures were apparently all right, and at the end forty leaves of supplementary matter. In another work, one of the earliest books of the first Paris press, without pagination, foliation or signatures, they discovered by means of water-mark collation that a leaf was missing from the heart of the volume, with the result that a work offered in the first place for £50 was eventually purchased for £5. Every book coming into the library should be carefully collated. As to the binding up of the original covers of a work, Mr. Guppy pointed out that it was not essential to bind in the heavy boards. The printed portion could be soaked off the boards and bound up in the same way as the title-page.

The PRESIDENT promised, on behalf of the Executive, that the recommendations based upon the paper and the discussion should be sent on to the publishers.

A Few Experiments at Glasgow.

Mr. F. THORNTON BARRETT, Librarian, Corporation Public Libraries, Glasgow, submitted a note respecting certain arrangements of a more or less experimental character in the recently opened library and news-room in the Gorbals district of Glasgow. The chief point, as regards the general reading-room, was that the reading tables are kept clear, and all reading matter—newspapers, periodicals and books—are kept on stands, or racks, or book-shelves. Readers find readily what they want, take it to any table they select, and when leaving restore it to its place. The result is an unusual degree of quiet and absence of dis-tracting movement. Several technical devices for facilitating the work were described, and as to the lending library a special system of numbering and marking, a new form of adjustable indicator, and other novelties were mentioned.

John Baskerville and his Work.

Mr. ROBERT K. DENT, Librarian, Public Library, Aston Manor, read an interesting and much appreciated paper on "John Baskerville and his Work".

Mr. H. R. TEDDER (London) said that as the writer of an article on Baskerville in the *Dictionary of National Biography* he was gratified that the subject of John Baskerville had not been omitted from their pro-gramme. He looked upon Baskerville as one of the greatest men the Birmingham nursery of great men had ever produced. His monument ought to stand by the side of that of Caxton, and his name ought never to be forgotten in Birmingham. Mr. Dent referred to Mr. Samuel Timmins, whose absence on account of the state of his health they all deeply regretted. All who had ever had to do with him would respect his memory. He made collections for a "Life of Baskerville," which he kindly placed at his (the speaker's) disposal, and anything that was useful in his article was entirely due to Mr. Timmins. He thought he was completely informed on the subject. But several facts were mentioned by Mr. Dent which he felt ought to be added to any future edition of his article. It was rash for one to think that his own biblio-graphy was complete. Only last week he found in a library not far from where they were assembled a book by Baskerville, published in 1767, and he had no doubt if he looked far enough he would find many more.

The conference then adjourned.

Luncheon at the Masonic Hall and Excursions.

At the invitation of the Local Reception Committee the members were entertained at luncheon in the Masonic Hall. In the afternoon a large party visited the Wolverhampton Exhibition, under the guid-ance of Mr. Whitworth Wallis. The Fine Art Section housed in the Horseman Gallery, the Municipal Art Gallery was explained by Mr. Laurence W. Hodson, the Chairman of the Section, and the visitors, after viewing the exhibition, partook of tea at the invitation of the Mayor of Wolverhampton (Mr. C. P. Plant). Another party visited Kenilworth.

Reception at the Council House.

A reception and ball was given in the evening by the Lord Mayor and Lady Mayoress of Birmingham, at which over 2,000 guests were present, including 250 members of the Library Association.   The rooms were beautifully decorated in red, white and blue in honour of the coronation.   Dancing commenced at the close of the reception, and an excellent musical programme was given in the Council Chamber by Miss Winifred Brightwell, Mr. E. Gordon Cleather and Mrs. Helen Trust.

WEDNESDAY, 24TH SEPTEMBER.

Second Session.

An Italian Librarian of the Seventeenth Century: Antonio Magliabecchi.

The second day's proceedings were continued at the Council House by the President, who was in the chair, calling upon:

Mr. W. E. A. AXON (Manchester) to read his paper, postponed from the previous day's session, on "An Italian Librarian of the Seventeenth Century: Antonio Magliabecchi," called the most learned of the learned librarians.   Born in ·Florence in 1633, he was one of two sons of a widow, who appeared to have brought up her sons in a very laudable manner.   His elder brother received a professional education, and obtained distinction as an ecclesiastic.   Antonio was apprenticed to a goldsmith, and remained a goldsmith until he was forty years old ; but he had a passion for knowledge, and long before his retirement his fame was known throughout Europe.   He then became librarian to the Tuscan princes, who treated him with great liberality.   They did not impose upon him any of the formalities of the Court, and when they wanted any assistance, as they often did, they went to his room and conversed with him as students with a teacher rather than as princes with a subject.   The stories told of his knowledge were so extravagant as to almost pass belief but for the testimony of learned men which showed it to be a fact.   He ate upon his books, he sat upon his books, he slept upon his books.   There were two great points in his career to interest librarians.   One was that he had acquired a method of getting to the heart of a book.   He examined the title-page and the index and hurriedly scanned the intervening pages, and could tell just what new information the author had to give on the subject.   It had been said that this method was not unknown to modern librarians.   The second feature which would appeal to them was that he realised more fully than, perhaps, any other learned man, the fraternity of learning, shown by the way in which he communicated information to all who sought him.   At the time of his death his own private collection consisted of 30,000 books and manuscripts, which now formed part of the library of Florence.

The Rate Limit and the Future of Public Libraries.

Mr. JOHN BALLINGER, Librarian, Cardiff Public Libraries, followed with a paper on the limitations of the functions of a library and the false economy of the 1d. rate imposed by the Libraries Acts.   Mr. Ballinger convincingly showed how many and how great are the public gains that would follow a slight increase of the library rate.   He pointed out that when the rate was first imposed, fifty years ago, the public

37

library was in its earliest experimental stage, and no one dreamed of the immense developments that lay before it. But "the spread of education has created demands upon libraries, both in range and extent beyond the most sanguine dreams of those who pioneered the movement, and to a very large degree the libraries have failed to supply the demands". They have so failed because they have been crippled by the restrictive Libraries Act. The general ideas of the functions of public libraries, said Mr. Ballinger, need revision and extension. He pointed to many directions in which their scope of action could be extended; for instance, they could further technical instruction by exhibiting choice collections of fine printing and bookbinding. The 1d. rate was false economy. At present books were bought out of the surplus that remained after the establishment charges had been met, an arrangement which seriously limited the usefulness of the library. An increased income would add to the power of improving the libraries out of all proportion to the extra rate levied. It would enable Corporations to build a sufficient number of branch libraries, and to provide in them the equipment which would be needed in the extended and nationalised library of the future. The idea of a library as a place where cheap fiction is doled out to casual ticket-holders is, of course, one which will have to go by the board. Mr. Ballinger showed, among other things, how much the library can do for the children of our towns by providing children's reading-rooms. "For want of a few pounds yearly," he said, "we are sacrificing the children generation by generation, and wasting to a large extent the benefits which ought to ensue from the immense sums expended on elementary education." Manchester had shown the way in this matter, and there the citizens had overridden the Imperial Act by local legislation, by which means the Manchester library rate is 2d. in the £. Mr. Ballinger dwelt on the need of more efficient staffing and organisation of libraries; and the need of increasing the remuneration of a worthy and self-sacrificing body of public servants. "Librarians, who are expected to possess qualities almost divine, are in most instances paid less than teachers in good elementary schools, and assistants are paid salaries which leave them without hope or pride," although, as Bishop Creighton had said, "a librarian has a greater and a higher educational opportunity than almost anybody else". Twenty-five towns had already been forced by the public need to override the limit by obtaining special powers, and their experience showed that there was no danger of wasteful expenditure resulting from greater generosity. As to the argument that to increase the rating power would prevent the adoption of the Libraries Act in some backward places, Mr. Ballinger thought it more likely that a general improvement in the library system would force these benighted towns into line. But even if this did not happen, "Are we to be dragged at the tail of the backward communities for ever?" Let them unite in a vigorous effort of library reform, whose aim should be to make the libraries really serve the wants and aspirations of the people. There were prejudices as to the very scope and purpose of a public library which must be eradicated. "The public library is not a philanthropic institution for the benefit of a class. It is a great co-operative effort of a community. At the outset the working man may have been mainly in the promoters' minds. That was fifty years ago. The idea is still prevalent, and to it is due much unfortunate prejudice against the library movement. We have not done all that we might to destroy the misconception. Far too many libraries are still mere newsrooms and circulators of large numbers of cheap books—excellent work enough as far as it goes. But the public library must be something much greater and more inspiring. It ought to minister to the reading wants of the whole community, to provide books of reference for all, to be a storehouse of learning for the scholar, a repository of every scrap of local literature, whether printed or manuscript, and every local print and drawing which can be brought together. All eyes should be turned to the library as a place where knowledge is stored and available for use. The greatest citizen should not be above the library, and the library should not be above the meanest of the citizens."

Alderman STOLTERFOHT (Liverpool) said many of the suggestions made in the paper had already been very beneficially carried out in Liverpool. From time to time members of learned and other societies had been invited to see some of their finest works. On Saturday afternoon especially a staff of assistants were reserved to show such parties round the library, and the privilege was not abused. On one occasion all the books referring to the history of Liverpool were exhibited, in addition to valuable water-colours relating to the same subject. The interest taken was so great that by general consent the exhibition was repeated on the following Saturday. Another suggestion carried out was the provision of catalogues for certain trades, as well as for the fine arts and architecture, and such catalogues had been found very useful. A special boys' reading-room was provided in all their branch libraries in addition to rooms for men and ladies. They had a rate of 1½d. in the £ with which to maintain the library, museum and art gallery, but the amount raised was quite inadequate. To give greater access to the books they had placed a large circular shelf in the centre of the great reference library on which all the newest books obtained were deposited. They could be obtained by readers without the necessity of going round to fill up cards. They were able to take them from the shelves themselves. The system had been attended with great success, and the total losses during the whole year did not exceed seven or eight volumes. He was sorry to say the public were not always quite honest.

Alderman BRITTAIN, J.P. (Sheffield), expressed a strong hope that the paper would prove a step towards securing unlimited power in the matter of rating. Speaking as the Chairman of the Sheffield Libraries Committee, he said they had by special Act of Parliament power to levy a rate of 2d. in the £. But as Mr. Ballinger pointed out it was not a matter of course that the full amount would be required. For instance, they had never found it necessary to ask for more than 1¾d. in the £. The trouble was that when they had to get a special Act, a single cantankerous individual could put them to great expense when the sanction of the ratepayers was sought by demanding a poll. Happily, when they made the application they were without the individual, and he attributed that to the confidence they had in their chairman. They badly wanted legislation to give them full financial powers to support their libraries. They now had four or five branches, and the committee were considering the addition of half a dozen other branches. They could not do that if they had only a 1d. rate producing about £6,000. But they had never found it necessary to use the whole of the 2d. rate, their expenditure being about £10,000. He hoped the discussion would lead to some practical step being taken.

Councillor ABBOTT (Manchester) thought the paper was so complete and comprehensive that no further discussion was necessary. He therefore moved the following resolution :—

"That having regard to the present condition and contemplated extension of public educational institutions in elementary, secondary and technical schools, and the greater demands of the age as to the equipment of the citizen, this Association is of opinion that the time has arrived for Parliament to revise the Free Libraries Act with a view to the removal of financial limitations, and that the Executive of the Association take immediate steps to secure such an amendment ".

The speaker suggested that those attending the congress should do their best to interest their Members of Parliament throughout the country. That would render great service in connection with the coming great struggle between education and ignorance which he feared awaited this country.

Mr. T. W. Lyster (Dublin) formally seconded the resolution.

Councillor Bowling (Leeds) expressed his regret that owing to the pressure of other municipal necessities they had been unable in Leeds to obtain more than a 1d. rate. They tried to get another ½d., but were defeated. But they had provided for their requirements by asking that whenever a fire brigade station was being erected a sufficiently large site should be obtained to accommodate a branch library. In this way they had got several magnificent sites free of cost to the Free Library Committee. As the Association were to meet at Leeds next year they would be able to show them that they were a very progressive city in the matter of libraries.

Mr. B. H. Mullen (Salford) advocated a more generous treatment of borrowers. For instance, the system of fines for overdue books might be abolished by a more extensive duplicating of popular books, and those borrowers who had been recommended and enrolled might have free catalogues.

Mr. C. Madeley (Warrington) held that any justification which might have existed of the limitation of the rate had now ceased. The initiative now rested almost entirely with the Town Council, and he could see no reason for limitation which would not apply equally to parks, baths or other municipal departments. The rateable value was no fair criterion. because it differed so greatly in towns of equal population, and the matter of assessment was one over which libraries unfortunately had no control. The question of population was that which regulated the needs of the libraries. Even if Warrington raised its 1d. rate it would get no more than Manchester would with a 1d. Yet Manchester had found it necessary to go up to 2d. In many towns, such as Liverpool and Warrington, museums and art galleries had to be maintained at the expense of the libraries. It would be more to the purpose if they got a 1d. rate for each. But, at present, they had to buy three loaves with the price of one. As to the assistants, the wages paid were not good enough for the work that had to be done. The hours also were too long and considerably above those of the same class of workers in other pursuits.

Mr. James Baker (Bristol) thought that the libraries of this country in regard to their equipment for scientific and technical education were pitiful compared with those almost throughout the continent of Europe. In other countries the libraries were attached to the technical classes. The question they had to decide was whether the public libraries in this country should be equipped to serve the same purpose. On the continent libraries ranged from 7,000 or 8,000 volumes wholly upon technical matters up to 70,000 or 80,000. He was at a place a few days ago with a population of 7,000 and having an agricultural school. They had a magnificent library wholly devoted to agriculture. Those engaged in scientific work saw very clearly how very far behind was this country. The library he referred to had not only text-books, but great and costly works of reference.

Alderman Southern (Manchester) thought the Corporations of the great towns were better able to judge as to what was necessary for their people than those extremely wise people who met at Westminster. The limitation should be altogether removed to enable the community to decide on the amount to be spent on the maintenance of libraries and the diffusion of knowledge. On that they were agreed, but when they came to talk about the best method of carrying out their wishes they were like children crying for the light, with no language but a cry. They needed to make the conference a bit more representative by introducing a larger proportion of the lay element as distinct from the professional, and in their various Corporations they should seek to develop the requisite public opinion to secure reform. He suggested that Chairmen of Free Libraries should be approached with a view to bringing influence to bear upon their Members of Parliament in favour of a change in the law.

Mr. T. DUCKWORTH (Worcester) suggested that from 10,000 to 20,000 copies of Mr. Ballinger's paper should be printed for distribution among members of the Town Councils, and especially among members of Free Libraries Committees. Unless they did something practical they might talk for ever.

Mr. G. H. ELLIOTT (Belfast) thanked Mr. Ballinger for his admirable paper, and said he would like the name of Belfast added to the list of those cities which had increased the 1d. rate. Three years ago Belfast, by a Local Act, raised the limit to 2d. At present they had a 1¼d. rate which might in the course of a year be increased to a 1½d. They were building one new branch library, and had two small branches housed in temporary buildings.

Councillor RODGERS (Newcastle-on-Tyne) thought all that was necessary was for local authorities to follow the example of Liverpool, Manchester, Cardiff and other towns. When going to Parliament, as they always were, they should introduce into their Bills a clause giving powers to raise an additional ½d., and the thing would be done.

Mr. J. PINK (Cambridge) said that in Cambridge they had power to raise what they liked, and no complaint of excess had ever been made. The people were so proud of their library they would go up to any amount short of actual extravagance.

Mr. H. GUPPY (Manchester) thought the question of local taxes was one of even greater urgency than the removal of the rate limit. There was an impression abroad amongst librarians that a library could claim exemption from rates under the "Literary and Scientific Societies Act of 1843". It was true that the Act was framed with the object of giving relief from the burden of rates to such institutions as libraries, art galleries, museums, etc., and that in many cities and boroughs the spirit of the Act was respected and exemption was granted, but in others the libraries still groaned under this burden of rates. It could not be denied that libraries were still at the mercy of the rating authorities — men, in many cases, of a very limited mental outlook, who go behind the spirit of the Act of 1843 and, on the most trivial grounds, refuse to recognise the perfectly legitimate claim to exemption which many libraries put forward. It would surprise many of those present to learn for the first time that the John Rylands Library had been assessed for rates—certainly the assessment was a so-called nominal one, but it reduced their powers of usefulness to the extent of about £250 per annum. A serious endeavour ought to be made to remove the uncertainty which hangs over all public libraries and similar institutions with regard to local taxes.

Alderman TOOTHILL (Bradford) thought the discussion showed the necessity for such a body as the Library Association.

The resolution was carried unanimously.

The Idea of a Great Public Library ; or, Bibliotheca Universalis.

Mr. T. W. LYSTER, Librarian, National Library of Ireland, Dublin, next read his paper on the "Bibliotheca Universalis," a title suggested by Cardinal Newman's *Idea of a University*. A word analogous to university in scholastic phraseology is needed in bibliothecal phraseology to distinguish the Great Public Library from partial, or special, or small, or proprietary, or local libraries. The concept of a Great Public Library is the concept of the librarian who aspires after the *Bibliotheca Universalis*. The would-be *Bibliotheca Universalis* bears to other libraries a relation somewhat resembling that which a real university bears to schools, or colleges, or scientific institutions, or institutes of specialised education. No *Bibliotheca Universalis* has ever been realised in the world; but the greatest libraries, the British Museum, the Bibliothèque Nationale, the Library of Congress—all National Libraries in fact— must be regarded as efforts at realisation of the idea.

This idea of a Great Public Library, or *Bibliotheca Universalis*, includes—

1. Universal Scope ; no subject of which books have treated, and no kind of book, being excluded.

2. Independence of Position is implied by the preceding thought. The *Bibliotheca Universalis* stands for itself. It is not the book-supply of a technical institute, nor of a museum, nor of a learned academy, nor even of a university college. Nor, without forfeiture of claim to the title, can it be the means of supplying books to a particular locality, where one kind of book is more needed than any other. In short, it must not be limited to any special set of requirements—for nothing human is foreign to it : it has its own right to exist, *it stands for itself.*

3. Huge Profusion in Possession of Volumes. Though universal possession be unattainable, huge profusion may and will be attempted.

4. Permanence of Existence—which implies that no book can be amiss, however dull or apparently worthless, since it awaits the time when it is needed, and the man who needs it.

5. The Function of supplying its books, both in the present and the future, to all who need them—and this implies all the organisation of a great library—(*a*) Building, furniture, staff and fittings for the proper preservation of the books; (*b*) suitable arrangements and staff for the reception and physical comfort of readers ; (*c*) keys to the collection of books, both registration as property and cataloguing as books, the cataloguing being both bibliographical and analytical ; (*d*) arrangement of the books in a way as nearly rational as possible, thus making a cosmos out of an original chaos, so that the collection shall have a life and unity, and shall *speak.*

Mr. Lyster pointed out that the idea of the *Bibliotheca Universalis* implies that in bringing together a collection of wide scope, of great size, as well chosen and admirably arranged as possible, there is the profit, not only the accumulated value of the separate books, considered separately, but also the increase of each separate book in worth due to its presence in one great organised collection. Nor is the increase in power of separate books alone to be considered. The books of separate faculties supplement, modify, balance each other, enlarging the views of those using them and employed among them, and justify us in attributing to the *Great Public Library* a character as compared with smaller libraries, resembling that of a university as compared with a school or technical college.

Dr. GARNETT C.B., said he had been struck with the great affinity between the last paper and that read by Mr. Ballinger. The latter was intensely practical in his suggestions, but he could hardly have been so, or have taken the keen interest necessary to produce such a paper if he had not been impressed by a high ideal. Mr. Lyster's paper, while ideal in its object, abounded in practical suggestions, ideas which if translated into practice would not be less fruitful than those put forward by Mr. Ballinger. Many libraries suffered from not having been in their original form upon a sufficiently expansive plan. The community did not see that it was going to expand, that the increase of popular study must inevitably lift the community as the water coming into the lock lifted the boat. All their libraries, including the British Museum, suffered from not having been founded on a sufficiently large scale. If they could show a local authority that it was the wisest and truest economy to build in accordance with a sufficiently liberal idea, they would have done a great thing. They needed to keep the idea of universality before it. The British Museum was bound to be universal as far as possible, not only in the literature of this country but of all countries. He had heard people say, why not leave to other countries, Austrians, Russians, Prussians, their own literature, and devote themselves entirely to English literature? Imagine the case of a searcher after information on the sociology of other countries finding it necessary to take a tour of Europe. He could not produce a proper work unless he went to all the libraries of all the countries. On the ground of economy alone it was better to get his information from the British Museum. It was still more important that the local libraries should be carried out on a generous scale. They all seemed to agree on the necessity of abolishing the rate limit, and he agreed on the desirability of proceeding on the line of least resistance. He was not prepared to say whether technical education was the highest point of attainment presented. But it happened to have laid hold of the people of this country who realised that it was a serious matter to fall behind in technical education. They might make the best of that line of argument. Considering with whom they had to deal, it would not be wise to deal too much with the ideal aspects of the question. Things they thought very valuable the community might not be prepared to receive. They would be like a character in Dr. Johnson's *Rasselas*. Rasselas called upon Imlac to define a poet, and when the definition was given at great length Rasselas said, "You have convinced me that no man can ever be a poet". They must not idealise so that people would say, "You can never have a library".

A short paper followed, by Mr. BEN. H. MULLEN, Librarian and Curator, Public Libraries, Salford entitled :—

Sight Indices for a Classified Library,

in which Mr. Mullen described a simple scheme, illustrated by means of diagrams, by which it was impossible in returning a volume to the shelves of a classified library to place it in a wrong position without the fact of the error being automatically and instantly shown by the volume itself.

Mr. L. S. JAST (Croydon) said the writer of the paper was evidently suffering badly from a disease called "tag". He had himself suffered from it. But there was nothing new in principle in this ingenious device. After lengthy experience he had come to the conclusion that the plain numbers put on bold labels or lettered on the backs of the books were amply sufficient. It was much more workable by the staff, and while the writer's devices were ingenious he regarded the invention as ingenuity misplaced.

The next paper in the programme :

Some Library Aids—Other than Mechanical,

by RICHARD W. MOULD, Librarian, Newington Public Library, Southwark, was, in the absence of the writer, taken as read.

Excursion to Oscott College.

In the afternoon an interesting excursion was made to the Roman Catholic Training College of St. Mary at Oscott. The members were received by the Principal who with a number of the students were at great pains in conducting the party through the building. Much time was spent in the library where had been laid out for inspection a number of the choicer of the manuscripts and other bibliographical treasures in which the library abounds, in addition to a number of very fine vestments, and a quantity of plate and sacred vessels. Tea was served in the refectory, at the close of which the thanks of the visitors for the kind and hospitable way in which they had been received and entertained were gracefully voiced by Dr. Garnett.

Third Session.

The Annual Business Meeting.

At the hour of 7.30 the members again assembled in the Council Chamber for the Annual Business Meeting, over which the President presided.

Mr. F. T. BARRETT (Glasgow) formally moved, and Mr. H. R. TEDDER (London) seconded, the adoption of the report, and the meeting then proceeded to consider the paragraphs *ad seriatim.*

The Annual Meeting of 1904.

In connection with the paragraph relating to the 1904 Annual Meeting,

Councillor FLOWERS (Newcastle-on-Tyne) said that the Public Free Libraries Committee of Newcastle had unanimously agreed that an invitation should be given to the Library Association to meet in the city in the year 1904, and Councillor RODGERS was present with himself as representatives of the City Council to support the invitation. Everybody who had seen their library in Newcastle praised it, and they would do their best to make the visit as agreeable as possible. He hoped they would enjoy their visit as thoroughly as they had enjoyed those to Bristol, Plymouth, Birmingham and elsewhere. They had many interesting historical objects to place before them, and in their library they had one or two rare books that could not be found even in the British Museum.

All the paragraphs in the report were approved without comment until the one relating to the election of Council was reached when

Councillor ABBOTT (Manchester) called attention to two paragraphs which he thought undesirable and out of place, if not out of order. He thought they would agree that it was undesirable that when an Annual Meeting had passed a resolution and the Executive had most laboriously endeavoured to carry the suggestion into effect by appointing a special committee to draft a resolution, that when the resolution came before them the following words should have been inserted respecting it :—

"It should be understood, however, that this proposal does not represent the views of the Council, and no member of the Council is in any way bound to support it. It is submitted, etc."

He did not think it necessary or nice of the Council, to tell them they did not approve of the sub-committee's work, and he moved that those words be deleted.

Mr. W. E. DOUBLEDAY (London) pointed out that the sub-committee had simply discharged the duty sent on to them.

The PRESIDENT said the members of the Council were quite willing to withdraw the sentences objected to.

Mr. G. T. SHAW (Liverpool) thought it quite as well the statement should go forth that the report referred to was not the unanimous decision of the Council. That would leave everybody at liberty to exercise his own judgment on a matter about which there was a difference of opinion.

The PRESIDENT: Without prejudice to the future action of any member of the Council, it is agreed by the Association that the two clauses commencing "It should be understood" and "It is submitted" be dropped.

On the question of publications Mr. T. DUCKWORTH (Worcester) expressed the hope that the question of publishing Mr. Ballinger's paper would not be lost sight of. He thought the paper should be sent broadcast throughout the country. It would prove one of the best means of educating the local authorities.

The PRESIDENT said the Hon. Secretary had made a note of the point, and would deal with the suggestion. Any resolution was therefore unnecessary. The other paragraphs having been approved,

Mr. H. R. TEDDER (hon. treasurer) presented his report and balance-sheet for the year, at the same time acknowledging the great help rendered by Mr. Agar. He was gratified to say the Association was in a state of financial happiness. The expenses of the year had been increased by the salary of the Assistant Secretary. But he thought the money had been extremely well laid out. He anticipated the surplus at the end of the current year would be about £54. He moved the adoption of the report.

Mr. B. KETTLE (Guildhall) asked how many members who had not paid their subscription were included in the total membership of 570?

Mr. TEDDER said he could not say off-hand. But the number of bad debts made during the past few years had been very few. Having been frequently urged by himself, the members had been most conscientious in paying subscriptions, and he saw no defaulter present. Subscriptions overdue on the 31st December only amounted to five guineas.

The remaining clauses having been adopted, the PRESIDENT formally moved the adoption of the report.

Mr. H. GUPPY (Manchester) asked whether they were to have a report from the North-Western District.

The Hon. SECRETARY explained that no report had been received, and that it had not been customary in previous years to mention districts omitting to report.

Mr. GUPPY replied that this was the first year in which the report had not appeared.

In reply to the PRESIDENT's invitation to move the addition of a sentence pointing out the absence of the North-Western report, Mr. GUPPY said that the Hon. Secretary of the Branch was present in the meeting, and therefore he need not say more.

The report was formally adopted.

On the proposition of Mr. J. CHURCHER (Alverstoke) seconded by Councillor ABBOTT (Manchester), Messrs. Blore and James were re-elected auditors.

Bye-Laws.

The HON. SECRETARY, on behalf of the Council, formally moved the following resolution, of which notice had been given :—

"That the following addition be made to bye-law No. 5 :—

"' Provided that at each annual election of Council, two London members and three country members shall be disqualified for nomination at the annual election in the following year, but shall become eligible again at the election in the succeeding year. The members so disqualified shall be those who receive the least number of votes.'"

Mr. J. K. WAITE (Bolton) seconded, and expressed the hope that the resolution would be carried.

The PRESIDENT thought he must ask all not actually members of the Association to withdraw during the discussion of this matter. It was essentially a subject for the Association. They need not go far away.

Mr. W. E. DOUBLEDAY inquired whether a librarian attending both as a member and delegate would vote once or twice.

The PRESIDENT said he would leave that to the democratic sense of the Association. They could not have more than one vote.

Mr. B. KETTLE (Guildhall Library, London) said that in view of the extraordinary way in which the resolution had been brought forward, which seemed to show the Council were rather ashamed of it, he would be willing to withdraw the amendment of which he had given notice if the Council would withdraw theirs.

The amendment of which Mr. Kettle had given notice read as follows :—

"To amend the addition to bye-law No. 5, submitted by the Council, as follows :—

"That all words after ' Provided that ' be struck out, and that the following words be substituted, *viz. :—*

"The thirty-two councillors be elected for four years, one-fourth (in the proportion of three London and five country members) retiring annually by rotation, who shall not be eligible for nomination either as councillors or vice-presidents for one year. For the purposes of bringing this new procedure into operation, councillors elected in 1903 shall retire as follows : The fourth then polling the highest number of votes shall retire in 1907 ; the next fourth in 1906 ; the next fourth in 1905 ; and the remaining fourth in 1904."

At the request of the President, Mr. KETTLE formally moved the amendment, which was seconded by Mr. T. DUCKWORTH (Worcester).

Councillor FLOWERS (Newcastle-on-Tyne) held that the withdrawal of the resolution was out of order ; the Council should have done so before the issue of its report. But the PRESIDENT declined to accept this, holding that the meeting had power to deal with something arising in a period subsequent to the passing of the report.

Mr. B. KETTLE was allowed, at his request, to make an explanation in connection with the withdrawal of the amendment. Since giving notice he had thought it might be better to deal with the whole question on different lines. The object sought was to have automatic retirement in a similar way to other societies. No doubt he was looked upon as a revolutionary—as one who sought to break up the Agapemone—but his object was to make the Association more useful. He did not ask them to get rid of their vice-presidents, while they never would wish to get rid of their President, but he asked them to take a broader view, and so apply the rules of the Association as to secure a greater change in the personnel of the Council. They had vice-presidents who had occupied the position twenty-five, twenty-four, twenty-one, eighteen, sixteen, thirteen and twelve years. It was very desirable to have country members on the Council, but there must be stagnation when they got members staying so long in the Council. The membership demonstrated the existence of the stagnation. It had only increased at the rate of eight per annum during the last twelve or thirteen years. Considering the enormous number of libraries that had sprung up all over the country, they ought not to be satisfied with a membership of 570. He was willing for his amendment to go back to the Council for reconsideration.

Councillor T. C. ABBOTT (Manchester) said he by no means shared the previous speaker's pessimistic views. They never had a finer gathering than this at Birmingham. The magnificent speech of the President, the admirable papers submitted and the sound financial condition all justified optimistic views. He agreed, however, that some of the Executive Meetings should be held elsewhere than London, say in the Midlands or the North. He thought they should vote for or against the resolution and amendment.

At the suggestion of the PRESIDENT both the resolution and the amendment were now withdrawn.

Councillor ABBOTT (Manchester) moved and Sir W. BAILEY seconded the resolution :—

"That the Council take into consideration the best means of enabling the country members to take a greater share in the work of the Council,"

and this was carried unanimously.

Dr. R. GARNETT formally moved the election of Mr. Frank Pacy as Honorary Fellow of the Association.

Mr. H. R. TEDDER (London) as seconder said the Association had reason to be grateful to Mr. Pacy for the work he did during four years at great sacrifice to himself.

Messrs. Roberts, Doubleday, Kettle and Martin were appointed scrutineers while the vote was being taken.

Votes of Thanks.

Mr. PETER COWELL (Liverpool) moved a vote of thanks to the local authorities as follows :—

"That the thanks of this Association be given to the local authorities and to those who have helped to entertain the members during the present meeting".

Mr. J. W. KNAPMAN (London) seconded, and the resolution was carried unanimously.

The PRESIDENT, replying on behalf of the local authorities, said they were very gratified at the visit of the conference to Birmingham, well knowing that it would be an advantage to the libraries of the city. The labour of those who had arranged for the visit was distinctly a labour of love. He hoped that the dinner on the following evening would be the most interesting entertainment they had ever had in the city, and at least as successful as any in connection with their conferences.

The PRESIDENT, having announced the election of Mr. Pacy to an Honorary Fellowship, congratulated the meeting on the friendly and expeditious character of the meeting.

This concluded the proceedings.

Smoking Concert.

At the conclusion of the Business Meeting the members adjourned to the Galleries of the Birmingham Society of Artists in response to an

invitation to a smoking concert issued by the members of the Midland
Arts Club and the Royal Birmingham Society of Artists. During the
evening a most interesting series of tableaux were shown, representing
many famous portraits by such well-known painters as Van Dyck,
Holbein, Titian, etc. The applause with which they were greeted was
in itself a sufficient indication of the appreciation of the guests. The
tableaux were interspersed with songs, recitations and musical sketches
to the evident enjoyment of all present.

THURSDAY, 25TH SEPTEMBER.

Fourth Session.

The conference was continued at the Council House at 10 o'clock,
with the President in the chair. Business commenced with the reading
of a postponed paper by Mr. J. POTTER BRISCOE, Librarian, Public
Libraries, Nottingham, on:

The Public Library and Reading Circles.

He said the average reader was omnivorous, and needed direction
if he was to derive the greatest advantage from his reading. Librarians
of rate-supported public libraries were some years ago regarded as
merely the custodians of books, but now they were expected to know
something of the contents of books, and to show a disposition to give
counsel to those who desired information respecting books. Other
machinery for influencing systematic reading had also been devised,
and there was now mooted a scheme to bring into close communion
with our free public libraries the National Home Reading Union. He
commended that movement to his colleagues, and appealed to them to
exert themselves in the immediate formation of reading circles in
connection with their libraries.

The remainder of the Session was entirely devoted to the important
subject of cataloguing.

Mr. F. THORNTON BARRETT (Glasgow) read a few notes entitled

More about Cataloguing,

in which he pointed out that whether the form of catalogue adopted
be classified or alphabetical, an effort should be made to secure as far
as possible the advantages specially pertaining to the other form. For
example, a good classified catalogue will have alphabetical indexes.
Similarly, the value of alphabetical catalogues may be much enhanced
by incorporation of the element of classification. This may be done
in two ways. A system of referencing of subject-headings occurring
throughout the catalogue, in which at each chief heading a list of subsidiary subject-headings is inserted, and at each sub-heading a list of
sub-sections, and at each heading a reference to the immediately
superior heading for a list of related subjects, gives to the catalogue
much of the advantage of classification, and this is augmented by pre-
fixing to the alphabetical catalogue a classified list of all the subject-
headings in the catalogue. Together these methods will guide the student
of any large division of literature to whatever resources the library may
possess in that department. Other points relating to cataloguing were
referred to.

Analytical Cataloguing for the Reference Library.

Mr. HENRY GUPPY, Librarian, the John Rylands Library, Manchester, read a paper on "Analytical Cataloguing for the Reference Library". He urged that it was well for them to be reminded from time to time that a collection of books, no matter what might be its size, was not of necessity a library. Not until it had been arranged and systematically and thoroughly catalogued could that term properly be applied to it. Until that point was reached it was little better than "a mob of books; a body without the breath of life".

While the majority of the smaller public libraries were rendered accessible to the public by means of the author and the subject catalogue in one form or another, the great reference libraries of the country, or many of them, had nothing beyond the merely alphabetical catalogue under authors' names—a catalogue which for purposes of research was in nine cases out of ten useless, because it did not enable the student of any topic to learn what the library contained suitable for his purpose. The result was that many of our fine libraries—libraries which were the pride of the nation—with their vast accumulations of literary wealth had been allowed to sleep, year after year, in dishonourable dust, until they had become little better than cemeteries of learning, or cities of buried knowledge, awaiting resurrection at the call of some intelligent and energetic librarian. Of late years there had been a tendency to develop specialised methods of reading—a tendency they all welcomed and encouraged. And in the larger reference libraries it was the student and the specialist for whom they had to cater, and in whose behalf they welcomed every new bibliographical aid which treated exhaustively and critically of the literature of a subject in a way that no catalogue could pretend to. But to suppose that such bibliographical aids could take the place of the subject catalogue was ridiculous in the extreme. The strongest argument urged against this was that a number of books in the bibliographies were not contained in any library, so that readers might waste a vast amount of time in making notes and in turning up or asking for books which they could not get. The man in a hurry would not bless such expedients as bibliographies; special bibliographies could never take the place of well-prepared catalogues. He argued that the catalogue of every library should at least enable the seeker to know what was in the library. Then, if it was deficient, the bibliography would enable him to know what had been written on the subject, and the catalogues of other libraries would show him where he could find the literature dealing with it. Coming more closely to the specific subject of his paper Mr. Guppy asked: Why should valuable works be buried and neglected, as they were, for want of an adequate catalogue, simply because by accident of birth they appeared in a volume with a number of equally important works, lumped together without any special title-page, and disguised under some misleading title? Every item recovered from the buried material and made accessible by means of a catalogue entry added to the available resources of the library, and in many cases was more valuable than the purchase of new volumes.

The ambition of every librarian should be to raise his small library to the dignity of a great one—great in usefulness, if not in extent. He did not think he was overstating the magnitude of the task when he said it was practically impossible to make an adequate analysis of the works contained in many of the greater libraries otherwise than by means of co-operation, and if only some means could be devised, some arrangement come to, whereby a duplication of work might be avoided, what a saving of time and energy would be effected. He suggested that the first step in this direction should be the issue of the revised code of cataloguing rules that the Association had for so many years promised to undertake. Unfortunately they were no nearer to these revised rules than they had been five years ago. He appealed to the Library Association to justify its existence in the appointment of a strong and representative committee to deal with this matter, so that when they came together in a year's time they might be able to congratulate themselves upon the accomplishment of some useful piece of work. There was no better way for a librarian to become acquainted with the contents of a library in his charge than by taking a personal part in the preparation of the catalogue, and no librarian could have a proper grasp of his library without an analytical subject catalogue in which was contained all the information he or his assistants were likely to need, and all the information the public were likely to require. A catalogue of this description would be a precious legacy to leave to their successors, enabling them to build upon the foundation they had laid without themselves finding it necessary to lay a new foundation to work upon. It was frequently remarked that as a nation we were far too easily pleased with ourselves, that we liked to estimate ourselves at our own value. But unfortunately it had to be confessed that in many branches and methods of work we were not as thorough as we should like for ourselves, and as we must be, if we were to command ultimate success or avoid ultimate failure. In preparing useful, well-prepared catalogues, librarians had no sinecure—it would make serious demands upon their time—but as librarians they must not shirk the responsibility.

Mr. GEORGE T. SHAW, Master and Librarian of the Athenæum, Liverpool, read a paper on:

The Cataloguing of the Contents of the Transactions of Learned Societies.

The object of the paper was to draw attention to the waste of time, space and money through librarians setting out in full in their printed catalogues the contents of the transactions of the learned societies to which their libraries subscribe. The societies all publish lists of their transactions, and a comparatively slight addition to these lists would serve the desired purpose in libraries, and render the printing of the contents in the catalogues unnecessary.

The Library Association Rules for Author Entries in Catalogues.

Mr. L. STANLEY JAST, Librarian, Public Libraries, Croydon, read a paper on "The Library Association Rules for Author Entries," in which he suggested that the cataloguing rules of the Association, which had been out of print for some time, should be revised and reprinted.

The discussions on the four last papers were taken together.

Mr. CECIL T. DAVIS (Wandsworth) strongly protested against various reflections on librarians in the course of the papers. One speaker said a reader might be fortunate enough to find a sympathetic librarian, while another said a librarian had no right to shirk his work. He protested against the suggestion that all librarians were not sympathetic, or that any of them shirked their work.

Mr. C. WELCH (Guildhall Library, London) doubted the value of a printed catalogue for the reference library. His library spent £1,000 in the preparation of one which was widely distributed, but he had now come very strongly to the conclusion that the money was largely wasted. It might have been better expended on card catalogues and in other ways. Card catalogues were so much cheaper, and his experience was that they were more used than an alphabetical catalogue. The reason the Royal Society's proceedings were not included in the catalogue was because they were not analysed. It was not the librarian's business to analyse any society's publications.

Dr. GARNETT, C.B. (London), said he always noticed that gentlemen who considered a special bibliographic index or subject catalogue unnecessary were specialists very deeply versed in the subject they had made their own. But on other subjects they would have needed a subject catalogue as much as anybody. He was impressed with the importance of a good subject catalogue in all libraries of any size. As to published indexes, such a book as Brunet's *Index* was expensive and difficult to procure, it having been out of print for some years. In fact, it would cost more to buy it than to make their own. If Mr. Carnegie or Mr. Passmore Edwards would devote a small portion of their benefactions to the production of such a work as Brunet's *Index*, they would do more for bibliography than by founding two libraries. A reprint of the index to *Notes and Queries* would be very desirable. The difficulty with all catalogues was to keep them up-to-date, in view of the rapidity with which new books followed each other from the Press. But if, when printing catalogues, they would have some printed on one side of the paper only, they would have no difficulty in cutting them, and forming from these their subject-index. If the subject-entries went *pari passu* with the catalogues they would never get out of date. Typewritten copies might also be got in duplicate or triplicate. If the British Museum adopted the card system it would be absolutely necessary that the card catalogue should be in continual circulation, to be carried about the room, and they could not ·carry cumbersome drawers of cards, though that might do for very small libraries. If country libraries would get a copy of the British Museum catalogue and copy the entries, they would find it would save them a great deal of expense and trouble. He would like to see a publication bringing together in one volume the rules in operation in standard libraries.

Mr. T. W. LYSTER (Dublin) thought the rules of the British Museum admirable, and they had latterly been greatly improved, but when they tried to improve their own catalogues, they were always met with the stone wall of expense. The remedy was undoubtedly co-operation but the difficulties of classification were tremendous. The card catalogue was in theory the right thing. But the public would prefer the large folio volume if it could be got up-to-date.

Mr. R. K. DENT (Aston, Birmingham) urged that the catalogue should be as simple as possible for the benefit of the large number who were not versed in bibliography. But the card catalogue did not give the opportunity for a large general view of a subject. A long series of cards would simply puzzle the reader.

Mr. W. E. DOUBLEDAY (Hampstead) thought it would be better if some scheme of co-operation could be devised so that the titles of books difficult of classification could be printed on slips or cards and circulated. They had just printed a catalogue by means of the monotype process, and instead of the metal being melted up it was being hired on a system of yearly rental, and when the new general catalogue was being printed the printer would work in the lines from the supplementary catalogue. That would mean a good deal of economy.

Sir WM. BAILEY (Salford) thought the solution of the problem lay in the co-operation in London of a paid staff representing and serving the city and the various municipalities. No discussion would prove more valuable than that upon these papers. The index they aimed at would focus the literary treasures of the world. The librarian's vocation was to hold up the mirror to his library and exhibit its contents.

Mr. W. E. A. AXON (Manchester) thought in view of the great variety of systems it would be better to adopt the code of rules now in use at the British Museum. If the Association took up the question of cataloguing they should follow those supported by fifty years' experience in the great National Library. There was nothing more useful to the bibliographer than the British Museum catalogue.

Mr. HENRY D. ROBERTS (St. Saviour's, Southwark) thought that this discussion seemed to turn to a large extent on the question of income, and that with the removal of the rate limitation it might be possible to produce better cataloguing work, or, at any rate, to allow more reference catalogues to be printed. On the question of co-operative work, it seemed to him that, while a lot of suggestions were made, no practical result was likely to be achieved unless the Council would take the matter up. He would like to see a co-operative index of poems in the English language compiled.

The HONORARY SECRETARY agreed with Mr. Lyster in observing that the public did not take kindly to card catalogues, and regretted that this should be so, in view of the great advantages which catalogues in that form undoubtedly possessed. He heartily endorsed Mr. Roberts' suggestion that co-operative efforts should be devoted to the preparation of indexes to special subjects, such as the authors and titles of poems and songs. Information of this kind was constantly being sought by readers, and librarians were not always able to furnish it.

Mr. P. COWELL (Liverpool), while appreciating the labour-saving suggestions made, pointed out that one disadvantage would be to deprive the assistant of the educational results following the collation and examination of new books.

Mr. E. W. HULME (Patent Office, London) agreed with Mr. Shaw that the serial entry was not justified, and he emphasised the necessity of a revised code of rules.

Mr. J. D. BROWN (Finsbury) moved the following resolution :—

"That a committee be appointed to take up the whole question of revising the Library Association rules—to consist of the readers of the various papers on the subject, and Messrs. Lyster. Doubleday, Tedder and Hulme."

Such a committee, he thought, would combine the progressive and conservative elements, and the result could be handed to the next conference and occupy the whole of a session for its consideration.

Mr. MINTO (Brighton), seconded the resolution, and on his suggestion Mr. Brown's name was added to the committee, to whom power was given to add to their number. The resolution was carried unanimously.

The readers of the papers next replied on various points raised, Mr. Guppy expressing his satisfaction at the formation of the committee. Mr. Jast deprecated the forming of a code of rules, on the ground that allowance should be made for differences in local circumstances. They would not do any good by imposing cast-iron uniformity, and personally, as he claimed to be superior to his own rules, he certainly should be to those of the Association.

The PRESIDENT congratulated the Association on having done a very useful morning's work.

This concluded the proceedings.

Visit to Coventry.

During the afternoon of Thursday an excursion was made to Coventry. The party, numbering about 100, arrived in the city shortly before three o'clock and proceeded to St. Mary's Hall, which was inspected with great interest. Here the visitors were met by the Mayor (Alderman A. S. Tomson), the Town Clerk (Mr. L. Beard), Dr. Lynes, J.P., Councillor West, the Rev. H. E. Bottomley, Mr. M. S. Wilkes (magistrates' clerk), and Mr. E. Brown (city librarian). The Mayor extended a hearty welcome to the guests, and Mr. Beard gave them a brief *résumé* of the mediæval history of Coventry, with special reference to St. Mary's Hall and its associations. Subsequently tea was provided at St. Mary's Hall, and the party returned to Birmingham after expressing pleasure at the kindness shown them in Coventry.

The Association Dinner.

The annual dinner of the Association took place on Thursday evening in the spacious dining-room of the Grand Hotel. The President occupied the chair, and was supported by the Lord Mayor of Birmingham (Alderman J. H. Lloyd), Dr. Garnett, C.B., Prof. B. C. A. Windle, Mr. Councillor Haines, Mr. Councillor Green, Sir William Bailey, Mr. Alderman Brittain, Mr. Councillor Plummer, Mr. H. R. Tedder, and other prominent members of the Library Association and their guests.

The PRESIDENT submitted the loyal toasts. In proposing "The King" he alluded gracefully to the vast amount of work done by the King and Emperor of a dominion wider than any known in history. Reference was made to those brothers in arms who had assisted in adding to this great territory. Throughout our own country and the whole Empire he believed and trusted the King would stimulate the minds of his subjects and give them as the years passed on even more reason to say, "The King, God bless him". The toast was responded to with great enthusiasm.

The PRESIDENT proposed "Queen Alexandra, the Prince and Princess of Wales and the Royal Family". It had been said that England was the home of practical men, and whether this was always the case or not, there could be no doubt that it was the home of practical women, in the front of whom was the example of our beloved Queen. Nothing was more distinguished in the characteristics of the English Royal family than their domesticity; this trait was the especial possession of our Queen, who was a perfect type of womanhood, the kind of woman to make a home. He coupled with the name of the Queen those of the Prince and Princess of Wales. This toast was also warmly received.

Dr. RICHARD GARNETT, C.B., proposed the toast of "The City of Birmingham". He remarked that it was now fifteen years since the last visit of the Association to Birmingham, and those of them who were present on that occasion would have a lively recollection of the extreme hospitality which they received, and of the pleasure and success which attended the meeting. When the Association came to Birmingham again they found the inhabitants of the city had done three things which had great interest to them as librarians. First of all they had built and stocked a splendid library; secondly, they had burnt it down; and thirdly they had rebuilt the library and restocked it with greater energy and magnificence than before. Then there were other matters which attracted them to Birmingham. They found a city, which fourteen or fifteen years before their previous visit had risen to a position of eminence—a city which had developed municipal, commercial and philanthropic life to a degree, which could be paralleled by very few English cities, under the guidance of Mr. Joseph Chamberlain and other eminent citizens, who were inspired, perhaps, by the example and teaching of one of the most effective popular teachers of a slightly preceding period—Mr. George Dawson. They found that Birmingham had made and was making enormous progress. During the last fifteen years, if the world had been moving, Birmingham had not been standing still. Many things had been done since then. They were now an incorporated body, Birmingham's Mayor had become a Lord Mayor, and Birmingham's College had become a University. These were all signs of gratifying progress, and should the Association revisit the city after another period of fifteen years he had no doubt but that they would find fresh developments. He had even heard some talk of a bishop, and, if a bishop, why not a cathedral? The Association is chiefly interested, however, in intellectual development, and they were very glad to find a refutation of that fallacy which maintained that industry, trade and commerce were utterly incompatible with intellect and culture. The University of Birmingham was a standing refutation to that argument. From very earliest times they found that analogy between the special arts which distinguished Birmingham and the cultivation of science and culture. They had heard of the two brothers in antiquity, one of whom was the instructor of every artificer in brass and iron, and the other the father of all such as handled the harp and organ—music standing in those early days as the symbol of everything that made for culture. That city had had representatives of whom it might well be proud. Though they could not indeed claim to have been the heralds of industry and culture, yet when they carried their eye back over the past of Birmingham, they found it had been remarkable for its men of intellectual eminence. They found the names of Joseph Priestley and James Watt, the high priests of applied science in their respective ways, and the Lord Mayor's name had been eminent in the intellectual history of the city. Birmingham possessed men of genius—which was less known— and not only first rate men of business. With their city could be associated such names us Coleridge and Cardinal Newman, Archbishop Benson, Bishop Lightfoot, Bishop Westcott, Sir Alexander Mackenzie, the late Sir Edward Burne-Jones and David Cox. Such names could not fail to make Birmingham a great city, acknowledged by all the world. The city had always taken a leading position in the country ; what Birmingham was thinking to-day possibly the people of England would be thinking too. To get Birmingham on one's side would be the best way to influence the people of England. Every one wished this influence would continue to be exercised by Birmingham and such cities, and that they would continue to hold the place in the nation which they filled at present. He was sure all present would join in wishing every possible success to Birmingham and would heartily join in the toast.

The LORD MAYOR in responding to the toast observed that on behalf of the city which for the time he represented, he thanked them most heartily for their very kind reception of the toast. He especially thanked Dr. Garnett for his generous and kind remarks on behalf of the city, which were particularly refreshing at the present time, when municipalities were coming in for a good deal of criticism. He hoped that it was the feeling of many present that there was life in the city, and great progress before them in the future. In *The Times* of that day he had seen a remark referring to what Dr. Garnett had said of Mr. Chamberlain, that though the spirit which those reformers brought with them still pervaded the city, there was reason for doubt whether the sam high standard of efficiency had been maintained. They did not grow Joseph Chamberlains every year; such men were not plentiful in any town. Mr. Joseph Chamberlain had, of course, immensely helped them by his far-sighted wisdom in the seventies, and had with the help of other men raised the standard of public life in the city. All of them who were keen for the welfare of their city were most desirous that that standard should be kept up. It was one thing to initiate vast works and quite another matter to carry them out successfully, but he was glad to think that they still had a large number of public-spirited men and women who were willing to take their share of public and philanthropic work for the citizens with whom they lived. Though it might be true that their influence was somewhat less on account of some gentlemen with means having made more or less money in the city, and retired into the surrounding counties, yet there were a great many left who were retaining an intense interest in Birmingham, and who helped it whenever they could. The success of Birmingham was not altogether due to its own citizens but on account of its cosmopolitan character which led the city to welcome men and women from other places, so they looked forward to greater progress, not only in Birmingham but in other places. There were many clever critics who found it easy to sit in their chairs and say what ought to be done, but to have the practical management and to have endless questions cropping up at committee meetings was a very different matter. The public had little idea of the extent of these difficulties. Birmingham had been very pleased to welcome the members of the Library Association, and hoped the meeting had accomplished useful results. He hoped the recreations, which had not been forgotten, would prove as beneficial physically as the meetings would prove to be mentally stimulating. He had very great pleasure in welcoming the Association and in wishing it every prosperity in the future.

Professor WINDLE proposed the toast of the Library Association. He remarked that it gave him more pleasure to propose this toast as it was one that called for no display of rhetoric on his part. He had examined the papers read by the members of the Association, which contained many excellent suggestions. He referred to some articles, "America at Work," appearing in the *Birmingham Daily Post*, and remarked that they appeared to him to tell them how to make the maximum amount of money in the minimum amount of time, with the least amount—he was afraid he must say—of commercial honesty. The articles had not yet advanced to the stage of libraries, and they must possess their souls in patience to see if there were any remarkable things to be told them in connection with American libraries. He supposed that some day or other this country would awake to the fact that the profession of librarian was not one which came like the senses of sight and hearing, and they had actually begun to discover that it might be an advantage for the person who was to teach to be taught how to teach. The position which educationalists and librarians occupied were somewhat similar in that respect. They were both coming to the conclusion that training seemed to be regarded as necessary; and he was glad to see that that Association had been to the forefront in instituting a training, with the inevitable examination. The functions which that Association carried out were of immense importance, and included the consolidation into a profession of a number of persons, who were previously isolated units. Those present who were not members of the Library Association would join in wishing every possible prosperity to the institution. He would couple with this toast the name of the President, of whose capacity the members had

had ample proof. He referred to the eloquence of the President's opening address, and to his extremely genial and courteous manner which had so largely contributed to the success of the conference.

The PRESIDENT in returning thanks said he confessed when he accepted the presidency of this Association, and glanced through the names of his predecessors, he was not a little alarmed at the responsibility he had undertaken and the weight of the task which had fallen upon his shoulders. He was not a little cheered to see on the toast list the name of Prof. Windle, who was his countryman. Prof. Windle had spoken of this Association in flattering terms, and he thought all must appreciate the skill and patience and industry shown by librarians in their work in this department of the public service. Their work was admirably done, and he was amazed and sorry that it was done so cheaply. Although English people did not pay too little for their books he was convinced they got their libraries for too little. Most people failed to recognise the extreme difficulty of a librarian's work, and the skill that was required properly to undertake the work of even a small library, and the public were inclined to grumble rather than to praise. Librarians did not work merely for the present, but for the future, and that generations yet unborn might have cause to bless their labours. One of their difficulties arose from the torrent of material poured in upon them ; not books alone, but periodical literature. What a task fell to the librarian to deal adequately with such a mob of gentlemen and ladies as our present writers. At times patience becomes exhausted when it appears that quantity will have to be accepted instead of quality. He would remind librarians that if there were difficulties in their profession there were also compensations. The President concluded by paying a touching tribute to the memory of the late Lord Dufferin, a former president. He thanked Prof. Windle for the extremely kind way in which he had proposed the toast. He foretold for the Association a great future of usefulness in the years to come.

Mr. HENRY R. TEDDER proposed "the Local Reception Committee and Officers ". He felt it a very great honour to propose this—which he considered *the* toast of the evening. At the annual dinner of the Library Association it was customary to return thanks to the gentlemen who had laboured so greatly to ensure the success of what was so important a part of the proceedings—the social side. The visit to Birmingham had been extremely agreeable and successful, which was due to the exertions of the Local Committee, headed by the President and other members, amongst whom reference ought to be made to Councillor Haines and Mr. G. J. Johnson, the Association's old friend in 1887, Mr. Capel Shaw, their fellow librarian, the Chairman of the Excursions Committee, Prof. Windle, the Honorary Secretary, Mr. George H. Morley, the Chairman of the Finance Committee—a very important office—Mr. Councillor Charles Green, Mr. Scarse, their energetic and active friend, and Mr. Pritchett, whose absence on this occasion was a matter of regret, the Association losing the opportunity of expressing their thanks for his exertions. The social entertainments had been most successful, and the enjoyment they had afforded and many other reasons justified agreement with the opinion generally received among philosophers that the social part was the most important part. He proposed very heartily the toast of the Local Reception Committee, with which he coupled the names of Mr. Councillor Haines and Mr. Councillor Green.

Mr. Councillor HAINES responded, and tendered, on behalf of the Reception Committee, their warmest thanks for the cordial manner in which the toast had been received. They had all done their best to provide varied amusements and to make the visit of the Association to Birmingham a pleasant one. The members had assisted in opening the Branch Reference Library at Harborne and had been present at the social functions held during the week. He believed that every one felt indebted to the President and Dr. Windle for their exertions. Their thanks were especially due to the President whose opening address would long live in their memory. The treasures of literature in the city of Birmingham had been opened to members, and the hospitality of the Lord Mayor had been generously dispensed at the Council House. At Oscott College illuminated manuscripts of the thirteenth century had been inspected and many other features of interest. The visit of the Association would conclude on the following day by an opportunity of worshipping at the shrine of our poet—the world's poet, William Shakespeare. He heartily thanked Mr. Tedder and the Library Association.

Mr. Councillor GREEN said he felt he was accepting thanks for which he had done nothing, since his labours during the week had been so light and his pleasure had been so great. His colleagues had had a great deal to do, and he felt sure all would agree that they had done it very well. His duties as Chairman of the Finance Committee had been very light owing to the liberality with which friends in Birmingham, the guarantors, had come forward. The President had said at the end of his speech to-night that he had to sound a note of sadness. He would like to carry this thought a little farther. When the Library Association came to Birmingham fifteen years ago he filled the same position, and his thoughts went back to the very pleasant meeting then held. How many of the bright faces then present were missing on this occasion. Some of their old friends had retired from public life, some had gone to other parts of the world to live, many had joined the great majority. After a lapse of fifteen years these changes and separations must always come. During these years we have seen this Association grow and prosper. These meetings give members the opportunity of meeting old friends and of making new ones. Whether we meet again here or elsewhere the Association will always have our best wishes, and we shall do our best to further its interests. He had been asked to mention one absentee from this gathering, our old friend Alderman Lee. He has expressed to the President his deep regret at not being present, and his assurance that nothing but business of the utmost importance would have kept him away. He thanked the Association for the hearty way in which they had received the toast and for their presence at Birmingham.

Sir WILLIAM BAILEY proposed the health of the President, and said it was his pleasant duty to invite his hearers to do justice to the toast of the chairman. The President had done his work well, and had won golden opinions from hosts of people. The members were all delighted with him—they had never had a better President—although they were in the presence of the Agamemnon of the Library Association, Dr. Richard Garnett, their former President. The Library Association felt they had never had a better President than William Macneile Dixon, the representative of a great city—great not wholly on account of its wealth and merchandise, but in realising the truth that a truly great city was one where every man was a law unto himself, and where each man looks upon his neighbour as a brother—a great city was where humanity existed. Sir William Jones in the middle of the eighteenth century had said a great city consisted of men and women, and that nation was the greatest where the best men and women existed. The function of this Library Association was to create intellectual activity amongst men and women, so that life might be made better worth living.   They had been engaged in useful work, in a patriotic duty, in furthering the objects of the Library Association.   In this work they had been assisted and encouraged in every possible way by their President, and he believed the Association would show their appreciation of his labours amongst them by joining most heartily in wishing the President long life and all prosperity.

The PRESIDENT in returning thanks said it had been said that no true friend was ever a flatterer, and he felt in a dilemma whether he must now end his friendship with Sir William Bailey after listening to his very kind words.   He thanked the Association for the very kind way in which they had accepted him as President of this Association—which he should never forget.

FRIDAY, 26TH SEPTEMBER.

Excursion to Stratford-on-Avon and Warwick.

The concluding day of the conference was devoted to excursions. A visit was first paid to the shrine of the best-loved poet of the English-speaking race.   The weather was beautifully fine, and the excursion proved very popular, practically all the members taking advantage of it. They arrived at Stratford by special train, about 10.30, and at once commenced a tour of sight-seeing under the genial direction of the President, who was indefatigable in his efforts to add the finishing touch to the success of the week's proceedings.   Dividing into two sections for convenience, they visited in turn Shakespeare's birthplace, the gardens, the site of New Place (the poet's last residence), the Guild Chapel, and King Edward's School, the Shakespeare Memorial Buildings, and the Church of the Holy Trinity.   At the Memorial, Mr. W. Salt Brassington (librarian) received them, and the party were also welcomed by Mr. Edgar Flower, Dr. Nason, and Mr. W. Hutchings, members of the Executive Council, who conducted them over the picture gallery, library and theatre.   Luncheon was served at the Golden Lion Hotel, and the party left by special train for Warwick shortly before three o'clock.   They visited the Castle, and afterwards had tea at the Court House, leaving by special train for Birmingham at 5.40 P.M.   No sooner was Birmingham once more reached than the spell which throughout the week had with strange power held the party together seemed to have broken, and the members, after much hand-shaking and leave-taking, were scattering in every possible direction, carrying with them many pleasant recollections of a meeting which must be pronounced an unqualified success.

APPENDIX.

REPORT OF THE COUNCIL.

Membership.

Since the last Annual Meeting 16 new members and 2 associates have been elected, and 4 libraries admitted to membership.

The losses by death and resignation number 3 fellows, 32 members, 2 institutions and 8 associates. The roll of membership now includes 19 honorary fellows, 13 fellows, 354 members, 155 institutions and 29 associates—a total of 570, as against 593 last year.

Obituary.

It is with much regret that we record the death of the following members, *viz.* : THE MARQUIS OF DUFFERIN AND AVA, Mr. B. F. STEVENS, Mr. A. J. BIRCH, Mr. E. FOSKETT, Mr. J. S. HOPWOOD, Mr. JAMES LEA, and Mr. C. WALL.

We have been unfortunate in losing a past President (Lord DUFFERIN) during the year. One cause of the success of the Association has been that it has been able to attach to itself a number of scholars and men of letters, lovers of books not directly interested in library administration. Among these perhaps the most brilliant example was the Marquis of Dufferin and Ava, who will be remembered among us not only as the delightful writer of *Letters from High Latitudes*, as the statesman and diplomatist whose public services to the Empire will never be forgotten, but especially as our President for 1894 at Belfast, where he delivered an address marked bv all the fine literary quality and charm of delivery which might have been expected from its distinguished author.

Mr. B. F. STEVENS, the younger brother of Mr. Henry Stevens, the well-known bibliographer, was a member since 1879. He took little active part in our work, but was a warm friend of the Association, to which he was frequently able to render indirect assistance. For about forty years he filled the honourable position of United States Government Despatch Agent in London. He will be known as editor of a remarkable publication, the series of *Facsimiles of MSS. Relating to America from 1773 to 1783*, in twenty-five folio volumes. He was greatly respected by all who had business dealings with him, and is held in affectionate remembrance by a large circle of British and American friends for his generous, kind and sympathetic nature.

Mr. ALFRED J. BIRCH, Librarian of the Great Western Railway Mechanics' Institution, Swindon, died 17th June, 1902, after a short illness. He was an original member of the Association, and a regular attendant at the Annual Meetings. Of a retiring disposition, Mr. Birch was much respected for his amiable and obliging manners.

Mr. Edward Foskett, Librarian of the Camberwell Public Libraries, was born in London in 1848, and previous to 1889, when he first devoted himself to library work, was a journalist and lecturer. In 1890 he became a member of the Association, and took an active interest in its affairs. He was the author of several works, chiefly poetical.

Mr. J. S. Hopwood, who died 27th November, 1901, was a member of the Wigan Library Committee, and a solicitor by profession. His father and grandfather had been Mayors of Wigan, and members of his family had held the same office in the eighteenth century.

Mr. James Lea, who died 31st October, 1901, joined the Association in 1900, and was a native of Wigan.

Mr. Charles Wall, editor of the *Wigan Observer*, had been a member of the Association since 1881, and died 8th June, 1902, aged fifty-one. He took a keen interest in all questions relating to public libraries, and was a member of the Wigan Library Committee.

Twenty-fourth Annual Meeting.

The twenty-fourth Annual Meeting was held in Plymouth and Devonport on 27th to 30th August, 1901, by the invitation of the local authorities. The attendance was good; the papers and the discussions were interesting and practical, while the arrangements made by the Local Reception Committee for the comfort and entertainment of the members of the Association were most satisfactory in every way. The peculiar advantages offered by the "Three Towns" and the neighbourhood were turned to the best account, and the thanks of the Council are due, and are hereby tendered, to the Local Reception Committee, and especially to the honorary secretaries, Messrs. W. H. K. Wright and F. W. Hunt, for their kind forethought and highly successful efforts to make the visit of the Association both serviceable and enjoyable to the members.

Annual Meeting, 1903.

The Council have accepted the invitation which was offered at the Plymouth Meeting by Councillor Bowling to the Association to hold its Annual Meeting in 1903 at Leeds. The following letter has since been received, and there is every reason to believe that the meeting at Leeds will prove as successful as the best of our Annual Meetings.

"Central Free Public Library,
"Leeds, 17th *June*, 1902.

"Dear Mr. Inkster,
"Referring to your communications of 13th March and 7th April, we have much pleasure to inform you that the invitation given at Plymouth to the Library Association to hold its Annual Meeting in Leeds in 1903 has been most heartily and unanimously confirmed by the Library Committee, and also by the City Council of Leeds.
"We are,
"Yours faithfully,
(Signed) "John Bowling, *Chairman.*
"Thomas W. Hand, *City Librarian.*"

Annual Meeting, 1904.

A letter, of which the following is a copy, has also been received conveying an invitation from the Libraries Committee of the City of Newcastle-upon-Tyne for the year 1904. The Council have much pleasure in recommending that this invitation be accepted, and congratulate the Association upon being able to make arrangements for the Annual Meetings so far ahead.

"NEWCASTLE-UPON-TYNE PUBLIC LIBRARIES,
"*2nd September*, 1902.

"DEAR SIR,
"I have pleasure in informing you that at the last meeting of the Public Libraries Committee it was resolved that a cordial invitation be given to the Library Association to hold their Annual Conference for 1904 in the city of Newcastle-upon-Tyne.

"The motion was made by Councillor Rodgers, who will be present at the Birmingham Meeting.
"Yours faithfully,
(Signed)   "BASIL ANDERTON.

"L. INKSTER, ESQ."

Monthly Meetings in London.

Monthly meetings were held at No. 20 Hanover Square, from January to May, 1902, at which the following papers were read:—

January 13th.—"The Provision of Books for the Blind," by Mr. Harry Rowlatt, Librarian of the Poplar Public Library.

February 10th.—"The Question of Net Books," by Mr. W. E. Doubleday, Librarian of the Hampstead Public Libraries.

March 10th.—"Library Service in London: Its Co-ordination, Development and Education," by Mr. Sidney Webb, L.C.C.

April 17th.—"Open Access," by Mr. L. Stanley Jast, Librarian of the Croydon Public Libraries.

May 15th.—"Indicators," by Mr. A. Cotgreave, Librarian of the West Ham Public Libraries.

Provincial Meetings.

In continuation of the plan recently adopted of holding special meetings from time to time in provincial towns, local gatherings have been held at the following places, *viz.*: Stoke-upon-Trent, Nottingham, Wigan and Richmond (Surrey). The proceedings in every case were both interesting and successful, and are briefly summarised below:—

March 19th.—Stoke-upon-Trent. Members were received at the Town Hall by the Mayor (Mr. T. R. Yoxall, J.P.), who presided over the meeting for a time, being succeeded by Alderman Leadbeater, Chairman of the Library Committee. Mr. A. J. Caddie, Librarian of the Stoke-upon-Trent Public Library, read a paper entitled "Some Further Notes on Co-operation for the Establishment of Reference Libraries". Luncheon and afternoon tea were provided by the Mayor, and during the day visits were paid to the Public Library and various manufactories in the town.

June 5th.—Nottingham. Under the guidance of Mr. Briscoe, visits were paid to many places of interest, and at the Exchange Hall the members were received by the Deputy-Mayor, Alderman Radford. The chair was taken by Mr. C. W. Sutton, M.A., and the following papers were read and discussed:—

"Library Lectures: A Retrospect and a Suggestion," by Mr. W. J. Willcock, Librarian of the Peterborough Public Library.

"The Reading-room in Connection with the Library," by Mr. A. J. Caddie, Librarian of the Public Library, Stoke-upon-Trent.

"Reference Libraries in Small Towns," by Mr. H. Walker,. Librarian of the Longton Public Library.

"The Library in Relation to the Elementary Teacher," by Mr. S. F. Kirk, of the Nottingham Public Library.

"Boy *versus* Girl Assistants," by Mr. Harriss, Birmingham.

The members afterwards proceeded to the Castle, where they were entertained at tea by Mr. Briscoe.

July 16th.—Wigan. The Mayor, Alderman Kellett, J.P., and the Vice-Chairman of the Public Library Committee, Councillor Gee, J.P., received the members at the Public Library. After visiting the Technical College and Standish Church, the members were entertained at lunch by Mr. Henry Flint. Mr. Gee presided at the meeting in the Reference Library, when Mr. J. P. Edmond read a paper on "Capitals". This was followed by a paper by Mr. C. W. Sutton, on "The Employment of Women in Free Libraries," and one by Mr. G. L. Campbell, J.P., on the new reading-room for boys at Wigan. Mr. Folkard described the catalogue of the Wigan Reference Library, and, the proceedings having been brought to a close, the Mayor entertained those present at tea in the old Council Chamber.

July 17th.—Richmond (Surrey). This meeting was largely attended, and differed from those described above inasmuch as the majority of those present were London members. After visiting the Public Library, the members were received in the Council Chamber by the Mayor, Alderman Aldin, J.P., who presided over the meeting. Mr. Alfred A. Barkas, Librarian of the Richmond Public Library, read a paper entitled " A Fifteenth-century Library at Richmond," and also submitted some notes on the Richmond Public Library. Afternoon tea was provided by the Mayor, in the Council Chamber, and a visit was then paid to the picture galleries at Doughty House, by the invitation of Sir Frederick Lucas Cook, Bart., M.P. The members and their friends were afterwards entertained to dinner at the Star and Garter Hotel, by the invitation of Councillor Clifford Edgar, Chairman of the Library Committee.

Public Library Movement.

During the year ended 30th June, 1902, the Public Libraries Acts have been adopted in the following places :—

Abersychan.	Holywell.
Aspatria.	Knutsford.
Birr (Parsonstown).	Mold.
Bowdon.	Montrose.
Buckley.	Newton and Parkgate.
Chelmsford.	Prestonpans.
Flint.	Stratford-on-Avon.
Haworth.	Wells-next-Sea.

London : Greenwich.

The Acts have also come into force in those parts of the following boroughs in which they had not already been adopted :—

Bermondsey.	Holborn.	Wandsworth.

Legislation.

THE PUBLIC LIBRARIES (IRELAND) AMENDMENT ACT, 1902.

The Association is to be congratulated on the successful passage of this Bill by Parliament in the same session as its introduction. It was only after its introduction in several sessions that the last English Act was passed, and then several clauses had to be withdrawn to meet the opposition. Some of these clauses affected Ireland, and it was principally to meet the reasonable complaints of Irish members and to redeem promises made to them that the present Bill was introduced. It is unnecessary to say that our Irish friends were asked to state the amendments they desired in the existing law, and, these having been ascertained, the Bill was drafted by the Hon. Solicitor of the Association to give effect to them. The Council desire to recognise the assiduous services of Mr. MacAlister in piloting the Bill through both Houses; of Mr. Fovargue, who with great skill drafted a Bill which, from a drafting point of view, could not be found fault with by the Parliamentary officials; and of Mr. Lyster, who exerted himself in securing for the measure the interest and support of representative persons in Ireland connected with libraries, education and literature.

Unfortunately, the Bill has been deprived of the provision which would have enabled library authorities to exceed the 1d. rate (an absolute essential to the complete success of the library movement in Ireland), but, even as it stands, it has been cordially welcomed by the friends of education in Ireland, and, as the main provision increases the number and extent of the areas in which the principal Act may be adopted, they hopefully anticipate a considerable extension of the public library movement in that country.

The new District Councils may adopt the Acts, and may combine for this purpose. In poor districts schools may be used for library purposes, and the teachers and other officials may be employed in management.

Another important clause permits County Councils to make grants in aid of libraries.

The Library Association may congratulate itself on a small but valuable addition to library legislation—the total cost of which does not amount to £20.

VARIATION OF THE PUBLIC LIBRARIES ACTS BY PRIVATE LEGISLATION.

Additions to list as printed in the LIBRARY ASSOCIATION RECORD, April, 1901, pages 199-201 :—

Bury, Lanc.	Bury Corporation Act, 1899, 62-63 Vict., ch. lxxx.	Limit raised to 3d. to meet expenditure on capital account, but rate for purposes other than capital account not to exceed 1d.
Kilmarnock.	Kilmarnock Corporation Order Confirmation Act, 1901, 1 Edw. VII., ch. clxxxvi.	Limit raised to 2d.

Education.

An important change in the management of the classes hitherto conducted by the Association has been agreed to by the Council, and will take effect in the session of 1902-3. By arrangement with the Governors of the London School of Economics and Political Science (University of London) these classes will in future be held at the new premises of the school (Passmore Edwards Hall, Clare Market, W.C.), under the control of a committee composed of two of the Governors of the School and two members of the Council of the Library Association.

The teachers of these classes will be nominated by the Council, with the approval of the Governors, who will defray all the expenses of management. The professional examinations will continue to be held by the Council as usual, and will be open to all persons who choose to present themselves, whether they have attended the classes or not. The first of the new classes will begin on 15th October, when Mr. J. D. Brown, Librarian of Finsbury, will deliver a course of ten lectures on "Elementary Bibliography". This will be followed early in 1903 by a similar course on "Cataloguing, Classification and Shelf Arrangement," by Mr. Franklin T. Barrett, Librarian of Fulham. The report of the Education Committee, which is printed on page 558, is the record of a year of useful work. The Council note with pleasure the reference to the examination held in May last. They are also pleased to think that the technical classes which have proved so successful in the past, though hampered for want of funds, are now about to be worked on broader lines, and feel sure that the results will be satisfactory to all concerned.

Library of the Association.

The Council for some time have had under consideration the necessity for re-organising the Library of the Association, and making it useful and accessible to members. This, of course, can only be done if suitable premises can be found in a central part of London, and the whole collection properly shelved and catalogued. Mr. J. D. Brown has kindly volunteered to accommodate the books at the Finsbury Public Library in Skinner Street, Clerkenwell, and to prepare a catalogue, and the Council warmly acknowledge their indebtedness to Mr. Brown for undertaking this onerous task. It is hoped that during the ensuing autumn and winter the work will be completed, and that the library will be at the disposal of members early in the year 1903.

Election of Council.

With a view to giving effect to the resolution which was passed at the last Annual Meeting on the method of electing the Council, a Special Committee was appointed to consider the subject, and upon their recommendation the Council decided to submit to the Annual Meeting at Birmingham the following motion, due notice of which has been given :—

"Provided that at each Annual Election of Council, two London Members and three Country Members shall be disqualified for nomination at the Annual Election in the following year, but shall become eligible again at the Election in the succeeding year. The members so disqualified shall be those who receive the least number of votes."

A majority of the members present and voting on the question is required to give this proposal, or any variation of it, the legal form of a bye-law.

Discount on Net Books.

At the Monthly Meeting held on 10th February, 1902, the following resolutions were adopted :—

"1. That this meeting of the Library Association—whilst heartily wishing the bookselling trade every success—regrets that, under existing trade arrangements, booksellers are prohibited from allowing libraries any discount from the published price of net books."

"2. That, having regard to the fact that libraries are extensive purchasers of new books, the Council be and hereby are requested to approach the Publishers' Association, or to take such other steps as may be deemed expedient, with a view of obtaining such freedom of action for the booksellers as they may desire in respect of the terms of discount to be allowed to libraries."

A circular letter was thereupon addressed to all the library authorities connected with the Association, asking their opinion on the subject, and the replies received show that there is an almost unanimous feeling in favour of asking the Publishers' Association to release booksellers from the existing restriction which prevents them from giving any discount on net books to public libraries. As the question is one of considerable importance, the Council think it desirable that it should be discussed by the Annual Meeting before any action is taken. If the resolutions adopted by the February Monthly Meeting are now confirmed, the Council will at once approach the Publishers' Association in the manner indicated.

Publications.

The Council have again much pleasure in acknowledging the valuable services rendered to the Association by Mr. H. Guppy, as Honorary Editor of their Official Journal.

Officers.

The office of Honorary Secretary having become vacant through the resignation of Mr. Frank Pacy at the Plymouth Meeting, the Council, on 20th December, 1901, appointed Mr. Basil H. Soulsby, of the British Museum, to succeed him. Mr. Soulsby took over the duties of the office on 1st January, 1902, but on the 10th February he relinquished them, as they proved to be more onerous than he had anticipated. On 28th February, 1902, Mr. Lawrence Inkster, Librarian of the Battersea Public Libraries, was appointed by the Council to the post of Honorary Secretary, being the ninth person who has filled that office since the Association was founded. On 1st November, 1901, the Council resolved to appoint an Assistant Secretary at a salary of £100 per annum, and in response to the advertisements 121 applications were received. Seven selected candidates were interviewed by the Council on 20th December, 1901, and one of them, Mrs. Kate Reilly, was appointed. The Council have pleasure in bearing testimony to the satisfactory manner in which the new Assistant Secretary discharges her duties.

The Council received with extreme regret the notification of Mr. Pacy's resignation of the office of Honorary Secretary, and feel sure that this regret is shared by all the members of the Association. Mr. Pacy very kindly consented to undertake the routine work until the end of the year 1901, when his successor was appointed. The Council desire to record their warm sense of the great services rendered by him to the Association since the time when he first took up the duties of his office at a critical period of their affairs, in 1898. As Honorary Secretary Mr. Pacy has shown great ability, industry, courtesy and self-denial, and his first object has always been to forward the best interests of his profession ; and the Council are deeply sensible of the loss they have sustained by the retirement of a loyal and conscientious colleague, to whose capacity and energy the Association is greatly indebted. The Council have given the necessary notice for the election of Mr. Pacy as Honorary Fellow at the Annual Meeting, and they feel assured that this proposal will be heartily supported by the whole body of their fellow-members.

Attendances at Council and Committee Meetings.

NAME.	Council Meetings held, 17.	Finance Committee Meetings held, 8.	Publications Committee Meetings held, 5.	Education Committee Meetings held, 6.	Library Committee Meetings held, 4.	Committee on Retirement of Council Meetings held, 1.	Number of Meetings Summoned to.	Number of Meetings Attended.
G. K. Fortescue (President)	7	...	...	...	...	...	41	7
The Earl of Crawford, K.T. ⎫ Past Presidents	...	...	...	...	...	...	17	...
Dr. R. Garnett, C.B. ⎪ serving on	...	...	...	...	...	...	23	...
Alderman H. Rawson ⎬ Council.	...	...	...	...	...	...	17	...
Alderman J. W. Southern ⎭	1	...	...	...	...	...	17	1
Sir W. H. Bailey	1	...	...	...	...	...	17	1
Francis T. Barrett	1	...	...	...	...	...	23	1
J. P. Briscoe	3	...	...	...	...	...	22	3
P. Cowell	1	...	...	...	...	...	17	1
Alderman F. Fox	...	...	...	...	...	...	17	...
J. W. Knapman	6	...	...	...	...	...	17	6
T. G. Law ⎬ Vice-Presidents.	...	...	...	...	...	...	17	...
T. W. Lyster	1	...	...	...	...	...	17	1
T. Mason	2	...	1	...	...	...	22	3
Rev. W. H. Milman	...	...	...	...	...	...	17	...
C. W. Sutton	1	...	...	...	...	...	17	1
W. H. K. Wright	1	...	...	...	...	...	28	1
H. R. Tedder (Hon. Treasurer)	17	8	2	3	4	1	41	35
H. W. Fovargue (Hon. Solicitor)	...	...	...	...	...	...	17	...
L. Inkster (Hon. Secretary)	17	8	4	2	3	1	37	35
LONDON MEMBERS OF COUNCIL.								
Franklin T. Barrett (app. Dec., 1901)	6	...	1	5	...	...	22	12
J. R. Boosé	7	2	...	...	...	...	25	9
J. D. Brown	13	...	3	...	...	1	23	17
F. J. Burgoyne	8	4	2	3	...	...	37	17
C. T. Davis	7	...	...	2	3	...	32	12
W. E. Doubleday	10	5	2	...	...	1	28	18
E. W. Hulme	12	...	1	...	4	...	22	17
J. Y. W. MacAlister	7	...	...	...	...	1	26	8
W. C. Plant (app. March, 1902)	7	...	...	1	...	...	10	8
A. W. Pollard	5	...	...	...	...	...	17	5
E. G. Rees (app. Dec., 1901)	12	...	...	3	...	...	17	15
H. D. Roberts	14	...	...	6	2	...	26	22
COUNTRY MEMBERS.								
B. Anderton	2	...	...	...	...	...	17	2
W. E. A. Axon	1	...	...	...	...	...	17	1
J. Ballinger	...	...	...	...	...	...	23	...
Alderman W. H. Brittain	...	...	...	...	...	...	17	...
G. L. Campbell	...	...	...	...	...	...	25	...
W. Crowther	2	...	...	...	...	...	17	2
R. K. Dent	1	...	...	...	...	...	23	1
J. P. Edmond	...	...	...	...	...	...	17	...
G. H. Elliott	...	...	...	...	...	...	17	...
H. T. Folkard	1	...	...	...	...	...	17	1
H. Guppy	1	...	...	...	...	...	28	1
T. W. Hand	1	...	...	...	...	...	17	1
C. V. Kirkby	2	...	...	...	...	...	17	2
A. Lancaster	2	...	...	...	...	...	17	2
C. Madeley	...	...	...	...	...	...	17	...
E. R. Norris Mathews	1	...	...	...	...	...	17	1
J. J. Ogle	1	...	...	...	...	...	23	1
A. W. Robertson	...	...	...	...	...	...	17	...
G. T. Shaw	1	...	...	...	...	...	23	1
B. Wood	...	...	...	...	...	...	17	...

Note.—The undermentioned non-members of Council were summoned to meetings of the Education Committee:—

Mr. E. A. Baker summoned to 6 meetings and attended 0.

Mr. L. S. Jast ,, 3 ,, ,, ,, 1.

Mr. F. A. Turner ,, 6 ,, ,, ,, 4.

Mr. Carnegie's Gifts.

The Council consider that this Report would be incomplete without some reference to the remarkable series of gifts to library authorities in all parts of the country which Mr. Andrew Carnegie has lately added to the long list of similar benefactions previously bestowed by him both in the British Empire and the United States. The library movement has been fortunate in attracting the munificence of many wealthy friends, especially in recent years, but it cannot be doubted that the enlightened liberality of Mr. Carnegie has exceeded in extent all previous donations of this kind, and education generally has found in him one of its most generous supporters. It would be impossible to include in this Report a circumstantial account of all that Mr. Carnegie has done and is doing for public libraries, to which the pages of the RECORD have borne witness for months past, but the Council think they may be allowed to give expression to the warm appreciation with which Mr. Carnegie's action is regarded, not only by the Library Association, but by all who are interested in the welfare of public libraries.

Expenses of Delegates.

The Council have been in communication with the Local Government Board on the subject of the payment by library authorities of the expenses of delegates attending the Annual Meetings of the Association. The Board state that there is no provision of law enabling local authorities to pay these expenses, and that they cannot give any general permission to local authorities to incur such expenditure.

Financial.

The Hon. Treasurer reports :—

"With the assistance of Mr. T. J. Agar, hon. accountant to the Association, I was able to place the balance-sheet and accounts, with all the books and vouchers, before the Auditors in April last, and the accounts were published, with the Auditor's Report, in the LIBRARY ASSOCIATION RECORD for May (see pp. 244-5).

"In my estimate of Income and Expenditure for 1901, I anticipated a surplus of about £90. The actual surplus on the year was £89 8s. In spite of the addition to the expenditure since January of the salary of an Assistant Secretary (to the usefulness of whose work I am glad to testify), I expect that the surplus at the end of the current year will not be less than £54.

"The amount invested in Consols at the end of 1901 was £365 16s. 3d., with £200 18s. 4d. in the Post Office Savings Bank, making a total of £566 14s. 7d. In June a further sum of £100 was invested in Consols."

ESTIMATE OF INCOME AND EXPENDITURE FOR THE YEAR 1902.

INCOME.				EXPENDITURE.			
Life Subscriptions (to be invested), £15 15s.				LIBRARY ASSOCIATION RECORD . . .	£175	0	0
Annual Subscriptions .	£535	0	0	Salary of Assistant Secretary	100	0	0
Dividends, Interest, etc. .	16	0	0	Rent	20	0	0
Sale of Publications .	10	0	0	Annual Meeting, Birmingham	45	0	0
				Education Committee . .	17	0	0
				Legislation Committee . .	15	0	0
				Expenses of Branch .	3	0	0
				General Printing . .	35	0	0
				Year Book . . .	23	0	0
				Annual Election of Council .	16	0	0
				Incidental and Sundry Expenses	58	0	0
				Balance, Estimated Surplus .	54	0	0
	£561	0	0		£561	0	0

Report of the Education Committee of the Library Association, 1901-1902.

The Education Committee was reappointed on 18th October, 1901, and was constituted as follows: Messrs. John Ballinger, Francis T. Barrett, F. J. Burgoyne, C. T. Davis, R. K. Dent, Dr. R. Garnett, C.B., Mr. H. Guppy, Miss M. S. R. James, Messrs. E. A. Baker, J. J. Ogle, Henry D. Roberts, G. T. Shaw, Fred. Turner and W. H. K. Wright; with the President, Hon. Secretary and Hon. Treasurer *ex officio*. At the next meeting of the committee Dr. Garnett and Mr. Roberts were respectively re-elected chairman and hon. secretary.

Messrs. Franklin T. Barrett, L. S. Jast, W. C. Plant and E. Rees were added to the committee during the year.

The fifth series of classes, the prospectus of which appeared in the February number of the LIBRARY ASSOCIATION RECORD, commenced on Wednesday, 26th February, the following being the classes and the number of students attending each: "Cataloguing" (Mr. J. Henry Quinn), nineteen students; "Classification and Shelf Arrangement" (Mr. Franklin T. Barrett), twenty-two students.

No class examination took place at the end of the series, but a professional examination in Section 2 of the syllabus of examinations (Cataloguing, Classification and Shelf Arrangement) was held in Belfast, Derby and London on 28th May, the examiners being Messrs. J. D. Brown, F. J. Burgoyne and L. S. Jast. Fifteen candidates entered for the examination, fourteen of whom presented themselves. The result was very satisfactory. Four candidates passed in "Cataloguing," one with merit; and nine in "Classification and Shelf Arrangement," two with honours, obtaining full marks, and three with merit. The list of successful candidates was printed in the July number of the LIBRARY ASSOCIATION RECORD, and reprinted, together with the questions set, in the current number of the *Library Association Year Book*. The report of the examiners concluded with the following paragraph: "The examiners note with pleasure a decided improvement in the quality of the papers".

In February another application was made to the Technical Education Board for aid in connection with the classes. This contained a history of the classes, statistics showing what use had been made of them, and a statement that the Council had no objection to their being held in connection with some educational institution such as King's College, University College or the London School of Economics. As a result a letter was received, in May, from the Secretary to the Technical Education Board, enclosing a report from Prof. Hewins on the educational training of librarians, and asking the committee to state to what extent the proposals made, and to which the Board were prepared to give effect, met the requirements of the Association. If the statement covered, or approximately covered, the ground desired, the Board would make arrangements to start classes in October. If in any way the suggestions fell short, the Board would like to be informed of the additional provision deemed necessary. The report of Prof. Hewins referred to went into considerable detail regarding the present means for the educational training of librarians, but included as necessary qualifications a number of accomplishments which the committee considered too advanced for the students who usually attend the classes. The report contained a suggestion that the classes might be held at the London School of Economics without further cost to the Association or the Technical Education Board.

At the same time, the Governors of the London School of Economics offered, in co-operation with the Library Association, to provide courses of instruction for library assistants, the whole to be managed by a small committee of the Governors, who would be prepared to co-opt two members to be nominated by the Council of the Association. After long and careful consideration, the Education Committee unanimously passed, and the Council afterwards unanimously adopted, the following resolution :—

"That the Library Association co-operate with the London School of Economics in conducting courses of instruction in :—

" 1. Bibliography and Literary History.

" 2. Cataloguing, Classification and Shelf Arrangement.

" 3. Library Management.

" Subject to the following conditions :—

" 1. That the Council of the Library Association nominate the lecturers in the three subjects.

" 2. That the Council continue to hold the professional examinations and to grant certificates.

" 3. That the classes be open to all-comers.

" 4. That the Council have an equal representation with the Governors of the London School of Economics on the sub-Committee of Management."

These conditions were agreed to by the Governors, and, until further notice, the classes will be held at the London School of Economics, Clare Market, W.C. They will be managed by a committee of four, on which Messrs. Sidney Webb and E. A. Whittuck represent the Governors of the School, and Messrs. H. R. Tedder and Henry D. Roberts the Library Association.

It has been arranged to hold a class in " Elementary Bibliography " on Wednesdays during the Michaelmas term, 1902, commencing on 15th October, the lecturer being Mr. J. D. Brown ; and on Wednesdays during the Lent term, 1903, on " Cataloguing, Classification and Shelf Arrangement," the lecturer being Mr. Franklin T. Barrett. It is also proposed that each of these courses shall be accompanied on the same day by another class suitable for those engaged in library work. In the ensuing term this will take the form of a series of lectures on " The Bibliography of Special Subjects," by specialists, which will probably be extended into the following term. Further particulars may be obtained from the Director of the School or from the Hon. Secretary of the Education Committee. The Association has agreed to pay half the fees of any students nominated by one of its members.

Since their last report the committee have held six meetings, the attendance of members being given elsewhere in the report of the Council.

The next professional examination of the Association will be held in centres to suit the convenience of candidates, in January, 1903.

A statement of the receipts and expenditure of the committee during the period covered by this report is appended.

On behalf of the Education Committee,

(Signed)   HENRY D. ROBERTS,

Hon. Secretary.

[Approved at a meeting of the Education Committee, held on 13th August, 1902.]

RECEIPTS AND EXPENDITURE OF THE EDUCATION COMMITTEE, 1901-1902.

RECEIPTS.		EXPENDITURE.	
To Fees received from Students attending the Fifth Series of Lectures . . £7 0 0		By Printing and Stationery . £8 5 6	
„ Grant from Association . 17 18 1		„ Advertising . . . 1 16 8	
		„ Petty Expenses . . . 4 5 11	
		„ Expenses of Lecturers . 10 10 0	
£24 18 1		£24 18 1	

HENRY D. ROBERTS,
Hon. Secretary.

Report of the Birmingham and District Library Association.

This Association has only met three times during the year commencing September, 1901. The Annual Meeting was held at the Reference Library, Birmingham, on Wednesday, 30th October, at which officers were elected. President, Mr. Howard S. Pearson (of the Birmingham Free Libraries Committee); Vice-President, Councillor William T. Davies (Chairman of the Oldbury Free Library Committee); Secretary, Mr. Robert K. Dent; Treasurer, Mr. William Downing.

At this meeting Mr. R. K. Dent read a paper on "The Annual Report in the Twentieth Century," which was followed by discussion.

A meeting was held at Aston Manor, 29th January, 1902, at which the President delivered a most interesting and instructive address on "The Story of the Invention of Printing," illustrated by lantern pictures.

A third meeting was held at West Bromwich, on Wednesday, 16th April, when a paper was read by Mr. R. K. Dent, introducing a discussion on "Open Access in Public Libraries, and some of its Advocates". It was resolved, in view of the coronation and other circumstances, not to hold a session of the Summer School during the present year. The interest in the Association is well maintained, notwithstanding the difficulty of completing the usual number of meetings, which may be attributed to the disturbing influences of the present season.

ROBERT K. DENT,
Hon. Secretary.

Report of the North Midland Library Association.

ANNUAL MEETING.—The twelfth Annual Meeting was held in Nottingham on 4th October, when the usual business was transacted, as reported in the RECORD.

ORDINARY MEETINGS have been held at Derby, Long Eaton and Lincoln; and the Annual Meeting is convened, as per rule, to be held at Nottingham on the first Thursday in October, to which members of the Library Association are hereby invited.

PAPERS.—The following is a list of papers read at the meetings:—

1. "Library Magazines and Bulletins" (Nottingham Meeting), by Mr. W. J. Willcock, Peterborough.
2. "The Literary Work of Calverley" (Long Eaton Meeting), by Mr. Lineker, Treasurer, Nottingham.
3. "A Bibliographical Work Epitomised, Prof. Ferguson's *Some Aspects of Bibliography*" (Long Eaton Meeting), by Mr. J. Potter Briscoe, Hon. Secretary.

4. " Dean Honeywood's Library '"[1] (Lincoln Meeting), by Canon Maddison, M.A.
5. " The Disinfection of Books and Papers " (Lincoln Meeting), by Chief Sanitary Inspector Curtin, Lincoln.
6. " Novel Reading: A Plea " (Lincoln Meeting), by Mr. W. Andrews, Hull.

LECTURE.—Mr. Briscoe gave a lantern illustrated lecture, with selected readings, on " The Homes and Haunts of two Nottinghamshire Poets—Byron and Kirke White," at Long Eaton, to which our hosts, the members of the Literary Institute, were invited.

DISCUSSIONS.—The papers were well discussed, and much useful information elicited.

VISITS.—In connection with the meetings, visits were made to local libraries, the Nottingham Fire Brigade Station, and Bemrose's Printing Works at Derby.

LIBRARY ASSOCIATION.—A Monthly Meeting of the Library Association was held at Nottingham on 5th June, a report of which has appeared in the RECORD.

MEMBERSHIP.—Two members have been elected during the year. There have been no deaths, removals or resignations.

CARNEGIE GIFTS.—Mr. Carnegie has promised to erect rate-supported libraries at Leicester, Kettering, Carlton, Mansfield and Ilkeston. All these places are within the North Midland Library Association district.

J. POTTER BRISCOE,
Hon. Secretary.

September, 1902.

Report of the Northern Counties Library Association.

The Executive Committee have the pleasing duty of submitting the second annual report, containing a summary of the work of the Association since the last meeting, held at Plymouth, 26th August, 1901.

The membership has increased during the year from 51 to 83. The libraries affiliated now number 51, and, excepting 3, every public library in England within the district of the Association (*viz.*, all libraries north of Hull, Huddersfield and Preston) is connected with the N.C.L.A.

The subscriptions received amount to £8 19s. 6d. The expenses, however, have been very heavy, and the committee have had to recommend an increase in the amount of subscription paid by chief librarians.

This, the Annual Meeting, is the Fourth Quarterly Meeting for the year. The other places visited have been Newcastle-on-Tyne, Leeds and Harrogate. Arrangements are being made for future meetings at Gateshead, Hull, Middlesbrough and Leeds (Annual Meeting).

The committee are gratified by the keen interest taken in the Association by its members, as shown by the good average attendance (38 members) at the meetings, and by the prompt manner in which papers have been supplied, and subjects for discussion introduced.

The formation of the N.C.L.A. has undoubtedly met a long felt want in the district, and very early in its history the Association has been called upon by local authorities, *viz.*, the new Borough of Wallsend, and the Urban District of Aspatria, to render assistance in establishing libraries under the Acts.

During the year a prize competition was held, open to all assistants

---

[1] Reprinted in the LIBRARY ASSOCIATION RECORD for August-September, 1902.

of under five years' experience.   Although the subject was difficult some good papers were produced.   Two prizes were awarded (value £2·10s. 6d.), Mr. D. W. Herdman, Newcastle Public Libraries, taking the first, and Mr. O. C. Hudson, Middlesbrough Public Libraries, the second.

In conclusion, the committee hope that in future the same interest in the work will be manifested by the members, and that librarians and assistants will do all they can to carry out the purposes which the Association has in view.

J. W. C. PURVES,
Hon. Secretary and Treasurer.

NOTEWORTHY BOOKS.

(Compiled by Guthrie Vine, M.A.)

The classification of each work according to Dewey's System of Decimal Classification is given in square brackets.

Allibone (S. A.). Dictionary of English literature and British and American authors. Supplement by J. F. Kirk. New edition. [016.8] 8vo. 5 vols. *Lippincott.* £4 14s. 6d.

Arc (Jeanne d'). Jeanne d'Arc, Maid of Orleans, deliverer of France: the story of her life, her achievements and her death, as attested on oath and set forth in the original documents. Edited by T. Douglas Murray. [944.026] 8vo. 424 pp. *Heinemann.* 15s. *net.*

Armstrong (E.). The emperor Charles V. [943.031] 8vo. 2 vols. *Macmillan.* 21s. *net.*

Arrhenius (S.). Textbook of electro-chemistry. Translated by John McCrae. [542.8] 8vo. 356 pp. *Longmans.* 9s. 6d. *net.*

Atkins (H. A.). The principles of logic. [160] 8vo. *Bell.* 6s. 6d.

Atkinson (A. A.). Electrical and magnetic calculations for electrical engineers and artisans, teachers, students and others interested in the theory and application of electricity and magnetism. [537] 8vo. 318 pp. *Lockwood.* 9s. *net.*

Baldwin (J. M.). Development and evolution. [575] 8vo. *Macmillan.* 10s. 6d. *net.*

Bale (G. R.). Modern iron foundry practice. Part 1. [672] 8vo. *Technical Publishing Co.* 5s. *net.*

Barron (T.) and Hume (W. F.). Notes on the geology of the eastern desert of Egypt. [556.2] 8vo. *Dulau.* 2s. *net.*

Bowers (R. W.). Sketches of Southwark, old and new. [914.21] 8vo. 544 pp. *Wesley.* 10s. 6d. *net.*

Brentano (F.). The origin of the knowledge of right and wrong. [171] 8vo. *Constable.* 5s. *net.*

Brouardel (P.) and Benham (F. L.). Death and sudden death. Second edition. [612.67] 8vo. 350 pp. *Baillière.* 10s. 6d. *net.*

Bullock (T. L.). Progressive exercises in the Chinese language. [495] 8vo. *Low.* 10s. 6d. *net.*

Burton (T. E.). Financial crisis and periods of industrial and commercial depression. [332] 8vo. 402 pp. *E. Wilson.* 6s. *net.*

Callendar (H. L.). Continuous electrical calorimetry. [536.6] 4to. *Dulau.* 4s.

Charlevoix (P. F. X. de). History and general description of New France. Translated from the original edition and edited with notes by Dr. John Gilmary Shea. With a new memoir and bibliography of the translator by Noah Farnham Morrison. .[971] 8vo. 6 vols. *F. Edwards.* £3 10s. *net.*

Coulson (H. J. W.) and Forbes (U. A.). Law of waters, sea, tidal and inland. [347.7] 8vo. *Sweet & Murray.* £1 12s.

DEFENDORF (A. R.). Clinical psychiatry: a textbook for students, etc. [616.8] 8vo. *Macmillan.* 15s. *net.*

DURAND (E. R.). An autumn tour in Western Persia. [915.5] 8vo. 266 pp. *Constable.* 7s. 6d. *net.*

ECKENSTEIN (L.). Albrecht Dürer. [927.6] 12mo. 274 pp. *Duckworth.* 2s. *net.*

FERRYMAN (A. F. M.). Annals of Sandhurst: chronicles of the Royal Military College from its foundation to the present day, with a sketch of the history of the Staff College. [355.07] 8vo. 328 pp. *Heinemann.* 5s.

FRÉMEAUX (P.). With Napoleon at St. Helena: memoirs of Dr. John Stokoe, naval surgeon. Translated from the French by Edith S. Stokoe. [944.05] 8vo. 266 pp. *Lane.* 5s. *net.*

FRENKEL (H. S.). Treatment of tabetic ataxia by means of systematic exercise. [616.7] 8vo. *Rebman.* 12s. 6d. *net.*

GOULD (S. Baring). Brittany. Illustrated by J. Wylie. (*Little Guides.*) [914.41] 12mo. 258 pp. *Methuen.* 3s.

GOWER (R. S.), *Lord.* Sir Joshua Reynolds, his life and art. [927.5] 8vo. 160 pp. *Bell.* 7s. 6d. *net.*

HAMER (W. H.). Manual of hygiene. [614.02] 8vo. *Churchill.* 12s. 6d. *net.*

HARRISON (F.). John Ruskin. (*English Men of Letters.*) [928.2] 8vo. 224 pp. *Macmillan.* 2s.

HARVEY (Henry). With Essex in Ireland. Extracts by the Hon. E. Lawless from the journal kept in Ireland during 1599 by Mr. H. Harvey, sometime secretary to Robert Devereux, Earl of Essex. With a preface by O. Maddox. [941.55] 8vo. 308 pp. *Methuen.* 6s.

HILBERT (D.). Foundations of geometry. Authorised translation by E. J. Townshend. [513] 8vo. *Paul.* 4s. 6d. *net.*

HORE (A. H.). The student's history of the Greek church. [281.9] 8vo. 562 pp. *Parker.* 7s. 6d.

IRVINE (R. Y.) and ALPERS (O. T. G.). The progress of New Zealand in the century. (*Nineteenth Century Series.*) [993.1] 8vo. 460 pp. *Chambers.* 5s. *net.*

KITTON (F. G.). Charles Dickens: his life, writings and personality. [928.2] 8vo. 520 pp. *Jack.* 5s. *net.*

KOLLER (Theodor). Cosmetics: a handbook of the manufacture, employment and testing of all cosmetic materials and cosmetic specialities. Translated from the German. [668] 8vo. 262 pp. *Scott, Greenwood & Co.* 5s. *net.*

LAVERGNE (Gerard). The automobile: its construction and management. [621.4] 8vo. *Cassell.* 10s. 6d. *net.*

LEWIS (Agnes Smith). Apocrypha: the Protevangelium Jacobi and Transitus Mariae. With texts from the Septuagint, the Corân, the Peshitta, and from a Syriac hymn in a Syro-Arabic palimpsest of the 5th and other centuries. With an appendix of Palestinian Syriac texts from the Taylor-Schechter Collection. [229.8] 4to. *Clay.* 15s. *net.*

LIDDELL (M. H.). Introduction to the scientific study of English poetry: prolegomena to the science of English prosody. [426] 8vo. 328 pp. *Richards.* 6s.

LONGFELLOW (W. P. P.). Applied perspective for architects. [729.15] 4to. *Gay & Bird.* 13s. 6d. *net.*

McCONNELL (P.). Elements of agricultural geology : a scientific aid to practical farming. [681] 8vo. 330 pp. *Lockwood.* 21s. *net.*

MACDONALD (H. M.). Electric waves. The Adams prize essay in the University of Cambridge. [587.1] 8vo. 200 pp. *Clay.* 10s.

McEVOY (B.). From the Great Lakes to the Wide West : impressions of a tour between Toronto and the Pacific. [917.1] 8vo. 288 pp. *Low.* 6s. *net.*

MASSEE (G.). European fungus flora : Agaricaceae. [589.2] 8vo. 280 pp. *Duckworth.* 6s. *net.*

MIDRASH Hag-gadol : a collection of ancient Rabinic homilies to the Pentateuch. Edited from various Yemen MSS., with notes and preface by S. Schechter. Genesis. [222.1] 4to. 468 pp. *Clay.* £1 10s. *net.*

MILLE (A. B. de). The progress of literature in the century. (*Nineteenth Century Series.*) [820.9] 8vo. 562 pp. *Chambers.* 5s. *net.*

MOOR (C. G.). Suggested standards of purity for foods and drugs. [614.3] 8vo. 260 pp. *Baillière.* 7s. 6d. *net.*

PATTILLO (T. R.). Moose hunting, salmon fishing and other sports in Canada. [799] 8vo. 308 pp. *Low.* 5s.

POOLE (R. Lane). Historical atlas of modern Europe. [912.4] Fol. *Frowde.* £5 15s. 6d.

ROBERTS (Morley). Immortal youth. [828.89] 8vo. *Hutchinson.* 6s.

ROME. Papers of the British School at Rome. Vol. i. [918.37] 8vo. *Macmillan.* 12s. *net.*

SCHOFIELD (A. T.). The force of mind : or, the mental factor in medicine. [615.851] 8vo. *Churchill.* 5s. *net.*

SCHUYLER (M.). Index verborum of the fragments of the Avesta. [491.52] 8vo. *Macmillan.* 8s. 6d. *net.*

SEGALL (J. B.). Corneille and the Spanish drama. [842.41] 12mo. *Macmillan.* 6s.

SEGLIMAN (E. R. A.). The economic interpretation of history. [901] 8vo. *Macmillan.* 6s. 6d. *net.*

STELWAGAN (H. W.). Treatises on diseases of the skin for advanced students and practitioners. [616.5] 8vo. 1,116 pp. *Saunders.* £1 5s. *net.*

SUFFOLK. Suffolk in the 17th century : the breviary of Suffolk, 1618, published from the MS. in the British Museum. With notes by Lord Francis Hervey. [914.264] 4to. 306 pp. *Murray.* 10s. 6d. *net.*

VALENTINE (E. S.) and TOMLINSON (F. L.). Travels in space : the history of aerial navigation. With an introduction by Sir Hiram Maxim. [588.6] 8vo. 344 pp. *Hurst.* 10s. 6d. *net.*

VILLAR (L.). Italian life in town and country. [914.5] 8vo. 274 pp. *Newnes.* 3s. 6d. *net.*

WALKER (F.). Aerial navigation : a practical handbook on the construction of dirigible balloons, aerostats, aeroplanes, aeromotors. [588.6] 8vo. 168 pp. *Lockwood.* 7s. 6d. *net.*

WIEL (Alethea). The story of Verona. Illustrated by N. Erichsen and H. M. James. (*Mediæval Towns.*) [945.3] 8vo. 330 pp. *Dent.* 4s. 6d.

WISE (S. S.). Improvement of the moral qualities. [170] 8vo. *Macmillan.* 5s. *net.*

ZIWET (A.). Elementary treatise on theoretical mechanics. [531] 8vo. *Macmillan.* 21s. *net.*

LIBRARY ASSOCIATION : NOTICES AND PROCEEDINGS.

Notice to Members of the Library Association.

THE FIRST MONTHLY MEETING of the Session will be held at 20 HANOVER SQUARE, W., on THURSDAY, 20th NOVEMBER, 1902, at 8 P.M., when Mr. H. R. PLOMER will read a paper on "THE BOOKSELLERS OF LONDON BRIDGE".

The following candidates for membership of the Association, having been approved by the Council, will be balloted for :—

Mr. William Easy, Bookbinder, 7 Greville Street, Holborn, E.C.

Miss M. C. Mondy, Secretary of the National Home Reading Union, Surrey House, Victoria Embankment, W.C.

Mr. Henry March Gilbert, Bookseller, 26 Above Bar, Southampton.

AS ASSOCIATE.

Miss Harriet Townsend, Assistant Librarian, Birmingham Library, Margaret Street, Birmingham.

Mr. B. Carter, Kingstown-upon-Thames, has given notice of his intention to ask the following question :—

At the Twenty-fourth Annual Meeting of the Library Association, 1901, the following motion was carried :—

"That this meeting recommends the Council to consider the desirability of drafting a set of bye-laws for submission, by way of suggestion, to the Local Government Board".

Has the Council taken any action in the matter, and if so, what has been done?

LAWRENCE INKSTER,
Honorary Secretary.

17th October, 1902.

Visitors will be welcomed to the meeting. Light refreshments will be served before the proceedings begin.

Programme of Monthly Meetings in London, Session 1902-1903.

The meetings will be held at 20 HANOVER SQUARE, W., at 8 P.M., ON THE THIRD THURSDAY OF EACH MONTH, unless otherwise notified in

the LIBRARY ASSOCIATION RECORD. The following arrangements have
been made by the Council, with the object of giving facilities for the
discussion of the everyday work of libraries, and a good attendance of
members is requested on every occasion.

LIST OF PAPERS AND AUTHORS.

1902.

November 20.—"The Booksellers of London Bridge." By H. R.
     Plomer, London.

December 18.—"Library Bookbinding." By Cyril Davenport, British
     Museum.

   This paper will open up the whole question of library binding,
        and especially the important matter of the quality and dura-
        bility of leathers.

1903.

January 15.—"The Educational Needs of Library Assistants." By
     Evan G. Rees, Westminster Public Libraries; Chairman of
     the Library Assistants' Association.

   Library Assistants are specially invited to attend this meeting,
        at which the question of professional training will be dis-
        cussed.

February 19.—"Librarians' Aids." By E. Wyndham Hulme, Patent
     Office Library, London.

   A discussion of the need for an intimate knowledge of profes-
        sional literature, with notes on useful books and periodicals.

March 19.—"Classification in British Public Libraries." By L.
     Stanley Jast, Croydon Public Libraries.

   This paper will raise the question of the application of syste-
        matic classification to all departments of public libraries.

April 16.—"Disputed Points in Cataloguing." By William C. Plant,
     Shoreditch Public Libraries.

   In view of the fact that the Library Association Cataloguing
        Rules are under revision by a Special Committee, a general
        discussion of difficulties and divergencies will prove useful
        and suggestive.

May 21.—"Public Libraries and Museums." By John Minto, M.A.,
     Brighton Public Libraries.

   A discussion of the connection between Libraries and Museums
        and Art Galleries, and their inter-relationships.

June 18.—"The Planning and Arrangement of Branch Libraries."
     By Franklin T. Barrett, Fulham Public Libraries.

   A discussion of general principles, and some novel arrangements
        contemplated for Fulham.

   NOTE.—At the conclusion of every meeting an opportunity will be
given members to raise any knotty point in librarianship or bibliography
which may have occurred in their daily practice. Such points or questions
should be written out and handed to the chairman, who will deal with
them in due course.

   *Light Refreshments will be served from 7.30 till 8 p.m., and visitors
will be welcomed. Library assistants in particular are urged to attend.*

JAS. DUFF BROWN,
Hon. Sec. Publications Committee.

October, 1902.

39*

List of Committees.

EDUCATION COMMITTEE.

Mr. E. A. BAKER.
Mr. JOHN BALLINGER.
Mr. F. THORNTON BARRETT.
Mr. FRANKLIN T. BARRETT.
Mr. F. J. BURGOYNE.
Mr. CECIL T. DAVIS.
Mr. R. K. DENT.
Dr. R. GARNETT, C.B.
Mr. H. GUPPY.

Mr. L. STANLEY JAST.
Mr. J. J. OGLE.
Mr. W. C. PLANT.
Mr. EVAN G. REES.
Mr. HENRY D. ROBERTS.
Mr. G. T. SHAW.
Mr. FRED TURNER.
Mr. W. H. K. WRIGHT.

With (*ex officio*) the PRESIDENT, the HON. TREASURER, the HON. SECRETARY.

FINANCE COMMITTEE.

Mr. J. R. BOOSÉ.
Mr. F. J. BURGOYNE.
Mr. G. L. CAMPBELL.

Mr. W. E. DOUBLEDAY.
Mr. J. Y. W. MACALISTER.

With (*ex officio*) the PRESIDENT, the HON. TREASURER, the HON. SECRETARY.

PUBLICATIONS COMMITTEE.

Mr. FRANKLIN T. BARRETT.
Mr. J. POTTER BRISCOE.
Mr. F. J. BURGOYNE.
Mr. J. DUFF BROWN.
Mr. CECIL T. DAVIS.

Mr. W. E. DOUBLEDAY.
Mr. H. GUPPY.
Mr. E. WYNDHAM HULME.
Mr. THOMAS MASON.
Mr. W. H. K. WRIGHT.

With (*ex officio*) the PRESIDENT, the HON. TREASURER, the HON. SECRETARY.

LEGISLATION COMMITTEE.

Lord AVEBURY.
Mr. F. THORNTON BARRETT.
Mr. C. C. BLORE.
Alderman W. H. BRITTAIN.
Mr. G. L. CAMPBELL.
Mr. H. W. FOVARGUE.

Sir. F. S. POWELL, Bt., M.P.
Mr. THOMAS MASON.
Mr. NORRIS MATHEWS.
Mr. FOSTER W. PROCTER.
Alderman H. RAWSON.

With all London members of Council.

With (*ex officio*) the PRESIDENT, the HON. TREASURER, the HON SECRETARY.

The Library of the Association.

PRELIMINARY NOTICE.

Some time ago the Council of the Library Association resolved to establish their library on a much broader and finer basis than before, and it was agreed to entrust Mr. Jas. Duff Brown, Finsbury Public Libraries, London, with the work of organising the library, on his offering to house and arrange it in the Clerkenwell Public Library.

The time has now arrived when this work can be conveniently commenced, and the following is the scheme proposed for the formation and equipment of the library:—

The library shall consist of all books or other publications relating to Bibliography, Library Economy, Classification, Cataloguing or other departments of a relative kind.

It shall be divided into two departments, reference and lending, under such regulations as may hereafter be made by the Council. The nucleus of the library exists in the form of a number of catalogues, a few books, a collection of plans, and a large group of forms illustrating charging systems. Various gifts of books have been promised, and a friend of the library movement and of the Association has agreed to look after the Bibliographical Section, and when it is completer than at present to deposit it with the Association on conditions to be afterwards arranged.

The present work of formation will, therefore, be largely confined to the collection of catalogues, plans, rules, and all kinds of books and documents dealing with the practical side of librarianship. It is proposed to make a collection of catalogues of all kinds of libraries, and donations are solicited for the purpose of building up the section. It is suggested that all catalogues be marked, behind the title-page, with the number and cost of the edition, as a guide to other librarians who may adopt the particular type or form. Plans of libraries are particularly required, and every librarian or library authority is urged to send drawings, reprints of architectural plans, or photographs of library buildings for the collection.

The rules of libraries will be collected, if sent in a convenient, separate form. Books relating to library administration will be accepted, and if those who are interested in the library are unable to think of a suitable book to send, a donation of money will be equally acceptable. Lists of donations will be published regularly in the Library Association Record, and full information will be given of the growth and use of the library. All donations should be sent to

Mr. Jas. Duff Brown,
Clerkenwell Public Library,
Finsbury, London, E.C.

Education Committee.

As already announced in our columns, the classes hitherto conducted entirely by the Education Committee will be held, until further notice, at the London School of Economics and Political Science. The inaugural meeting of this session of the Library Assistants' Association was held at the school on Wednesday, 8th October, with Mr. Inkster in the chair, when the Hon. Secretary of the Education Committee read a paper on " The Technical Training of Library Assistants," more particularly in relation to the new classes. An interesting discussion followed, when the Library Association and the Education Committee came in for a certain amount of good-natured criticism.

An interesting programme of classes, which might be attended with profit by those engaged in library administration, has been issued, containing, in addition to the three courses already announced, fifteen other classes. It is interesting to note that thirty-five students are attending Mr. Brown's series of lectures on "Elementary Bibliography ".

The Education Committee has been re-appointed by the Council, and that body has added Mr. Evan G. Rees and Mr. R. B. Wood to represent the Library Assistants' Association on the Committee. It has been decided, in view of several representations made to the Council, to alter the date of the next professional examination from January to May, 1903.

North Midland Library Association.

The thirteenth Annual Meeting of this organisation was held at the People's Hall, Nottingham, on Thursday afternoon and evening, 2nd October. There was a large attendance of members. Mr. Crowther, Public Librarian of Derby, presided. The hon. secretary, Mr. J. Potter Briscoe, presented an interesting record of the year's work, from which it will be seen that meetings had been held at Derby, Long Eaton and Lincoln; that six papers on library and literary topics had been read and discussed, in addition to a lantern-illustrated lecture of a semi-public character, on " Byron and Kirke White" by Mr. Briscoe; that the membership was stationary, that Mr. Carnegie had promised to erect rate-supported libraries at six places within the district, and that since the formation of the N.M.L.A. in 1890 forty-five meetings had been held. Mr. Briscoe, who had occupied the position as hon. secretary for eight consecutive years, sought to retire. The following resolution, moved from the chair, was at a later stage unanimously carried :—

> "That the members desire to acknowledge the obligations which they were under to Mr. Briscoe for the zeal and ability he has displayed in their interests during the past eight years, and their pleasure that he has been induced to reconsider his determination to withdraw ".

The report of the treasurer, Mr. Lineker, Nottingham, which was regarded as very satisfactory was adopted after a report from the auditor had been given. The annual elections then took place, with Messrs. Dent and Kirk as scrutineers. There were contests for several offices, the result being as follows: President, Mr. F. Shakespeare Herne, Leicester Permanent Library, who had previously occupied the position; Vice-President, Mr. J. T. Radford, Nottingham Mechanics' Institution Library; Hon. Secretary, Mr. J. Potter Briscoe, for the ninth time; Treasurer, Mr. Lineker, Bromley House Library, Nottingham, re-elected; Auditor, Mr. Thomas Dent, Sub-Librarian, Nottingham Free Public Libraries; Representative to the Library Association, Mr. A. Easom, People's Hall Library, Nottingham. The retiring President made some appropriate remarks on installing his successor, and the new President gave a short address on assuming the presidential chair. Mr. Crowther also reported, in an admirable and exhaustive manner, on the proceedings at the Annual Meeting of the Library Association recently held at Birmingham. Mrs. Lineker was elected to membership. Two papers were read, by Mr. T. Dent, on the "History of the People's Hall at Nottingham," and by Mr. Corns, City Librarian of Lincoln, on "Readers and Librarians," for which they were heartily thanked. The decision as to the place for the holding of a meeting on the first Thursday in January was relegated to the Executive.

Society of Public Librarians.

The Annual Meeting of the Society of Public Librarians was held at "Rozel," Manor Road, Forest Hill, S.E., on Wednesday evening, 8th October, when there was a good attendance of members. All the officers were re-elected, viz.: Chairman, Mr. W. C. Plant; Vice-Chairman, Mr. F. E. Chennel; Hon. Treasurer, Mr. H. S. Newland; Hon. Secretary, Mr. C. W. F. Goss.

Souvenir of Coventry.

We have been requested to announce that woven copies of the Address by the City of Coventry to the King on his Coronation can be purchased at 10s. 6d. each from W. W. Curtis, Hertford Street, Coventry.
When the Association visited Coventry, some of our members expressed a desire to purchase copies of this address, and a promise was made to them that the necessary particulars would be obtained and printed in the RECORD for their information.

FOR NOTICE OF NEXT MEETING, SEE PAGE 629

VOL. IV.   DECEMBER, 1902   NO. 12

THE

Library Association Record

A MONTHLY MAGAZINE OF LIBRARIANSHIP AND BIBLIOGRAPHY

THE LIBRARY, ASSOCIATION

EDITED BY

HENRY GUPPY, M.A.

LIBRARIAN OF THE JOHN RYLANDS LIBRARY, MANCHESTER

London:

PUBLISHED BY THE LIBRARY ASSOCIATION

AT WHITCOMB HOUSE, WHITCOMB STREET
PALL MALL EAST, LONDON, S.W.

Price One Shilling Net

CONTENTS.

LAMBERT'S PATENT
PERFECT ADJUSTING SHELVING

For Public and other Libraries.

THE BEST AND MOST ECONOMICAL ON THE MARKET.

Supplied to
THE INDIA OFFICE LIBRARY,
NEW PATENT OFFICE LIBRARY,
ROYAL OBSERVATORY, GREENWICH,
SYDNEY BOTANIC GARDENS,
MANCHESTER TECHNICAL INSTITUTE,
BRISBANE PUBLIC LIBRARY,
And many others.

Full particulars from

W. LUCY & CO., LIMITED,

SHELVING IN IRON, STEEL, WOOD, ETC.

Eagle Iron Works,
OXFORD.

The Library Association Record,

DECEMBER, 1902.

ANALYTICAL CATALOGUING FOR THE REFERENCE LIBRARY.[1]

BY THE EDITOR.

THE question of paramount importance to the librarian is: How best to render accessible to readers and students the stores of literature which are to be found upon the shelves of the library?

It is well for us to be reminded from time to time that a collection of books, no matter what may be its size, is not of necessity a library. Not until it has been arranged and systematically and thoroughly catalogued can that term properly be applied to it. Until that point is reached, it is little better—as I think it was Justin Winsor who once said—than a "mob of books, than a body without the breath of life".

There may be some truth in the oft-repeated assertion that the best guide to the library, or that the best catalogue of a library is the librarian. But it is equally true that the knowledge of the most accomplished librarian is after all but very imperfect, though acquired at the cost of many years of labour and study, and at best dies with him unless he has taken the precaution of treasuring it up in the form of a catalogue.

---

[1] Read at the Annual Meeting of the Library Association, Birmingham, 25th September, 1902.

It follows then that the great desideratum of the library, and more particularly of the greater reference libraries, is the catalogue, or catalogues, in which the authors and subjects represented upon the shelves are accurately described and made accessible to readers.

It has been claimed for the smaller libraries, and not without a certain amount of justice, that they are much better provided for in the matter of catalogues than the larger ones. For while the majority of the smaller public libraries are rendered accessible to the public by means of the author and the subject catalogue, in one form or another, the great reference libraries of the country, or many of them, have nothing beyond the merely alphabetical catalogue under authors' names—a catalogue which for purposes of research is in nine cases out of ten useless, because it does not enable the student of any topic to learn what the library contains suitable to his purpose. The result is that many of our fine libraries—libraries which are the pride of the nation—with their vast accumulations of literary wealth, have been allowed to sleep year after year in dishonourable dust, until they have become little better than cemeteries of learning, or cities of buried knowledge, awaiting resurrection at the call of intelligent and energetic librarians.

In every one of these libraries there are thousands of works which have never been opened, because nobody knows they are there for want of proper catalogues. Whereas, by the aid of judicious cataloguing these neglected volumes may be opened up, and in innumerable instances it will be found that they disclose information which would have been sought elsewhere in vain, though all the time it was so near at hand.

In justice to the greater libraries it must, however, be pointed out that the comparison is not quite fair, since the circumstances of the cases are so completely dissimilar. For the ordinary public library, with its initial stock of five, six or perhaps ten thousand volumes of current popular literature, growing at the rate of a few hundreds or even a thousand volumes per year until it reaches twenty or thirty thousand volumes, it is an easy matter to furnish its readers with every facility in the way of catalogues. In the case of the greater libraries, with their vast accumulations of literature and their constant stream of accessions, it is quite another matter.

Mr. Fortescue, it is true, has done fine work in removing the reproach from the British Museum, in so far as the current literature since the year 1880 is concerned, by the publication of those invaluable subject-indexes so familiar to most of us; but the vast accumulations down to 1880 remain still to be dealt with, and constitute a problem not easy of solution.

I have heard it said that with the great multiplication of bibliographical aids of all kinds, and the wider recognition of the value of such helps, the need of elaborate subject catalogues is considerably reduced, that the compilation of such catalogues is labour lost, since it is duplicating what is done elsewhere. It has been proposed even that we should do without subject catalogues and rely upon bibliographies!

Of late years there has been a tendency to develop specialised methods of reading—a tendency we all welcome and encourage. In the larger reference libraries it is the student or the specialist for whom we have to cater, and in whose behalf we welcome every new bibliographical aid which treats exhaustively and critically of the literature of a subject, in a way that no catalogue can pretend to. Indeed, to my way of thinking, this bibliographical collection should occupy a very prominent place in every such library. In the John Rylands Library we are paying particular attention to these aids with a view to be able to place in the hands of the specialist the bibliography of his subject, when, of course, such a bibliography exists.

But to suppose that such bibliographical aids can take the place of the subject catalogue is ridiculous in the extreme.

The advocate of such a plan fails to recognise that there are not now, and will not be for many years, any bibliography of value upon a very large number of subjects; that such bibliographies as we have do not include the latest and to many students the most important contributions to their subject. The most serious drawback in all bibliographical work is that by the time, and even before the work is published and in circulation it has fallen into arrear and cannot be said to be *au courant*.   Perhaps the strongest argument against this plan of making the bibliographies do duty for the subject catalogue is that the majority of the books in the bibliographies are not contained in any one library, so that readers would waste a vast deal of time in making note of and turning up or asking for books which they cannot get.

The man in a hurry will not bless such expedients as bibliographies!   Special bibliographies can never take the place of a well-prepared subject catalogue.   It is the subject catalogue that shows the resources of a library better than anything else, and enables us to answer the question : " What does the library contain upon such and such a subject ? "   If the library is not furnished with a full subject catalogue, how is that question to be answered ?   How is the student to find what he is seeking ?   He will be as helpless as a traveller without a map or a guide-book.   The catalogue of every library should at least enable the seeker to know what is in the library.   If the library is deficient, then the bibliography will enable him to know what has been written upon the subject, and the catalogues of other libraries will show him where he can find literature dealing with it.

For the sake of argument let us take the case of a student arriving from a distance at one of the great libraries, with the object of looking up some particular subject which he believes to be well represented.   He may be fortunate in finding a sympathetic librarian who can help him to what he seeks, but in many cases—alas, too many—he is directed to the author catalogue, and after many hours of turning it over he retires weary and disappointed if not disgusted.

Take the case of another library where everything is carefully classified upon the shelves, and where a student is allowed access to the shelves to seek for himself the knowledge he desires.   The chances are against his finding what he seeks, for the simple reason that it is hidden in the heart of a book whose title does not indicate it.   I am not over-stating the case, for quite recently a student came to the library with which I am associated for the express purpose of referring to the text of *The Gelasian Sacramentary*. He was astonished to find—as well he might—that according to the printed catalogue the library did not contain that important liturgical text. He was taken to the shelves, but even there it was not to be found in the place where the classification provides for it, and yet all the time it was in the library, twice over, but buried in the heart of volumes of collected works. Yes! some one will say, but if that student had known the literature of his subject he would have known that Muratori: *Liturgia Romana Vetus . . .*, or Migne: *Patrologia Latina*, was likely to contain what he wanted. How few students do know the literature of their subjects ; and, indeed, it does not necessarily follow that because a student wants to refer to such a text that it is his subject. Such are the interrelations and overlappings of every department of knowledge, whether science, literature or art, that to know one subject well it is necessary to know something of a thousand others, and it may be that "liturgiology," or *The Gelasian Sacramentary*, was one of the thousand subjects surrounding the main subject in which he was specialising.

That brings us face to face with the real subject of my paper, which constitutes one of the most difficult problems with which we have to deal—the analytical cataloguing of composite works, such as the transactions of learned societies, the great historical collections and so forth.

Why should valuable works be buried and neglected as they are for want of adequate cataloguing, because by an accident of birth they appear in a volume with a number of other equally important works, lumped together without any special title-page, and disguised under some misleading title ?

The component parts or papers of the transactions of many of our learned societies, or of such composite volumes as : *Contentio Veritatis ; by Six Oxford Tutors . . .*, 1902 ; *An English Miscellany presented to Dr. Furnivall . . .*, 1901 [49 studies]; *Mélanges Julien Havet: recueil de travaux d'érudition dédiés à la mémoire de J. Havet*, 1895 [54 studies], to mention three that are at this moment before me, constitute so many separate books, and in many cases are of much greater importance to the student and specialist than many of the more imposing but less trustworthy works that are granted more space on our shelves and in our catalogues than they merit.

Every item recovered from this buried material and made accessible by means of the catalogue-entry adds to the available resources of the library, and in many cases is more valuable than the purchase of new volumes. The smaller the library the greater the need to have its resources in this way expanded. It should be the ambition of the librarian of the small library to raise his small library to the dignity of a " great library "—great in usefulness if not in extent.

There never has been a question as to the desirability of getting at this hidden material, but the question of ability to carry out the work with the limited resources at our disposal has long taxed our ingenuity. I do not think I am overstating the magnitude of the task when I say that it is practically impossible to make such analysis of the works contained in many of the greater libraries otherwise than by means of co-operation.

If only some means could be devised, some arrangement come to whereby the duplication of work might be avoided, what a saving of energy would be effected. For example, to my own personal knowledge, within the last few years several sets of Pertz: *Monumenta Germaniæ Historica* have been independently analysed by as many different libraries. To appreciate the waste of energy involved in this case it needs only to be pointed out that to properly analyse Pertz something like three thousand slips or entries have to be made. Now, supposing those libraries had entered into a friendly arrangement whereby one undertook the analysis of Pertz: *Monumenta Germaniæ Historica;* another the analysis of Muratori: *Scriptores Rerum Italicarum;* a third that of the *Patrologia Latina* and *Patrologia Græco-Latina*, edited by the Abbé Migne, or his *Encyclopédie théologique*, and had made carbon copies of the slips to the number of the co-operating libraries possessing sets of the various works, what a saving of energy would be effected. In this way two or more collections such as those to which reference has been made might be analysed at little more than the cost of time and labour required to analyse one set.

It is quite obvious, however, that before such an arrangement could be entered into some system would have to be devised for securing uniformity of treatment in the carrying out of the work. The first step in that direction should be the issue of the revised code of cataloguing rules that the Library Association has for so many years promised to undertake. Unfortunately, we are no nearer to those revised rules than we were five years ago, and that in spite of the reminders that the Council have received from time to time. What have we been doing as an Association during the past years, or what are we doing? Let us justify our existence in some way. Let us, for example, here, in Birmingham, and now, appoint a strong and representative committee to deal with this matter of revision, so that when we come together next year we may be able to congratulate ourselves upon the accomplishment or the inauguration of some useful piece of work. We might also with advantage undertake a revised list of subject-headings similar to that issued by the A.L.A., but in a cheaper form.

What an advantage it would be to have such tools ready made and procurable at small cost, so that we might be able to place in the hands of our assistants a really useful set of working tools. It would enable us to overcome the difficulty that we all experience in some degree, especially those with a staff of cataloguers each having ideas of his own, and wanting to work on his own lines unless some clearly defined system is in this way laid down for his guidance.

There is very much more that might be said upon this subject with reference to form of catalogue, method of work and so forth. But the real object of my somewhat disconnected remarks will have been attained if I succeed in calling attention to the urgent need for recovering the thousands and thousands of "books" which are year by year diverted from the natural stream of literature because they are published as subordinate parts, papers, essays, articles in collected works or in the transactions of the learned societies.

The ideal catalogue would also include an analysis of

the important historical, philosophical, classical, philological, theological, and literary magazines and reviews. Since that is quite out of the question, I draw the line at the transactions of learned societies to the exclusion of other periodical literature.

In conclusion, let me say there is no better way for a librarian to become acquainted with the contents of the library under his charge than by taking a personal part in the preparation of the catalogues; furthermore, that no librarian can have a proper grasp of his library without an analytical subject catalogue in which is contained all the information he or his assistants are likely to need, and all the information the public are likely to require.

A catalogue of this description will be a precious legacy to leave to our successors, enabling them to build upon the foundation we have laid, without finding it necessary to lay a new foundation to work upon.

Let us try to raise the standard of the work in which we are engaged. Let it be our endeavour to produce work to which we shall be able to point with ever-increasing pride.

It has frequently been remarked that as a people we English are far too easily pleased with ourselves, that we like to estimate ourselves at our own value. Such an attitude of mind is most harmful!

Unfortunately, it has to be confessed that in many branches of work and methods of work, we are not as thorough as we should like to think ourselves, and as we must be if we would command ultimate success, or avoid ultimate failure. The "good enough" policy may perhaps impose upon the world for a time, but the day must come when it will be found out and exposed as a fraud and a sham.

The labour of making a careful and really useful analytical catalogue is no sinecure. It will make large demands upon our time and our skill; but as librarians we must face it. We have no right to shirk it because bibliographies are likely to appear, which at best, if we are really in earnest in our work, will be but clumsy tools as compared with our own provision for our readers.

THE LIBRARY ASSOCIATION CATALOGUING RULES.

By L. Stanley Jast, Librarian, Croydon Public Libraries.

AS I understand it, I am not here to read a paper on the Cataloguing Rules of the Library Association, but to contribute a sort of prefatory note to a discussion upon the rules and upon the question of reprinting them. The first general question upon which your views are desired is, Is it well to reprint them at all, in view of the several codes, covering the same ground, which are to be obtained ? While I do not think that a mere reprint would be of any particular value, even so they should certainly be reissued, because they *are* the official rules of the Association, and, as such, should not be allowed to remain out of print. But if—and this is the second question before us—the decision be taken to thoroughly revise and, where desirable, enlarge the rules, an opportunity offers to make a distinct and helpful contribution to bibliographical science, and to supplement in a few directions all the existing codes.

It was in 1883, nineteen years ago, that the rules were revised at the Liverpool Meeting. We have not stood still —at least some of us haven't—in those nineteen years, and the rules do not adequately answer to the practice and needs of to-day. It is not proposed that their scope should be enlarged to include the " new cataloguing," *i.e.*, annotating and evaluing. I do not agree with those who consider that it is impossible to usefully codify descriptive cataloguing, though it is undoubtedly very largely personal to the cataloguer—one must annotate, as Opie mixed his colours, with brains mainly—but the time is not yet ripe for work of this sort to be done by this Association. But whatever are the advances or changes which have been or will be effected in cataloguing, the author-entry is still, and must remain, the cataloguer's sheet-anchor, whatever additional references are made or descriptive matter is appended to it.

Coming to the rules as they stand, the necessity for revision may be shown by one or two examples. In Rule 7 the imprint particulars are classified into obligatory and optional. Among the latter are illustrations, maps and portraits. The best modern practice always gives these— formerly ignored, with very few exceptions, in public library cataloguing—and if the rules are to be in accord with the best models they should be specified as obligatory. On the other hand the edition and place of publication which are declared obligatory should be regarded as optional. I don't suppose one library in fifty supplies this information. The edition is occasionally useful—and in my own library we occasionally record it—but of what value is the place of publication to any one other than the bibliographer? Rule 12 directs that books are to be entered " under the pseudonyms of the writers," not, be it observed, if better known than the real name but always, contrary to any current practice as far as I am aware. Many rules require amplification, but I need not adduce further examples to make out a case for revision.

Exactly how we should set about this task is a matter for careful consideration. It will have to be done, so far, at any rate, as a draft revision is concerned, by a specially appointed committee, and the smaller this committee so long as it is representative the better. The views of this meeting as to the various points submitted will be a most valuable help to that committee, especially if we can come to some agreement on the general lines of its work. As to these I have a few suggestions to make with which I shall conclude this note.

First as to what we may call the focus of the rules, the particular kind of catalogue with regard to which the code is more especially compiled. The focus of the existing code is rather the bibliographical than the average library catalogue, but in the revision the requirements of the latter rather than of the former should, in my opinion, be kept steadily in view. We are all familiar with the cookery book which caters for the rich and poor alike by the simple but not invariably satisfactory process of leaving out all the expensive ingredients in the recipes. Nor do you get an altogether satisfactory popular code of cataloguing rules by simply reducing a code intended for more or less exact bibliographical work.

The next point I have to bring before you is one upon which I would lay particular stress, and upon which alone a paper might be written. In the preface to Cutter's *Rules for a Dictionary Catalogue* he states that the rules are by no means so complex as they might seem, but result from the application of a few general principles. It is much to be regretted that neither Mr. Cutter nor any other writer, I believe, has seen fit to state what these principles are, with the result that these elaborate codes are regarded as a series of multifarious and largely disconnected injunctions special to each case, beads with no thread of principle upon which they can be strung. Yet if cataloguing is a science, it must be reducible to principles, and if we can bring these out in our new code, arranging particular rules under the wider covering rules from which they naturally flow, we shall have rendered their mastery comparatively easy, and laid the foundation of an intelligent—the only intelligent—method of teaching cataloguing.

As a rough illustration of what I mean take this :—

General Principle :
Enter under latest name.
Therefore :
Noblemen under title not family.
Married women under husband's name.
Saints, popes and friars and ruling princes under forename, which becomes latest name by the dropping of the surname.

Here are three rules reduced to one; in this case one of four words only. I don't say that a whole code can be arranged just in this manner, but something like it is possible, and in the interests of logical order and sound tuition something in this direction should be tried.

In drawing up a code of cataloguing rules one is constantly faced by alternatives, between which a choice has to be made, and in choosing, the principle which should be followed is to select that alternative which will bring the rule into line with some other rule or rules, unless some very strong reason to the contrary can be shown.   In the above example, entry of noblemen under title is preferred to entry under family name, not so much because British noblemen are known by their titles, but because entry under title brings the rule under the covering rule of "latest name".

The most important of the directions in which the present code requires amplification is that of the cataloguing of official publications.   Owing to the vagueness of the rules there is much uncertainty and difference in the cataloguing of works of this class.   What is wanted is a definition of authorship sufficiently clear and comprehensive to be capable of application to all cases of corporate authorship.   Cutter's definition, " Bodies of men are to be considered as authors of works published in their name or by their authority," requires a further definition of what precisely is meant by " in their name " and " by their authority ".   Almost immediately he violates this covering rule by directing that " Calendars of documents, regesta, etc., are to be entered under their maker, with a series-entry under the department which orders the publication ".   The whole subject of corporate authorship is unsettled and unsatisfactory and needs attention.

The cataloguing of music and maps are other directions in which the code should be extended.

The rules should be illustrated by examples, and it might be well to give alternatives where there is good authority for the variation.

In concluding this note, I would suggest that the discussion be confined to the general questions raised.

IS IT NECESSARY TO PRINT IN REFERENCE LIBRARY CATALOGUES LISTS OF THE CONTENTS OF THE PUBLICATIONS OF LEARNED SOCIETIES? [1]

By George T. Shaw, Master and Librarian, The Athenæum, Liverpool.

THE subject of this paper has been referred to by various writers when dealing with the cataloguing of the transactions of learned societies, but it has never received the direct attention that I think it deserves. The few references which have been made to it may be regarded as negative answers to the question I have selected as a title, but these *obiter dicta* cannot be expected to supersede a custom which appears to be more rigid than the cataloguing rules justify. A brief examination of this custom will prove that it is either extravagant or inconsistently economical. The general practice in our reference libraries is to print in the catalogues lists of the contents of the publications of those societies which issue a work in one or several volumes, and to ignore the publications of those societies which issue several works in one volume. The contents of the publications of *The Camden Society*, *The Early English Text Society*, *The Ray Society*, and others published in a similar form, are fully listed under the names of those societies in the catalogues of the libraries subscribing for them, while in the same catalogues the contents of *Archæologia* and the *Philosophical Transactions of the Royal Society* are ignored. If a reader desires to consult any work published by *The Camden Society* he will find it entered in these library catalogues under the name of the author, under the subject, probably under the title of the book, and, according to the present practice, under the name of the society; but

---

[1] Read at the Annual Meeting of the Library Association, Birmingham, 25th September, 1902.

if a reader wants to consult any paper published by either *The Royal Society* or in *Archæologia*, the same catalogues will not render him the slightest assistance. It is not any consideration of the comparative value of these publications which prompts this extraordinary selection, for if either *The Royal Society* or *The Royal Society of Antiquaries* were to start to-morrow and publish their works or papers separately, they would be catalogued like the publications of the other societies that I have named. Surely it is absurdly illogical to allow the form of publication to influence our cataloguing in this way.

I will first deal with those transactions the contents of which are printed in our catalogues, and I ask any librarian to state, if in his experience the number of references to the contents justify the expenditure of time, labour and money, so printing them entails? We must bear in mind that these series are already very long, and are increasing every year, thus making a search through their lists of contents a labour from which an ordinary man shrinks, particularly as he can obtain the information elsewhere; while the printing of pages of contents in nonpareil, or any small type, adds very largely to the cost of the printing of a catalogue. In my opinion this is an expenditure that is not only unauthorised by our cataloguing rules,[1] but unjustified by experience, and I sincerely hope that a definite expression of opinion by my fellow-librarians may stop it.

If, however, the opinion on this point should be opposed to that which I have expressed, I venture to suggest a means by which lists of these publications may be obtained, and the printing of them in our catalogues avoided.

It is, I presume, known to all of you that the societies I am now referring to issue regularly, generally with their annual reports, lists of all their publications, and subscribing libraries can always obtain copies of them. They are, of course, sale lists, and for use in our libraries have one defect, *viz.*, they do not indicate how many parts a work is complete in, nor the number of the volumes of the transactions in

---

The Library Association Rule (9) is as follows: "*Contents of volumes are to be given when expedient*".

which the various parts are published. Let me make this point clear by referring to one of the publications of *The Early English Text Society.* A reader desiring information about the early English version of the *Cursor Mundi* may consult the list of that society's publications, and he will have to read the title of every work issued by the society before he can be quite sure that he knows how many parts the said work has been published in. The first part of the *Cursor Mundi* was issued in 1874, and the seventh and final part in 1893. Between the publications of parts five and six there was an interval of twelve years. What is wanted to make these lists suitable for use in our libraries is a system of references from and to the various parts of a work. Thus, under the entry of the first part of the *Cursor Mundi* could be added the words, " continued in vols. 59, 62, 66, 68, 99 and 101 ". I may say that *The Royal Historical Society* do this in the list of the Camden Series, and that our friend Mr. C. W. Sutton, as hon. secretary of the Chetham Society, has revised the list of that society's publications in accordance with my suggestion.

There is no selfishness in making this suggestion, because the lists when thus amended will be better adapted for the purpose for which the societies publish them, while the cost of the extra printing will be infinitesimal. With regard to the clerical labour entailed, I suggest that the alterations should be recommended by the Council of our Association to the Councils of the various societies, and that we should offer to make the necessary alterations in the lists published (the work could easily be carried on in future years by the annual revisers of the lists). I will gladly undertake to make the suggested alterations in the lists issued by *The Surtees Society*, *The Ray Society* and *The Palæontographical Society*, the latter being one of the most complicated lists printed, and I trust that other librarians will show public spirit enough to offer their assistance. Should any of the societies refuse to adopt this suggestion when made to them, I would still recommend that their lists be taken and that the alterations be made by librarians. The objection to referring a reader from the catalogue to a separate list need not be taken very seriously, as in some libraries (*e.g.*, the London Library) lists of the contents of transactions of learned societies and other long sets are printed in a supplemental volume. The advantage of referring a student to the latest official list, rather than to a supplemental catalogue, probably ten years old, must be obvious to all. The lists issued by the societies are always up-to-date, while the lists printed in your catalogues never can be later than the dates of the catalogues.

Before leaving this part of my paper, let me also recommend that the Government lists of *The Rolls Series* and *The Historical MSS. Commission*, which can be obtained from Messrs. Eyre & Spottiswoode for the cost of postage, should be taken regularly in all reference libraries, and that the printing of the lists of those series in our catalogues be abandoned.

I now turn to those societies the contents of whose transactions are not printed in our catalogues. These may be classified as follows: The *Transactions of the Royal Society*, representing scientific societies, and *Archæologia*, as representing the various archæological and literary societies all over the country. In no library catalogue have I ever seen the contents of the *Philosophical Transactions of the Royal Society*. In only one catalogue have I seen the contents of *Archæologia* set out. The catalogue is a small quarto in size, and the contents of forty-four volumes of *Archæologia*, printed in small type, occupy ten and a half pages. It is also to be noted that although these contents are so carefully set out, only a selection are catalogued under author and subject. Generally speaking, the contents of the transactions of these societies are left alone, and the extraordinary result is, that in a library where *Archæologia* and the publications of *The Early English Text Society* are taken, a student will find an obsolete English tract carefully entered in several places in the catalogue, while *Bruce's Report of the Committee on the Authenticity of the Paston Letters;* or the carefully compiled and elaborate work by Messrs. Fox and St. John Hope on the excavations at Silchester, will not be entered in the catalogue. This very weak spot in our system of cataloguing calls for instant attention, and should not be tolerated by any association of librarians.

The subject of general cataloguing is outside the object of my paper, but I may be permitted to say that when our Association takes up the subject of cataloguing, consideration will have to be given, not only to the cataloguing of the contents of learned societies' transactions, but also to the cataloguing of the contents of such long sets as those collected by *Pertz, Muratori,* and the *Abbé Migne.* How far are we justified in turning every reference library catalogue into an index of sets for which specially compiled and elaborate indexes are obtainable? The three great works I have named above, and many other sets, will be found indexed in the compilations by *Potthast*[1] and *Mas Latrie*[2] far more thoroughly than can be done in any library catalogue. The solution of this problem is, in my opinion, foreshadowed by the way in which our reference libraries now treat the students who wish to consult the *Philosophical Transactions of the Royal Society, Archæologia,* or magazines and reviews, *viz.,* refer them to the special indexes in existence.

Since the publication of *Poole's Index to Periodical Literature,* the practice of printing the contents of magazines and reviews has been discontinued. *The Catalogue of Scientific Papers compiled by the Royal Society* should, and does, render unnecessary the cataloguing in our library catalogues of the transactions of scientific societies, while the *Index to Archæological Papers,* which is published by Messrs. Constable & Co. under the direction of the Congress of Archæological Societies, should render a similar service for antiquarian publications. This index began in 1891 and has been published annually since. Parts are bound up in the volumes of the subscribing societies, but copies can be obtained from the publishers at a cost of 1s. per part. The index of papers published prior to 1891 is nearing completion, and will be published at an early date—price 30s. These indexes should be subscribed

[1] Potthast, A., *Bibliotheca historica medii aevi. Wegweiser durch die Geschichtswerke des europäischen Mittelalters bis 1500.* 2 v. Berlin, 1896.

[2] Mas Latrie, J. M. J. Louis de, *Trésor de chronologie d'histoire et de géographie pour l'étude et l'emploi des documents du moyen âge.* Fol. Paris, 1889.

for by all libraries, as they will do for the transactions of archæological societies what *Poole's Index* has done for periodical literature.

The printing of the contents of the proceedings of local societies may be left to the discretion of the local librarians. It is not probable that much space in the catalogue of a library in a midland town will be allotted to the contents of the transactions of a purely local society in the north or south-west of Great Britain. So far as the archæological work of local societies is concerned, that will be made generally accessible by the index above referred to.

Before concluding my paper I desire to refer to the indexes to *Notes and Queries*. We all know the value of that publication and the amount of useful and miscellaneous information contained in its numerous volumes. It is the finest dictionary of verified quotations in existence. More libraries I fear possess sets of the periodical than sets of the indexes. There are now eight indexes to *Notes and Queries*, and a complete set costs about £20. Some of the indexes—which were published at 6s. each—are quite out of print, and if obtainable at all will cost about £5 or £6 each. These high prices, I think, indicate that there is a demand which will justify the publishers in combining the indexes and reissuing them in one alphabet and, if possible, in one volume.

I must say that I make this suggestion with reluctance, because I realise that I am giving the editor of *Notes and Queries* an opportunity to retort that "indexing like charity should begin at home". I think that we must all admit that any student requiring to consult a paper published in any of the transactions or journals connected with our Library Association, must either have an exact reference, or else plenty of time and patience. We may consider ourselves a hopeless failure as an association if at the end of twenty-five years our proceedings are unworthy of a good index. For some years there has been talk about co-operative work amongst us. It would be appropriate to commence that co-operative work by compiling an index to our own publications.

In the discussion which I hope my paper will be considered worthy of, I shall be glad if the speakers will answer the following questions :—

1. Do the references that are made to the lists of contents of transactions of learned societies printed in our library catalogues justify the expenditure of time, labour and money that the printing of them involves?

Of those who may answer the above question in the affirmative, I further ask :—

Will it not be more convenient and economical to substitute for the lists printed in library catalogues those issued by the various societies, but amended in accordance with the suggestions indicated in this paper?

Even if a majority of my fellow-librarians decline to accept my suggestions for economy, I shall still be gratified if I succeed in drawing a satisfactory defence of what now appears to be an extravagant and inconsistent practice.

PUBLISHERS AND PUBLISHING.[1]

By Walter Powell, Sub-Librarian, Free Libraries,
Birmingham.

IN coming before you to say a few words on the subject of
publishing, I do so in the hope and belief that I am
bringing forward a subject that has not yet reached the
hackneyed stage, although it may not be new. The gentlemen who read papers at the first Conference in 1877 had a
much easier task in choosing their subjects than we have in
1902.

Publishing can be looked at from at least three points
of view. Looked at from the publisher's own side it is no
doubt a very different matter from what it is when looked
at from the point of view of the author, or from a librarian's
standpoint.

I have no qualifications to discuss the matter from the
publisher's or author's side, but a long experience in collating
books for our great Reference Library has persuaded me that
from the librarian's point of view, publishers are guilty of
many sins which should be brought home to them. To the
ordinary reader who thinks of a book only as a production of
the brain, and not as a production of the press, a book seems
a very simple thing. It consists of paper, printer's ink and
binding, and there does not seem to be much scope for
anything either superlatively good or bad as regards its
manner of production, especially if we leave the binding out
of the question. And yet to those who are constantly
dealing with books as productions of the press, there are
many ways by which a good production can be distinguished
from a bad one. The paper, the ink, the illustrations, the
pagination, the stitching, the trimming of the edges, the
binding, should all receive thought and careful attention, so

---

[1] Read at the Annual Meeting of the Library Association, Birmingham,
23rd September, 1902.

that they may be not only good in themselves, but in harmony with one another.

Probably no one will dispute that it is just as reasonable to expect "value for money" when buying books as when buying furniture. If we want a table or a book-case it is comparatively easy to get just what is wanted. One may be too cheap and another too dear, but between the two there is almost sure to be something that is satisfactory.

It is not so with books: there is (generally speaking) no going up in easy stages and getting the same thing on better paper, or with better illustrations, or improved in some other respect, for a trifle more money. The book must be taken just as it is produced by the publisher, or done without altogether. If it is such that it is a credit to the publisher, whether it suits individual ideas or not, there is little to be said: allowance must be made for taste. If on the other hand it is produced in such a way that it reflects credit on no one the case is different, and there is just cause for complaint.

My special object to-day is to call attention in the first place to the unnecessary irregularities which are so frequently to be found when books are collated, and also to the many books which are so padded, either by the use of thick paper or large type, as to form volumes two or three times larger than is necessary, apparently with the object of justifying an unreasonable price.

Turning now to the component parts of a book, there is in the first place the paper on which it is printed. The varieties and qualities used at the present day are numerous. Much of it is very bad, but there is no need to despond and think that paper cannot be made to-day as it was made in the sixteenth century. Many books are printed on excellent paper. The Trustees of the British Museum have recently set an example by having one of their books printed on an admirable permanent paper. On the other hand, however, much of the paper used nowadays is shocking. There is that beautifully "ribbed" paper on which the eye has such a tendency to partly follow the ribs on the paper and partly the line of type, the result being dazzling in a somewhat similar manner to that produced by a "double impression" on a newspaper. Then again there is the thick spongy paper on which so many books are printed at the present day. If thickness were proof of durability, that paper ought to last for ever. Unfortunately thickness is not synonymous with strength, and the paper in question is so soft and spongy that it can scarcely bear the stitches which are designed to hold it together. This paper, however, should be a good friend to the publisher, as it has the power of making a pamphlet into a book, and a book costs more than a pamphlet. It should also meet with approval from those who disapprove of modern fiction, as no author whose books are printed on it can hope for immortality.

As you are aware, however, the question of paper has recently been taken up by the Society of Arts, who appointed a committee to report on the subject. It is sincerely to be hoped that good results will come from this.

Having disposed of the question of paper there is next the collation of the work. I think all books which are intended for permanent preservation, either in a private or public library, should be carefully collated when received. It is in this process that the various vagaries of publishers come to light. The volume should contain two paginations, one in Roman figures for the preliminary matter, the other in Arabic figures for the book itself and its index. The preliminary matter consists of the sub-title-page, the title-page, and anything of a like nature. This sounds simple enough, and it *is* simple enough; yet the unnecessary exceptions are very numerous. Some publishers, for instance, leave the first *leaf* (not page) blank, but yet calculate it in the pagination. While the book remains in the publisher's case it is generally easy to see that the blank leaf is part of the sheet, and therefore it may be presumed to count in the pagination. If the book is rebound, however, 99 binders out of every 100 would carefully remove the blank leaf and thus unconsciously render the work imperfect. The possibility of this could be removed by the very simple expedient of not including blank leaves in the pagination.

Another stupid departure which is sometimes, but fortunately not often adopted, is to have only one pagination. In such cases it is usually thought desirable to have a dividing line between the preliminary matter and the book, and this is accomplished by using Roman figures for the preliminary matter, and Arabic figures for the book as usual. What advantage there is in having only one pagination I am not able to say; it is easy, however, to point to a serious disadvantage. As you are aware, the preliminary matter is usually the last part of the book to be made up: consequently the amount of space it will require has to be estimated. Supposing it is likely to occupy sixteen pages, the book is commenced at page seventeen. On the principle, however, that "there is many a slip 'twixt the cup and the lip," it not infrequently happens that it is necessary to either extend or curtail the intended preliminary matter. In such cases the book must inevitably appear either with a leaf or so too much or too little, and consist of say pp. i-x, 17-300; or i-xx, 17-300.

Much more frequent irregularities are the omission of (1) List of Contents, (2) List of Maps or Plates, or (3) Index. The first is not very common. Most books are provided with a list of contents, although it is sometimes describable as "of a sort". The omission of a list of plates is much more common ; it is a particularly irritating practice, because it would be such a small matter to make a book complete in this respect. As an example of the stupidity shown in this direction, I may cite the new volumes of the *Encyclopædia Britannica*, which contain a number of plates of which there are no lists. It seems incredible that in this the twentieth century the publishers of such an undertaking actually print lists for the guidance of the binder, and yet do not include them in the volumes for the benefit of the purchaser. Yet this is what is actually done.

I am sure the members of the Library Association will be glad to hear that for years past it has been the custom here to write to the publishers of every book that comes into the Reference Library deficient in this respect and inquire (1) whether any list of plates was issued, and if not (2) what plates the volume should contain. The publishers usually courteously reply in full, and the inquiry thereby answers two useful purposes, inasmuch that it supplies the library with an MS. list of what should have been printed, and at the same time gives the publisher a hint that the omission has not passed altogether unnoticed. It is not altogether unknown for such an inquiry to result in the subsequent publication of a list of plates. As a sort of offshoot of this practice, there is the inaccurate or incomplete list of plates which is more common than desirable. Mistakes are particularly rife in those books which contain a large number of illustrations, some of which are included in the text, the others being full-page plates. In such cases there is often only one list of illustrations in which the words "*facing* page" are supposed to appear to signify the full page plates; frequently there is only supposition. Again there is the incomplete list. It is not at all uncommon for a book to be provided with a good list of illustrations, maps, etc., which utterly ignores folding tables and such-like matters which are often to be found in works of a statistical character. Surely if a map, or a plate, or a folding table, or an extra leaf, forms an integral part of a book, there is no reason why any publisher should be ashamed to say so.

Another point in connection with the beginning of books to which I wish to draw attention is the undated title-page, which was once so well described by a witty bookseller, who said of an undated work, "The publisher has done his best to make the work immortal by omitting all reference to time". I suppose a title-page is often left undated from commercial considerations, as it is no doubt much easier to sell a book which is ten years old if the intending purchaser thinks it is new. Apart from this, however, there are innumerable cases of books without dates for which no satisfactory reasons can be given. The Shakespeare Memorial Library in Birmingham contains 584 complete editions of Shakespeare's works in English; these are arranged on the shelves and in the catalogue in chronological order. If those who are responsible for the publication of editions of Shakespeare with undated title-pages had the responsibility of ascertaining that any undated edition which is offered to the library is not already there, they would realise one of the lesser difficulties which the omission causes. The evil, however, is so widespread that I am afraid that there will be no improvement until His Majesty's Government ranges this crime with murder and high treason and makes it a capital offence.

Title-pages, by-the-way, have undergone a complete change from the days when they were about half as long as the book itself. The present tendency is to introduce eccentricities, which appear to be very doubtful improvements. In some cases practically all the information is put in a square, and the title, author's editor's or illustrator's names are all run on without any spacing or punctuation ; moreover, it is often necessary to divide two or three words or names on one title-page so as to make them fit the square. The result is very similar to Mr. Pickwick's celebrated antiquarian discovery of Bilst um pshi s'm. ark.

It is very surprising to find that there is a strange jumbling of the information usually given on the title-page in so important a work as *The Victoria History of the Counties of England* (160 volumes, costing £240). As one would expect, each volume contains two handsome title-pages, but unfortunately they are almost duplicates, and in the earlier volumes at least, the principal information (*i.e.*, the editor's name and the number of volumes in which the particular county will be completed) is relegated to the back of the sub-title-page where it appears in very small type.

These are the chief defects at the beginning of books.

At the end, the omission of an Index is comparatively common, especially in works of travel and biography. This, I presume, is rather the fault of the author than the publisher, but that is immaterial to the purchaser.

It is a matter for congratulation that at least one influential literary paper (*The Athenæum*) never fails to call attention to the want of an Index and so lends its support to the remedying of this defect.

There is one more frequent defect at the end of a book, and that is an abrupt termination. It is usual to signify the end of a volume by the words "The End" or by the printer's imprint, or other obvious means. Certain books, however, have no such guide. They simply stop: it must be taken for granted that the last page is the legitimate end, because there is no more. Surely it is never impossible to put one or other of the usual devices for indicating the end, however full the last page may be.

I have now had my say as regards the interior of books and would venture to make a suggestion. Would it not be well to try to induce publishers to print in every book, say on the back of the title-page or other convenient place, its own collation? It would be a very simple thing to do, would be very little trouble and no expense to the publishers, and would be an inestimable boon to bibliographers. Moreover, it would have the further advantage of preventing any doubts as to completeness in the minds of collators, even in those cases where the publishers felt that they really must indulge in one or more of the vagaries to which I have called attention. A step has been taken in the right direction by Messrs. Macmillan & Co., who already print full collations in their lists of new publications. It would certainly be a great advantage to have this information made more accessible and guaranteed longer life. Publishers' monthly catalogues have a happy knack of eventually finding a resting-place in the waste-paper basket.

As regards the exterior or binding of books there is not so much to be said. There is not the same objection that you must take it as it is, or go without altogether. If you do not like the binding of a book, you can have it re-bound, where you could not have it reprinted. At the same time there are directions in which publishers' bindings might be improved. In the first place the cutting down of the edges is too frequently done recklessly; it seems to me that in cases of books of importance it would be better to leave them entirely uncut, even if for no better reason than that it is always possible to trim an uncut book, while there would certainly be considerable difficulty in replacing the full margins on a book which has been cut down.

Passing lightly over several barbarous methods adopted for holding the sheets together, such as wire stitching, india-rubber backing, unnecessary overstitching, etc., I think a word of protest should be entered against several recent brilliant ideas as to lettering the backs. The *Civil Service Year Book*, for instance, has the briefest possible lettering, that is none at all. The proprietors of the *British Almanac* appear to have arrived at the conclusion that the popular prejudice in favour of lettering a book near the top of the back was founded on wrong principles, and consequently they now have their volumes lettered at the foot, where the publisher's name is usually stamped. As a further variety those responsible for the *Baptist Year Book* tried a novel idea a few years ago. Lettering was considered a necessity, but apparently there was no reason for it to bear any relation to the contents of the book. Any one being so unreasonable as to expect to know from the back of the book what it was about, was informed in large letters that "Silk Banners" could be obtained at a certain address, information which struck me as being akin to the observation of Mr. F.'s aunt in *Little Dorrit*, who, referring to nothing in particular, suddenly announced, "There's milestones on the Dover Road".

These, however, are specific examples; reverting to the general question of lettering there seems to be a tendency to indulge in extremely ornamental backs to books, in which the title is so carefully interweaved and hidden, that it would sometimes seem that the words "puzzle, find the title" should have been stamped on the back.

Lastly, on the subject of publishers' bindings there is a growing practice of giving information on the binding, which is not to be found in the book. For instance, Messrs. Dent & Co.'s pretty little volumes of "Mediæval Towns" are only so named on the cover. In the books themselves there are no indications that they form part of a series, and consequently when they are rebound the information will often be lost.

A still more flagrant case is the "Edinburgh Folio Shakespeare" now in course of publication. This handsome edition is to be in forty parts, costing altogether £10 net. In the original prospectus and in the publisher's advertisements it is described as the "Edinburgh Folio Shakespeare". This title, however, appears only on the paper boards in which the parts are issued. The title-page gives no further information than "The Works of Shakespeare, edited by W. E. Henley". When the parts are subsequently made up into volumes and bound it will certainly not be convenient to bind in the heavy boards on which the title is printed. Consequently the name of the edition by which it has been so largely quoted will be entirely lost, and apparently future generations will be unacquainted with it under the name by which the publisher intended it to be known.

The points to which I have alluded so far are all comparatively small matters, and are probably more attributable to want of thought than to any other cause. They could be easily remedied with no loss to the publisher, and with great gain to the book-lover. There are, however, other, and in some ways more important grounds on which there is cause to complain of publishers. First and foremost is the dishing up of old wares as new matter. The *Cyclopædia of Home Arts*, edited by Montagu Marks, issued in 1899, reappeared in 1901 as the *Home Arts Self-Teacher*. The *Young Sportsman* is a work made up of articles from *The Encyclopædia of Sport*, and was issued, I believe, without even the permission or knowledge of the authors of the articles. Mrs. Little's *Land of the Blue Gown*, published a short time ago, includes, without any acknowledgment of the fact, an entire work issued in 1898 under the title of *My Diary in a Chinese Farm*. These are merely instances of three of the methods adopted to get old stock off.

There is, however, another way in which the unlucky buyer finds himself "sold" of which brief mention has been made. By the use of large type and thick paper many books are padded out to an utterly unreasonable extent. A recent "Autobiography" contains 270 such pages, and is published at 16s. net. It could be read in a few hours. Another work issued a short time ago in two volumes contains 470 pages in all, with only one pagination, and is to be had for the ridiculously small sum of 32s. If the two volumes were bound together they would form one of ordinary thickness, but then 32s. would seem rather a high price for one volume. The one pagination seems a curious departure, but no doubt there is method in the madness. Unless I am much mistaken the idea is to subsequently cancel the two title-pages, bind up the unsold sheets with a new title-page, and issue the work in one volume as a " cheap edition "—say at 8s., actually the same book with the exception of the title-page as was originally sold at 32s. !

Three more grumbles and I have done. In the first place, is not the modern craze for " Series " being very much overdone. What chance has an author to do his best work when he is so restricted as he must of necessity be when writing for a series. The work must not be too long (which is one thing in favour of a series), or too short, or go beyond a certain date, and altogether is often so restricted in scope as to make good work, or at least best work, impossible. Secondly, a protest should be entered, I think, against the practice of booming a book by a preface from another hand. The particular objection is that, generally speaking, there is just preface enough to make it describable on the title-page and in the advertisements which are de-signed to sell the book. A curate writes a book which is ushered into the world by his vicar; the vicar in his turn calls upon the dean to boom his wares, while eventually the dean is moved by the Spirit to commit his thoughts to paper, and he persuades the bishop to try to persuade the public to buy the thoughts. It is surprising to find how many recognised authorities on various subjects allow their names to be made use of in this way, but pity the poor purchaser who buys the book for the preface, and more often than not finds that it runs to about a page and a half.

The remaining point to which I would call attention is the changeableness of the publishers of periodicals and the publications of various learned societies. Some of them have a positive passion for beginning a fresh series. Some-times there is good reason for it, as, for instance, in the cases of *Notes and Queries* and *The Expositor*, which begin a new series at certain regular intervals with the very laudable object of issuing general indexes to each series as completed. Even in these cases, however, it does not seem absolutely necessary to begin afresh each time. The *Quarterly* and *Edinburgh Reviews* have existed for nearly a hundred years each, have never yet found it necessary to begin life afresh, and yet have issued their indexes regularly. But let that pass: I will not say anything against a practice that has for its object the multiplication of indexes. Other periodicals, however, begin a new series apparently with no better object in view than to bewilder those who preserve them, and to distract those who try to make a workable index to them. If this brilliant idea had not come into existence, and all sets had been issued with a consecutive volume numbering, there would have been no necessity for that complicated conspectus at the beginning of *Poole's Index*, which forms such a stumbling-block to some of our readers.

As a specimen of the "New Series" craze the now defunct *Theatre* is interesting. A set consists of vols. i. to iii.; New Series, vols. i. to iii.; New Series, vols. i. to vi.; New Series, vols. i. to xxiii.; and from that time to the end of its existence anything you like, as all reference to series was "dropped" with that delicacy which caused Silas Wegg to "drop," in the presence of Mrs. Boffin, the explanation of the difference between the Rooshan and Roman Empires.

But what shall be said of an Association, hereinafter called the Blank Association, which ought to be a leader in such matters. It issued a journal under the title of *The Blank Chronicle*. After five years the title was altered to *The Blank*, and a fresh volume numbering was begun. After ten years another change seemed desirable, and the title was again altered to *The Blank Association Record*, and this time a further variety was imparted to the set by increasing the size of the volumes by an inch or so, apparently with the laudable object of preventing them from standing on the same shelf as their predecessors. This title has now existed for nearly three years, so a further change may be confidently looked for at an early date. At the present time, by the way, the title-page and index for the volume for 1901 have not been issued. The same Association issues a *Year Book* at spasmodic intervals, and is very un-decided as to whether its *Proceedings* should be issued in volume form or not. I will say no more, or some of you may guess what " Blank " stands for.

Gentlemen, I have had my say.

On reading over my paper I find it sounds extremely pessimistic. If I could read it as an outsider, I should gather that publishing generally is in a very bad way, and that there has never yet been a book issued that was quite satisfactory. Believe me, gentlemen, I do not feel like that. I do not even think that the proportion of unsatisfactory books is alarmingly large. My object in preparing this paper has been to call attention to these matters, because I think that many of them could be remedied if joint action were taken by some influential body with a view to educating the offenders. It is of little use for one voice here and there to be crying in the wilderness. Co-operation is required, and surely if anything can be done in the matter it can best be done by the Library Association.

I would recommend that they begin with a fierce on-slaught on the Blank Association.

CAUSERIE.

Functions of a University Library.—The subjoined paragraphs are extracted from a report recently submitted by the Aberdeen Library Committee to the University Court :—

"Objections made to the Committee's expenditure by students and by outside readers are largely due to a misapprehension of the functions which a University Library is intended to perform ; and the Committee believes it to be advisable to specify what, in their opinion, are and are not the true aims of the Library.

"(i.) It is *not* the province of the University Library to furnish, still less indefinitely to multiply, the text-books required by the ordinary student. To a certain extent the supply of these must always lie with the student himself, but the institution of Class Libraries, which he can join on payment of a small subscription, helps to reduce the demands on his purse.

"(ii.) It is *not* the province of the University Library to compete with the Public or the Circulating Library in the supply of contemporary literature of interest to the general reader but more or less ephemeral in character. It is along special rather than along general lines of reading that the Library should be found serviceable.

"(iii.) It should be the aim of the Library to supply treatises and books of reference in the several branches of University study, as recommended by the teachers and other experts who are willing to help the Committee with their advice. Apart from such books it is impossible for research to be carried on by graduates and advanced students, as well as by members of the University staff, without frequent reference to Libraries in London and elsewhere.

"(iv.) It should be the aim of the Library to supply Transactions of learned Societies and the leading journals devoted to special branches of knowledge, access to which is nowadays absolutely indispensable for those engaged in research. The number of such periodicals must be large, and the set of each must be made as complete as possible. Nor can they be restricted as to language without serious loss to workers in the University. There is much information of great value that cannot be found in English books or periodicals. It cannot always be gathered from even the leading European languages : reference must be made at times to papers in Dutch, the Scandinavian and the lesser Latin tongues ; while in the Eastern hemisphere Japanese is now establishing a claim to be reckoned with. As a matter of fact, all periodicals purchased by the Committee for the Library are in English, French or German, except one in Italian on Mathematics. Other languages (Latin, Modern Greek, Spanish, Portuguese, Dutch, Swedish, Norwegian, Gaelic, Japanese are represented only among the periodicals purchased from the Wilson fund or received in exchange or gift. The expenditure on account of some special subjects, such as Zoology, is large in comparison with that for others, but the literature in those subjects is relatively more costly.

"(v.) It should be the aim of the Library to acquire all publications bearing upon the district—Scotland north of the Tay—of which the University of Aberdeen is the natural centre. The collection thus formed should include not merely all books and pamphlets relating to or published in the North of Scotland, but all books or pamphlets written or edited by graduates or alumni of Aberdeen. The sum that can be set aside from general Library funds for this purpose is small, and the Committee confidently appeal to former studetns to present to the Library copies of any publications which they may write or edit."

Public Libraries and Sunday Schools.—A suggestion is thrown out by a writer in the *Sunday School Chronicle* which we venture to think is worthy of consideration by the public library authorities of this country : "The American libraries are extending their usefulness by invading the Sunday Schools and using them as the means for the distribution of good literature in the homes of the people. A hundred books are offered for a month by the local library to each Sunday School in the town, the schools becoming responsible for the transit and care of the books. Freedom of choice is given to the schools, though the free library reserves the right of withholding any book in great demand. The need for loan libraries has long been felt by the Sunday School Union and met as far as is practicable. Naturally the expense of travelling libraries worked from one centre is much greater than would be the case if every town had its own supply on the spot. The Sunday School must not abandon its effort to influence the choice of the scholars' reading, and must also keep the control, as far as possible, in its own hands. It may be contended that the existing control is not very effective, but we have, in the Sunday School Library, the means of supplying good literature, and we are not destitute of some power of getting it read. The affiliation of the School Library to the Public Library, under adequate inspection from the school authorities, might revive the prosperity of the former institution, and give it a new lease of life."

An Interesting Parish Church Library.—In a recent number of the *Church Times*, communicated to us by Mr. R. D. Prosser, we find a short account of a most interesting parish church library, apparently unknown to collectors, which is situated in the parish of Shipdham in the county of Norfolk. The "Peripatetic Parson," who is responsible for the article in which the library is described, writes as follows :—

"The special feature of this church is the remarkably good library housed in the parvise over the south porch. There can be no doubt, we think, that this is the most valuable library that any parish church in England possesses. It is passing strange that no bibliographer has produced any catalogue of these books, or even any description of its rarities. Through the courtesy of the rector we were able to spend a hasty half-hour amongst them. The most valuable is probably *The Floure of the Commandmentes of God*, printed by Wynken de Worde, 1509. We also noticed a Richard Pynson of 1517, as well as several fifteenth-century printed books. The collection also includes one or two manuscripts, among them being a copy of Ovid's Epistles. The extraordinary thing is that no one has any idea who was the collector of these books or the donor of them to the church. The fly-leaves of these volumes, which number some hundreds, are silent on the subject."

Topography of London.—Lord Rosebery's address to the London Topographical Society at its Annual Meeting, which was held at the headquarters of the Society of Antiquaries, Burlington House, on the 15th October last, was one of those happy little excursions with which he occasionally diversifies the arid labour of political letter-writing. He has long been, like Dr. Johnson, an ardent lover of the town, and the eulogy which he pronounced upon the work of the Society over which he presides was that of an expert. This modest little organisation was established only four years ago, yet, despite public indifference and a restricted income, it has already established solid claims to the gratitude and support of those who take an intelligent interest in those memorials of the past which are fading so rapidly away, and leaving the Capital of the Empire splendid, perhaps, but all too new. Lord Rosebery commented, with not undeserved sarcasm, upon the comparatively small appreciation which the Society's efforts to preserve graphic remembrances and accurate records of vanished buildings have hitherto met with in London itself. In the last two years only two Metropolitan Free Libraries have become members, though five American libraries have joined it in the last twelve months. If we except Paris in the hands of Baron Haussmann and his imperial patron, no great city has ever altered so much and so quickly as London in the last quarter of a century. Even Rome, which has been jerry-built almost out of recognition since the collapse of the Temporal Power, retains practically all its great classical and historical landmarks. Far otherwise is it on the banks of the Thames. Since 1874, when the modern era of demolition began with the destruction of Northumberland House and the cutting of the gloomy avenue that occupies its site, innumerable buildings, not merely familiar to generations of Londoners, but conspicuous in the history of the English people, have been swept away—sometimes, it is to be feared, without overwhelming necessity. Nor has the process stopped with the disappearance of isolated buildings. Whole streets have been obliterated, as in the recent case of King Street, Westminster—in some respects the most historic thoroughfare of the town. The narrow way along which Charles I. passed to his trial, as he had gone to his coronation, has been destroyed as utterly as the old Royal Mews that once stood where Landseer's lions simper and the Municipal fountains occasionally squirt their soapy-looking water. The city has suffered heavily, especially in the matter of churches, which have been pulled down wholesale. At this moment the most sweeping alterations of the generation are taking place in preparation for that "anonymous Crescent" for which Lord Rosebery twitted his friends at Spring Gardens with being unable to invent a name. Regret it as we may, it is, as Lord Rosebery reminded us, generally inevitable. The least we can do, for our own credit, and for the behoof of posterity, which always values that of which the generation in possession makes light, is to preserve complete records, in word and picture, of the structures that we remove from our path. The London Topographical Society has already begun the publication of a record of changes, but it is hampered by lack of means. The suggestion its president made yesterday that the Capital ought to possess a special library of books relating to its own past is excellent, but is somewhat of a counsel of perfection. Such a collection would be very large, for the bibliography of London is infinite, and the modern revival of topographical literature provides almost daily accessions. The city possesses, in effect, such a library at Guildhall, as regards the area of its own jurisdiction, while the stores of the British Museum may be supposed to be almost exhaustive. In preserving memoranda of that which is destroyed year by year the Society has before it quite enough work to occupy all its energies, and to enable it to make good use of much wider support than it at present enjoys.

English Ornamental Initial Letters.—At the November meeting of the Bibliographical Society, Mr. Charles Sayle read a paper on "English Ornamental Initial Letters". Their use in printed books, which was a direct consequence of the illuminated letters in manuscripts, seems to have been introduced by Caxton in 1480, at a comparatively late period in his life. He did not trouble himself greatly about the ornamentation, being much more interested in the books themselves, though on the Continent this branch of the art of book production had made considerable advance. The period covered by the lecturer was about 120 years—till 1600. From 1480 to 1500 might be considered as one period; from 1501 to the end of the century it would be advisable to reckon by decades, and after the close of the sixteenth century the value of the work began to decline. The letters themselves might be divided into groups, according to the character of the ornamentation. Thus they might be called floriated when the letter was surrounded with floral decoration; heraldic, when a coat-of-arms or badge was inserted; historiated, when the subject of the book was illustrated in the treatment of the initial; teratological, when monsters were introduced in the ornamentation; and the term " factotum " was used to denote a pierced ornamental block in which any letter of the alphabet in movable type could be inserted. The lecturer spoke of the work of the University presses, and those of Tavistock and St. Albans, during the different periods under consideration, exhibiting and describing specimens of the different types of letters, and urged the necessity for the study of our old initial letters and printers' marks in order to elucidate the history of book ornamentation in this country. A collection of drawings and early printed books was displayed in the room.

The Second Folio Shakespeare.—A writer in the *Manchester Guardian* called attention recently to a curious anomaly in the bibliography of some early editions of Shakespeare, and very pertinently points out that every schoolboy has a certain acquaintance with this subject nowadays. He knows that the First Folio was printed—very badly—in 1623, that many quarto editions of separate plays had preceded it, and that there were three later folio editions, of which the Second was distinguished by containing the memorial verses of Milton and being the favourite companion of the Royal Martyr, whilst the Third, in 1663, was the first to contain the seven more or less doubtful plays, of which all but " Pericles " have since been banished from the standard editions. Thus far the schoolboy. But there are lower deeps, greater niceties of distinction, to one of which attention has just been called by the litigation about a certain copy of the Second Folio. The general public, as Mr. Roberts truly says, does not quite understand the fine shades which make one folio differ from another in glory, so that, while an ordinary copy of the Second Folio is worth about £100, that which was the subject of dispute appears to have fetched £615 at Sotheby's last June. It is not merely a question of tallness and condition, though of course these eminent bibliographical qualities have something to say in the case. The distinction is really due to a peculiarity of the publishing trade in the seventeenth century, which Mr. Roberts lucidly explains. The Second Folio was the speculation of five booksellers who united to make a profit out of Shakespeare's derelict plays—and incidentally to enshrine their names for ever in bibliographical prefaces. The colophon states that it was "printed at London by Thomas Cotes for John Smethwick, William Apsley, Richard Hawkins, Richard Meighan, and Robert Allot ". Each of these speculative booksellers took the trouble to have a special title-page printed for his copies, bearing his own name alone.

The majority of the copies which are still extant bear the title-page thus prepared by Robert Allot, who seems to have been the leading man among the five. Consequently the others are more valuable. The copy which is now in question bore the name of Smethwick, and consequently gained a fictitious value from its comparative rarity—

though the useful compilation known as *Book-Prices Current* records the sale of six similar copies in the last fifteen years, at prices varying from £30 to £690. The very wide discrepancy in price at once shows what a difference is made by the condition of a book; evidently the £30 one was a mere fragment or *torso* of a book, whilst the one which fetched £690 was a "very fine and unwashed copy". The editor of *Book-Prices Current* lends his authority to the description of the Smethwick title-page as "extraordinarily rare," which is more than Mr. Roberts will say of it. The British Museum does not possess a copy with this title-page, but there is one in the Cambridge University Library, one in the Lennox Library at New York, and probably several others in public and private collections. The mere alteration of a name in the title-page seems hardly basis enough for the demand which has been made that the British Museum should take steps to acquire a copy with this slight variation. There is this to be said for the interest taken in the Smethwick copies, that he was the only bookseller who helped to bring out both the First and the Second Folio. But at the best it is a somewhat factitious interest. Still, if a millionaire will present one of the Smethwick copies to the British Museum, and another to our own John Rylands Library, there will be no reason to quarrel with his taste for minute details of this kind.

The *Index Expurgatorius.*—The new number of the *Quarterly Review* contains an interesting article on the past history and the present position of the *Roman Index of Prohibited Books*. It is called for by the publication of a new and much amended edition in which many ancient errors and misunderstandings have been corrected. It was obviously unseemly and tending to merriment in the enemy that orthodox Roman Bishops and other dignitaries should remain side by side with Voltaire and Renan upon a list in which they were originally inscribed by mistake. The *Index* was never a really original Roman work, but was, through a great part of its history, a compilation that incorporated the titles of books prohibited by the Catholic Sovereigns. The first real *Index Librorum Prohibitorum* was that published in 1546 at Louvain by direction of Charles V. To this was added shortly afterwards a further *Index*, emanating from the University. It was adopted by Spain as its own, and Venice presently also took it over; eventually all the books contained in it were "censured" by Rome *en bloc*. When the first Vatican *Index* was published by Pope Paul IV. in 1559, it consisted of various catalogues of this kind, with numerous additions arrived at in the most haphazard way. Lists of mediæval "heretics" were taken, and the whole of their books included. In the beginning, editions of the Scriptures in the vulgar tongue, and the myriads of controversial volumes produced by the religious ferment that so soon followed the relatively extensive use of the new art of printing, were nearly all placed upon the *Index*—if censors chanced to come across them. In time the impossibility of keeping thought in leading strings became obvious; but, hateful as the endeavour seems to us now, there was nothing so very intolerant in it, according to the lights of the times. It was not the Vatican alone that proscribed and burned books of which it did not approve. The Temporal Sovereigns did the same thing. Henry VIII., even, began by discouraging the English Bible, and actually prohibited the books of Luther and Tyndale, just as though he had been a Dominican compiling an Index, and when Calvin burned Servetus because he considered that his books were heretical, he only went a step further. On the whole, the world took but little notice of the swingeing reprobation of the Roman censure. Fine and excommunication—at one time the penalties went towards the fabric fund of Bramante's Basilica—

were, no doubt, sometimes inconvenient to individuals; but the area of jurisdiction was small. Spain insisted upon supremacy in her own house—even Philip II. treated Papal Bulls with contumely, when it suited him; the non-Spanish Italian States were restive; France would allow of nothing to which the King had not given his *imprimatur;* Germany was a difficulty from the first. For the last three centuries the *Index* has been chiefly the portion of Roman Catholic writers whose orthodoxy has been denounced—there has been no machinery for seeking out heresy, and, indeed, many heretics have escaped condemnation. Galileo is, of course, a leading case, and from 1624 to 1757 every *Index* contained the comprehensive rubric, " All books forbidden which maintain that the earth moves and the sun does not "; and it was not until 1835 that the faithful were tacitly permitted, by the removal of his name, to regard Galileo as orthodox. Some strange company is still found in the new *Index.* Henry VIII. and Anne Askew share its pages with George Sand and Darwin; there we find both the Dumas; Rabelais, of course, Voltaire and Pascal, and even Fénélon; Heine for the *Reisebilder,* and Hobbs for *Leviathan,* Sir Thomas Browne for the *Religio Medici,* and Gibbon for the *Decline and Fall.* Hugo and Michelet were too Revolutionary for the Roman censors, and it has even not been thought fit to liberate Goldsmith's *History of England* and Sterne's *Sentimental Journey* from their purgatory. The old penalties, however, are removed, and the power of excommunication for reading forbidden books is reserved to the Pope alone. Altogether, it would seem that even Rome herself now regards the *Index* rather as an interesting historical relic than as a practical weapon.

LIBRARY NOTES AND NEWS.

ABERDEEN UNIVERSITY LIBRARY: *Lady Assistants.*—Mr. Frank C. Nicholson, M.A., has resigned the assistant librarianship at Marischal College, and the University Library Committee have resolved to appoint a lady as his successor. It is understood that Aberdeen (which has thrown open to women all its classes, prizes and degrees) was the first University in the United Kingdom to introduce lady assistant librarians. Two, still in office, were appointed more than eight years ago; a third was appointed four years ago; and Mr. Nicholson's successor will be a fourth.

BEVERLEY: *Municipal Election to be fought on the Library Question.*—The municipal contest at Beverley is being fought upon two subjects only—the Corporation's electric light scheme and a free library and museum, but chiefly upon the latter. An anonymous donor has offered to build and equip a library and museum for the town, providing the Corporation will find a site and agree to maintain it, and this latter point is the one which engages public attention for the moment. Of the eleven candidates for municipal honours, three have declared themselves to be opposed to the scheme. The rest, whilst alluding to it in guarded terms, offer no definite opinion. On the 30th October a meeting was held in the Corn Exchange in advocacy of the library, and so great was the interest manifested that many were unable to obtain admission, whilst the doors of the hall remained open throughout. Alderman Hobson presided, and on a crowded platform were the Mayor, several members of the Town Council, professional men, and other prominent residents. The Mayor proposed a resolution in favour of the offer, and urging upon the Town Council the desirability of taking the necessary action to secure its acceptance. The resolution was carried by an overwhelming majority, there being only one dissentient.

BRIGHTON: *Opening of the New Public Library, Museum and Art Galleries.*—On the 5th November the Mayor of Brighton (Mr. Alderman Stafford) opened the new Public Library, Museum and Art Galleries in Church Street, Brighton, in the presence of a large assemblage. The buildings have been erected by the Corporation on the site of the old Victoria Public Library adjoining the Dome and Pavilion at a total cost of £41,000. The exterior of the buildings is quite in harmony with the peculiar architecture of the Pavilion, and presents an exceedingly handsome appearance. The interior is magnificently fitted up. The newsroom and libraries are spacious apartments, and a very fine suite of rooms has been prepared for the picture gallery. A loan collection of pictures, which will remain open three months, and which comprises many valuable pictures lent by various noblemen, gentlemen and corporate bodies throughout the country was also opened by the Mayor. Altogether 228 pictures have been hung, of which 216 are oil and water-colours, and the remainder etchings.

BRISTOL: *The New Central and Reference Library.*—Out of sixty-one designs for the new Central and Reference Library sent in, that of Mr. H. Percy Adams, of 28 Woburn Place, Russell Square, London, has been selected. The assessor says that other designs were of high quality, but several involved too great a cost, or in other ways did not comply with the regulations of the competition. Mr. Adams was architect to the Bristol Guardians for the infirmary scheme which was rejected a few weeks ago, after long consideration, on account of the unwillingness of a majority of the board to spend so much money on provision for the sick poor as the scheme involved. The proposed building is to cost £25,000, or one-half of the Stuckey-Lean bequest which the Library Committee received a few years ago. The site is now being cleared—that of the old Deanery, adjoining the Norman gateway. It has been purchased from the Dean and Chapter on a fee-farm rent of £120 a year, which is to be met by setting aside £4,000 of the capital. The building will be of Bath stone, with Forest of Dean stone to give variety of colour, and the roof will be covered with green Westmoreland slates. The design is intended to harmonise with the surroundings of the site, and it is treated with a Gothic rather than a classic feeling. A sum of £5,000 is to be spent on furniture and fittings, £5,000 more on books, and a third £5,000 is put down for contingencies. Further, in order to reduce the burden of maintenance, the committee have wisely decided to invest £6,000, which will bring in, say, £180 a year. These items account for the whole £50,000, which was payable, less legacy duty. But it has taken so long to find a site and get thus far with a scheme such as the testator had in mind that the interest has probably more than made up the amount of the duty.

CARDIFF: *A Year of Growth in the Public Library.*—The public library movement in Cardiff has now reached its fortieth year and Mr. Ballinger's annual report enables one to see at a glance what progress has been made, and what is being done at the Central Library and its branches. The stock of books is now 107,669 volumes, and the school libraries contain 9,550. The circulation exceeds largely that of any previous year, the total circulation during the year ended 31st October, being 567,199. Twenty years ago the circulation was only 72,976, much of the increase being due to new departures, such as the branch and school libraries. The Reference Library shows a similar growth. Ten years ago the number of books used in the department was 18,886; this year it was 108,616. An important collection of early printed books has been presented by Mr. John Cory, D.L., J.P., of Duffryn. An unusual number of valuable donations were received during the year. Mr. Ballinger gives a detailed account of the Wooding Library, purchased by the committee, which bibliographers will read with great interest. Mr. Wooding was a general merchant at Beulah, Brecknockshire, and a lifelong collector of books, and people used to take Welsh books to him to be exchanged for cash or goods from the shop. The total number of volumes in his collection is over 5,000, and rather more than half are Welsh or relate to Wales. The collection is rich in Welsh elegies. The history of the printing press in Wales is illustrated and elucidated by a number of books, some hitherto unrecorded. The *Public Library Journal* retains its popularity, and has now completed its sixth year of publication. Children attending the classes for the blind in the elementary schools were supplied with books in the Braille character from the Central Library. Some important and valuable books and manuscripts have been added to the Reference Library, a list being given in the report. For many years books in French and German have been circulated in the Central Lending Library.

CARDIFF: *The School Libraries.*—At a meeting of the Cardiff School Board on the 5th November, the annual report upon the school libraries by Mr. Ballinger was read, and was considered by the chairman and Mr. H. M. Thompson of a most satisfactory character. It appeared that the total circulation for the year had been 169,314 volumes, whereas in 1900-1901 it was 153,528. Having regard to the time the books had been in use they were in a very satisfactory state. Mr. Ballinger also remarked: " During the year just closed the scheme for a closer union between the school and the public library has been carried as far as it is possible to go under existing conditions. The main idea is that during school life the children shall acquire, under the supervision of the teachers, a love of good books, and be shown how, and what, and when to read." Mr. Ballinger was thanked for his interesting report.

COGAN : *Opening of a New Reading-room.*—A new reading-room, which has been built in the centre of Cogan by the Penarth Urban District Council, at a cost of £640, was opened to the public on Saturday the 1st November. The opening ceremony was performed by Mr. S. Thomas, J.P. Mr. Thomas gave a review of library work, after which he was presented with a gold key by the contractor, Mr. J. Pickford. Mr. Thomas then declared the room open to the public. Subsequently a luncheon was provided at Cogan Schools.

CORK: *A Correction.*—The librarian of the Cork Free Public Library (Mr. James Wilkinson) has been good enough to call our attention to an inaccurate statement with regard to Mr. Carnegie's offer, which appeared on page 433 of the RECORD. The sum offered by Mr. Carnegie was £10,000 instead of £1,000 as stated. This the Corporation have decided to accept. A public library has been established in Cork upwards of nine years.

DALKEITH: *The Library Question.*—A year ago there was a proposal that the Dalkeith Scientific Association should be dissolved, but as an offer had been made to the Burgh of Dalkeith by Dr. Carnegie of a gift of £4,000 for the erection of a library, it was felt that opportunity should first be afforded to the Town Council of taking action in connection with the adoption of the Free Libraries Act if they thought fit. Dr. Carnegie made the offer as the result of certain proceedings of several of the officials of the Scientific Association, and it was contemplated to hand over the 1,300 volumes belonging to the scientific library as a nucleus. Provost Chisholm and the late Councillor Storie, the president of the Scientific Association, and others, also offered assistance. The Town Council have done nothing in the matter, and the directors of the Scientific Association, who have now completed another financial year, at a slight loss, held a meeting last month, and after discussion resolved to summon the whole of their members to a meeting of the Association in view of the necessity of dissolving the library, as the membership has gradually been decreasing during the last twenty years, and the funds have also naturally decreased. The Association was formed in 1835, and was for a long period kept abreast of the times by additions to its library of the best works in science, history and general literature.

DUNFERMLINE: *The Year's Work at the Carnegie Library.*—At a meeting of the committee of the Carnegie Free Library, Dunfermline, held on the 20th November, the annual report of the librarian was submitted. The report stated that the total number of books issued during the year amounted to 72,643. Of these 68,953 were from the lending department, and 3,690 from the reference department, making the total number of books issued since the opening 1,288,669. As compared with last year this shows an increase of 1,977. The average daily issue was

255. During the year 491 books have been added to the library, 488 by purchase and 3 by gift. Of these, 454 had been placed in the lending department, and 37 in the reference department. There were now in the former 14,109, and in the latter 2,875, making a total of 16,984.

FALKIRK: *Opening of the New Library.*—Mr. Andrew Carnegie visited Falkirk on the 9th October in connection with the opening of the new Falkirk Public Library, erected in Hope Street, towards the cost of which Mr. Carnegie very generously gave £3,000. The library, which is likely to cost about £7,000, provides commodious as well as convenient premises.

GLASGOW: THE MITCHELL LIBRARY: *A Noteworthy Record.*—At one o'clock on Friday, 21st November, 1902, the library reached a somewhat interesting point in its history. Just at that hour the number of volumes which have been issued to readers reached ten millions. The first book was issued at ten o'clock A.M. on the 5th November, 1877, so that the issue of ten millions has occupied a fortnight more than twenty-five years, an average over the whole period of 400,000 a year. The table below gives the number of volumes and percentage of issue in each of the eight main classes in which the work is recorded.

	No. of Vols.	Percentage.
Theology, Philosophy and Ecclesiastical History	866,531	8·67
History, Biography, Voyages and Travels	2,088,501	20·89
Sociology (Law, Politics, Commerce, Education, etc.)	429,862	4·30
Arts and Sciences	2,160,768	21·61
Poetry and the Drama	568,354	5·68
Linguistics	230,219	2·30
Prose Fiction	891,575	8·91
Miscellaneous Literature	2,764,190	27·64
	10,000,000	100·00

It may be of interest to note the number of days required for the completion of each successive million.

Millions.	Date of Completion.	No. of Working Days.
First	14th January, 1881	982
Second	1st September, 1883	808
Third	4th December, 1885	693
Fourth	8th March, 1888	693
Fifth	20th May, 1892	816
Sixth	13th June, 1894	626
Seventh	15th May, 1896	591
Eighth	2nd July, 1898	653
Ninth	27th October, 1900	712
Tenth	21st November, 1902	637

The fifth million, which occupied 816 days, included the long interval between the quitting the old premises in Ingram Street and the opening of the present building in Miller Street. The later figures tell eloquently that the available accommodation does not permit further development, for since the completion of the seventh million there has been no general increase in the use of the library.

It should be noted that the number of volumes reported above as issued is quite independent of the very large use which has from the commencement been made of the selected periodical publications in the magazine-room, a use which is little less than that of the books issued over the counter.

GREENOCK: *Opening of the New Library.*—The Greenock Public Free Library, towards which Mr. Andrew Carnegie contributed £8,000, was formally opened by Mrs. Carnegie on the 10th October. The Free Libraries Act was adopted in Greenock on the 9th March, 1900.

HAWARDEN: *Opening of the St. Deiniol's Library.*—On the 14th October Earl Spencer opened the St. Deiniol's Library at Hawarden which has been built as a national memorial of Mr. Gladstone. The great statesman himself caused to be erected an iron building quite near the old parish church of Hawarden and hard by what was once the Grammar School. The school was made into a hostel for occupation and use by students of any age, " or others desiring times of rest," and in the iron building near it Mr. Gladstone himself stored the 30,000 books which he had for many years collected and afterwards gave " for the promotion of religion and sound learning". The church, as everybody knows, stands in the heart of the village, which everywhere bears associations with the name of Gladstone. The committee formed for the purpose of raising a national memorial to Mr. Gladstone decided to devote a sum of £10,000 for the erection of such a library—in which the books might be placed for all time—as would stand as a fitting memorial of the great man and one of the kind that he probably would have most desired. The new library has been built in front of the older iron building, and it is really joined to the hostel. It is built on the brow of the hill which overlooks the broad valley between Hawarden and Cheshire, and from it one can see right away over the farm land to the estuary of the Dee. The foundation-stone was laid by the late Duke of Westminster, and the stone-laying was one of the last public celebrations that was attended by Mrs. Gladstone. The inscription on the stone really tells the story of the foundation of the library. It reads: " In this building, erected to his memory by a grateful nation, is preserved the library of William Ewart Gladstone, who, eminent no less as theologian than as statesman, established this foundation for the advancement of Divine learning ". The inscription on the stone also states that it was laid in the presence of "the Bishop of the Diocese by the Duke of Westminster, K.G., on 5th October, 1899; G. E. Joyce, warden ". The library is designed in the Gothic style, with mullioned windows. Externally the building is faced with Helsby stone, a red sandstone, and the roof is covered with dark green Buttermere slates. The interior of the building consists of two large rooms, one for the " Divinity" and the other for the " Humanity" sections of the library, according to the scheme outlined by Mr. Gladstone. There are galleries, and the roof is of oak, open-timbered. The building also has rooms for the use of those in the hostel and for the warden. The floors are laid with oak blocks, and the columns which support the gallery as well as the front of the gallery itself are finely carved. It is interesting to know that the oak book-case fittings, which project from the walls and are quite simple, have been done after the plan of the fittings devised by Mr. Gladstone. They are placed as he would have had them—conveniently for the student or reader and without any waste of space. Many of the books too are made the more interesting through the markings and annotations and marginal references made by Mr. Gladstone. The library design is the work of Messrs. Duglas & Minshull, architects, of Chester. The plans include a new hostel and warden's house, and these will be built when funds are available.

The proceedings commenced with a short service of a simple character at the parish church, at which the Bishop of St. Asaph, in an eloquently worded eulogy of the late statesman, said they would always recall with thankfulness the fact that the profound and permanent influence of the character of Mr. Gladstone was ever on the side of what he believed to be purity, truth and justice.

Earl Spencer, in declaring the library open, said he thought he could claim a longer friendship of the deceased statesman than either Mr. Morley or Lord Rosebery. He could remember being taken to the House of Commons when he was a mere boy, and there was pointed out to him the rising man of the political world. That was Mr. Gladstone. He would never forget the impression which the great statesman then made upon him, and he knew no man who had shown so noble an example to his fellow-countrymen and to the world. He desired to speak of Mr. Gladstone as a Christian man, and as one who always acted on principle. Men might sometimes put forward high principles at the wrong time and on the wrong occasion, and then the lofty principles which they advocated did not always have their proper effect, and might even do harm to the great cause which they desired to prevail. Now Mr. Gladstone was more farseeing in the way in which he thought principles should be applied. He could name several occasions when this was shown, but he would mention only one—the question on which this wonderful power of his came out more powerfully than on any other perhaps—the great dispute which occurred in the House of Commons with regard to Mr. Bradlaugh. They must remember that Mr. Gladstone was a man of the deepest religious feeling, and they all knew the view that Mr. Bradlaugh took of religion. No one regretted the non-religious views of Mr. Bradlaugh more intensely than Mr. Gladstone, and yet because he thought that principle was being violated he incurred the odium of the House of Commons by taking what at the time was thought to be the side of the Atheist. He vigorously opposed the popular view, and introduced a measure into the House of Commons to rectify what he considered was wrong. He (Earl Spencer) was in the Cabinet at the time, and he would never forget the deep earnestness of feeling and determination of Mr. Gladstone on the subject. He laid down what he considered to be just and equitable laws, and though he differed entirely from Mr. Bradlaugh on religious matters he was willing to incur the most violent opprobrium and attack in securing justice for him. That example showed not only the farseeing wisdom Mr. Gladstone could apply to principle, but the great, remarkable and indomitable courage which he always displayed on the great questions which he propounded. It was fitting that this memorial should be raised near Mr. Gladstone's home. That was a home of moral love and purity, which was an example to every home in the country. Mr. Gladstone, in bequeathing that library for the effective promotion of Divine learning, explained that while the principles of the institution would be those of the historic Church of this country, and while the governing body would be worked on that idea, it was his earnest desire that the hospitality of the institution as far as possible might be available for persons beyond the pale of the Anglican Church, or even of the Christian religion. Those words, Earl Spencer proceeded, explained more eloquently and forcibly than he could the desire which Mr. Gladstone had in view. They were noble words which illustrated Mr. Gladstone's respect for, and devotion to, religion.

The Rev. Stephen Gladstone on behalf of the trustees and wardens accepted the gift. He said he could assure them that his father would have rejoiced to see that day.

Mr. Andrew Carnegie moved a resolution expressing veneration for Mr. Gladstone's life and character. He said Mr. Gladstone's fame extended far beyond the wide boundaries even of the British Empire, and embraced the entire English-speaking race. It was truly said by an American when Mr. Gladstone died, "The world lost its greatest citizen".

LEWISHAM : *Opening of New Library.*—On Saturday, the 29th November, Lord Baring, who was accompanied by Lady Baring, opened the Manor House, Lee, as a free library in connection with the borough of Lewisham. The estate was purchased some two years ago from Lord Northbrook (who was prevented by indisposition from performing the opening ceremony) by the London County Council and the Lewisham Borough Council, and the grounds were opened on Whit Monday last as a public recreation ground. The house was adapted at a cost of about £1,000 as a library. Lord Baring, in declaring the library open, said that the estate passed into the possession of the Baring family in 1796, and besides other members of the family previously Sir Francis Baring (afterwards Lord Northbrook) lived in the house from 1838 to 1848, and while Chancellor of the Exchequer used to ride backwards and forwards to his office in London. His lordship, on behalf of Lord Northbrook, his father, offered to the Libraries Committee portraits of members of the Baring family who had lived in the house for hanging on the walls. The books at present in the library number 7,369.

LIVERPOOL : *Mr. Carnegie Opens a New Branch Library.*—At the invitation of the Library, Museum and Arts Committee of the Liverpool Corporation, Mr. Andrew Carnegie, on the 15th October, opened a new branch library and newsroom, erected for the benefit of the residents in the Toxteth district of the city. Upwards of £12,000 have been spent upon the building, which is in the English Renaissance style, and contains reading-rooms for ladies, men and boys, and also a lending department. Mr. Carnegie, in the course of his address, remarked that no ceremony could be more congenial to him than to open a public library, one feature of which commended itself with special force to him—it was the property of the whole people. Scotland was now almost finished as a field for founding libraries, and applications for such institutions in that country were now few and for small communities. They were not so far advanced in England, but they would soon be supplied if the applications continued to come in as they had done during the past few months. In July 226 applications were received, nearly all for England and Ireland, though one came from Dunedin, in New Zealand, and another from Hobart, in Tasmania. The great want of the toiling masses was comfortable homes, and the lack of a quiet room in which the husband could spend his evenings was one of the strongest roots from which intemperance sprang. The best club in the world for any man was his own home, but the public library, with its reading-room, should supply this greater want to many of the best of working men. Especially should the treasures of the library appeal to young men as a substitute for the allurements of the public-house. As to the excessive love of fiction, Mr. Carnegie urged that it was a great point when any one was attracted to anything at all in the form of a book, unless it were distinctly pernicious.

LONDON : NEWINGTON : *Valuable Bequest to the Public Library.*— By the will of the late Mr. H. Syer Cuming, F.S.A. Scot., vice-president of the British Archæological Society, whose death was recently announced, the Newington Public Library, Walworth Road, received a valuable addition to its resources. The Cuming Museum, founded in 1782, and constantly enriched by purchases from practically all the notable collections dispersed during the first three-quarters of the nineteenth century, including the Leverian, Arundel, Portland, Belzoni and Stainforth collections, and a valuable library, rich in topography, together with £8,000 for the maintenance of the museum, have been bequeathed by Mr. Cuming to this the largest of the Southwark Public Libraries. The Walworth Road Library already contains upwards of 30,000 volumes, of which 20,000 are works of reference.

LONDON: PADDINGTON: *The Question of Adopting the Acts.*— The question of the adoption of the Public Libraries Acts in Paddington, and consequent acceptance of Mr. A. Carnegie's offer of £15,000, will be considered by the Borough Council at a special meeting next week. Meanwhile, a report of the Libraries Committee, of which the Mayor (Alderman H. A. Harben) is chairman, has been issued which recommends the adoption of the Acts and of the maximum rate of 1d. in the £ on the rateable value. The committee remark that " Mr. Carnegie's proposed gift, generous though it be, will form but a comparatively small contribution to the total cost of carrying out the Acts, as the Council, by accepting the Acts, would be pledged to provide not only the sites for two libraries, but to provide for their equipment and subsequent maintenance in perpetuity ".

MANCHESTER: BLACKLEY FREE LIBRARY: *A Successful Year's Work.*—The Blackley Library and Institute, which is the youngest of the branch libraries administered by the Manchester Corporation, has just completed its first year's working, and has proved to be in every way successful. That the people of Blackley and the surrounding district appreciate the library is shown by the fact that the number of the volumes issued for home reading and for use in the reading-rooms has amounted to 107,785, whilst the number of borrowers' cards in use is 2,549. The stock of volumes has been increased during the course of the year from 6,000 to 7,543, which includes a number of duplicate copies of the most popular works. In connection with the library a short course of lectures was arranged last season to be given in the adjoining hall. These lectures were attended by crowded and enthusiastic audiences, and proved instrumental in quickening interest in the contents of the library. Indeed such was the success of the first series that the committee have arranged for a second series during the present season. We must congratulate the Manchester Free Libraries Committee upon the success of the youngest member of their large and growing family of thriving offspring—a success which we are glad to hear, is due to the able and energetic administration of the librarian in charge (Mr. Billings).

MANCHESTER: PUBLIC LIBRARIES: *Mementos of the First Librarian.*—Mr. Thomas Greenwood has made an interesting and valuable gift to the Free Libraries of a large collection of books which he has formed with great care as a memorial of Mr. Edward Edwards, the promoter of municipal libraries, and the first librarian of the Free Library at Manchester. The collection embraces copies of the various books and pamphlets written by Edwards, and several hundred volumes from Edwards' private library. It includes also a transcript of Edwards' catalogue of the parochial (Bray) library at Whitchurch, Hants, and a large number of original letters, diaries, notes and other manuscripts, all carefully and methodically arranged and bound. There are, besides, some interesting personal relics, such as seals, rings, etc. The whole will be placed in a handsome book-case to be provided by Mr. Greenwood. The gift was referred to in terms of high appreciation at the City Council meeting on 3rd December by Mr. Henry Plummer, chairman of the committee.

NEWRY: *To Adopt the Libraries Act.*—At the monthly meeting of Newry No. 2 (Co. Armagh) Rural District Council, on Saturday the 18th October, the Council, in pursuance of the Act which received the

Royal Assent in August last, decided to adopt the Public Libraries (Ireland) Acts, and the clerk was instructed to make inquiries as to the best means of working the Acts in the district.

NORMANTON : *Offer of a Site for Public Library.*—At a meeting held last month of the Normanton Urban District Council the chairman announced that the Council had received an offer of a suitable site on which to erect the proposed free library offered by Mr. Carnegie. It was, however, thought desirable by the Council that a public meeting be held to take the opinion of the ratepayers on the matter.

NEWTON ABBOT : *New Library and Technical School.*—The foundation-stones of a new public library and county technical schools were laid at Newton Abbot on Thursday, the 9th October, the first by Mr. Passmore Edwards, the donor of the library, in memory of his mother, who was a native of Newton, and the other by the Earl of Morley, chairman of the Devon County Council. The two institutions will practically form one building, although all the departments are separate. The library building comprises a very spacious general reading-room, a magazine-room, librarian's-room, reference library, general lending library, borrowers' lobby, committee-room, and the various subsidiary rooms necessary to the proper equipment of a public library. On the second floor there will be a good residence for a caretaker. The technical schools may be considered the chief portion of the building. They comprise excellent accommodation for chemical, physical, biological and mechanical science, and an art department. There will be suites of classrooms, and an excellent general lecture-hall, with good approaches and stairways. The architect is Mr. Silvanus Trevail, F.R.I.B.A., and the builder is Mr. Henry Goss, of Torquay. Speaking at the luncheon, Mr. Passmore Edwards said it was surprising to him that Devonshire, with its roll of illustrious men, had been a little behind Cornwall in the development of institutions such as those they saw established that day. We had arrived at a moment in the period of our history when it was not only desirable these things should be done, but necessary. Unless England woke up, it would be beaten in the race of nations. Americans during the past two or three generations had been attending to primary education and secondary education. One of the results was that they had thrown Germany in the shade, and were beating us at the present time. Was that to be so in the future ? He believed not. Particularly if other towns in Devonshire and England would follow what was now being done at Newton Abbot.

PERTH : *Grant to the Library by the Town Council.*—The Perth Town Council has agreed to contribute to the Sandeman Public Library a sum of £50 from the Residue Grant for the current year.

SOUTH SHIELDS : *The Year's Work.*—The committee of the South Shields Public Library, Museum and Art Gallery have issued their annual report, in which they state that during the past year they have purchased a greater number of books than usual. The 818 books which have been bought during the year now bring up the total number of works in the libraries to 26,868. There have been 53 volumes presented to the committee, and these added to the number bought show an increase of 871. In the total issues there has been an increase of 10,478. The number of volumes issued was 113,693, the daily average being 428. During the previous year the total issues were 103,215, while the daily average was 388. The stock in the lending library now comprises 17,621 volumes. From this department 97,039 volumes were lent for home reading against a total last year of 87,880. The percentage of prose fiction for the year was 63·89. During the year 871 volumes were bound and 106 volumes were replaced. The year shows a considerable increase in the number of new readers. 1,658 vouchers have been signed, this being 591 more than last year. This includes applications for students' tickets. The total number of readers now enrolled is 9,249. In the juvenile department there are now 9,247 volumes. During the year 16,554 volumes were consulted. Special attention is drawn to the "open-access department" of the reference library. Book-cases have been made for the accommodation of 500 works of reference, which may be consulted without filling in the usual application form. These volumes comprise such works as cyclopædias, dictionaries, atlases, histories, books of local interest, etc. They were glad to report that the attendance of readers in the reference library and students' room was steadily increasing.

STEEPLE CLAYDON: *Opening of the New Free Library and Public Hall.*—Saturday, the 1st November, witnessed the opening of the handsome block of buildings that Sir Edmund and Lady Verney have erected at Steeple Claydon as a Free Library and Public Hall at a cost of some £1,700, exclusive of furniture, etc. These buildings are an addition to and partly in substitution for the old Chaloner Schools. The old buildings were given to the parish of Steeple Claydon in the year 1656, and were purchased last year from the Chaloner Trustees by Sir Edmund Verney, who has now added a room 45 feet long by 25 feet wide, and 23 feet high, exclusive of a fixed platform or stage 16 feet wide by 10 feet deep. This room will be used as a village hall, in connection with the Public Library, the latter being housed in the original portion of the premises. The new room is built from designs by Mr. Raymond Unwin, architect, of Buxton, and forms a striking addition to the buildings of the village. The chief external features are a colonnade running nearly the whole length of the room, and containing benches for use in fine weather, with a long roof cut up by dormer windows of unique design. The interior is chiefly notable for the construction of the visible roof timbers, the maple block floor, and the wood dado, surmounted by a shelf specially designed to carry pictures, vases and other decorative objects ; also for the arched ingle having a fireplace on the hearth, and the rustic benches on either side. The backs of these benches are fitted with very old oak carved panels from Claydon House. The building is warmed with hot air. It is built of red brick, with red stone dressings from the Penrith quarries, and tiled roofing.

Sir Edmund Verney opened the proceedings with a brief historical sketch, saying that Steeple Claydon was the dowry of Katherine of Aragon, first wife of Henry VIII. Her daughter, Queen Mary, inherited it, and in 1557 granted it to the first Sir Thomas Chaloner, a great diplomatist. Their benefactor, Thomas Chaloner, was the third son of the second Sir Thomas. Thomas Chaloner was born at Steeple Claydon in 1595 ; after leaving Oxford he went abroad, and "returned from foreign travel a perfect gentleman". He married a Miss Sothabie, whose brother "died from drinking too much sack ". He was M.P. first for Richmond and then for Scarborough. In 1651 he became Master of the Mint. He and his brother James (M.P. for Aldborough and Governor of the Isle of Man) both signed Charles I.'s death-warrant. In 1656, at Steeple Claydon, he " built a house with a clock for children to be taught in, and impaled part of the waste about the said house which was called the school-yard, and planted trees within the pale for the defence of the house, and settled £12 per annum for maintenance of the schoolmaster ". At the Restoration he was excluded from the amnesty, and fled to Holland, where he died in 1661, aged 66. Charles II. granted the estate to Richard Lane, who had enabled him to escape after the battle of Worcester. He obtained the title deeds, and refused to pay the endowment, greatly to the dismay of the parishioners, who vainly petitioned for it. Subsequently the Chaloners bought back the estate and lived there until they sold it to the Verneys in 1705. His father Sir Harry Verney, who found the playground used as a bull-ring and the school in ruins, repaired and floored it in 1838. In 1841 he bought the adjoining property from Mr. Grace, pulled down that house, and built the schoolmaster's residence. In 1856 Lady Dunsany, aunt to his mother, Eliza Lady Verney, added an additional classroom to the single room of which Chaloner's School had hitherto consisted. In 1901 the Public Libraries Act was adopted in the parish, and the library was immediately opened in a small villa. The disused school buildings were afterwards sold to him by the trustee; they had now been added to and adapted for their new purpose. In about ten days' time there would be a meeting of the Parish Council, when Lady Verney and he hoped that the premises would be hired at a nominal rent for parish use, and that the Council would undertake their control and management on behalf of the parishioners. The only condition they made was that they should be available impartially for all, without distinction of religious or political opinions. It was a happy circumstance that their opening had fallen on All Saints' Day, which has been observed on the 1st November ever since the year 834 A.D. They had saints living in England that day whose names were as sacredly venerated as those of any holy men or women of old: specially connected with that library was the name of Florence Nightingale, whom he regarded as their pious founder, and whose portrait and autograph were in the adjoining room.

This is not the first time we have had to record the generosity of Sir Edmund and Lady Verney in promoting the cause of village libraries, and we offer to them, in the name of the Library Association, our grateful and appreciative thanks for this practical demonstration of their great and growing interest in so deserving a cause as that of providing rural districts with the means for mental improvement and healthy and helpful recreation. We venture to express the hope that many other wealthy landowners up and down the country may be induced to follow the example of Sir Edmund and Lady Verney by promoting similar institutions which must have an incalculably good effect upon the people of our villages and smaller towns. The most pleasing feature of Sir Edmund Verney's work is that very far from pauperising the people as was too often done in the past, he is putting them in the position to help themselves by generously equipping the library and so inducing them to adopt the Libraries Act.

TAUNTON: *Adoption of the Libraries Act.*—At a meeting of the Taunton Town Council, held on the 31st October, it was unanimously resolved to adopt the Free Libraries Act in the borough, and that the maximum rate under the Act be levied. A site was at the same time conditionally accepted. This action of the Council entitles the borough to £5,000 which Mr. Carnegie had offered on the usual conditions.

OBITUARY.

TIMMINS (Sam).—It is with deep regret that we announce the death of Mr. Sam Timmins which took place at his residence at King's Heath on the 12th November. The deceased gentleman, who had been in failing health for some time, was among the best-known men in Birmingham in the days when George Dawson, Vince and Dale were seeking to give educational opportunities to the working classes of the town of that period. Born in Birmingham on 27th February, in 1826, Mr. Timmins was educated under Dr. Ryall at the Proprietary School. His grandfather founded the firm of Richard Timmins & Sons, which was established a century ago for the manufacture of steel toys, and subsequently Mr. Sam Timmins conducted the business until his retirement eighteen years ago. It is, however, in connection with literature that the deceased gentleman obtained the widest popularity. From his earliest years he was an enthusiastic lover of books, and an old book-stall always appealed to him, and many a time has his well-known figure been seen pouring over the shelves at the various second-hand shops in the city. It was in 1842, when but sixteen years of age, that he commenced to write for the press, and five years later he visited France, Holland, Germany, Italy and Greece. The account of his travels on the Continent was afterwards graphically described in the columns of the Birmingham *Journal*, and the vivid and attractive character of his writings at once claimed public attention. The many and delightful articles from his pen which subsequently appeared in the Birmingham *Daily Post* also attracted much attention, and from the first issue he edited the valuable series of articles entitled " Local Notes and Queries," which were published in the *Weekly Post*. His knowledge of the history of the city of Birmingham and its environments was surpassed by none of his contemporaries. When only nineteen years of age Mr. Timmins took an active part in the work of the Public School Association. This was in 1845, and twenty years later he was an energetic member of the National Education League. The Mechanics' Institute, the Polytechnic, afterwards the Midland Institute, and suburban institutions all claimed his time, and the wonder is how he succeeded in devoting so much to the work of improving the educational facilities of the people. The Old Library, at his instigation, was subjected to startling but necessary reforms and twice he was made president. For twenty-three years he was a member of the committee appointed when the town adopted the Free Libraries Act, and so valuable were his services that when, in 1883, he tendered his resignation the Town Council unanimously decided that he should be reappointed. At the same time they relieved him of all committee work with the exception of that connected with the choice and purchase of books, and he was accordingly elected chairman of the Book Committee. Forty-four years ago, at the Shakespeare birthday dinner, Mr. Timmins suggested the formation of a Shakespeare collection. The idea met with general approval, the collection was formed, and one can imagine the state of mind of the originator of this valuable acquisition to the literature of the city when it was destroyed by fire in 1879. However, he was not cast down, and in a very short time a new Shakespearean library was formed, which remains to-day one of the finest in the world. Going back once more to the earlier days of his life, Mr. Timmins was, in 1853, elected president of the Edgbaston Debating Society; from 1853 to 1864 he and the late Mr. George Dawson conducted the institute classes in English literature and history. Six years later he was chosen president of the then newly-formed archæological section, while ten years previously he edited a reprint of two texts of " Hamlet ". In 1860 he wrote a series of forty interesting articles entitled " Rambles Around Birmingham," which were published in the Birmingham *Journal*, and in 1861 edited a volume dealing with *The Resources, Products and Industrial History of Birmingham and the Midland Hardware District*. Perhaps, however, one of his very best literary productions is his *History of Warwickshire*. Mr. Timmins was a Fellow of the Society of Antiquaries, a Fellow of the Anthropological

Society, and belonged to the New York Shakespeare Society, the German Shakespeare Society, and the Historical Society of Pennsylvania, and an Hon. Fellow of the Library Association. The Birmingham Sunday Lecture Society was really founded by him, and for many years he was one of the best lecturers. Mr. Timmins was for many years a Birmingham magistrate and one of the visiting Justices.

OFFICIAL GAZETTE.

Cooper (Frederick W.), chief assistant of the Cheltenham Public Library, has been appointed sub-librarian of the Public Library, Port Elizabeth, South Africa.

Heaton (Ronald W.), M.A., formerly director and librarian of the Bishopsgate Institute, London, has been appointed librarian of the Government Library, Pretoria.

THE FREEDOM OF THE CITY OF MANCHESTER TO BE CONFERRED UPON ALDERMAN RAWSON.

A T a meeting of the Manchester City Council, held on Wednesday, the 3rd December, it was unanimously, or, rather, should we say, enthusiastically decided, that the freedom of the city should be presented to Mr. Alderman H. Rawson.

For the past half-century Mr. Rawson has taken a large share in the public work of the city of Manchester. He was born in Manchester in 1820. One of the first of the useful public organisations which he helped to develop was the Manchester Mechanics' Institution. His father was one of the Manchester men who attended the public meeting held in the Queen's Theatre, Spring Gardens, in 1825, when the Institution was founded. The son became a member while yet a youth, and he was thus first a student, afterwards a director, and then chairman of the board of directors of the Institution. Mr. Rawson first became a member of the City Council in 1856. Two breaks have been made in the continuity of his service, one in 1861 and the other from 1865 to 1884. During the years which have passed since 1884—years which have seen many memorable events in the city—Mr. Rawson has done Manchester notable service. He was for some years chairman of the Free Libraries Committee, and his administration of this important office was large and liberal. During the early years of the free library movement he distinguished himself by establishing the first of the branch libraries, which have become so useful and popular. He took an active part in the movement for opening the libraries on Sunday, a reform that was not carried through without difficulty. He helped the development of the work of technical instruction in Manchester, he is one of the life governors and a member of the Council of the Owens College, and he has done much to aid public movements for the physical and moral advantage of the thickly populated parts of the city. His more recent and great services as chairman of the Watch Committee are common knowledge. When, after public inquiry, it was decided to reorganise the police force, the City Council turned to Mr. Rawson as the man best fitted for the control and guidance of such a work. He accepted the appointment, and the manner in which he carried out the duty he had undertaken needs to-day no explanation. His interest in library matters has never flagged. He was president of the Library Association in the year of the Buxton Meeting. He still occupies a seat on the Free Libraries Committee of Manchester, and lastly, but by no means the least in importance, is chairman of the Council of Governors of the John Rylands Library.

The Manchester roll of honorary freemen is rarely opened. Since 1888, when the late Oliver Heywood became the first freeman of the city, only ten names in all have been inscribed on the list, and nine of those were borne by citizens of Manchester. The honorary freedom has thus come to be regarded as a rare distinction reserved almost exclusively for those inhabitants of Manchester who have shown an exceptional measure of civic virtue. The surviving freemen who have qualified in this way for the honour number only four—Dr. A. W. Ward, Mr. Herbert Philips, Mrs. Rylands, and Mr. R. D. Darbishire. None will question the right of Alderman Rawson, who has been engaged in public work for half a century, to be added to this select company of eminent citizens.

We are quite sure that every member of the Library Association will rejoice with us that the city of Manchester has chosen our esteemed past president to receive the highest honour that it has to bestow, and will join with us in wishing him still many years of happy and useful _ife.

NOTEWORTHY BOOKS.

(Compiled by GUTHRIE VINE, M.A.)

The classification of each work according to Dewey's System of Decimal Classification is given in square brackets.

ALGER (J. G.). Paris in 1789-94; farewell letters of victims of the guillotine. [944.04] 8vo. 564 pp. *G. Allen.* 10s. 6d.

ARISTOTLE. Aristotle's psychology: a treatise on the principles of life. Translated by W. A. Hammond. [150] 8vo. lxxxvi, 339 pp. *Sonnenschein.* 10s. 6d. *net.*

AUSTIN (H. H.). Among swamps and giants in Equatorial Africa: surveys and adventures in the southern Sudan and British East Africa. [916.6] 8vo. 366 pp. *Pearson.* 15s. *net.*

BACON (Roger). The Greek grammar of R. Bacon and a fragment of his Hebrew grammar. Edited from the MSS., with introduction and notes by Edmond Nolan and S. A. Hirsch. [485] 8vo. 298 pp. *Clay.* 12s. *net.*

BEDFORD (W. K.) and HOLBECKE (R.). The order of the Hospital of St. John of Jerusalem: being a history of the English Hospitallers of St. John, their rise and progress. [929.711] 8vo. *F. E. Robinson & Co.* 7s. 6d.

BOOTH (A. J.). The discovery and decipherment of the trilingual cuneiform inscriptions. [492.1917] 8vo. 478 pp. *Longmans.* 14s. *net.*

BOSANQUET (H.). The strength of the people: a study in social economics. [331] 8vo. 358 pp. *Macmillan.* 8s. 6d. *net.*

BOTTONE (S. R.). Galvanic batteries, their theory, construction and use, comprising primary, single and double fluid cells, secondary and gas batteries. [537.86] 8vo. 392 pp. *Whittaker.* 5s.

BOUTROUX (Émile). Pascal. Translated by E. M. Creak. [273.7] 8vo. lxxvi, 211 pp. *Manchester, Sherratt & Hughes.* 5s. *net.*

BROOKE (Stopford A.). The poetry of Robert Browning. [821.83] 8vo. 554 pp. *Isbister.* 10s. 6d.

BROWNELL (C. L.). The heart of Japan: glimpses of life and nature far from the traveller's track in the land of the rising sun. [915.2] 8vo. 314 pp. *Methuen.* 6s.

CARLETON (James G.). The part of Rheims in the making of the English Bible. [220.52] 8vo. *Clarendon Press.* 9s. 6d. *net.*

CARPENTER (J. E.). The composition of the Hexateuch: an introduction and select lists of words and phrases; with an appendix on laws and institutions by George Harford. [222.1] 8vo. 554 pp. *Longmans.* 18s. *net.*

CLARK (W.). Pascal and the Port Royalists. (*World's Epoch Makers.*) [273.7] 8vo. 246 pp. *T. & T. Clark.* 3s.

Conway (*Sir* M.). Aconcagua and Tierra del Fuego : a book of climbing, travel and exploration. [918] 8vo. 264 pp. *Cassell.* 12s. 6d. *net.*

Curtiss (S. I.). Primitive Semitic religion of to-day : a record of researches, discoveries and studies in Syria, Palestine and the Sinaitic peninsula. [299.2] 8vo. 288 pp. *Hodder & Stoughton.* 6s. *net.*

Cunningham (A.). The French in Tonkin and South China. [959] 8vo. *Low.* 5s. *net.*

Dalton (T.). The role of the unconquered : an historical narrative of the courtship of Henry of Navarre and Marie de Medici. [944.031] 12mo. *New York.* 7s. 6d.

Dante Alighieri. The vita nuova : or, new life. Translated from the Italian by Francisco de Mey. [851.15] 16mo. 132 pp. *Bell.* 2s. 6d. *net.*

Das (S. C.). A journey to Lhasa and Central Tibet. Edited by the Hon. W. W. Rockhill. [915.15] 8vo. 300 pp. *Murray.* 10s. 6d. *net.*

Day (L. F.). Windows : a book about stained and painted glass. [748] 8vo. 432 pp. *Batsford.* 21s. *net.*

Demetrius, *Phalereus.* Demetrius on style : Greek text of Demetrius de elocutione. Edited, after the Paris manuscript, with introduction, translation, etc., by W. R. Roberts. [808] 8vo. 328 pp. *Clay.* 9s. *net.*

Dickinson (E.). Music in the history of the western church. With an introduction on religious music among primitive and ancient peoples. [246.7] 8vo. 436 pp. *Smith, Elder.* 10s. 6d. *net.*

Diplock (B.). A new system of heavy goods transport on common roads. [656] 8vo. *Longmans.* 6s. 6d. *net.*

Dobson (A.). William Hogarth. With an introduction on Hogarth's workmanship by Sir Walter Armstrong. With plates in photogravure and facsimile. [759.2] Fol. 262 pp. *Heinemann.* £5 5s. *net.*

Everett (C. C.). Psychological elements of religious faith. [201] 8vo. *Macmillan.* 5s. *net.*

Federn (K.). Dante and his time. With an introduction by A. J. Butler. [851.15] 8vo. 328 pp. *Heinemann.* 6s.

Gardner (E. G.). The story of Florence. With 40 illustrations by N. Erichsen and many reproductions from works of Florentine painters and sculptors. [945.5] 8vo. 450 pp. *Dent.* 10s. 6d. *net.*

Havelok, *the Dane.* Lay of Havelok the Dane. Re-edited from MS. Laud Misc. 108 in the Bodleian Library, Oxford, by Walter W. Skeat. [821.19] 12mo. 232 pp. *Frowde.* 4s. 6d.

Howe (W. H.). Castles and abbeys of Great Britain and Ireland : their history and legendary lore. Illustrated by Harry Evans. Vol. i. [918.42] 4to. *Dicks.* 7s. 6d.

Journal of the National Literary Society of Ireland. Vol. i. Parts i.-iii., 1900-2. [820.6] 8vo. *Dublin, O'Donoghue & Co., 31 South Anne St.* 1s. *each part.*

Kennedy (E.). The black police of Queensland : reminiscences of official work and personal adventures in the early days of the colony. [994.3] 8vo. 298 pp. *Murray.* 10s. 6d. *net.*

Konody (P. G.). The art of Walter Crane. [740] Fol. 162 pp. *Bell.* £3 3s. *net.*

LANG (Andrew). James VI. and the Gowrie mystery. [941.05] 8vo. 294 pp. *Longmans.* 12s. 6d. *net.*

MACLEAN (Magnus). The literature of the Celts: its history and romance. [891.6] 8vo. 400 pp. *Blackie.* 7s. 6d. *net.*

MALLET (B.). Mallet du Pan and the French revolution. [944.04] 8vo. 368 pp. *Longmans.* 12s. 6d. *net.*

MALLOCK (W. H.). Religion as a credible doctrine: a study of the fundamental difficulty. [201] 8vo. 287 pp. *Chapman & Hall.* 12s.

MATHIESON (W. L.). Politics and religion: a study in Scottish history from the Reformation to the Revolution. [941] 8vo. 2 vols. *Glasgow, Maclehose.* 21s. *net.*

MAUNDER (E. W.). Astronomy without a telescope. [520.2] 8vo. *Office of Knowledge.* 5s. *net.*

MILLER (F.). Pictures in the Wallace collection. [708.2] 8vo. 228 pp. *Pearson.* 10s. 6d. *net.*

MOELLER (W.). History of the Christian church, A.D. 1-600. Translated from the German by Andrew Rutherfurd. [270] 8vo. 558 pp. *Sonnenschein.* 15s.

MONTAIGNE (M. E. de). Essays. Translated by Charles Cotton. Entirely new edition, with a fresh English rendering and a careful revision of the text throughout: to which are added some account of the life of Montaigne, notes, and a translation of all letters known to be extant. Edited by W. C. Hazlitt. [844.81] 8vo. 4 vols. *Reeves & Turner.* £2 2s.

PASTON (G.). Side-lights on the Georgian period. [942.07] 8vo. 312 pp. *Methuen.* 10s. 6d.

PAWLOW (J. P.). The work of the digestive glands. Translated by W. H. Thompson. [611.8] 8vo. 208 pp. *Griffin.* 6s. *net.*

PHIN (J.). The Shakespeare cyclopædia and new glossary. With the most important variorum readings, intended as supplement to all ordinary editions of Shakespeare's works. With an introduction by Edward Dowden. [822.88] 8vo. 456 pp. *Paul.* 6s. *net.*

PLATO. The republic of Plato. Edited by J. Adam. [888.4] 8vo. 2 vols. *Cambridge University Press.* 15s. *net.*

POLLARD (A. W.). Old picture books: with other essays on bookish subjects. [010.4] 8vo. *Methuen.* 7s. 6d. *net.*

POYNTING (J. H.) and THOMSON (J. J.). A text-book of physics: the properties of matter. [530] 8vo. 236 pp. *Griffin.* 10s. 6d.

ROBERTSON (W. G.). Old English songs and dances. [784.4] 8vo. *Longmans.* £2 2s. *net.*

ROXBY (P. M.). Henry Grattan: the Gladstone Prize Essay in Oxford University, 1902. [941.57] 8vo. 192 pp. *Unwin.* 3s. 6d. *net.*

SASTROW (B.). Social Germany in Luther's time: memoirs of B Sastrow translated by A. D. Vandam. [943.03] 8vo. 376 pp. *Constable.* 7s. 6d. *net.*

SHEPHERD (E. H. Archer). Three bulwarks of the faith. [239.8] 8vo. 234 pp. *Rivington.* 5s. *net.*

SIDGWICK (H.). Lectures on the ethics of T. H. Green, Herbert Spencer and J. Martineau. [170.4] 8vo. 418 pp. *Macmillan.* 8s. 6d. *net.*

SMITH (G. Gregory). Specimens of Middle Scots; with introduction, notes and glossary. [891.68] 8vo. 451 pp. *W. Blackwood.* 7s. 6d. *net.*

SUPERNATURAL religion : an inquiry into the reality of divine revelation. New edition. [211] 8vo. *Watts.* 6s. *net.*

THOMAS, *Aquinas, Saint.* Apology for the religious orders. Edited with introduction by J. Procter. [271] 8vo. *Sands.* 6s. *net.*

TOWNSEND (W. G. P.). Plant and floral studies : for designers, art students and craftsmen. [741] 8vo. 152 pp. *Chapman.* 5s. *net.*

WARTENBURG (Y. von), *Count.* Napoleon as a general. [944.05] 8vo. 2 vols. *Paul.* £1 10s.

WHITMAN (Walt). Complete writings of Walt Whitman. Camden edition. [811.88] 8vo. 10 vols. *Putnam.* £1 5s. *net.*

YEATS (W. B.). Cathleen Ni Hoolihan : a play in one act and in prose. [822.8] 12mo. *A. H. Bullen.* 5s. *net.*

LIBRARY ASSOCIATION: PROCEEDINGS AND NOTICES.

Monthly Meeting, 20th November, 1902.

THE First Monthly Meeting of the Session was held on Thursday, 20th November, at 20 Hanover Square, at 8 o'clock.

Mr. J. Potter Briscoe presided in the absence of the President. About thirty members and visitors were present. Messrs. Johnston and Frowde having been nominated scrutineers, the following candidates approved by the Council, were duly elected:—

As MEMBERS.

William Easy, Bookbinder, 7 Greville Street, Holborn, E.C.

Miss Maria Charlotte Mondy, Secretary, National Home Reading Union, Surrey House, Victoria Embankment, W.C.

Henry March Gilbert, Bookseller, 26 Above Bar, Southampton.

As AN ASSOCIATE.

Miss Harriet Townsend, Assistant Librarian, Birmingham Library, Margaret Street, Birmingham.

Mr. B. CARTER (Kingston-on-Thames) asked the following question, of which he had given notice:—

"At the Twenty-fourth Annual Meeting of the Library Association, 1901, the following motion was carried:—

" 'That this meeting recommends the Council to consider the desirability of drafting a set of bye-laws for submission, by way of suggestion, to the Local Government Board '.

" Has the Council taken any action in the matter, and if so, what has been done ? "

The HON. SECRETARY replied that the Council had considered the matter and come to the conclusion that it was not desirable to draft such a set of bye-laws. At the request of Mr. H. D. Roberts (St. Saviour's) he undertook to apply to the Local Government Board for a copy of their model bye-laws, with a view to their publication in the LIBRARY ASSOCIATION RECORD.

Mr. H. R. PLOMER then read a paper on "The Booksellers of London Bridge," of which the following is an abstract:—

The Booksellers of London Bridge.

The first bookseller's shop on London Bridge of which we have any certain knowledge was that opened by William Pickering at St. Magnus' corner, that is close to the church of St. Magnus at the north end of the bridge. He continued there until 1571, being succeeded in the same house by Richard Ballard, Hugh Astley and John Tap.

Before the close of the sixteenth century a second shop was opened "neer the gate," that is at the southern end of the bridge, by Thomas Gosson. Thomas Gosson died in 1600 and was succeeded in 1607 by his son Henry, who carried on the business until 1641. We have also a glimpse of a third bookseller on the bridge in the first quarter of the seventeenth century. This was John Spencer, whose imprint is found in a chap book entitled *Love's Garland*, published in 1624.

In 1633 a fire destroyed many buildings at the northern end of the bridge, including, it is believed, the shop at St. Magnus' corner, then in the occupation of John Tap.

A fourth bookseller, of whom we have a solitary record, was Stephen Pemell, who in 1635 printed Scott's *An Essay of Drapery*.

During the Civil War the booksellers' shops on London Bridge appear to have been closed, but in 1659 trade revived and a bookseller named Charles Tyus is found at the sign of the "Three Bibles" on the middle of London Bridge. He was succeeded by Thomas Passinger who died in 1688, leaving his business to a kinsman, another Thomas Passinger, who can be traced there till 1695. During the eighteenth century this house was in the occupation of Ebenezer Tracy and his sons.

The fire of London in 1666 again destroyed the buildings at the northern end of the bridge, but they were quickly rebuilt and the bridge became more popular than ever with the booksellers. Amongst the signs met with between 1660 and 1750 are "The Seven Stars" in the New Buildings, that is the buildings rebuilt after the fire, "The Red Lion," in the hands of A. Bettesworth, "The Golden Bible" in the occupation successively of T. Parkhurst and Joseph Collyer, The "Hand and Bible," by T. Taylor and Elizabeth Smith, The "Sun and Bible," in the Low Buildings, by J. Williamson and H. Green, and the "Black Boy," near the drawbridge, where John Back was succeeded by M. Hotham. There was also a house in the New Buildings apparently without a sign in the occupation of Benjamin Hurlock. But the most important house, during the first half of the eighteenth century, was the "Looking Glass". Its first tenant from 1670 to 1706 was Josiah Blare, after which it appears to have been in the occupation of Thomas Norris and James Hodges; but there seems to have been another house with the same sign, and it is most difficult to distinguish between the various tenants of the two houses. The most important of them appears to have been James Hodges, who was in 1750 elected deputy for Bridge Ward Without, and afterwards held the position of town clerk of the City of London. In 1758 he was knighted by George II.

Owing to the ruinous condition of the bridge it was decided by the Corporation to remove the houses. The work began in 1758, which therefore marks the close of the history of the booksellers of London Bridge.

Coming to the literature sold by these booksellers our attention is naturally first drawn to the ballads which formed so large a portion of their stock. William Pickering and Henry Gosson appear to have been the most prolific of ballad publishers, but before the year 1640 the ballads had been made into a "stock" by the Company of Stationers and therefore no special entry in the registers was necessary, and it is quite likely that Thomas Passinger or Thomas Norris issued quite as many ballads as either Pickering or Gosson.

These ballads were afterwards collected into book form and known as "Garlands". Jest-books were also largely sold by the London Bridge booksellers, but the literature which more than any other set its seal upon them were the "three sheet histories" and "peny histories" but which are better known as chap books. In this form we meet with *Reynard the Fox, Valentine and Orson, Thomas of Reading, The Seven Champions of Christendom, The Tragical History of Doctor Faustus*, and scores of others.

Much useful literature was also to be met with on the bridge. To Thomas Passinger belongs the credit of having issued the first edition of Cocker's *Arithmetick*, and from the same house came Gervase Markham's *Masterpeece, containing all the knowledge belonging to the Smith, Farrier or Horse Leech*, a work that long remained the best of its kind on the subject.

Books on the science of navigation were to be had at the shops of John Tap and Benjamin Hurlock.

Again, amongst the host of trivial works issued by James Hodges, were many of a higher order, notably a collection from the poets, entitled the Muses Library, issued in 1737, and the works of William Tansur the musician.

The CHAIRMAN said the Association was much indebted to Mr. Plomer for his very interesting paper, especially interesting to us who are antiquaries ; and to librarians generally the subject must have been of very great interest. He might say he had been interested in bridges from a very early period of his life. When a boy he took out and read with great interest Thomson's well-known book on London Bridge. From that time he had been interested in the whole subject ; had contributed a paper on the bridges which had crossed the Trent at Nottingham from early times to the Royal Historical Society's Transactions ; and lectured upon the subject of bridges generally. The illustrations Mr. Plomer had shown had added to the interest of his paper. With reference to buildings on the bridge he pointed out that a chapel was a feature which prevailed very largely on the other bridges, erected in many cases for the purpose of prayer for people who were going out into the wilderness. A number of these chapels on these bridges were endowed so that priests were kept there to celebrate services and offer masses from time to time. There is a very fine gothic chapel on the bridge at Wakefield. John Bunyan was imprisoned in a Bridge Prison at Bedford. It would be very useful and interesting if the Library Association were to publish a catalogue of books actually produced upon London Bridge from time to time. Let each member present look through his own shelves and find the books printed on London Bridge and send the result to Mr. Plomer. It would be very interesting to see the number of illustrations of the bridge from simple woodcuts to the more elaborate coloured illustrations, which would also show the design of the outstanding tradesmen's signs varying greatly in form, design and colour. He had great pleasure in proposing a vote of thanks to Mr. Plomer for his instructive paper.

Mr. ROBERTS (St. Saviour's) seconded the resolution. He did so with great pleasure, and he had listened to Mr. Plomer's paper with a great deal of personal interest, as half of London Bridge happened to be in the parish of Southwark. A large number of people would look forward to this paper being printed and to obtaining copies of it. The subject had never been so fully treated before. He would have brought his collection of prints had he known an exhibition would be available, and he would be only too pleased to show them to anybody who called at his library and whose interest in the subject had been stimulated by Mr. Plomer's paper.

The HON. SECRETARY supported the vote of thanks, and referred to the fact that more than ten years had elapsed since the Association had been favoured with a paper by Mr. Plomer. In that to which they had just had the pleasure of listening, many facts of varied interest had been given relating to the printers as well as the booksellers of London Bridge. Papers such as Mr. Plomer's were always welcome at their meetings, and frequently opened up as many practical questions as did other papers which appeared from their titles to bear a more technical character. It was impossible to listen to Mr. Plomer for any length of time without discovering that he spoke with authority on the subject of printers and printing in Old London. His present paper abounded with interest, and suggested openings for research in many directions. If the librarians present were to do no more than devote their spare time to the collection of books published by the printers of London Bridge, they would find a very wide field open for them, although the number of such books to be met with must necessarily diminish year by year. He heartily joined in the vote of thanks to Mr. Plomer.

Mr. GEORGE POTTER (Highgate) exhibited a considerable number of books issued upon London Bridge, and in the course of the discussion drew special attention to the long series of editions of Cocker's *Arith-metick*, including the first, and still rarer "second impression" issued the same year, which bear slightly varied London Bridge imprints (*vide N. & Q.*, vi., 1-502, June, 1880).

In returning thanks Mr. PLOMER said for his own part he was rather out of conceit with his paper. He feared it had become too much a catalogue of titles. He was very much indebted to Mr. Potter for bringing his collection of books, and as a matter of fact Mr. Potter knew more of the subject than he did. He was very much indebted to the Chairman for his remarks on the chap books at Nottingham. He (Mr. Plomer) should find out a little more about the chap books of London Bridge. By 1624 it had been turned into warehouses and used for all sorts of purposes, so it had not got so many romances attached to it as the bridge at Nottingham.

The meeting terminated with a cordial vote of thanks to the Chairman.

Notice to Members of the Library Association.

THE SECOND MONTHLY MEETING of the Session will be held at 20 HANOVER SQUARE, W., on THURSDAY, 18th December, 1902, at 8 P.M., when Mr. CYRIL DAVENPORT, of the British Museum, will read a paper on "LIBRARY BOOK-BINDING". Members are invited to bring any specimens they can produce of good-wearing and bad-wearing bindings.

The following candidates for membership of the Association, having been approved by the Council, will be balloted for:—

Mr. H. Tapley Soper, Librarian, Royal Albert Memorial Public Library, Exeter (*Now an Associate*).
Mr. William Bolton, Borough Engineer, Wigan.
Mr. Richard Johnson, J.P., Ince Hall, near Wigan.
Mr. F. S. Hockaday, Highbury, Lydney, Gloucestershire.
Mr. Richard Hargreaves, Librarian, Public Library, Stock-port.

LAWRENCE INKSTER,
Honorary Secretary.

5*th December*, 1902.

Visitors will be welcomed to the meeting. Light refreshments will be served before the proceedings begin.

List of Committees 1902-1903.

EDUCATION COMMITTEE.

Mr. Franklin T. Barrett.	Mr. L. Stanley Jast.
Mr. J. D. Brown.	Mr. J. J. Ogle.
Mr. F. J. Burgoyne.	Mr. W. C. Plant.
Mr. Cecil T. Davis.	Mr. Evan G. Rees.
Mr. R. K. Dent.	Mr. Henry D. Roberts.
Dr. R. Garnett, C.B.	Mr. G. T. Shaw.
Mr. H. Guppy, M.A.	Mr. Fred Turner.
Mr. T. W. Hand.	Mr. R. B. Wood.
Mr. E. Wynlham Hulme.	

With (*ex officio*) the President, the Hon. Treasurer, the Hon Secretary.

FINANCE COMMITTEE.

Mr. T. Aldred.	Mr. W. E. Doubleday.
Mr. H. Bond.	Mr. H. D. Roberts.
Mr. J. R. Boosé.	

With (*ex officio*) the President, the Hon. Treasurer, the Hon. Secretary.

PUBLICATIONS COMMITTEE.

Mr. T. Aldred.	Mr. W. E. Doubleday.
Mr. Franklin T. Barrett.	Mr. H. Guppy, M.A.
Mr. H. Bond.	Mr. E. Wyndham Hulme.
Mr. J. Duff Brown.	Mr. L. Stanley Jast.
Mr. Cecil T. Davis.	

With (*ex officio*) the President, the Hon. Treasurer, the Hon. Secretary.

The Education Committee is arranging for a special series of technical lectures to assistants and others during the earlier months of 1903. The first will be given by Mr. C. T. Jacobi, of the Chiswick Press, on "Printing," and will take place on the 21st January, 1903. The date and hour will be announced in our next issue.

Professional Examination of the Library Association.

The next professional examination of the Association in Section 1, Bibliography and Literary History, and Section 3, Library Management, will be held at centres to suit the convenience of candidates on Wednesday and Thursday, 14th and 15th January, 1903. Intending candidates should send in their names, accompanied by a fee of 10s. (which may be returned at the discretion of the Education Committee), in good time, to the Hon. Secretary of the Education Committee, Mr. Henry D. Roberts, 44A Southwark Bridge Road, London, S.E., who would be glad to send a copy of the examination syllabus to any person not possessing one already. Under the new regulations Section 1 may be taken in three parts, *viz.*: 1, Bibliography; 2, English Literary History; 3, Literary History of another country. It is hoped there will be a good attendance of candidates, particularly in the first part of Section 1, for which Mr. Brown's lectures are proving such an admirable preparation. The examination in Section 2 has been deferred until the end of Mr. Barrett's course of lectures next year. The date will be announced in good time.

There is a possibility of establishing a class in French or German specially for library assistants in London and district, at very low fees. The class will be held at the Birbeck Institute, and any assistants who care to enter for the same are requested to place themselves in communication with the Director of the School of Economics, from whom particulars can be obtained.

North Midland Library Association.

For the forty-seventh time during the last thirteen years the librarians constituting the North Midland Library Association met on Thursday afternoon, 4th December. This meeting was held in the St. Paul's Institute, Burton-on-Trent. In the absence of Mr. F. Shakespeare Herne, the president, Mr. J. T. Radford, vice-president, occupied the chair. The hon. secretary, Mr. J. Potter Briscoe, read the minutes of the Annual Meeting, which was held at the People's Hall, Nottingham, on 2nd October. There were elected to membership Mr. Caddie, Free Public Library, Stoke-on-Trent; and Mr. Grose, Free Public Library, Burton-on-Trent. The hon. secretary reported the gift of a copy of Mr. C. Gerring's work entitled *Notes on Printers and Booksellers*, from the author, and of Mr. Baker's *Descriptive Handbook to Prose Fiction* from the compiler—both donors being members of the N.M.L.A. Thanks were accorded for these gifts. Mr. Grose gave an account of the public library movement in Burton-on-Trent; Mr. Caddie read a paper on " A Small Practical Reference Library "; Mr. E. A. Baker, M.A., contributed one on " Derbyshire in English Fiction "; and Mr. Radford on " Photography and Libraries ". These papers were severally discussed by Messrs. Briscoe, Radford, Lineker, Dent, Dennis, Caddie, Baker and other members. The readers of papers were heartily thanked for their interesting and useful contributions, and Mr. Grose for facilitating the local arrangements. After tea had been served, the Institute was inspected, and the librarians returned to their respective towns. Before the meeting was held the Free Public Library and St. Paul's Church were visited. The next meeting will probably be held at Leicester on 12th February.

Northern Counties Library Association.|

The Quarterly Meeting of the above Association will be held at Gateshead, by invitation of Ald. L. H. Armour, J.P., Chairman of the Library Committee and a Vice-President of the N.C.L.A., on Wednesday, 17th December 1902.

PROGRAMME.

12.15.—Meeting of Executive Committee at the Town Hall.

1.30.—Assemble at the Town Hall. Members will be received by the Mayor (Councillor Walter de Lancey Willson, J.P.) and Ald. Armour, J.P. (Chairman of Public Library Committee).

2.0.—Business Session : Papers and Discussions :—

    (1) The President's Address.

    (2) " The N.C.L.A. and its Junior Members," by Mr. A. Hair, Sub-Librarian, Tynemouth.

    (3) " Libraries and Lectures: a Suggestion," by Mr. B. R. Hill, Librarian, Sunderland.

(4) Questions :—

   (*a*) What are anonymous books, and how should they be treated ? (Mr. B. Anderton, B.A.).

   (*b*) Do our juvenile readers receive the attention to which they are entitled ? (Mr. A. Errington).

   (*c*) Are newsrooms an acquisition, and is the money well spent on daily, weekly and monthly papers ? (Mr. A. Watkins).

   (*d*) What is the best method of registering replacements and disposing of worn-out books ?

4.0.—Visit to North-Eastern Railway Locomotive Works, by permission of Wilson Worsdell, Esq.

5.15.—Tea in the Assembly Room, Town Hall, by invitation of the Chairman of Public Library Committee.

6.15.—Visit Public Library.

6.45.—Smoking Concert in Lecture Room of Library,

J. W. C. PURVIS,
Hon. Secretary.

Society of Public Librarians.

A meeting of the Society of Public Librarians was held at the Bishopsgate Institute, E.C., on Wednesday evening, 5th November, when Mr. F. E. Chennell read a paper on " The Selection and Retention of Assistants ".

INDEX TO *THE LIBRARY ASSOCIATION RECORD.*

VOL. IV., 1902.

COMPILED BY OLIVER J. SUTTON, ASSISTANT IN THE JOHN RYLANDS
LIBRARY, MANCHESTER.

Contents.

General Index.
Bibliographies of Persons.
Bibliographies of Subjects.

The month is given after the page reference, it being advantageous to know the month in which the article appeared. The abbreviations are Ja.-F., Mr.-Ap., My., Je., Jl., Ag.-S., O.-N., D.

GENERAL INDEX.

A.

Aberdeen Public Library, annual report, 61, Ja.-F.; annual financial estimate, 213, My.
    Gift of £6,000 from A. Carnegie, 162, Mr.-Ap., 293, Je.
    New central reading-room, 213, My., 239, Je., 342, Jl.
    Proposed branch at Torry, 213, My., 293, Je., 342, Jl.
Aberdeen University Library, 163, Mr.-Ap., 602, 608, D.
Acton, Lord, his library presented to John Morley by A. Carnegie, 410, Ag.-S.
Adoptions of Public Libraries Acts, list, 552, O.-N.
Advocates' Library, Edinburgh. *See* Edinburgh.
Africa, South, public libraries. *See* CAPE TOWN LIBRARY. KIMBERLEY PUBLIC
    LIBRARY.
Airdrie, gift of £500 by A. Carnegie for a public library, 53, Ja.-F.
America. *See* UNITED STATES.
American History, The Literature of. Edited by J. N. Larned: notice, 458,
    Ag.-S.
American Library Association. *See* LIBRARY ASSOCIATIONS, A.L.A.
Analytical cataloguing. *See* CATALOGUING.
Anderton, Basil. Books brought into relation with each other and made opera-
    tive: paper, 382, Ag.-S.
Annan, gift of £3,000 for a public library, 53, Ja.-F.
Archer, William, librarian of the National Library of Ireland, 96, Mr.-Ap.
Architecture, library, 73, Ja.-F.
    The planning of some library buildings in the United States: précis of
    paper by S. K. Greenslade, 204, My.
Art books in the Hammersmith Public Libraries: address by Sir W. Richmond,
    110, Mr.-Ap.
Australasia, public libraries. *See* MELBOURNE. SYDNEY.
Australasian Library Association. *See* LIBRARY ASSOCIATIONS.
Axon, W. E. A., on Edward Edwards, 1, Ja.-F.
    An Italian librarian of the seventeenth century: Antonio Magliabecchi:
    précis of paper, 527, O.-N.

IV.   44

B.

L.

N.

U.

United States of America—
    Forty new libraries given by A. Carnegie, 218, My.
    Planning of some library buildings in the U.S.: précis of paper by S. K.
        Greenslade, 204, My.
    See also BROOKLYN. NEW YORK. WASHINGTON.
University libraries, functions of, 602, D.
    In Scotland, helped by A. Carnegie, 160, Mr.-Ap.

V.

Vatican Library, Leonine Reference Library, 414, Ag.-S.
Verney, Sir Edmund, opens Steeple Claydon Public Library, 617, D.
    Letter *re* use of library by persons living outside the district, 76, Ja.-F.
Victoria University confers honours on four members of the L.A., 178, Mr.-Ap.
Village libraries, 420, Ag.-S.
Vine, Guthrie, on the National Library of Ireland, 95, Mr.-Ap.
    Noteworthy books, 82, Ja.-F., 183, Mr.-Ap., 225, My., 302, Je., 355, Jl.,
        465, Ag.-S., 563, O.-N., 622, D.

W.

Wakefield, offer of £8,000 by A. Carnegie for public library, 443, Ag.-S.
Walker, H. Reference libraries in small towns: paper, 327, Jl.
Wall, Charles, obituary, 445, Ag.-S., 550, O.-N.
Wandsworth Public Library, bazaar in aid of, 441, Ag.-S.
Washington, Congressional Library, catalogue, 52, Ja.-F.
Washington, D.C., U.S.A., Public Library, annual report, 73, Ja.-F.
Waterford, gift of £5,000 by A. Carnegie for a public library, 53, Ja.-F.
Waterloo-with-Seaforth Public Library, annual report, 301, Je.
Water-marks in paper, 207, My.
Webb, Sidney. The library service of London: paper, 193, My.; discussion,
    231, My.
Westminster Public Libraries, annual report, 441, Ag.-S.
    Rate limitation removed, 66, Ja.-F.
Whitchurch Public Library and Museum, inauguration in new building, 172,
    Mr.-Ap.
Willcock, W. J. Library lectures: a retrospect and suggestion: paper, 394,
    Ag.-S.
Wolverhampton Public Library, opening of new building, 173, Mr.-Ap.
Women as librarians—
    In Aberdeen University Library, 608, D.
    In Cardiff Public Library, 158, Mr.-Ap.
    B. Reuz at Munich State Library, 423, Ag.-S.
Woolwich Public Library, offer of £14,000 by A. Carnegie for two branch
    libraries, 442, Ag.-S.
Workhouse library at Lambeth, 170, Mr.-Ap.
Workington, gift of £7,000 by A. Carnegie for a public library, 350, Jl.

BIBLIOGRAPHIES OF PERSONS.

APIAN, Pierre.—Van Ortroy, F. Bibliographie de l'œuvre de Pierre Apian (1902), 457, Ag.-S.

BUONNARROTTI, Michel Angelo.—Montaiglon, A. de C. de. Essai de bibliographie michelangelesque. In *Gazette des Beaux Arts*, 2nd series, vol. xiii., 1876, 457, Ag.-S.

DOBSON, Austin.—Murray, F. E. A bibliography of Austin Dobson (1901), 81, Ja.-F.

KEENE, Charles.—Pennell, J. The work of Charles Keene (1897), 457, Ag.-S.

LEECH, John.—Chambers, C. E. S. A list of works containing illustrations by John Leech (1892), 457, Ag.-S.

MORRIS, William.—Forman, H. B. The books of William Morris described (1897), 458, Ag.-S.

NAPOLEON.—Kircheisen, F. Bibliographie Napoléons, 458, Ag.-S.

OSSIAN.—Tombo, R., *jr*. Ossian in Germany (Columbia University Germanic Studies, vol. i., No. 2), (1901), 458, Ag.-S.

PARMENTIER, A. A.—Balland, A. La chimie alimentaire dans l'œuvre de Parmentier (1902), 458, Ag.-S.

RUSKIN, John.—Jameson, M. E. A bibliographical contribution to the study of John Ruskin (1901), 458, Ag.-S.

WASHINGTON, George.—Library of Congress. A calendar of Washington MSS. (1901), 81, Ja.-F.

WHISTLER, J. A. McN.—Albany: University of the State of New York, State Library Bulletin, Bibliography No. 1, 1895. Guide to the study of J. A. McN. Whistler. Compiled by W. G. Forsyth and J. Le R. Harrison (1895), 458, Ag.-S.

IV. ᵣ

BIBLIOGRAPHIES OF SUBJECTS.

To Publishers, Booksellers and Library Furnishers.

●●●●●●●●●●●●●●●●●●●●●●●●●●●●●

THE attention of Publishers, Booksellers and Library Furnishers is called to the advantages of The Library Association Record as an effective advertising medium.

The Journal, which is published regularly each month, is the official organ of The Library Association, and circulates in no fewer than 600 libraries up and down the country, as well as amongst the more prominent book-lovers and collectors.

Furnishing, as it does, the transactions of The Library Association, with notices of forthcoming meetings, in addition to library notes and news from all parts of the world, it is eagerly looked for and scanned each month by librarians, being, in fact, their official medium of intercommunication.

Not only does the Record circulate in the United Kingdom, it has a much wider sphere of influence, having subscribers in most of the British Colonies, as well as in the principal Countries of Europe.

Our aim in making this announcement is to secure a representative set of advertisements which may serve as a Directory of Library Furnishers, whether in fixtures, stationery, books or other accessories. The advantages of such a medium must be quite obvious to all firms in any way catering for the library, enabling them, as it does, to keep themselves constantly before not only librarians but members of Library Committees and book-collectors.

No advertisement will be received which is not strictly in keeping with the character of the Journal.

◆ ◆ ◆

SCALE OF CHARGES.

	Page.	Half Page.	Quarter Page.
Back of Cover - - - -	£3 0 0	£2 0 0	£1 5 0
Inside Cover and Pages Facing			
Matter or Cover - - -	2 2 0	1 7 6	0 17 6
Any other Page - - - -	1 11 6	1 1 0	0 13 4
Less than Quarter Page, 4s. per Inch Single Column.			

Reduction on a Series of	Three.	Six.	Twelve.
Insertions - - -	5 per cent.	10 per cent.	20 per cent.

Advertisements should be sent to the Assistant Secretary at the Offices of the Association, Whitcomb House, Whitcomb Street, Pall Mall East, S.W.; or to Mr. A. E. Bennetts, 176 Milkwood Road, London, S.E., not later than the 20th of each month.